P9-DXM-367

DATE DUE

AG 9'0			

DEMCO 38-296

THE ISRAELITES

12

THE
ISRAELITES

B.S.J. Isserlin

With 159 illustrations

THAMES AND HUDSON

Riverside Community College
·00   Library
MAY   4800 Magnolia Avenue
Riverside, CA 92506

DS 121 .I87 1998

Isserlin, B. S. J.

The Israelites

In memory of my wife Hilda,
who helped me so much

Any copy of this book issued by the publisher as a paperback is sold subject to the
condition that it shall not by way of trade or otherwise be lent, resold, hired out
or otherwise circulated without the publisher's prior consent in any form of binding
or cover other than that in which it is published and without a similar condition
including these words being imposed on a subsequent purchaser.

© 1998 Thames and Hudson Ltd, London

All Rights Reserved. No part of this publication may be reproduced or
transmitted in any form or by any means, electronic or mechanical, including
photocopy, recording or any other information storage and retrieval system,
without prior permission in writing from the publisher.

British Library Cataloguing-in-Publication Data
A catalogue record for this book is available from the British Library

ISBN 0-500-05082-1

Printed and bound in Slovenia by Mladinska Knjiga

Contents

Preface

This book attempts to present a picture of ancient Israel 'in the round'. The subject has not been comprehensively covered before, though W.G. Dever's *Recent Archaeological Discoveries and Biblical Research* (1990) and R.L. Harris's *Exploring the World of the Bible Lands* (1995) are among works offering surveys of value. There is, however, a model: Donald Harden's *The Phoenicians* (1962), which the present volume closely follows, down to the chapter divisions, and the author of this work also finds himself echoing Harden's comments on the apparently unending time needed for the book; and his thanks to the publishers for what appeared to be inexhaustible patience and helpfulness and to the ever-present encouragement and sympathy of his wife.

In some respects, the approach followed in this book is a little unusual: it deals essentially with ancient Israel only, with reference to neighbouring countries or the Levant as a whole being reduced to a minimum. This is against the present tendency not to treat Palestinian archaeology on its own; but one may recall that V.G. Childe, whom no one can accuse of parochialism, also wrote *The Prehistory of Scotland* (1935). On the other hand, as far as information permits, and as far as seems apposite, the subject is treated in the same way one might approach a topic in (e.g.) European history or archaeology, though with due regard to Near Eastern features. This, in a way, is applying the angle of vision acquired by the writer when he took a degree in History with Archaeology in Edinburgh, to the field of Oriental Languages in which he took another degree in Oxford. He is very much aware of the debt he owes to his teachers in both, especially, in Edinburgh to V.N. Galbraith (History), V.G. Childe (Archaeology) and N.W. Porteous (Hebrew), and in Oxford to H. Danby and G.R. Driver (Hebrew) and H.A.R. Gibb and A.F.L. Beeston (Arabic), besides C. Rabin (Semitic languages). It is hoped the result will be found acceptable, especially to readers of the three great monotheistic religions for whom ancient Israel and her religion are of special interest. All readers will have to accept frequent references to uncertainty: documentation is strikingly patchy compared with that available to historians of Europe.

I am grateful to my late parents and elder sister for stressing the necessity of backing hypotheses by facts, and the need to consider individual humanity in a world overmuch taken up by social or economic 'laws'. This book is dedicated to the memory of my wife Hilda, whose very sudden death deprived her of the chance to see this book completed. She had offered valuable suggestions and encouragement and support over many years, putting up with the stresses and strains it caused. We, and the readers of this book, are much in her debt.

Introduction

Ancient Israel is far more familiar to a wider public than most other ancient nations: religious instruction absorbed in childhood has seen to that, which also means it is viewed in a special way. Yet when we turn to the picture of ancient Israel presented by recent scholarship (composed from non-scriptural as well as scriptural data) we are faced with a disturbingly altered scene. Not only are familiar features in the landscape surveyed from different viewpoints, but quite fundamental traits in it are obscured by clouds of doubt, or blotted out entirely. To begin with the most basic question, was there really an entity called Israel which comprised the territories of both the United Monarchy of David and Solomon, and of its successor states, as well as the earlier confederation of tribes?

Many recent scholars feel there was not really such a comprehensive entity, and that the name 'Israel' should be applied only to the region of the northern kingdom. Furthermore, is it permissible to draw a picture of Israel and Judah and their histories on the basis of biblical texts? For these (many now maintain) were written largely in a very late period – the time of the Exile and of the restored Second Commonwealth (i.e. the Persian and Hellenistic eras) and from late points of view. Being removed, therefore, by many centuries from the events with which they deal, they are in this interpretation of doubtful trustworthiness. Moreover, biblical texts are works of literature and thus, it has been held, affected by the tendency of literary works to select and present their narrative data according to certain literary canons. Would it not, then, be advisable to distinguish between biblical literature on the one hand – to be judged according to literary standards – and archaeology and history on the other – based on truly historical foundations such as non-biblical Palestinian and other Near Eastern texts – rather than attempting to combine them into a construct called 'the history of ancient Israel' which must be fundamentally flawed?

While such matters will concern us below, the vital question as to whether we are justified in talking of an Israel comprising both Judah in the south and the region of the northern kingdom requires an immediate answer. That biblical texts assume it cannot here be adduced as an argument, for, as already noted, many recent critics regard them as mostly late and of doubtful evidential value. It seems to this writer, though, that there are at least two main arguments in favour. Firstly, Judah and northern Israel acknowledged the same national deity, written in the Hebrew Bible with the consonants YHWH, and commonly pronounced by scholars as 'Yahweh', though they differed substantially in worship and theology. Now, in the ancient Near East the worship of a common high god went with common nationality – Moabites worshipped Kemosh, Ammonites Milkom, etc. It is, furthermore, a striking fact that the deity worshipped in the temple at Jerusalem is referred to (especially by Isaiah) as 'the God of Israel', but never as the god of Judah. Had the two kingdoms been utterly separate then one would have expected such a difference in title. Secondly, as we shall see, archaeology now indicates that the origins of Judah are linked with a substantial immigration southwards from the Israelite heartland to the north. Such immigrants might well have retained the knowledge that common (Israelite) descent tied at least some later Judeans to their northern neighbours. These considerations lend weight to the biblical assumption of a hereditary link between the two regions, and we therefore feel justified in referring to a long-standing entity called Israel which comprised both north and south, in spite of their substantial differences. (The case of ancient Greece is somewhat analogous.) Against this, it is difficult to understand why post-Exilic Judeans should have begun calling themselves Israelites (as many now propose): the northern kingdom had been an object of dislike to pre-Exilic Judeans because of what they thought were its separatist and heretical practices, and there is no reason to assume this attitude had changed.

To turn to another aspect of our subject – ancient Israel tended to regard herself as unique, a people dwelling apart, and not reckoned among the nations. This view about her is still held by many, though others think that hers was a poor and provincial civilization containing little which could not be paralleled among her neighbours. Such issues will occupy us later; here we must define what Israel herself thought her uniqueness consisted in, and why her view should have remained influential and she herself a topic of interest when many of her contemporaries were only recently rescued from near oblivion by the decipherment of their records and the unearthing of their remains. Uniqueness was after all claimed by certain other ancient nations also, on such grounds as excellence in civilization or military might. Israel, a small nation inhabiting the Palestinian hill country in the late second and early first millennia BC, was only intermittently of political or military significance, and though her culture compared fairly well with that of many of her neighbours, it was not for this either that she was remembered. Her claims were grounded in religion: the Israelites were, they thought, special by virtue of their exclusive covenant with the Lord their God, which was indeed the foundation of their very national existence.

This central tenet in Israelite religion was to be diffused by the spread of the faith: both achieved international impact on world history. Quite early on, the deity worshipped by Israel was respected in nearby countries. Later, the Israelites were more widely regarded as the 'People of the Book'. Their sacred scriptures, laws and customs intrigued and at times attracted the ancient world. Christianity, as it grew, adopted as its Old Testament (in Greek and Latin translation, mainly) the Hebrew Bible treasured by the Jews and in due course familiarized much of mankind with its contents. European thought, literature and art were much influenced by it while, at the same time, the rise and spread of Islam (in which a number of biblical traditions are paralleled) introduced additional multitudes to such topics. Personages like Abraham, Moses, David and Solomon – to name but a few – are thus familiar to adherents of the three great monotheistic religions round the world.

Not unnaturally, there were attempts from quite early times onwards to learn more about people, places and events referred to in the Bible by drawing on literary or material evidence from outside it. Yet the illumination of Scripture is not the only reason for such an approach. Biblical traditions may also be viewed as potential documentation for the wider subject of ancient history, placing Israel's religion in relation to its general spiritual and material culture. The Bible itself would thus have to be investigated and evaluated as a historical document, rather than esteemed as a foundation of faith. A book on the ancient Israelites must, accordingly, keep in mind the different needs of two kinds of readers: those interested mainly in the elucidation of the Bible, and those concerned primarily with Israel as an ancient Near Eastern nation. Our aim in what follows will be to offer as concise a picture of Israel and her intellectual and material culture as emerges from the combined study of the Bible, extra-biblical texts and archaeology, in the light of recent scholarship.

Definition of the subject

A number of additional preliminary points should be made. The first of these concerns the period within which our study is to be confined. The fundamental query as to whether Israel existed within these limits as an entity sufficiently coherent to form a single subject of study has been briefly discussed above. We note here the main tenets of Israel's traditions about her past. She constituted a unified entity only during the short period of the United Monarchy under David and Solomon. Before then, the south lived in comparative isolation from the centre and the north, while after Solomon's death, the United Monarchy split into two separate kingdoms – Judah and a northern state which took the title of Israel. The two never again became one, yet there was throughout a feeling of a common Israelite identity, which survived even the end of the sister kingdoms – that of Israel in 722 BC and the subsequent Exile. Indeed, when Cyrus allowed a group of Judeans to return to their homeland, they referred to themselves on occasion as Israelites, and the habit persisted. We shall have to review these traditions in the light of scholarly discussion later on.

As for time, then, we shall begin at the point where an entity called Israel first appears on the stage of history in the late thirteenth century BC. Israelite traditions enshrined in the Bible trace it much further back, however – to Jacob, a common tribal ancestor who was given the honorary name of Israel after an epic contest with a mysterious angelic stranger, and ultimately to the patriarch Abraham. We shall consider these accounts in a later chapter, comprising as they do such remarkable events as the period of oppression in Egypt, the Exodus, the giving of the Law at Mount Sinai and the conquest of Canaan. Here we may say that they cannot at present be convincingly documented within the framework of what is known from historical sources. For an ending, we shall not go beyond the fall of the Kingdom of Judah in 586 BC, except for background references: the 'Second Commonwealth', founded after the return from Exile, was a community that lived under a theocratic constitution based on strict adherence to religious law and was in many ways different from what had gone before – some have indeed seen the origins of Judaism at this stage.

Where boundaries in space are concerned, we shall restrict ourselves to Israel in its Palestinian homeland, therefore not dealing with Israel in Egypt, and referring only marginally to those groups of Israelites and Judeans found before or after the fall of Jerusalem in Egypt and Mesopotamia. At the same time, our subject cannot be treated in total isolation. In order to understand Israel some reference is needed to the Near Eastern world of which it was part, both in order to obtain an idea of the extent to which they shared a common development and also to see where Israel followed a line of its own.

The sources and their limitations

We must also consider the sources available to us: what can we learn from them and what are their limitations. The Bible and archaeology in particular require detailed discussion while other sources can be dealt with more briefly.

The Bible

Strictly speaking, the Bible (Old Testament) is not one book but a collection of books. According to most modern reckoning there are 39, though early Judaism counted fewer, for a number of books now separate were then combined. It is mainly written in literary Hebrew, for which it is indeed our primary source; hence we shall refer to it as the Hebrew Bible, even though small parts of it – found for the most part in the books of Ezra and Daniel – are in Aramaic (a related language). Comprising 300,000 words arranged in 23,100 verses, the Bible is one of the most sizeable representatives of ancient oriental literature. Nevertheless, though it is four times the size of the Koran, its bulk is equal only to about a third of the combined works of a single English author, William Shakespeare.

Traditionally it is divided into three main sections: the five Books of Moses (known as the Pentateuch in western parlance, or in Jewish terminology as the Torah); the (Former and Latter) Prophets; and the Writings. These are arranged in the order of their canonization as Scripture, rather than according to their dates of origin. Written partly in prose and partly in poetry, the Bible deals with a considerable variety of subjects: Israelite and Jewish history; religious and civil laws (according to modern classification); hymns and prayers for public and private worship, and other poetry; prophetic utterances; proverbs and other expositions of wisdom. These works are the relics of a larger literature now lost, as biblical references to a number of titles show. They include some of the most outstanding poetic and prose texts of world literature; in addition, they reflect the beliefs and practices of their authors and of the world in which they originated. However, they are not an encyclopedia offering a complete conspectus of ancient Israelite life and thought. The Bible was put together for what we would call a religious purpose: it was intended to teach Israelites about the relation between their God and his people with whom he entered into a covenant; his guidance of them according to his divine plan through history; and the hope that, in the end, the faith and worship instituted for Israel would become the centre of religious attraction for mankind. A dispassionate discussion of rival religious loyalties must not be expected here, and the views of those not in agreement with this outlook are not expounded. The Bible is thus a very important source, but a limited one. If the books, now lost, to which the Bible refers its readers for further reference were available to us, together with a larger body of other contemporary documentation, we should be better able to obtain a comprehensive picture.

Yet even if such limitations are accepted, we have to face further problems concerning the biblical text and its history. For fundamentalist orthodoxy, both Jewish and Christian, the accepted standard text is immutably fixed though with regard to its meaning and wider interpretation recourse may be had to long-standing traditions. This attitude is still important but, since the nineteenth century especially, western scholarship has largely followed an alternative, critical approach. According to this, the biblical text has to be investigated like any other ancient document. The possibility of scribal errors, additions, or accidental or intentional shortenings and other changes has to be recognized; moreover the combined evidence from ancient versions, and now also of variant readings in the Dead Sea manuscripts, sometimes suggests that in the period before the present standard text became obligatory (*c.* AD 100) a number of rival manuscript traditions existed.

In addition, the question of the original date of composition of a given text (as well as its literary genre and social setting), and of its later development has to be addressed. Comparison with similar works in other ancient Near Eastern literatures is also required, both at the linguistic and at the cultural level, in order to elucidate and assess the text in question. All these topics are the subjects of an extremely large literature expressing varied and frequently changing opinions. Nevertheless, some views have been widely shared, especially concerning the authorship and date of biblical books. Thus, while traditional orthodoxy regards the Pentateuch as the work of Moses, and the prophetical writings mostly as the work of those whose names they bear, critical scholars mostly feel that little, if anything, in the Pentateuch as we have it goes back to Moses or his age (perhaps the thirteenth century BC); similarly, prophetic books may include sizeable later additions or reworkings (thus nothing in the book of Isaiah after chapter 39 is the work of the eighth-century prophet, and perhaps even very little before). The Book of Daniel (scholars argue) was even composed as late as the second century BC – the time of the Maccabean rising – and that century marks the closing stage of the growth of the scriptures which may have begun about a thousand years earlier. Works or passages written after the Exile are perhaps of less relevance to us here than those composed before. This applies in particular to the Books of Chronicles which are widely believed to illustrate thinking in their own period, possibly the fifth to third centuries BC, and whose value as a source for the pre-Exilic age is often disputed.

Concerning the times when individual biblical books came into being, opinions are generally in a state of flux at present. Where the origin of the Pentateuch is concerned, the 'documentary' hypothesis proposed in its classical form in Germany, especially by J. Wellhausen in the last century, was for long almost universally accepted; and with some modifications it is still influential. According to this, the Pentateuch arose from the combination of selections from four originally separate written sources, usually abbreviated as J, E, D and P, by a succession of redactors. (An alternative view – the 'supplementary hypothesis' – which suggests that the texts grew by accretions rather than combinations, has been less popular.) All four differ somewhat in vocabulary, style and outlook. J was regarded as the oldest source, composed in Judah during the tenth or ninth century BC. It was given its name because of its preference for the divine name 'Yahweh' (Jahweh in the German spelling), the learned vocalization for the four consonants YHWH which express the name of the lord no longer pronounced by the Jews for reasons of reverence. It was held to reflect the thinking of a simple, self-assured society either during the great days of the United Monarchy or just after. E, dating from the eighth century BC, a northern – Ephraimite – source, received its name from its tendency to call the Deity by the Hebrew word 'Elohim', meaning 'God'. Theologically more sophisticated it is also more critical. D stands for 'Deuteronomy' (or its core), a book marked by a special brand of rhetorical prose and by its hostility to influences potentially harmful to Israel's faith. It was identified with the book found in the Temple in 622 BC which provoked King Josiah's religious reform concentrating all worship there. Considered initially to be little older than the date of its discovery, Deuteronomy was later thought to enshrine much older writings, perhaps of a northern Israelite origin. P, lastly, stands for a 'priestly' source much interested in ritual but also in genealogy, world chronology and the unfolding of the divine plan and the place of Israel within it. It was thought to be post-Exilic, though involving older materials.

Development of this documentary hypothesis has included not only further refinement, such as the division of J and E into several constituent strands, but also the attempt to trace the sources beyond the Pentateuch, perhaps as far as the Book of Kings: D's ideas are widely considered to have been elaborated into a philosophy of divine reward and punishment involved in the historical process, traceable especially in the 'Deuteronomistic' framework from Joshua and Judges to Kings. This overall scheme corresponded nicely with an evolutionary vision of Israel's development from simplicity to sophistication. It has, however, more recently been queried not only in this latter regard – Israel developed, as archaeological and textual discoveries have shown, as part of a very advanced Near East and was affected by this from the start – but more fundamentally and on other grounds. An increasing interest both in oral traditions and in purely literary aspects of biblical writing has led to some questioning of source divisions and the introduction of other material for assessment.

In addition, radical changes in dating have been proposed. J, which for some time has been thought to be based on earlier, partly oral, materials, as well as D, is now regarded by some as a late (Exilic or even post-Exilic) book, the end of a process of gradual accretion perhaps, in which E (never an independent work) and P are just ingredients. Late datings for other parts of the Bible are now widely (though not universally) followed: even the story of David's court life and succession (2 Samuel 9–20; 1 Kings 1–2), long regarded as the oldest history writing anywhere and drafted by a contemporary, has now been viewed as a post-Exilic 'novel' of no great historical value. According to such views, inculcating theological lessons mattered more to biblical writers than historical detail. One cannot, then, at present, rely on agreed source datings as writers a generation ago did; but where Hebrew historical texts are paralleled by extra-biblical evidence (the character and veracity of which has of course to be assessed before it can be used) they can be employed with some confidence, and there are others where the time or place to which they belong is in little doubt. Such texts are, however, mostly from times nearer the end of Israel's history than its beginnings.

Epigraphic evidence

Compared with the multitude of texts of the most diverse kind unearthed in other Near Eastern countries (Egypt and Mesopotamia in particular), epigraphic finds from Israel have been few, though their number is increasing with the progress of excavations. They are also restricted in respect of the types represented. Public inscriptions on stone are rare, and since formal, public or private documents were mostly on perishable papyrus, they are practically non-existent. There are in particular no remainders of literary or religious (especially biblical) texts ancestral to biblical books, though the discovery of the Ketef Hinnom amulet discussed below (p. 258) may argue for their existence. What has survived in the main are informal notes or drafts written on potsherds (*ostraca*), besides short texts on seals or objects.

The available materials are unequally distributed also in time and space. Hardly any pre-date the eighth century BC, while most come from late pre-Exilic Judah rather than northern Israel. Such as they are, these writings do nevertheless offer insight into varied topics – administrative and military ones in particular. Epigraphic discoveries in neighbouring lands supplement those from Israel significantly but again selectively. Egypt and Mesopotamia understandably figure most prominently, but not exclusively. Among texts found since the 1930s, besides the collections of cuneiform tablets from the Mesopotamian Bronze Age city of Mari on the upper Euphrates, those from the Bronze Age city of Ugarit in northern Syria and now also Ebla are of special interest to us, in view of the significant and wide comparative background they provide on social, religious, literary and other aspects. Cultural and historical information is also available from Iron Age Egypt and Mesopotamia. Israel's immediate Levantine neighbours, on the other hand, have provided far less documentation, and with the exception of the victory stela of Mesha, King of Moab (*c.* 835 BC) (pl. 35) and fragments of a victory stela put up apparently by King Hazael of Damascus at Dan in the ninth century BC (pl. 36), no text from there refers to Israel by name, or illustrates relations with her in peace or war.

Extra-biblical literary works

Learned interest in the Jews and their country in the Graeco-Roman period gave rise to works containing information which is still of value. Some of more general scope, such as Strabo's *Geography* or Pliny's *Natural History*, tell us about the Palestine of their time; others by earlier Greek writers survive only in quotations. However, in the first century AD, the Jewish historian Flavius Josephus composed several books (*Jewish Antiquities*, *Jewish War* and *Against Apion*) which support his account of the past of his people by occasional references to texts now lost, such as the 'Annals of Tyre'.

Jewish religious writers were also interested in identifying biblical places, and such geographical as well as historical interests were taken over by the early Christian church. Thus biblical history and sacred geography were deeply researched by Bishop Eusebius of Caesarea in the fourth century AD, the former in his *Chronicle*, the latter in his *Onomasticon*, in which he located biblical sites with reference to the contemporary Roman road system. This book, re-edited in a Latin translation by Jerome in the fifth century AD, remains an essential source. Later, another type of literature became dominant as continued interest in the holy places throughout the Middle Ages gave rise to a multitude of pilgrim accounts and geographical works which offer much valuable information about the country and places as they were then.

Antiquarians turned their attention to Palestine during the seventeenth and eighteenth centuries, but the foundations of comprehensive scholarly knowledge of a modern type were laid in the nineteenth. Biblical interests were now combined progressively with economic and political ones, linked with the general desire to explore the world scientifically – the Near East in particular. At the same time, the horizons of classical and biblical scholarship were broadened by the discovery of Egyptian and Mesopotamian monuments and by the progressive decipherment of texts found there, which proved to be of great value also to biblical scholarship. In Palestine, this led to progress in a number of directions – travellers and explorers visited parts of eastern and western Palestine long inaccessible to westerners; there were attempts to map the country; and its geology, scenery, fauna and flora were progressively described.

Of special interest for biblical studies were the results obtained by Edward Robinson and Eli Smith who, during their travels in 1838 and 1852, systematically noted analogies between biblical and Arabic place-names, thus helping to fix the approximate location of many biblical sites. Such individual efforts were, however, to be outclassed before long by those of newly founded learned societies and institutions specially devoted to biblical and wider Syro-Palestinian investigations, and able (if sometimes with difficulty) to raise the financial means to send out capable field investigators.

The first in the field was the British Palestine Exploration Fund, founded in London in 1865. It sponsored the first comprehensive scientific mapping of western Palestine (undertaken in 1871–77) which was accompanied by voluminous memoirs detailing, for each sheet, not only geographical and human features but also the antiquities then still visible. Both maps and memoirs remain of considerable value. East of the Jordan, however, circumstances permitted only partial surveys. The Fund also promoted archaeological excavations in Jerusalem and elsewhere, including Flinders Petrie's pioneer work at Tell el-Hesi in the coastal plain in 1890.

Other nations quickly joined in such work: German, French, Austrian and American excavators worked at such sites as Megiddo, Taanach, Jericho, Samaria and Jerusalem. The Turkish administration then in control of the region regulated their activities under an antiquities law, though local circumstances sometimes caused difficulties. Exploration increased during the period of enlightened and active British antiquities administration after the First World War, and still more with the arrival of the two independent states of Israel and Jordan following the Second World War.

Archaeology and ancient Israel

Archaeological activity has now gone on in Palestine for more than a century. Not unnaturally its aims, methods and standards of achievement have changed during that time, leaving us with a body of information varying in kind, aims and value. Before, and indeed after the First World War, it was overwhelmingly Bible-orientated (a number of its practitioners were theologians or Hebrew philologists and historians by training). Objects of excavation were mainly towns of biblical interest, and within these, buildings and finds of possible religious significance or that could be ascribed to biblical personages, were particularly sought.

More recently, interest has veered from biblical to more general Palestinian archaeology, with an increasingly sociological and ecological slant. What is being looked for now is documentation of the social structure and mode of life of the ancient population of the country and its dependence on the natural or man-made conditions in which they found themselves. This has led to interest in non-urban settlement – an interest which began between the two World Wars with regional surveys exploring patterns of settlement, the individual sites being dated mainly by samples of surface pottery. Surveys on a large scale intended to cover the whole territory of Israel and Jordan are now a major aim, in order to integrate urban sites within their surroundings. To assess the latter, and the use made of them, scientists such as botanists, zoologists and geologists have joined the trained archaeological staff in excavations.

Scientific analysis of finds is now routinely employed, sometimes on the basis of preserving everything found, and computer analysis is increasingly coming to the aid of archaeology. Air and satellite photography offer valuable assistance to archaeologists; underwater exploration, moreover, has joined land-based archaeology. Team-work has thus largely replaced individual effort.

All told, archaeological activity including excavation has, since the Second World War, grown on an unforeseeable scale, though publication, regrettably, lags behind fieldwork. In another development local archaeologists have, especially in Israel, largely replaced foreign investigators. Sociological interpretation of excavation results is common to all of them, if to a varying degree.

Methods of archaeological excavation and interpretation

We must now consider more closely the methods of excavation applied during the period. We can be brief where the earliest attempts – those by C. Warren in Jerusalem in 1867–70, and later diggings there by F. Bliss and R.A.S. Macalister in 1901 – are concerned. They all excavated largely by underground shafts and tunnels (pl. 4), revealing valuable architectural details, but still lacking the means to date them.

Such were, however, provided for the first time by W. Flinders Petrie's brief but epoch-making work at Tell el-Hesi. Petrie observed that the mound there consisted of the superimposed remains of a number of settlements – *strata*. The pottery associated with them changed from earlier to later, and some of it (as well as other finds) could be dated from its similarity with analogous objects of known age found elsewhere, for instance in Egypt, Greece or Cyprus – *cross-dating*. The concepts of stratigraphic sequence and of dating by associated finds, especially by a sequence of datable pottery forms, have remained fundamental ever since.

Petrie also provided a section drawing (as well as plans), in which surviving buildings were treated somewhat schematically as single units from foundation levels to surviving wall-tops: individual layers in the soil were sometimes noted but not systematically separated, leaving walls to be linked, at times theoretically, by roughly horizontal lines added to the observed section. Petrie maintained this approach after the First World War, and it influenced both his pupils and others. Yet by then a more sophisticated technique was already available, pioneered (though not fully applied) by G.A. Reisner in his excavations at Samaria in 1908–10.

Anticipating later excavation methods by a generation or more, Reisner understood the importance of soil layers and their functional distinction – foundation trench fills and masons' debris, floor make-ups, floors and floor occupation deposits, destruction and thus decay layers, fills in pits, robber trenches and so on. All these were to be excavated separately and competently indicated on trench-side section drawings, which thus provided a far more differentiated record than Petrie's. Detailed documentation, including photography and the assignment of finds to their proper contexts, were other tasks for the trained excavation staff. Yet for the time being, Reisner's example was not fully followed.

Discerning soil layers and understanding their meaning is indeed often not easy and the difficulties are greatest in the hill country where most Israelite settlements are located. Here, buildings were not so often constructed from mud-bricks, as in the plains belt, but more frequently totally or partly from stone. This was apt to be robbed out later as ready-made building material, with much consequent disturbance in the stratigraphic sequences.

A method of overcoming such problems (at a price, as it turned out) was developed by Reisner's former architect colleague, C.S. Fisher, in his large-scale excavations at Megiddo from 1926 onwards (low labour costs made the investigation of extensive areas feasible then, for a time). Fisher was mainly interested in revealing and recording buildings; any feature regarded as significant associated with them – such as a group of pottery on a surviving floor area – was styled a *locus* and given a *locus* number, and these *loci* were fixed in space by plan references and absolute heights. *Loci* with similar and presumably contemporary finds were then assigned to a stratum. This 'architectural' or '*locus-to-stratum*' method was widely adopted, and it still influenced American and Israeli archaeologists after the Second World War, since it seemed suited to the recovery of architecturally significant features in large urban areas. Yet it is liable to serious flaws. In individual *loci*, the absence of systematic attention to separate layers, significant differences between under-floor make-up and floors, deposits on floors and later debris cover might not be noted; nor might disturbances between *loci* grouped together be given due consideration. There being no detailed sections, walls shown in schematic profiles might seem to 'float in space', being grouped according to absolute height rather than because they were stratigraphically linked – another possible source of error, as strata are rarely absolutely level. In addition, some individual buildings might stand for centuries while their neighbours were rebuilt or demolished.

It is not surprising that this method has recently been called 'proto-scientific'; earlier, Sir Mortimer Wheeler, the pioneer of modern stratigraphic digging, had expressed himself about its results in very unflattering terms. His own method was transferred to the region by his pupil Miss (later Dame) Kathleen Kenyon who used it before the Second World War at Samaria and later on a large scale in her excavations at Jericho (1952–58) and at Jerusalem (1960–67). Her model has come to be adopted almost universally since then, sometimes in combination with *locus* registration. Essentially, this 'stratigraphic' method is based on the systematic distinction and separate excavation and registration of all individual soil layers visible and documented in carefully drawn sections. These may be along the sides of single search trenches, but to cover larger areas a grid system or square digging areas divided by baulks is used. Running sections along these allow the sequence across the whole excavated area to be read. To be employed successfully this method needs well-trained staff. It has proved most helpful in establishing the history of sites, provided always that sweeping conclusions about these are not based on isolated small trial excavations. Applying it to the excavation of large areas with a view to revealing entire architectural complexes is, however, a demanding task.

Methods of dating

In Israelite sites closely dated objects such as inscribed seals and scarabs belonging to known historical persons are rare in the period under discussion, while inscriptions indicating that a certain ruler put up, or restored, a building, are at present unknown. The occurrence of datable pottery forms is the main means of building up an archaeological chronology. Datable objects made from metal or other valuable substances have survived much more rarely, but even discarded potsherds often prove useful aids. The pottery chronology constructed between the World Wars by W.F. Albright and elaborated later by R. Amiran in a standard volume is thus still basic.

There are, however, limitations to the usefulness of pottery for dating purposes. Unlike certain later non-Palestinian fabrics (such as Greek red-figured wares which often can be dated from a knowledge of the artist who painted them), Israelite fabrics and shapes were frequently in use for several generations and the times when they went in and out of fashion may be ill defined, although statistical frequency may help locally, when it is known. Moreover, though the mass-produced pottery from the later part of our period probably spread over large marketing areas fairly quickly, older techniques or forms might also survive. Regional fashions opposed general tendencies. Poorer backwaters probably received new fashions only after delay, or not at all. The correlation of pottery sequences with known historical events or individual reigns of kings is thus rarely a straightforward task, especially since the identification of sites with towns mentioned in biblical texts may be in dispute. The search for Solomonic or Davidic monuments in particular has led to few agreed results, and datings for whole stratigraphic sequences, like those at Megiddo, Samaria or Lachish, have been the subject of long-standing and recurring disagreements. Even such events as the foundation of Samaria or the rebuilding of Hazor by Solomon offer no really fixed points. Nor do destruction layers provide unfailing help – though the destruction of Jerusalem in 586 BC can be archaeologically matched with certainty, many others cannot be dated with such confidence.

Architectural fashions, such as in town gates, offer similarly imprecise dating criteria. Scientific tests, for instance the radiocarbon method, are not yet available to a significant extent for our period. Broad rather than close dating is thus often the best which can be obtained. Archaeological charts must thus remain somewhat hypothetical and approximate even though representing a wide consensus on inter-site correlations. Moreover, there is no general agreement concerning the way in which the Bronze and Iron Ages should be subdivided, or the exact regnal dates of the kings of the United Monarchy and of the twin states of Israel and Judah thereafter; a compromise solution is accordingly followed here.

There has also been disagreement about the use of datable finds in the dating of strata. One school, following Kenyon, holds that the time when floors in buildings were laid down is decided by the latest datable finds *below* them; another, represented by some American and Israeli excavators, regards deposits *on* floors as chronologically decisive. A compromise between these positions may be the best solution. Finds below or in floors may be much earlier than the date when the buildings concerned were erected; on the other hand, since floor deposits often represent the last rather than the initial phase of use, they may be rather later. Together deposits below, in, and on floors may thus offer a time span of variable length; a more exact construction date within these limits may sometimes be suggested by historical or other considerations, but all too often it remains indeterminate.

Conclusion

To sum up – our sources, both biblical and archaeological, are not sufficiently ample or exact to provide as comprehensive, detailed and specific a picture of ancient Israel as we might wish; moreover, their interpretation is frequently a matter of dispute. Israel's intellectual development and social and political history remain fragmentary, but a more general picture of ancient Israelite life-styles and of the main stages of their development can be drawn. However, correlation of individual events known from the historical record with evidence from archaeology and elsewhere is rarely possible.

The increasing use made of various scientific techniques in recent years has shed new light on a number of aspects of ancient Israelite life. For example, the ancient environment, in which the Israelites lived and the use they made of it, is better understood and the same is true for various aspects of ancient Israelite technology and trade. Available results of analyses are as yet few and too patchy for an overall picture, but much enlightenment may be hoped for from this direction in the future.

Finally, another factor needs to be considered concerning our ability to comprehend the world we are studying and attempting to recreate, and the way in which it was viewed by the ancient Israelites. We experience no fundamental difficulties in understanding the politics of the period – the division of the Levant in the late second millennium BC between two imperial powers, Egypt in the south and the Hittite Empire to the north, to be followed during the first millennium by a 'concert' of medium-sized and small states, which later collapsed before the irresistible advance of the Assyrian superpower which was replaced in its turn by the Babylonian Empire. Some details in this story look indeed quite startlingly modern, like the dispatch by the Egyptians of ship-loads of grain as famine relief to the collapsing realm of their former Hittite rivals, late in the thirteenth century.

Yet the time when this took place falls within the very period when many would set the appearance of Israel in Palestine, and the sequence of events this involved – the Exodus from Egypt, the desert wanderings and the Conquest of the Promised Land – are by biblical tradition firmly ascribed to a direct Divine Intervention which continued thereafter.

Again, we have no real trouble when considering the existence of an international system of trade conducted under conventions of law, the evidence for the available technological equipment or Israel's social organization. Our difficulties arise when we come to consider ancient Near Eastern thought and beliefs, some of which were shared by Israel though others were rejected. This is partly due to the fact that what textual evidence exists is one-sided, largely representing the views and literary conventions of the intelligentsia, while the material evidence which might cover a wider spectrum permits only limited insight into the intellectual world of those who left it. But it is also because much of what we do know – about, for example, popular beliefs in evil spirits and the efficacy of charms or the belief in the divine sonship of kings, prophecy and oracles or ordeals, and a strict theological view of historical events – is alien to our modern western thinking. The effort to recreate this part of any ancient society is indeed hard, but we should not be deterred from attempting it.

In a field where the gaps in our information are enormous, it must be remembered that attempts to fill them with hypotheses are no more than that, and that a simple profession of ignorance may at times be best. We should also be wary of using dogmatic assertions drawn from other Near Eastern societies as, for example, that literacy in Israel must have been essentially confined to a scribal class, because that was the case in Mesopotamia and Egypt. Parallels, or the use of models drawn from outside, can be most suggestive but should not be employed to 'prove' the existence of features in Israel which are not attested. Indeed, the writer is more inclined than most to think that students dealing with ancient Israel can profitably make use of ethnographic parallels by examining the history of the Arabs who entered Palestine some 1800 years after the Israelites. Such studies might apply, for instance, to the questions of Israelite conquest and immigration and of early literacy outside a scribal class, and particularly to the problem of the conflict between traditional lifestyles and political practices based on 'reasons of state' on the one hand, and the stringent and revolutionary demands of religion on the other. In the case of Israel, the picture presented in the Bible of such a conflict has sometimes been regarded as an overdrawn retrojection of later views into the past. However, the fate of the first 'Ummayad Arab state shows us just how such a conflict did ruin a dynasty – insufficiently 'orthodox', it fell (shades of Jehu) to a military onslaught inspired by religious propaganda. Such an event (differing from the political machinations of discontented priests) was not 'normal' in the ancient Near East, but brings us back to the basic question of how 'normal', in terms of its time and location, ancient Israel really was.

CHAPTER ONE

Geography: The Land and its Resources

The country in which the Israelites lived is small – western Palestine between Dan and Beersheba is comparable in size to Wales or Massachusetts – and its natural resources are limited. Within this compass it comprises, however, a remarkable variety of scenery and living conditions, and though its borders in some directions are fairly definite, the lines of communication with the greater world outside are very significant. Tensions apparent in Israel's history, such as the conflict between isolation and international involvement, between the austerity of the desert and the attractions of a settled lifestyle, between regional or tribal separatism and strivings for overall unity, are related to geographical factors.

Position

Israel's homeland forms part of the land bridge linking Eurasia and Africa and, more particularly, of the 'Fertile Crescent' – a discontinuous belt of fertile areas extending from the Nile Valley to the Euphrates and the Tigris. Within this, Israel's separate identity was circumscribed by the Lebanon and Anti-Lebanon to the north, the desert to the east and south, and the Mediterranean Sea in the west. Yet these borders were not impenetrable for they were crossed by some of the main arteries of international communication. The great trunk road from Egypt to Mesopotamia and beyond traverses Palestine from the south to the northeast. Southeastwards, caravan tracks led across Arabia to the Indian Ocean; the parallel sea route from the head of the Gulf of Aqabah down the Red Sea was indeed open, but uninviting, owing to unpredictable squalls and treacherous reefs fringing inhospitable shores. Westwards, along the Mediterranean coast, conditions for shipping were better. Though nature did not provide harbours as good as those enjoyed by the great maritime trading towns in Phoenicia, a number of little bays, river mouths or shelters behind reefs made the Palestinian coast accessible to the small craft of antiquity. These plied routes to and from Egypt, Phoenicia, Cyprus and lands further west as far

NOTE: Place names are given in the forms found in the Revised Version and in the New English Bible. However, Israeli spellings are increasingly used in the relevant literature. They are sometimes very different, as in Ashkelon for Ascalon; more commonly *b* after a vowel becomes *v* (as in Negev for Negeb) and final *-ah* may be given as *-a*. There are other minor differences.

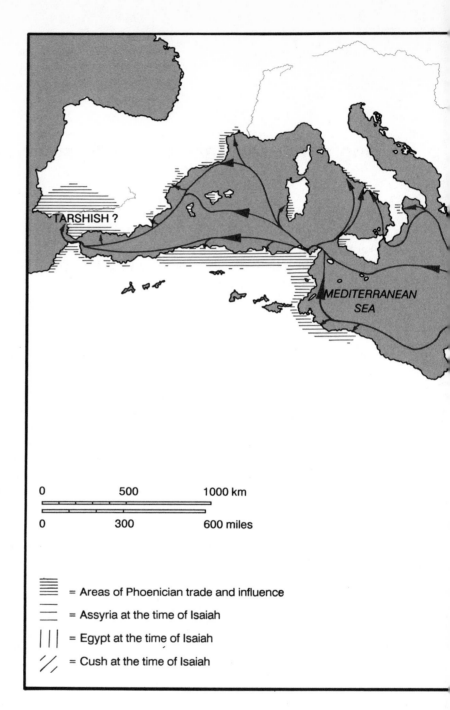

TARSHISH ?

MEDITERRANEAN
SEA

0   500   1000 km

0   300   600 miles

≡ = Areas of Phoenician trade and influence

≡ = Assyria at the time of Isaiah

||| = Egypt at the time of Isaiah

// = Cush at the time of Isaiah

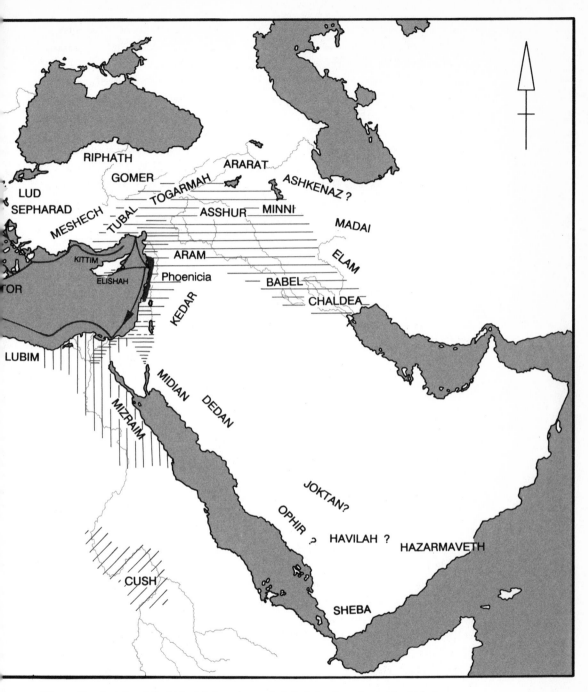

1 The world as Isaiah and Ezekiel might have known it. It includes the regions with which the neighbours of Israel – Egypt, Assyria and Phoenicia – were in contact, and from whom the Israelites presumably drew information.

away as Spain. Israel's separate identity was thus balanced by her economic and cultural contacts: it is not by accident that Israelites knew of Tarshish, of Ethiopia or of Ararat. Yet such a position also brought danger. Egypt to the south, and Assyria followed by Babylonia to the north, repeatedly sought to invade or annex the country; Midianites raided it from the east and Philistines to the west dominated much of it for a while. Israel, on her side, at times sought to expand beyond her borders or even to establish empire. However, only occasionally did she achieve any significant success. Nature seemed rather to suggest that between Egypt and Mesopotamia there should be a number of small or medium-sized states, of which Israel would be one. Barring imperial intervention from the outside, local disputes would be unlikely to lead to permanent major changes in the regional balance of power.

Israel's knowledge of the world

Though Israelites knew their own country best, they were remarkably aware of the wider circuit encompassing it. The 'Table of Nations' contained in Genesis 10 in particular offers a good view of what was known to them between the eighth and sixth centuries BC (and sometimes much earlier). Their world extended from Arabia to southern Spain, and from Anatolia and Greece to Libya, Egypt and Ethiopia (an area of something like 6500 km (4040 miles) from east to west, and about half that distance from north to south); it was occupied by a mixture of pastoralists and nomads, agriculturalists and towns-folk and seafarers, grouped as descendants of Shem, Ham and Japhet. Such a picture seems to reflect Israelite contacts with the spheres of Assyro-Babylonian, Egyptian and Phoenician dominance or influence. Curiously, distant Anatolia seems reasonably well known, but apart from the names of the capital cities of Syrian regional states there is little detail about nearby Syria, and the comparative profusion of data concerning northern and southern Arabia (though admittedly information on the north is rather more exact than that concerning the south) is puzzling since the Arabs at this time seem to have excluded outsiders from their caravan trade. Perhaps the growth in commercial contacts between Arabia and the Levant from the late eighth century BC onwards nevertheless afforded Israelites and others some chance to enquire more closely about the places of origin of the goods they obtained from their Arab trading partners. Again, though the Bible mentions Tarshish (which many locate inland from Cadiz) it shows little definite knowledge of the way there; though there are hints that the Israelites were not unfamiliar with Phoenician sea lanes. The rest of continental Europe, Africa and Asia seem to have been outside their ken, even though they and their neighbours benefited from long-established trade with India, Sri Lanka and perhaps beyond, to the east, and just possibly from the import of tin from Britain in the west. At the furthest limits of their known world the all-encircling ocean set the ultimate boundary, paralleled by the waters of the deep below the earth and the rain-giving waters above. Concerning the locations of mysterious far-off entities such as Paradise and its four rivers, their opinions seem indefinite and those of ancient and modern commentators have ranged widely: thus both Armenia and the marshlands near the Gulf Coast of Iraq have been suggested recently as locations of Paradise.

The mechanics of communications

Though this world was large and diverse, communication between its different parts had long taken place and Israel was not excluded. Contacts with the Phoenician world would be assisted by the close relation between the Hebrew and Phoenician languages. Aramaic, increasingly important as a medium for international trade as well as Assyrian and Babylonian administration, was known to upper-class Israelites; Egyptian was taught to those who needed it, but Assyrian and Ethiopic remained strange tongues. The speed of commercial exchanges was, so far as can be judged, within the range accepted before the Industrial Revolution in Britain in the eighteenth century. Records concerning distances covered per day on foot, by donkey or camel caravans or by carts or wagons are few, but they can be filled in by reference to classical, medieval and modern analogies. A rate of 25–30 km (15½–19 miles) per day seems to have been perfectly feasible but greater speeds could be attained: 40 km (25 miles) on foot and 40–60 km (25–37 miles) by camel caravan between desert halts in particular. Ships hugging the coast between nightly landings would cover modest distances, but when travelling directly between ports by day and night they might achieve *c*. 100–150 km (62–93 miles) in 24 hours, as indicated by a two weeks' return journey between Byblos in Lebanon and Tanis in Egypt, referred to in the eleventh-century BC story of Wen-Amon.

We may thus venture some guesses concerning the time needed to reach the limits of the world known to Israel, referring to instances familiar in popular lore. Jonah, fleeing from the face of the Lord to Tarshish (Jonah 1, 3), might, with exceptionally favourable winds, have needed roughly a month to get there

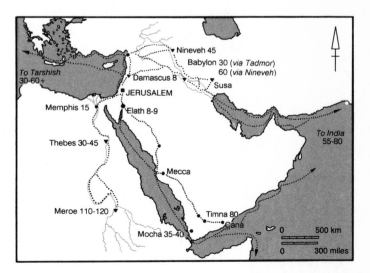

2 The presumed duration of travel (measured in days) from Jerusalem to various towns and regions in the ancient world. This is estimated, on land, according to caravan speed and at sea following main sailing routes at average speed – where feasible by uninterrupted 24-hour sailings.

(contrary winds and currents on the outward journey might easily have doubled or even tripled the journey time, but speedier progress was more likely on the homeward journey). However, the much shorter journey to Nineveh (Jonah 3, 3) could have taken him a month and a half. Again, the fabulous Queen of Sheba might have required some two and a half months to reach Solomon in Jerusalem if she travelled by land from South Arabia (1 Kings 10, 1–13), but the fleet sent by Solomon and Hiram of Tyre from Ezion Geber (Jeziret Far'aun near Aqabah) to Ophir (1 Kings 9, 26–8) would have needed only some 20–25 days to get there if Ophir was in South Arabia. If it was in India or on the Somali coast, as some think (which would imply overcoming the difficult conditions near the Bab el-Mandeb straits), an additional 20–40 days might have been needed. Two to three months of continuous travel would probably have sufficed to reach most points in Israel's world (only the journey to Ethiopia seems to have been much lengthier), but frequent intermediate stops and the need to await favourable seasons for the return trip would have extended the time required quite considerably.

While armies and any prisoners they conveyed would normally have journeyed slowly, travellers in a hurry and bearers of important messages could move fast, at double the normal speed or more, over long distances. Thus when Nebuchadnezzar was informed while campaigning in Syria of his father's death and the need to return to Babylon at once, both the messenger and the crown prince seem to have averaged some 60–80 km (37–50 miles) per day on their respective trips from and to Babylon. From the later Assyrian period onwards, speedy official travel on main roads appears to have been assisted by relays at stations permitting change of horses – precursors of the Persian postal system described by Herodotus – but even so, a message between Palestine and Nineveh might have taken some two to three weeks to reach its destination. Chains of stations for fire and smoke signals were also known, and these could be transmitted at very high speeds. An experiment in England at the time of Napoleon proved that beacon signals could be conveyed over 60 miles in eleven minutes, while post-biblical Jewish sources refer to astonishingly fast transmission of fire signals from Jerusalem to Babylonia. It seems nevertheless likely that signalling codes could deal with very basic messages only, and bad weather or inattention might prevent them being forwarded. Whether carrier pigeons were employed in our period remains uncertain. Any speedy transmission of news would in any case have been available only to a very restricted élite. People excluded from the system might have had to wait a long time before they heard even about important events: Ezekiel in his Babylonian abode only received news of the fall of Jerusalem some five months later from a fugitive (Ezekiel 33, 21).

Geographical regions

Physically, the land of Israel is divided into a number of regions forming part of wider geographical entities, the outlines of which were determined in the distant geological past. Originally part of the Arabian tableland, Palestine was transformed during the Tertiary Period (between 65 and 1.64 million years ago) into four main parallel zones running from north to south, as the result of processes of folding, rifting and volcanic activity which were active in the whole region from the Orontes Valley to the north via the Red Sea into East Africa to the south. The most westerly of these zones is the Palestinian coastal plain fringing the Mediterranean. It is wide in the south, in Philistia – where an area of low ground, the Vale of Beersheba, branches off from it eastwards – but less so in the Sharon sector in the centre; thereafter it is reduced to a narrow band by Mount Carmel, which occurs again further north where the present border between Israel and Lebanon meets the sea. In between these two points, it

3 The main geographical sub-regions of Palestine. Their character is determined by the relief and geological make-up of these regions, climate, vegetation cover and internal and external communications.

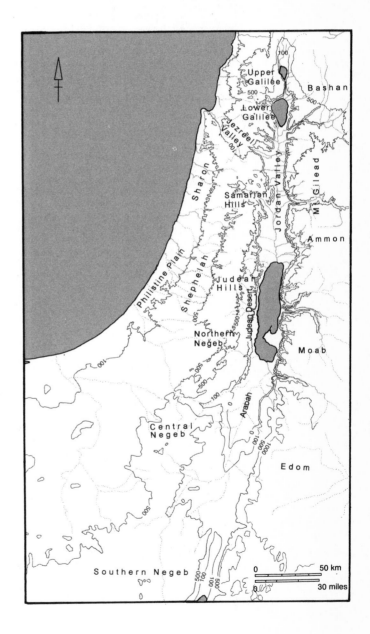

widens into the crescent-shaped plain between Haifa and Acco, linked to the east with the Vale of Jezreel allowing access to the Jordan Valley.

Eastwards, the plain abuts on the second main constituent zone, the belt of uplands and hills which occupy most of western Palestine. (Locally, though, between the latitudes of Beersheba and Aijalon, a row of low foothills – the Shephelah – precedes the main range from which it is separated by a longitudinal valley.) The uplands themselves are divided into three main parts: the hill country of Judea; that of Samaria; and across the Vale of Jezreel, the hills of Lower and Upper Galilee. In Judea, the land attains a level of *c.* 1000 m (3280 ft); in Samaria the average is less, but it rises again northwards in Upper Galilee, where Har Meron (Djebel Djermaq), the highest mountain in Cisjordanian Israel, attains a height of *c.* 1200 m (3937 ft); across the Jordan, Gilead ('Adjlun) rises somewhat higher still. While the western flank of this belt of high ground ascends gradually, there is everywhere a steep drop from it eastwards to the next main geographical zone. This is the long rift valley, the northern section of which contains the River Jordan while the centre is occupied by the Dead Sea and the south by the Arabah. Much of this remarkable trough, which deepens towards its centre from both north and south, is below sea level, the surface of the Dead Sea being set at −394 m (−1293 ft). From the eastern edge of the rift valley there is a steep ascent up rugged slopes to the fourth and final zone, the highlands of Transjordan. Essentially this consists of a plateau or tableland sloping gradually towards the east, though the western part is much dissected, and indeed subdivided by the deeply incised valleys of rivers tributary to the Jordan or Dead Sea, into a number of isolated blocks – Gilead, Moab and Edom in particular. Locally, higher mountain massifs dominate the scene, as especially in the cases of Mount Seir in the far south, and the Hauran mountains some distance to the east of the Lake of Tiberias. An area of somewhat lower ground nearer the latter opens up the intervening plain of Bashan.

Geological features

The basic geological make-up of the country is simple. In the highland zone, much of the visible rock structure consists of Cretaceous formations, either the hard Turonian and Cenomanian limestone and dolomite, or the softer and often chalky Senonian. The former has given rise to steep-edged and craggy scenery, the latter to rolling hills and flat valleys, except where interstratified bands of flint resulted in stepped slopes in the Judean desert. In the mountain limestone region of Judea in particular similar sequences of softer and harder layers have given rise to stepped hillsides, which later invited adaptation into agricultural terraces. Post-Cretaceous Eocene rocks form somewhat irregular hill country, as in the Shephelah; ancient lava flows connected with the genesis of the great rift valley are found to the east and west of the upper Jordan, in Galilee and in the Hauran mountains. As against this, the underlying older rock formations remain mostly deeply buried, only occasionally outcropping: the reddish-brown 'Nubian Sandstone' in particular forms a conspicuous feature of the eastern flank of the Arabah Valley (the 'rose-red city' of Petra is carved into it, hence its title). Even older granites and other ancient metamorphic or plutonic rocks are revealed in the Negeb and in Mount Seir where they are responsible for some very wild and rugged desert scenery recalling Arabia. Further north, the main limestone upland formations, being permeable, are not rich in springs, which tend to occur nearer the edge of the hill and plain (mostly on the western flank, though a few like those of En Gedi are on the eastern side). The deeply entrenched river valleys which now serrate the highlands were probably formed at times when rainfall was ampler, during pluvial periods linked with the European Ice Age sequence.

All along the Mediterranean coast, wind-borne dune sand has encroached to a varying extent on cultivated land within historical times. Inland, some geological features of the country which are of importance for human settlement and land use go back to a geologically fairly recent past. In the southern coastal plain, wind-borne clayey dust has formed deep layers of so-called 'loess' in the northern Negeb near Beersheba (Tell es-Saba): when well watered it is fertile, but otherwise provides only grazing for sheep and camels. Further north, the coastal plain is floored by pans of potentially fertile red clayey sand (or sometimes swamp soil) between parallel ridges of 'kurkar' sandstone resulting from the fossilization of ancient dunes, extending from north to south. These provide dry ground fit for habitation and travel even in the wet season, and also some rather mediocre building stone. Another kind of fairly easily worked but inferior stone is provided by the 'nari' crust which has formed over chalky deposits in the hill country. There are several varieties of mountain limestone which are superior, but more difficult to cut and dress. Elsewhere in the hills red Mediterranean earth has formed on much of the limestone country, offering good opportunities for the production of grain and wine and for olive cultivation; grey-brown soils elsewhere in the hills mostly offer less favourable conditions. Reddish-brown earth developed over basaltic lava deposits in the north of the country can be very suitable for cereals and other crops. On the other hand, the 'lisan marls' – laminated deposits of marl, gypsum and other substances, left behind in the Jordan Valley by the gradual shrinkage of the Dead Sea from a gigantic prehistoric lake to its present size – are generally of little agricultural use, unless improved by irrigation, a fact which applies also to saline soils.

From the geological conditions outlined above it follows that minerals useful to early man are few. The Bible mentions that iron and copper could be dug in the hills of the Promised Land (Deuteronomy 8, 9). The latter is known to occur in significant quantities only in the Nubian Sandstone on the flanks of the Arabah, especially in Edom, where it was extracted in antiquity. Iron ore occurs more frequently, as in northern Galilee and in Gilead, where it appears likely that it was mined during our period. Rock salt and bitumen could be obtained in the Dead Sea region, but gold, silver and the tin prized by the ancients are not present in the country in workable quantities.

Climate

Most of Palestine lies within the zone of Mediterranean climate characterized by hot, very dry summers, and cool, wet winters. Rainfall is concentrated mainly in the period between October–November and February–March and the initial downpours may be particularly heavy and thundery. These are the 'former rains' of the Bible, while the 'latter rains' (April–May) are the final showers of the wet season. In the hill country, snow may then replace rain. Summers are completely rainless, to the extent that a thunderstorm in summer was regarded as an awesome miracle (1 Samuel 12, 17–18). Heavy dew formation may, however, help to sustain plant life during that period – the Israelites regarded it as a gentle blessing.

Such overall tendencies are nevertheless combined with marked regional climatic diversity, the sharpness of which within such a limited area is astonishing. There are two reasons for this. Firstly, rain-bearing air streams come in mainly from the west (easterly and southerly winds tend to be hot and dry) and their effect decreases from north to south. Precipitation is thus substantial in Galilee and respectable in central Israel, but the Beersheba region further south is semi-arid, and only occasional downpours relieve the prevailing drought in the Negeb. Secondly, rainfall is directly related to land relief. Air masses passing eastwards from the Mediterranean cool as they rise over the hill country, and drop their moisture over its western slopes. When crossing the Jordan rift valley thereafter, they descend and warm up so that rain is rare on the eastern downslope, including the Judean desert, and in the rift valley north and south of the Dead Sea. Most of the small Palestinian rivers flow westwards, and only a few towards the east. Continuing on its easterly course, the air rises yet again when ascending the eastern slopes of the great depression and significant amounts of rain are released over the western edge of the Transjordan highland belt but rainfall then decreases eastwards, except where the air currents funnelled in through the zone of low ground east of the Lake of Tiberias meet the Hauran mountains. There are thus two main belts enjoying high precipitation east and west of the Jordan Valley – the eastern area extends further south than the western one, due to the effect of the mountains and high plateau in Edom – divided by a dry belt which also envelops them to the east and south. Variations in relief also have other climatic effects. In summer, the coastal plain may be subject to an enervating damp heat, but the uplands, while hot during the day, enjoy a healthier drier air and may be refreshingly cool at night; the region near the Dead Sea, mild in winter, can be intolerably hot in summer, while in the arid zone there are extreme differences between cold nights and very hot days. All told, the hill country which formed the homeland of the Israelites may be regarded as climatically favoured.

Yet climate is subject to fluctuations and long-term changes. Even in recent times sequences of rainy years have varied with periods of drought, and these can be disastrous, particularly in districts that are only marginally favourable anyway. That such was also the case in the Israelite period we know from the

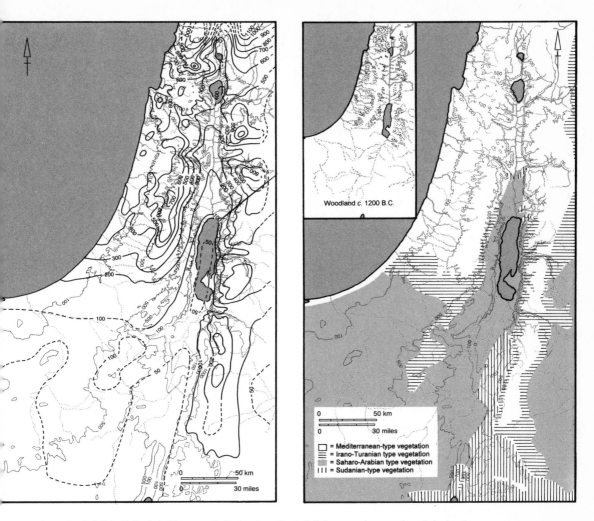

Woodland c. 1200 B.C.

0   50 km
0   30 miles

□ = Mediterranean-type vegetation
   = Irano-Turanian type vegetation
▓ = Saharo-Arabian type vegetation
| | | = Sudanian-type vegetation

4 Annual rainfall in Palestine. The overall diminution of rainfall from north to south and the local occurrence of a west to east sequence of zones of heavy precipitation, linked with the western slopes of high ground, are clearly visible.

5 The vegetation zones of Palestine, and the distribution of woodlands c. 1200 BC (inset). These depend on relief, geology and the opportunities offered to various plant communities.

Bible (e.g. Ruth 1, 16; 1 Kings 17ff.). The question is, however, whether there were, within this time, variations from the present climatic regime of greater significance and duration. There is much discussion and disagreement, but on present evidence it appears that the Chalcolithic and the earliest part of the Bronze Age enjoyed a somewhat wetter climate than now prevails, but that drier conditions came in by the thirteenth century BC if not before, and that these have remained dominant ever since. On the whole, therefore, it seems that the Israelites would have encountered climatic conditions and regional variations similar to present ones. It should be noted, though, that climate may be modified to some extent by human activity, especially by the clearing of forest or the removal of plant cover through over-grazing. The latter, it has been estimated, might raise local temperatures by as much as 6°C (11°F), with drastic environmental conseqences.

Vegetation

That the vegetation found in the various climatic provinces should vary in agreement with prevailing conditions is natural. However, the actual composition of the plant and animal communities which occur is determined by another factor also – the previous connections between Palestine and various continents in the geological past, and particularly by its geologically more recent location on the land bridge between Eurasia and Africa. As a result, the country is connected with several of the world's major phytogeographical divisions, and is endowed with an impressive variety of plants and animals.

Of the outside linkages, those with temperate and northern Europe and Asia (Euro-Siberian) are the least significant, being mainly restricted to scattered occurrences in upper Galilee and Golan. More importantly, those parts of Palestine enjoying a Mediterranean climate, including a reasonable amount of rainfall, belong, not surprisingly, to the region with Mediterranean vegetation (with some local variations due to differences in relief, soil types and underlying rocks). Forest once covered much of the ground. In the hills, there was a mixture of trees including in particular the evergreen oak, terebinth, juniper, cypress and hawthorn. Softer, chalky limestone regions were covered by pine trees, but it seems the cedar tree was never at home here (though some grew in the mountains of Edom). Forests of a somewhat different composition were found in the foothills and in the Sharon Plain.

For centuries, however, man has attacked and progressively destroyed or transformed this vegetation by removing trees for timber and charcoal, or by clearing ground to create farmland for grain, olive and vine cultivation, and pasture for animals. As a result, only a few forested areas have survived into the modern period and the woodlands have been widely replaced by areas of mixed shrubs, by ground covered with thorny plants or even by bare rock – a process which had begun even before the Israelites arrived on the scene. Though in the backwoods of Galilee they apparently still had to make their homes in forest clearings, elsewhere (as at Ai and Khirbet Raddaneh north of Jerusalem, or at Tell Beit Mirsim and Lachish to the south) fields and pasture had long replaced the forest. The clearing continued during the Israelite period, especially in the western Samaritan hill country, in order to provide additional ground for settlement (cf. Joshua 17, 14–18). By the eighth century BC, much of this region was rich farmland, as surveys have shown, though trees still grew in the hills near Jerusalem well after the Exile. At Tell el-Ful (Gibeah of Saul?) excavations have helped to date the gradual thinning of the tree cover during the Iron Age. When the first fortress was built there in the tenth century BC, cypress and pine wood were available for rafters, but in the seventh/sixth century almond wood had to be used because proper timber was apparently no longer available locally.

1 Landscape near Bethlehem. The underlying soft rock is easily weathered, creating gently undulating scenery: open country rather than tree cover is typical.

2 Landscape near Bittir, traversed by the railway line to Jerusalem. The terraces on the hillside (right) replace slopes fit only for grazing with a sequence of level surfaces useful for fields and gardens.

3 Charles Warren (right), seen talking to Yakoub ash-Shellaby, the leader of the Samaritan community at Nablus. Warren made important contributions to the exploration of Palestine.

4 *(Below)* This illustration recalls the early exploration of underground Jerusalem by shafts and galleries sunk into the ground. Charles Warren is shown touching a stone with typical Herodian dressing in a gallery next to the south-east corner of the Temple Platform.

Archaeology of ancient Israel

5 Jerusalem: view of the entrance chamber to 'Warren's Shaft' and the beginning of the sloping access tunnel.

6 *(Left)* Jerusalem: the 'Tomb of the Royal Steward' in the necropolis at Silwan, facing the 'City of David' across the Kidron Valley. Depressions in the facade of the tomb mark the place where, in 1870, inscribed panels (now in London) were cut out by C. Clermont-Ganneau.

7 *(Below)* Jerusalem: the 'Tomb of Pharaoh's Daughter'. The visible remains consist of a rock-cut, cube-shaped monument, ending in a cornice, once topped by a masonry pyramid. It was originally free-standing. The burial chamber inside, which has a gabled ceiling, contained niches for burials and stone couches.

8, 9, 10 *(Above)* Jerusalem: City of David Excavations (Area G, looking south). The foundations of the 'House of Ahiel' overlie the older, sloping foundations of the Canaanite or Davidic citadel building (near the top). The house (named by Y. Shiloh after a person mentioned twice on ostraca found here) is unusual in having a privy. *(Below)* The stone toilet fitting is in the rear right-hand corner of the room. Wooden toilet fittings above a cesspit may have been more common.

11 Remains of one of 'Solomon's Stables', of which there are several groups at Megiddo. They date from the time of Ahab, though some examples of Solomonic date have been discovered more recently.

12 Megiddo: the Stratum IV gate, viewed from the north. Note the use of ashlar, which in places enclosed horizontal beamwork.

13 Fragments of carved wood (burnt) from
Y. Shiloh's City of David excavations in
Jerusalem. They may have come from furniture
or wall panelling: the motifs match those in
Phoenician ivory carvings.

14 Ivory carving from Nimrud, Mesopotamia,
featuring the 'woman at the window'. This
motif is found repeatedly among Phoenician-
style ivory carving at various sites. Note the
window balustrade with its dwarf columns
which imitated actual ornamental windows
(see 15).

15 A stone window balustrade with dwarf
columns from the palace at Ramat Rachel,
which recalls the example depicted in 14.

16 Painted stone lamp or brazier found at Megiddo, imitating a composite column capital with pendant leaves. It has been suggested that the twin columns (Jachin and Boaz) which stood in front of Solomon's Temple had similar capitals.

17 Proto–Aeolic capitals, such as this one from Ramat Rachel, were employed in important public buildings in Israel. Those in Judah tend to be stylistically superior to examples in the Northern Kingdom, but related to ones in Moab.

18 Base for a throne or statue (originally surrounded by four columns supporting a canopy); the ornament on the column bases is of North Syrian type. The whole fixture was placed in front of the inner gate at Dan.

19 View of the massive stone foundations of the palace-fort at Lachish.

20 Lachish: the Level IV–III gate, looking outwards. The partitions on the near side of the gate room are clearly visible. The rougher walling at the back on each side of the gate opening belongs to the later Stratum II.

In the coastal plain, mixed oak forest survived in Sharon and as far south as Jaffa into the nineteenth century, but human activity during our period changed its composition. Curiously enough, the Philistine plain further south appears always to have been comparatively treeless.

Where the rainfall diminishes on the southern and eastern borders of the western Palestinian hill range, and similarly on the southern and eastern borders of the Mediterranean vegetation region of Transjordan, a second vegetation zone, the Irano-Turanian, is encountered. While in the transitional districts parklands with some trees, such as terebinth, may be observed, tree growth in the Irano-Turanian region proper is scarce, and low shrubs like wormwood predominate. Excavations in southern sites like Beersheba and Arad show that trees growing in this zone were also cut for timber by the Israelites.

The part of Palestine provided with the least rainfall forms the Sahara-Arabian zone. This includes the central and southern Negeb and much of the Dead Sea and Arabah regions, as well as the eastern flank of the Transjordanian uplands, and also the coastal dune strip along the Mediterranean. It is by far the largest part of Palestine in all. Much of it is desert, with ground only sparsely covered by plants except where wadi beds provide some moisture; tamarisks, broom and thorny acacias related to those found in the Sudan may be found. Near Elath, *dom* palms like those found in Arabia also occur. Remarkably, even here the results of the destructive activity of man can be discerned: though the bedouin might plant the odd tree for shade, over-grazing has widely removed the type of vegetation preferred by their flocks and left plants unpalatable to animals.

One more type of plant community should be mentioned, found especially in the rift valley in isolated warm and well-watered patches or oases as a survival from a warmer and wetter pre-Tertiary geological period, namely the Sudanian (Sudano-Zambesian). The lotus tree or 'Christ thorn' (*zizyphus spina Christi*) belongs to this assembly, and date palms and Jericho balsam can be grown in this environment. Surviving remnants of former expanses of papyrus reeds, once characteristic of the (now drained) Lake Huleh on the upper Jordan, are an impressive reminder of past connections between Palestine and Nilotic Africa.

Animal life

The diversity of relief, climate and vegetation in the country in turn affected animal life. External connections with Eurasia and Africa were again influential in the selection of various zones by a multitude of different species, though animal mobility is apt to blur borders, and the main division tends anyhow to be between forested as against desert or semi-desert regions. An example taken from the Bible will illustrate this point. When David recalled (1 Samuel 17, 34–36) that in order to protect his father's flock he had killed a bear and a lion, he was referring to creatures living in different habitats – the bear is a woodland dweller, the lion more an inhabitant of savannah and steppe country. Scripture in fact offers quite a few examples of animals found in these two main regions and their subdivisions (a few are also linked with the Sudanian zone). Biblical writers liked to use animal characteristics and habits (which they keenly observed) for similes and metaphors in poetry and prose.

Archaeological discoveries, together with observations by classical and later writers and reports by more recent travellers and scientists, allow a further picture. They also show that the rich animal life found in the past has been progressively impoverished, particularly since the arrival of modern firearms. We may begin with two surprising inhabitants: hippopotami and crocodiles were apparently found in the coastal plain during the Iron Age – as indicated by finds of bones of the former, and by the survival of living specimens of the latter in the Zerqa (Crocodile) River south of Haifa until the end of the last century. At the eastern and southern flank of Palestine, in Transjordan, in the Negeb and in the Arabah, there was a different world. Here ostriches, wild asses or onagers, oryx and gazelles roamed the steppes or deserts, while the hyrax (the biblical coney), wild goat and ibex were found on rocky ground; lions and wolves, followed by hyenas and jackals, could find their prey here. These animals might penetrate surprisingly far westwards; during the last century, ostriches were seen west of Amman, and gazelles near Jerusalem, while the roar of the lion was still heard by a medieval pilgrim not far from Haifa. The most arid remote desert was also made fearsome by snakes and scorpions (cf. Deuteronomy 8, 15). Desert locusts issuing in swarms from Arabia or Africa could be a devastating plague from time to time.

The central region covered by forest or bush was different again. Here lived red, fallow and roe deer and the aurochs (wild ox) and wild boar – except for the latter, all are now gone. Predators included foxes, wolves, cheetahs and leopards (the latter two also found in the rift valley), besides the bear, which was resident in the woods near Bethel in Elisha's time (2 Kings 2, 24); they sometimes strayed from Lebanon into northern Israel in the nineteenth century, as did wolves.

Of the very many kinds of birds, resident or migratory, partridge might be found in the dry regions, while quail alighted in the Sinai desert on their journeys. Other migrants, like storks, preferred well-watered places. Birds of prey abounded, particularly in the desert.

Among freshwater creatures, tortoises and fish in the Jordan and in the Lake of Tiberias deserve notice; among the latter were some Nilotic species. Fish in the Mediterranean included the occasional whale and the *murex* molluscs from which purple dye was produced. In the Red Sea, besides many kinds of fish, the dugong, which may have furnished the prized *taḥaš* leather mentioned in the description of the Tabernacle, might be found, besides *tridacna* shells (used as cosmetic containers) and corals.

Man found many species among this multifarious fauna desirable as prey, though against others he would have to wage war. The varied habitats of the wild animals would also suit the domesticated species – cattle, sheep, goats, camels and donkeys, as well as the adaptable dog, all of which were in the service of people by the end of the Bronze Age, though camel riding may then have been a very recent art. Domestic fowl appear to have been introduced only during our period, and the time when the cat (long-esteemed in Egypt) may have decided to join human company in Palestine is still a mystery.

Communications

The natural conditions outlined above largely determine the country's lines of communication and their respective importance. The fact that the four main belts of high and low ground extend from north to south means that four trunk roads on the same alignment are feasible. Of these, the most westerly runs up the coastal plain along the Mediterranean, the second follows the crest line of the western hill country, the third goes down the Jordan Valley and, after a gap caused by the impassable shores of the Dead Sea, continues southwards along the Arabah Valley to Elath and the fourth traverses the belt of fertile land in the Transjordanian uplands between their steep western edge and the desert border to the east (a parallel loop line positioned further east on the steppe–desert border is an additional possibility). As for transverse routes running between east and west, which have to overcome some considerable differences in altitude between highlands and lowlands, numerous river valleys descending westwards (or more rarely eastwards) from the ranges offered easier going, especially when leading to saddles of lower ground interrupting the mountain ranges and inviting crossing. Transverse routes are thus more numerous though of varying significance. The road network made up in this fashion would have helped to exploit and exchange the products of various zones of the country and permit the inhabitants to respond to the consequences of local climatic differences – for example, the early or late ripening of crops, local droughts, or the need to move flocks some distance to more permanent pastures as the vegetation of the steppes shrivelled up with the coming of summer (cf. Genesis 37, 12–17).

In addition to such internal functions, certain routes were specially apt to carry important international commerce into or across the country. These seemed predestined, unfortunately, to be used also by foreign invading armies.

The most important artery of trade traversing the country was the long-established road which came up from Egypt – the 'Way of the Sea' or *Via Maris*. Up to the neighbourhood of Jaffa it mostly followed a range of fossilized dunes offering dry ground underfoot, but thereafter it ran by preference further east, along the border of hill and plain, thus avoiding the marshes and forests of Sharon. Similar reasons also caused travellers to shun the constriction of the coastal plain where Mount Carmel nearly reaches the sea. It seemed preferable to cross the Carmel range by one of the passes leading to Megiddo, Jokneam or Taanach. From here, a route was available to Acco and so to Tyre, Sidon and the north, but this was again hemmed in, and the main line struck across to Beth Shean or, preferably, up to the western shore of the Lake of

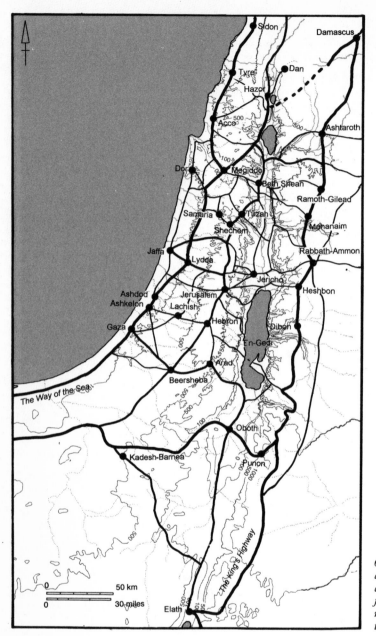

6 *Map showing the principal roads in ancient Palestine. International lines of communication crossing the country, and first- or second-class regional or local roads are indicated by progressively thinner lines.*

Tiberias. Though further travel northwards through the valley between Lebanon and Anti-Lebanon to Hamath, Aleppo and the Euphrates was feasible, both this and the Beth Shean route led by preference to fords crossing the Jordan, the road continuing thereafter to Damascus and ultimately to Mesopotamia.

The road along the crest of the western uplands was not of the same long-standing international significance, though it gained importance as a line of access to, and communication (or sometimes confrontation) between, northern

Israel and Judah. Southwards it continued to Beersheba, and a track might be followed from there to Egypt; northwards, however, the difficult hill country in Galilee forbade an extension beyond the Vale of Jezreel. The tracks flanking the Jordan on its western and (preferably) eastern sides were likewise not of major significance during our period, though the route down the Arabah did carry important traffic at least at times when a strong government could provide safety (a factor significant also with regard to roads in the neighbouring Negeb). The trunk road crossing Transjordan from south to north, known as the 'King's Highway', however, was another main artery of international commerce along which caravans bringing incense, spices and other valuable goods from South Arabia and beyond travelled to Damascus.

TOWNS WITHIN ISRAEL							
West		North		East		South	
To	**Days**	**To**	**Days**	**To**	**Days**	**To**	**Days**
Acco	5	Dan	7	Ramoth-Gilead	5	Elath	8–9
Dor	4	Hazor	6	Mahanaim	3½	Beersheba	2½
Jaffa	2	Megiddo	3½–4	Dibon	3	Arad	2
Ashdod	2+	Beth-Shean	3½–4	Heshbon	2	Lachish	2-
Ascalon	2½	Samaria	2½	Jericho	1-	Hebron	1+
Gaza	3	Shechem	2				
NEARBY FOREIGN CAPITALS							
West		North		East		South	
To	**Days**	**To**	**Days**	**To**	**Days**	**To**	**Days**
Tyre	6½	Damascus	8–9	Rabbath-Ammon	3–4	Bozrah	5½–6

7 Approximate travelling times from Jerusalem at caravan speed (25–30 km per day).

Lines of communication between east and west were of varying importance. Upper Galilee could be crossed by a circuitous track linking Hazor with Tyre. Further south, there was the route known until fairly recently as the *'Darb el-Hawārneh'*, which allowed camel caravans carrying grain from the Hauran region by tracks flanking the Yarmuq Valley to traverse Lower Galilee on their way to Acco. South of the main route across the Vale of Jezreel (linking the Mediterranean coast with the Jordan region), a number of valleys allowed access to the district of Shechem and Samaria from the west; eastwards, however, the Wadi Far'ah provided the best line of descent to the Jordan Valley. Across the river, the valley of the Jabbok offered a way past Succoth, Mahanaim and Penuel to the Transjordan plateau. Further south, several openings permitted access from Jaffa and Philistia to the central part of the western uplands and to Jerusalem. From there, rather steep tracks led down to Jericho, and then, across the Jordan fords, there were routes up into the Transjordan plateau and onwards to the Ammonite capital, or alternatively to Heshbon. Hebron could be reached by a number of routes from the Philistine plain, while eastwards a track descended towards the narrow waist of the Dead Sea, which could be forded at that point by camel caravans; these could then continue to make their way up into Moab.

Of much greater significance was another east–west route linking Philistia and Transjordan via Beersheba and Arad, and a parallel track further south past Kadesh Barnea to Punon and Bozra. These linked the 'King's Highway' with the west, allowing the caravans carrying South Arabian incense and spices access to the port of Gaza; the southern route might also be used to convey copper westwards from Punon. Kadesh Barnea was connected by desert tracks with the Gulf of Aqabah and Elath. Such profitable trade routes were liable to become objects of political dispute, and arouse the desire for conquest. Peaceful or warlike, however, travel in the country was not time-consuming: to get from Dan to Beersheba might take above a week, on to Elath another, while traversing the country from east to west was only a matter of three to five days.

Human geography

While it is true that much of the lowland zone is better endowed than the highlands, if more exposed to danger, only the Philistine plain had sufficient resources to become a region of international significance. The climate might be unpleasant, but the cultivable area was large and productive, and important trading links by land and sea offered benefits. Relations with Israel are of special interest. F. Braudel has taught us to expect a well-endowed lowland zone to dominate poor highland neighbours. We must keep an eye on this question since Israelite traditions seem not to support the thesis entirely. Further north, Sharon, the coastal plain north of Mount Carmel and the Vale of Jezreel were all dependent, or at times disputed, areas.

Among the upland districts which were blessed with a more bracing climate but where greater effort was needed to gain a livelihood, Galilee was too little provided with cultivable land to count for much. Some of its inhabitants might have had to seek work in neighbouring Phoenicia – an example perhaps of the general tendency of hill folk to seek their livelihood in the richer plains nearby, when conditions did not permit this at home. Ephraim and Manasseh further to the south offered their inhabitants better conditions: areas suited to farming were sizeable and could be expanded, and trade could enter from a number of directions – so, unfortunately, could enemy forces. Judah in the south was less well endowed, but also more isolated and thus perhaps more secure. Both these hill countries would tend also to be closely linked with the plain to the west, invading sometimes or being invaded, but also entering into economic links which archaeology is only just beginning to reveal. The Shephelah acted as a frontier zone for such military or peaceful contacts.

Across the Jordan, Bashan was rich but lacked defensible frontiers – trade might cross it, but invasion and annexation were also likely consequences of such openness. Its southern neighbour Gilead, however, a well-endowed mountain stronghold closely connected with Israel across the Jordan, long held its own. Yet, in spite of the fact that the deeply incised river valleys descending westwards provided apparently natural frontiers, the balance between the various political entities on the Transjordan plateau – Ammon, Moab and Edom as well as Israel – was fluid and the intervention of imperial forces from outside (Egyptian momentarily at the time of Sheshonq's campaign, Assyrian and then Babylonian) was an overpowering factor, here as elsewhere. Development of the resources of the desert zone in the Arabah and the Negeb would similarly be at the mercy of political circumstances favouring now one and now another of the interested parties – Edom, Egypt, Arabian and other tribes, and Judah in particular. These regions acted as zones of transit, so that, for example, Edomites were found at times in the Negeb as well as in Transjordan, having expanded across the zone.

Factors of human geography also affected the pattern of settlement. The lowland belt offered greater advantages for urban growth than the uplands, where significant cities were few, though villages and hamlets came to abound, except in Galilee. Some formerly Canaanite towns continued to flourish in our period as before, due to their special functions. Megiddo, for instance, was situated by an important road junction, besides controlling the chief pass across the Carmel range. However, it seems that here as elsewhere the fact that government had selected the place as a military or administrative centre was influential. Choice was also an element in the selection of capital cities. Thus, though the best region to place a northern Israelite capital seemed fairly circumscribed, Shechem and Tirzah were contenders for the honour before Samaria was selected. Similarly, while an all-Israelite capital for a United Monarchy seemed best located on neutral ground near the middle of the upland belt, a site in Benjamin, rather than Jerusalem, might have attained this rank had the house of Saul, who was of that tribe, ruled longer; Gibeon still functioned in important pan-Israelite religious ceremonies even after the accession of Solomon (1 Kings 3, 4ff.). Geography might present (or seem to deny) opportunities, but the use made of them was determined by the historical process.

CHAPTER TWO

Origins and Affinities of the Israelites

In spite of intensive scholarly activity for more than a century, the origins of Israel remain obscure. The history of Israel, many feel, cannot be traced back beyond the twelfth and eleventh centuries BC, the period of the Judges (and some even think not beyond the time of the Monarchy in the tenth century). A generation ago it appeared that valuable information about Israel's ancestry was being obtained by placing data from the biblical narratives within the framework of ancient Near Eastern history and social and material evolution. Lately, however, many of the results of such a combined approach have been queried and fundamental reservations have been voiced about the legitimacy of arguing from a combination of scriptural and archaeological sources. At the same time, recent information, including in particular the results of large-scale archaeological field surveys, has opened new perspectives, and novel ways of interpreting and synthesizing the known facts on sociological lines have come to the fore. It follows from this that in order to assess what can be said about Israel's prehistory, an outline of the biblical record and its scholarly interpretation must be presented separately from a succinct account of the historical and archaeological data. The main views expressed by scholars as to how, in the light of such information, Israel appears to have come into being also need reviewing.

The 'patriarchal period'

The Bible, and in particular the Book of Genesis, contains accounts of how Israel came into being, and how it was related to its neighbours. In spite of some difficulties in detail the main story is fairly clear and coherent. The Israelites are descendants of Abraham (originally called Abram), a Hebrew or wandering Aramean, who, under divine guidance, forsook his home town of Ur in Mesopotamia and after a stay further north at Haran travelled with his family to Canaan. There he entered into a covenant with the Deity and was promised that his offspring would become a great nation and inherit that country. It was at this time that his name was changed from Abram to Abraham. He and his descendants, Isaac and Jacob, are described as moving about the land with their flocks (with occasional reference also to agriculture); their relations with the local inhabitants are depicted as friendly at times, hostile at others. Localities in the central hill country (Shechem, Bethel) and in the far south (Beersheba, Mamre) are associated with their wanderings and acts of worship, while the family burial cave was at Hebron.

A number of neighbouring nations are described as related to Abraham by descent: the Arameans collaterally, the Ishmaelites and other Arab tribes directly, the Edomites through his grandson Esau, and the Ammonites and Moabites as the somewhat irregular offspring of his nephew Lot. The main interest, however, is centred on the descendants of Jacob, who received the name Israel after a remarkable contest with a superhuman stranger by the ford across the river Jabbok near Penuel in Transjordan. Jacob's favourite but precocious son Joseph was sold by his jealous brothers to a caravan of merchants, who took him down to Egypt. There, after many tribulations, he finally obtained high office at the court of the pharaoh and was thus able to obtain permission for his father and 11 brothers to sojourn in the district of Goshen during a famine alleviated by his own inspired foresight. Here the offspring of the 12 brothers multiplied in time, to become the 12 tribes of Israel.

Scholarly attitudes to these accounts have, in recent years, been increasingly affected by doubt. We have seen that the biblical text had a long and complicated history, and that it is often thought now that much of the present text is late, and reflects the general situation and preoccupations of that time. To what extent it might then preserve correct information about an age long gone by is unclear, even if it is accepted that Abraham, Isaac and Jacob did exist as real persons, rather than representing theoretical eponymous ancestors of tribal groups (and not all scholars do accept this). It has also been suggested that the patriarchal traditions are not unitary in origin, but go back to different antecedents – even those about Jacob and Israel have been held to have separate derivation. In this case, it is thought, the stories would have been preserved at various holy places and combined and reshaped later by later editors.

It is similarly difficult to obtain a proper assessment of the historical realities involved in the patriarchal accounts by viewing them against the historical and archaeological background now known. No mention is made in ancient Near Eastern texts of persons identifiable with members of the patriarchal family although it has in the past been noted that the names of several – Abram and Jacob, for example – occurred in documents from the second millennium BC, and that places mentioned in the stories also existed then with similar names. Furthermore the general milieu seemed right, in that the eighteenth-century BC cuneiform documents found in the city of Mari on the upper Euphrates showed that part of the countryside was occupied by largely pastoralist tribes whose lifestyle might be compared with the one found in the patriarchal accounts. Indeed, they even included a tribal group whose name was read as *Banu-Iamina*, or 'Benjaminites'. Again, slightly later documents, such as those found at Nuzi, which is some distance from Mari, seemed to show that social and legal customs in the patriarchal traditions could be matched in early Mesopotamia.

The wanderings of Abraham might also have been connected with donkey nomadism and donkey-borne trade, while within a larger canvas they might relate to migrations of peoples linked to Abraham's family by kinship. Some have suggested connections with the supposed arrival of the Amorites, forerunners of the Arameans, in Palestine near the start of the second millennium BC (reflected, it was thought, in the intrusive Palestinian Middle Bronze I culture). Others have made connections between the unsettled group transcribed in Akkadian texts as *Ḥabiru*, in Egyptian as *'Apiru*, and the Hebrews. Dates offered by scholars for the patriarchs ranged mostly between the nineteenth and thirteenth centuries BC, with the eighteenth favoured; biblical chronology, subject to variant reckonings and dependent in the last resort on the disputed date of the Exodus from Egypt, allows some latitude.

More recently, such attempts to confirm the biblical accounts have been subjected to numerous criticisms. Names found in the patriarchal stories occur not only in the second but also in the first millennium BC, and some would be more natural in the latter period. In particular, the puzzling occurrence of Hittites in patriarchal Palestine, as at Hebron, has been linked with the use of the term 'Hittite' to denote inhabitants of the Levant in Late Assyrian and Babylonian texts. References to the Mari texts, while instructive, are distant both in space and perhaps also time. The pastoralists there referred to are not true nomads on the way to settling down, and the reading *Banu-Iamina* needs qualifying. As for alleged parallels between legal and social customs in the patriarchal stories and those found in documents from Nuzi and elsewhere, some are thought to be based on misunderstanding while others, it is claimed, can be established better in the first millennium BC. Suggestions that Abraham was a donkey-caravan merchant are now discounted, and his connections with suggested Amorite migrations or their archaeological attestation are also not accepted – during Middle Bronze I, a number of localities referred to in the Abraham stories were apparently not inhabited. The Arameans are not really attested before the thirteenth century BC, and the use of the term 'Hebrew' without a derogatory tinge seems to have become current only in the later books of the Bible. The possibility of anachronisms would thus have to be kept in mind. Some feel that there was, in fact, no patriarchal period, but that the story we have combines events and persons separated in time by remodelling and telescoping accounts. Such scepticism is, however, balanced by recent arguments showing that there are points in favour of a patriarchal age datable to the first half of the second millennium BC, and for a thirteenth-century Exodus.

The sojourn in Egypt, the Exodus and the wanderings in the desert

Our sources for these events are found mainly in the books of Exodus, Leviticus, Numbers and Deuteronomy. According to Exodus (12, 40) the Children of Israel stayed in Egypt for 430 years (other figures are given elsewhere and a much shorter stay may be implied by certain genealogies, like that of Moses in Exodus 6, 16–20). Their rapidly increasing numbers alarmed the Egyptians to such an extent that an unnamed pharaoh decided to oppress them with heavy task-work – in particular by forcing them to build his new cities of Pithom and Raamses. Pharaoh also ordered all new-born males to be killed, but one boy-child survived miraculously – set adrift in a rush-basket in the Nile, he was noticed by an Egyptian princess, saved and adopted by her, and given the name Moses. Later, however, he had to flee the country after killing an Egyptian whom he saw ill-treating fellow Hebrews. He took refuge in Midian and married one of the daughters of a local priest. Subsequently, at Mount Horeb, he received a divine call to lead his people to freedom, with the assistance of his brother Aaron. Moses returned to Egypt, where the new pharaoh at first resisted his pleas to let the Israelites leave Egypt, but divine intervention, manifested in the 'Ten Plagues', forced him to relent. When, thereafter, he decided to send his troops in pursuit of the Israelites, the latter were miraculously delivered at the Sea of Reeds, whose waters temporarily divided to let them pass but returned and drowned the pursuing Egyptians. Moses then led his people to Mount Sinai (synonymous with Horeb). Here they were given, in an awesome divine revelation accompanied by thunder, lightning, earthquake, fire, smoke and the sound of trumpets issuing from the mountain, first the Ten Commandments and later many civil and religious ordinances, including the order to make a tent sanctuary or tabernacle. Miraculously sustained in the wilderness but nevertheless rebellious – the making of the Golden Calf was an especially grave lapse – the Israelites had to wander in the desert for 40 years (including a stay of some length at Kadesh) before they were allowed to enter the Promised Land.

This account has presented scholars with considerable problems to which there is at present no obvious solution. The biblical text is again regarded as a compound of a number of traditions: the description of the route of the Exodus, for example, is thought to contain traces of several different versions, and some elements in the story have been thought to be affected by backward projection of later conditions. Thus the background of the Joseph story may fit the Egypt of the first millennium BC better than that of the second, the description of the tent sanctuary has often been thought to be modelled on Solomon's Temple in Jerusalem (but it has been pointed out recently that in its reported setting and constructional features it fits Bronze Age Egyptian prototypes); and the Golden Calf was perhaps simply derived from the 'calf' images put up by Jeroboam after the split of Solomon's kingdom. The question of possible anachronisms is, however, more serious. There is no agreement among scholars over how much of the religion allegedly proclaimed by Moses in the biblical accounts may really be credited to him. Much of the ritual legislation is regarded by many as being of a much later origin, while monotheism itself is, some think, not the starting-point of Israel's beliefs but rather the end-product of a long evolution. Some indeed doubt whether Israel preserved any common ancient traditions about Moses, for it has been noticed that – outside the Pentateuch – he is mentioned only rarely in texts from the time of the Monarchy, and more perhaps in northern Israel than in Judah, where the dynasty of David featured largely in religious thinking. Problems are also caused by what seem to be improbabilities in the Exodus accounts – for example, the very large numbers of Israelites who reportedly sojourned in the desert (Numbers 1 and 26 both give approximately 600,000 adult males).

Lastly, it has been observed that elements of folklore and comparative literature are enshrined in the traditions: thus the remarkable preservation of the infant Moses recalls an almost identical Mesopotamian tale about the early childhood of Sargon the Elder, the legendary founder of the Empire of Akkad. All told, it is hard to identify authentic elements in the Exodus story.

Recourse to extra-biblical information is unfortunately of limited use. Though Semites are known to have lived in Egypt, Egyptian records do not attest the existence of Israelites, the Oppression or the Exodus. Nor can an individual clearly corresponding to the biblical Moses be identified, though the name Moses is found – it is Egyptian, being a short form of a name like Thutmoses or Ahmoses. (The occurrence of other Egyptian names such as Hophni, Phinehas and Merari among the Levites to whom Moses belonged is indeed an indication of early links with Egypt but it is uncertain when they were adopted.) The statement that the Israelites built Pithom and Raamses has been used as a chronological peg. Since building with conscripted labour was carried on during the long reign of Ramses II in the thirteenth century BC, he has often been identified as the pharaoh of the Oppression and perhaps of the Exodus (his successor Merneptah is also considered in the latter connection). Yet a thirteenth-century date for the Exodus, long popular, cannot be securely established on that foundation because the use of the names Pithom (probably Tell el Maskhuta) and Raamses (now identified with Tell el Dab'ah/Qantir) may be an anachronism, and the building operations envisaged may have taken place before Ramses II – indeed, Pithom may no longer have existed in his day. Such a dating is also in conflict with the biblical statement that the Exodus took place 480 years before the fourth year of Solomon's reign (1 Kings 6, 1, cf. also Judges 11, 26), which would date it to *c.* 1446 BC. Genealogical and other arguments have, on the other hand, been adduced to show that the time-span involved was much less than 480 years. The suggestion that the Exodus occurred still earlier, and was linked with the expulsion of the Hyksos from Egypt, goes back to the Hellenistic period and is discounted by many, though some still regard it possible.

Such discrepancies may be due to differing Israelite traditions, now combined. Some believe the Exodus did not occur at all, or that only a small group of followers of Moses was involved; others maintain that not all the Israelites ever left Canaan for Egypt, and returned from there, but only either the Leah or Rachel tribes (going by the grouping of the sons of Jacob according to his wives and their concubine maids in Genesis 35, 23–26); yet others have suggested that several tribal groups entered Egypt and left it again at different times. In addition, many feel the fully developed system of 12 Israelite tribes cannot have existed before Israel was established in Palestine, i.e. at the inception of the Monarchy or not much earlier. All told, a proper historical treatment cannot be attempted, and there is not much more certainty about what followed.

Leaving aside the puzzles offered by the miraculous delivery of the Israelites at the crossing of the Sea of Reeds (some other body of water near Tell el

Dab'ah – now identified with Raamses – rather than the Red Sea may be what is referred to), and of the routes followed thereafter, we must say something about the central event of the divine revelation, covenant and law-giving at Mount Sinai. The tradition that this took place at one of the high peaks in the south of what is now called the Sinai Peninsula cannot be traced back beyond the early centuries of the Christian era, and two alternative locations have been considered by scholars. Some look for the mountain of the Revelation not far from Kadesh, about 80 km (50 miles) south of Beersheba. Others, impressed by the similarity between the phenomena attending the Revelation and those accompanying volcanic eruptions, would see Sinai in northwestern Arabia – ancient Midian – for here volcanic activity reportedly still occurred in the Middle Ages. Habbakuk (3, 1–7) and Judges (5, 4–5) may point in that direction (or to a region in southern Transjordan) but the matter is still unresolved.

Whatever the exact geographical location of Sinai, the Israelites later held the belief that it was there that the God who had delivered their ancestors from Egyptian bondage constituted them his special people, and that he was the one whose name was written with the consonants YHWH (pronounced, scholars think, Yahweh – Yeho, Yahu, Yo and Yah being shortened forms). This name seems to have been attached to a locality in southern Transjordan in two Egyptian texts of the fourteenth and thirteenth centuries BC respectively (later, in the ninth century BC, we hear of Yahweh of Teman (Edom) in a text found at Kuntillet 'Ajrud). Whether the cult of YHWH was at home there, or among the Midianites further south remains a subject for speculation, as do alleged occurrences of the name elsewhere in the second millennium BC. On present evidence, a southeastern derivation seems likely in general terms.

Other divine names used by the Israelites have different associations. The name El in particular was widely used among Canaanites and others in the second millennium BC to designate the High God heading the pantheon. It was also an element in the formation of names, and it is in particular enshrined in the name Israel, which may mean 'El contends victoriously' (the explanation in Genesis 32, 28 seems secondary). The name is also known to have been borne by persons mentioned in extra-biblical documents from Ugarit and Ebla during the Bronze Age.

Archaeologically, the tradition about Mount Sinai and the desert wanderings remains unsupported. Though early camp sites or burials may now sometimes be detected in desert conditions, none which could be ascribed to the wandering Israelites are known at present. It must of course be borne in mind that nomads may also be 'archaeologically invisible'.

The conquest of Canaan and the tribal settlement

According to the Bible, the Israelites gained the Promised Land by conquest: first, under the leadership of Moses, they took northern Transjordan; later, under his successor Joshua, they invaded western Palestine. The first stage, involving the conquest of the kingdoms ruled by Sihon and Og is described in

Numbers 21, Deuteronomy 2 and 3, and Judges 11, the second in Joshua 1–12. In both cases there is reference to the united action of all Israel under one supreme leader, followed by his allotment of territory to the tribes. Joshua is stated to have gained control of most of the western hill country through a series of co-ordinated campaigns (the plain belt remained largely in Canaanite hands). The accounts are particularly specific about the conquest of the Benjamin region: we are told about the miraculous fall of Jericho, whose walls came tumbling down, about the conquest of Ai by stratagem and the compact with the Gibeonites obtained by deceit. Elsewhere, we learn about a campaign against the kings of the southern hill region, and another against Galilee which led to the taking of Hazor. The conquered land was then allotted to the tribes, and a covenant ceremony at Shechem was followed by the dismissal of the forces and finally by Joshua's death. However, in Judges 1 there is another account of various local conquests and settlements, especially in Judah, resulting from individual actions. Some have taken these to represent various 'mopping-up' operations in the wake of Joshua's campaigns, but many feel the account may be a fragment of an alternative tradition according to which the Israelites gained their land, not by concerted action but piecemeal, as and where circumstances allowed them to assert themselves. Lastly, some think Numbers 14, 44ff. and 21, 1–3 reflect the entry of various groups into Judah from the Kadesh region.

Problems involved in the assumption of a conquest

The date and historical veracity of the accounts in these sources have been much debated. A generation ago, their basic truth was generally accepted. Although the Book of Joshua especially might contain material of varying age – some quite late – including aetiological sagas (as in the cases of Jericho and Ai) and although Judges 1 might offer a truer picture of how Canaan was conquered, it was widely believed that the Israelites were intruders from the east, and that military action accompanied their coming. At present, however, there is a tendency to stress that our sources, Joshua in particular, represent late – possibly Exilic or post-Exilic – reconstructions of Israel's early history intended to illustrate theological principles. Even the account in Judges, some now think, is of less historical value than was once believed.

As the amount of credence placed in the biblical sources has altered, so the assessment of the testimony offered by extra-biblical textual and especially archaeological evidence has changed too. That this points to the reality of an Israelite conquest has been increasingly queried and alternative views have gained ground. The question must be studied within its general cultural and political setting. During the Bronze Age, Palestine was covered by a network of small city-kingdoms, closely spaced in the plains but more widely in the hill country, which controlled the nearby villages and, when possible, the pastoral nomads found in parts of the district, with whom they lived in economic symbiosis. Urban settlement also existed throughout the period in

Transjordan, though rather doubtfully in the south, where it became important only from the ninth–eighth century BC onwards. Though the ruling classes had come to include some Indo-European and Hurrian speakers, this urban civilization may be called basically Canaanite. Biblical distinctions between Canaanites and Amorites among the pre-Israelite inhabitants of the country need not be pursued here and, except perhaps for the Horites, who may have had some connection with the Hurrians, other pre-Israelite nations mentioned in the Bible remain in the shadows.

Egypt was an early influence on the country. Following the expulsion of the Hyksos from the Nile delta, the Egyptians chased them northwards, and the destruction of many Palestinian towns about 1550 BC is often attributed to the invading Egyptian armies, though this cannot be proved. Palestine was thereafter incorporated into the Egyptian empire in Asia, and from the fifteenth century into the twelfth, Egypt remained in control there to a varying extent (more in the strategically and economically important lowlands than in the less vital hill country). Though there were some Egyptian garrisons and governors and a system of strategically placed 'governors' residences' the Egyptians largely allowed the system of petty kingdoms to continue as long as they furnished taxes and services, particularly in support of the Egyptian forces stationed in the country or present there on campaign. Canaanite civilization also continued, though affected by Egyptian and other foreign contacts. Important towns in the regions directly controlled by Egypt remained wealthy – the rulers of Megiddo for instance were able to amass some remarkable art treasures, especially carved ivories – but elsewhere, in outlying districts in the hill country in particular, decline set in. Settlements became fewer, smaller in size and the quality of material civilization declined. Egyptian exactions may be to blame, but also the insecurity caused by unsettled marauders and outlaws. Among these, a group featuring repeatedly in the Amarna letters – the international diplomatic archive of clay tablets written in Akkadian found at el-Amarna in Egypt and dating from the early fourteenth century BC – has been much discussed. Styled *Ḥap/biru* (corresponding to the transcription *'Apiru* in Egyptian documents), they were at first related by scholars to the biblical Hebrews; the fact that they were active particularly in the western hill country and in league with the ruler of Shechem seemed to support the equation. However, it has since been shown that the term refers to a much wider class of 'displaced' people found from Mesopotamia to Egypt during the second millennium BC. Some took service as labourers or mercenaries, others became brigands; and runaway peasants might swell their ranks – the term was not mainly an ethnic one. Some connection with the Hebrews of the Bible cannot be ruled out completely. The case seems similar with another group of unsettled freebooters – the Shasu or Shosu of Egyptian texts, who were active particularly in southern Transjordan in the thirteenth century BC. The place-name Y-h-w is located in their region, and some people think they played a part in the formation of Israel, but this remains hypothetical.

The late thirteenth and early twelfth centuries BC confronted the Egyptian empire in Asia with increasing difficulties. It survived to an astonishing extent until *c.* 1150 BC or even later, having somehow accommodated itself to the settlement of groups of Aegean marauders – the Philistines and other 'Sea Peoples' – in the coastal plain belt *c.* 1174. Yet repeated campaigns were needed to retain influence in the western hill country, the Arabah (where the copper mines at Timnah continued under Egyptian control) and in the uplands of Transjordan, the aim of several punitive expeditions. That there is no hint of all this in the biblical records is most remarkable for by now, many think, there was an Israelite presence in Canaan, which would have been ringed by the Egyptian-controlled zone. This assumption is based on the 'Israel stela' (*ANET* 378), erected in Thebes by Pharaoh Merneptah (pl. 34). In it he records that in the fifth year of his reign (1207 or alternatively 1219) he campaigned in Palestine, defeating among others a people whose name is read by most, though not all, as 'Israel'. Most scholars admit the campaign did take place and that an entity called Israel, small perhaps, was in the country – perhaps in Galilee, or the central highlands, or even in the whole highland zone. Israelites, it has also been claimed, are figured on a relief ascribed to Merneptah. One recent suggestion is that Merneptah referred to an Israel still outside Palestine, perhaps in Egypt. Israel would then have entered the Promised Land only in the twelfth century. This hypothesis (which has been proposed before) has some advantages, but it would involve a drastic shortening of the period of the Judges and of biblical chronology beyond what is generally accepted. Yet if an Israel was in Palestine *c.* 1207, questions arise of how long had the Israelites been in the country before they were mentioned, and how had they got there?

Concerning the time when Israel appeared on the scene in Palestine, there is again a wide diversity of opinion. Most still date it to the thirteenth century BC, though it has been pointed out that it must have taken time for the Israelites to adopt the mode of agriculture and stock-rearing developed by the Canaanites. Few, however, would go back as far as the sixteenth century BC or as late as the twelfth. As for the way in which Israel arrived there, problems have increasingly been raised concerning the biblical report about an Israelite entry into the country from outside by conquest, partly on the basis of archaeological discoveries. As a result, those who still assume an Israelite entry either by conquest – very few now – or by infiltration, possibly followed by military action locally – a much larger number – have now been joined also by a third group who think Israel came into being in Canaan as a result of sociological processes (thus essentially abandoning the biblical accounts).

Until fairly recently, many followed W.F. Albright's assumption that the Israelites, or an essential part of them, were establishing their presence in the country by conquest in the second half of the thirteenth century, especially around 1230 BC, and the destruction of a number of towns in the hill country around that time, revealed by excavations, was quoted in confirmation. This was taken as a corollary of a thirteenth-century Exodus, with the archaeological record apparently in agreement with the biblical one. There were admittedly some difficulties, most strikingly in the cases of Jericho, Ai and Bethel as mentioned in Joshua. At Jericho, the town that was defended by powerful fortifications had fallen *c.* 1550 BC, while recent re-examination of the archaeological evidence has confirmed that there was only a very limited and increasingly impoverished settlement, apparently unwalled, between *c.* 1425 and 1275 BC, after which the site was, it seems, abandoned. Ai, located by fairly wide consensus on the mound of et-Tell near Beitin (regarded by many as the successor of biblical Bethel) presented another problem, for the site was unoccupied between *c.* 2400 BC (when the Early Bronze Age city fell) and the foundation of a short-lived village in the twelfth century BC. Attempts to find an alternative location with a more suitable archaeological record have not so far been successful. Again, at el-Jib, the presumed location of Gibeon, excavations have produced no indications of the existence of a substantial city here during the Late Bronze Age. In recent years the difficulties arising from the view that there was a unified Israelite conquest about 1230 BC have multiplied. The time when towns were destroyed now stretches from *c.* 1250 BC (Hazor) to *c.* 1150 BC (Lachish). The original sites of some other towns mentioned in the conquest narratives were apparently not occupied in the thirteenth century BC. Still others may have existed in the Middle rather than the Late Bronze Age. Though not perfect, the correspondence between towns reportedly taken by the Israelites and Middle Bronze Age settlements is indeed rather better than that for Late Bronze Age sites. It has accordingly been suggested by J.J. Bimson that the destruction of Middle rather than Late Bronze towns was the work of the Israelites. This suggestion, however, which involves shifts in archaeological chronology, has also failed to find general acceptance.

There are, moreover, further fundamental difficulties about linking the burning of Canaanite towns with the Israelite conquest reported in the Bible. Firstly, the firing of towns was not, according to the biblical record, a general Israelite practice (cf. Joshua 11, 13). Secondly, where it did occur, others may have been responsible – Egyptian punitive expeditions, for example, inter-Canaanite feuds or Philistine raids – and accidental conflagrations or earthquakes should also be considered. Moreover, the present writer has argued, conquests may in any case not always be recognizable from archaeological indications. It is, for instance, very difficult to document the Muslim conquest of Palestine archaeologically. Since cultural continuity prevailed then, the continuity which similarly prevailed on both sides of the Jordan during the late thirteenth/early twelfth century may not in itself rule out an Israelite conquest. Vice versa, where ceramic changes did occur, as at Tell Deir 'Alla, they cannot be linked with the arrival of new population groups of known origin. It also does not necessarily follow that the poor rustic settlements that arose on the ruins of some destroyed Canaanite towns signify that Israelite newcomers with only a primitive material culture were taking over there. After all, in a number of cases, as at Tell Beit Mirsim, such simple villages seem to have housed people with an essentially Canaanite cultural tradition. The question as to whether within the impoverished and coarsened lifestyle which prevailed –

especially in the hill country – during the transition from the Bronze to the Iron Age there may not be features hinting at the rise of something new, will occupy us later. Meanwhile, we may still note the progressive deletion of the alleged hiatus in settlement in Transjordan before the thirteenth century BC. This used to be regarded as a support for the hypothesis of an Israelite conquest in the thirteenth century, since before then there would have been no Edomite and Moabite kingdoms obstructing the direct route as described in Numbers 21–22 and Deuteronomy 2. This time-limit is now removed, but the question of whether an Israelite conquest of Transjordan did occur at any period cannot, at present, be answered from extra-biblical sources, although indications of fresh settlement in or just before Iron I, followed by destructions, in the Central Jordanic uplands may prove relevant.

Alternative hypotheses

Faced with this disconcerting situation, many have turned away from the conquest hypothesis in search of other models which might explain the rise of Israel. Among these, one first proposed by A. Alt as long ago as 1925 and thereafter adopted by M. Noth in his influential *History* was to become increasingly popular. The Israelites, it was suggested, did indeed enter Canaan, but not as invaders, rather as groups of pastoralists who peacefully infiltrated sparsely settled regions following a pattern of transhumance between the desert and the hill country. They gradually settled down and took up agriculture, thus coming into competition with the Canaanites. This led to occasional and local violent conflicts and it was these that gave rise to the tradition of an Israelite conquest, which would in this case properly represent not the initial but the second stage in the rise of Israel in Canaan.

A totally different hypothesis, first put forward by G.E. Mendenhall in 1962 and later somewhat modified and elaborated by N.K. Gottwald (most significantly in 1979), rapidly gained adherents but also attracted criticism. According to this, there was neither a conquest from outside, nor a numerically significant semi-nomad infiltration into Canaan. Rather, there was widespread revolt by the oppressed Canaanite peasantry against their urban masters. Withdrawing into the fairly uncontrolled backwoods country in the hills as 'drop-outs', they found freedom there in conjunction with other outlaws – the *Ḫabiru* marauders – and were able to organize themselves into a new egalitarian proto-Israelite society. Mendenhall and Gottwald accepted that a point of crystallization for this process was provided by the religious ideas which a group of followers of Moses brought with them (Gottwald thought they became effective after the social revolution had started). More recent adherents of this view seem little interested in such a factor, and the rise of Israel is for them largely the result of social developments among the Canaanites.

None of the hypotheses outlined above account satisfactorily for the rise of the peculiar local entity which was Israel, nor is there support for them in biblical traditions. The origins of Israel may in fact have been far more complex, involving not only conquest by a limited group with a novel religion, but also some peaceful infiltration, as well as the adhesion of dispossessed elements. Such a combination would not be entirely without parallels.

The evidence of 'type fossils'

However Israel may originally have come into existence, there are some archaeological facts which have been linked with its establishment in its histor-ical homeland. The first of these is a striking increase in the number of settle-ments in the highland zone of western Palestine from the late thirteenth century BC onwards, whereas previously their number had been small. This phenomenon has been associated with the settling down of the Israelites. Secondly, the introduction of new cultural traits – such as the appearance of 'four-room' houses (see below, p. 124), sometimes after a phase of flimsy huts and pits, and of new pottery types, in particular the 'collared-rim' store jars (see below, p. 168) – have been regarded as 'type fossils' indicating the presence of Israelites. Small unfortified settlements, sometimes consisting of houses grouped around a circular or oval open space have been similarly interpreted. Such views are, however, subject to criticism.

In the highlands, for example, Israelites may have shared the same material culture as others. Furthermore, both 'four-room' houses and 'collared-rim' store jars were also to be found in non-Israelite regions and towns (though the latter are rare in Galilee). It is true, though, that these indicators are found pre-ponderantly in Israelite territory and that where they do occur outside, their presence may at least in some cases indicate the admixture of Israelites in a non-Israelite population, as has been suggested for Megiddo. And in the Valley of Jezreel, the presence of both 'collared-rim' store jars and Philistine ceramics might correspond to a presence of Israelite dependants among 'Sea People' rulers, though such a hypothesis is not at present favoured. It is also true that the highland culture being discussed here developed, without any detectable later intrusions, into that of historical Israel.

The testimony of archaeological surveys

Recently, results of comprehensive archaeological surveys of Israel and to a lesser extent Jordan, combined with discoveries in new excavations in the western hill country in particular, have led to yet another view of Israelite origins. On the basis of a detailed regional study I. Finkelstein has proposed that the original heartland of historical Israel was the Ephraim–Manasseh region in western Palestine, where almost 70 per cent of all early Israelite settle-ment sites are located. Other early foci were in Gilead and in the Jordan Valley (where some sites may have been occupied only seasonally). In western Palestine, an Israelite presence (whose antecedents will occupy us shortly) becomes tangible in the late thirteenth or early twelfth century in part of

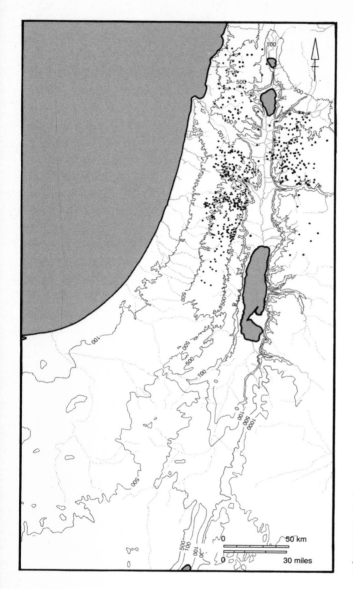

8 Distribution of settlements in the eastern and western highland zones, during the Early Iron Age. Those west of the Jordan will have included 'Proto-Israelite' elements; in Transjordan the situation is less clear but precursors of the tribes of Reuben, Gad and Eastern Manasseh may have been present.

Manasseh and especially in the section of Ephraim extending from the eastern desert fringe to the central hill spine.

These districts offered facilities suitable for pastoralists turning to a settled mode of life: in the north they would have found accommodation between the Canaanite towns, while in the rougher and originally sparsely inhabited southern sector they would have been more on their own. In accordance with their mainly pastoral economy these people did not at first rely on the construction of agricultural terraces, nor were cisterns needed for water supply in these areas. Both these technical features, long taken as new inventions basic for the establishment of an Israelite population in the hills (but actually known in the preceding Bronze Age), only came into their own during a second stage of

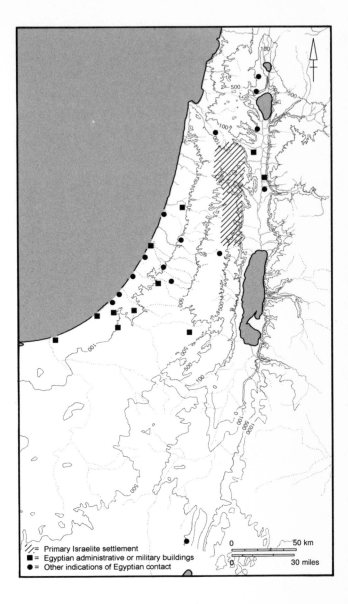

9 *The main area of presumed primary Israelite settlement in western Palestine* (after Finkelstein). *It is assumed to have been concentrated at first in the eastern parts of Ephraim and Manasseh, and to have spread out from there. Finkelstein's views are widely (though not universally) followed. Note that the primary Israelite territory was practically surrounded by Egyptian strongholds until* c. 1150 BC.

settlement, in Early Iron II, when population increase led to the establishment of agricultural settlements in originally forested land on the western hill slopes, where springs are scarce.

Israelite lifestyle showed a mixture of features, with some borrowed from their Canaanite neighbours and others supposedly going back to their pastoral past. Their small settlements – mostly unfortified – tended to comprise a roundish or oval open central area (where herds, especially sheep and goats, could be kept in safety) surrounded by buildings – an arrangement tentatively traced back to nomad camps. There were also hamlets and isolated farmsteads. The pillared 'four-room' house favoured among Israelites is similarly thought by some scholars to descend ultimately from rectangular pastoralist tents.

Pottery was largely derived from Canaanite prototypes though the repertoire was much reduced and technical standards were coarser. The 'collared-rim' storage jars, an important feature of Israelite material equipment produced in many local varieties, were found particularly in those districts devoted to garden cultivation, where they were chiefly used as containers for wine and oil, though they could also be used to store water, which might have to be fetched from some distance. During the early period grain was kept mostly in the numerous stone-lined silos dug into the ground within settlements, or just outside; later, other forms of storage came into use. In cereal-producing districts, storage jars in houses may also have served for this purpose.

The Israelite population, though probably not very numerous (see below, pp. 95–6) would gradually have spread out from the central hill country, both northwards into Galilee and, particularly, southwards into Judah. The latter region had been very thinly populated during the Bronze Age and only came to have a notable Israelite population around 1000 BC, when it also attained political significance. The gradual decline in the comparative importance of sanctuaries in the central uplands in favour of more southerly ones is thought to be associated with this southward shift.

Finkelstein's views agree well with the general importance of the people in the central hill region during the early Israelite period as shown in the biblical record. His opinion that this archaeologically attested Early Iron Age population, whatever its derivation, is the essential root from which the Israelites of the period of the Monarchy sprang is also reasonable. Where it comes to their origins, however, he argues that these early upland dwellers came there neither as conquering invaders, nor as mainly pastoralist immigrants from the east, nor as similarly displaced peasants from the west. Instead, they were mostly descendants from the local population of the Middle Bronze Age period, who, after the destruction of their towns c. 1550 BC turned to pastoralism, but reverted some three centuries later to a settled mode of life. This part of his interpretation remains undemonstrated, and among his Israeli colleagues A. Zertal, for instance, would opt for immigration from the Jordan Valley. Until such supposed pastoral nomad elements are traced archaeologically the question must remain undecided.

Other data are likewise ambiguous. For example, the occurrence of the name Asher in Egyptian records of the fourteenth and thirteenth centuries may, but need not, have links with the tribe of that name in the Bible. The fact that Israelite place-name types include some not in use in the pre-Israelite period, and that an Aramaic element has sometimes been postulated within the Hebrew language (which otherwise is largely derived from Canaanite speech), may be adduced in support of the entrance into the country of an outside element (possibly by conquest), but the latter still needs to be established more firmly (see below, pp. 217ff.). Beyond this, appeal has to be made to general probabilities. The belief among Israelites that they were descended from liberated slaves is most unusual – ancient nations tended to claim descent from gods or heroes. The story should thus have some factual foundation (some deny this

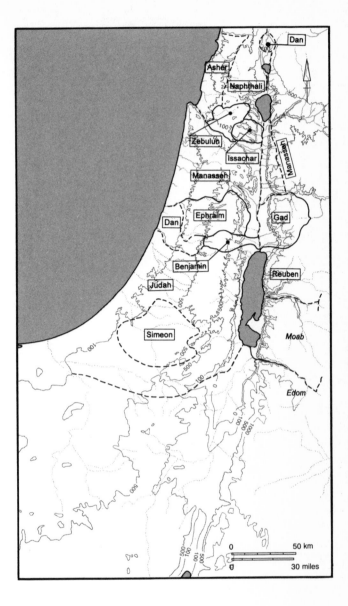

10 The territories of the Twelve Tribes, as they might have been at the time of the rise of the United Monarchy (some shifts did occur both before and after this period). The tribe of Gad may have been present in the Jordan Valley right up to the Lake of Tiberias, possibly intermingled with elements of Manasseh who occupied the high ground on both sides.

but the analogies to which they refer are not compelling). Similarly Israel's beliefs in Yahweh and the Covenant are unlikely to be the result of cultural diffusion alone; they should have been introduced by a process not totally dissimilar from what the Bible tells us. Lastly, the ancient writers to whom we owe the biblical records had presumably more information available than we do now, and their audience might not have accepted newly invented stories clashing with long-established traditions. Here opinions will be divided; for the moment scientific evidence cannot really carry us back beyond Merneptah's victory stela of the late thirteenth century.

Whatever their origins, the Israelites needed time to consolidate their hold on the land and their society. They had, for a time, no coherent territory:

Galilee was linked precariously to the central hill region across the Vale of Jezreel, while southwards Judah was isolated from its brethren to the north until David conquered Jerusalem. In the uplands, Canaanite or other enclaves remained in being until the time of the Monarchy and the lowlands stayed solidly non-Israelite. In the far south, Amalekites and others still retained much of the Negeb. Nor was the Israelite population static. Migrations kept changing the map – Ephraimites and Manassehites moved across the Jordan (others from the same region may have crossed over into Galilee), Dan migrated to the north and, according to some, elements of Ruben lost their original hold in western Palestine. Hand in hand with this, smaller groups were being progressively absorbed into larger units. The Judah of history came to include Kenites, Kalebites, Jerahmeelites and Simeonites, among others. The ideal community of the Twelve Tribes is, it seems, based on the combination of traditions from various stages of development, and tribal borders probably did not become finally established much before the coming of the Monarchy. Similarly, some ancient external ties such as those between clans in Judah and families in Edom, Moab and the Negeb, or between Israel and the Arameans, or even between Israelites and the Sea Peoples – some would trace the tribe of Dan to the Danuna among the latter – were probably gradually superseded with the rise of national states.

All this took place, however, in a scene which had changed drastically since the time when Canaanites with a fairly homogeneous civilization were under a single Egyptian overlordship. In spite of widespread cultural and ethnic Canaanite survivals, the new Palestinian world was culturally, and ethnically, fragmented, with sharp regional differences between hill and plain people. Among the latter there were regional distinctions between Philistines in the southern coastal plain, Sikels in the Sharon, and Sherdana in the Acco plain, all descendants of Sea People invaders progressively assimilated to local Canaanite stock (and similarly, perhaps, we saw, Danuna/Danites). These differences often dominated history during our period and indeed thereafter: only by the Classical or even the Arab period had they lost their old significance.

CHAPTER THREE

History

The sources

The task of outlining the history of Israel may at first sight appear easy, for it is dealt with fairly fully in the Bible. The historical sequence from the time of Israel's settlement in Canaan, down to the fall of the kingdom of Judah is treated in a number of biblical books – Judges, 1 and 2 Samuel, 1 and 2 Kings, and 1 and 2 Chronicles. They deal with events sometimes in detail, sometimes summarily, within a chronological framework of some precision. We are occasionally offered references to sources, and frequently historical judgments. Additional historical information is available, moreover, in prophetical books such as those of Amos, Hosea, Isaiah, Jeremiah and elsewhere.

Scholars have nevertheless experienced some difficulty in constructing on such foundations a history of Israel which would satisfy modern interests and critical principles. Sources referred to by biblical writers are lost to us, so that we cannot judge whether the excerpts included are representative or to what extent they may have been modified in transmission. The whole genesis of the texts concerned is often in dispute, and the present tendency to attribute many of them to the Exile or later has led to a questioning of how much reliable information they carry about times long past. Biblical chronology is likewise problematic – apparent inconsistencies (compare, for example, 1 Kings 16, 8 with 2 Chronicles 16, 1) may reflect different chronological systems, and attempts to achieve overall coherence are faced with a number of obstacles.

There are other sources of difficulty too. As the biblical historians who composed the texts show in their judgments, their purpose was not to offer a comprehensive record of past events, but rather to exemplify a religious thesis, namely that the Lord guided His people according to His promises and threats, punishing backsliding but rewarding obedient fulfilment of His commands. Much historical detail was thought irrelevant to such aims and passed over with references to works now lost, where readers could inform themselves more fully. While the 'great days' of the United Monarchy received ample coverage, important rulers like Omri and Ahab are not recognizable as the international figures that they were. Our knowledge is thus often tantalizingly incomplete. Furthermore, Israelite historians, like ancient historians in general, were not interested in the workings of impersonal social or economic processes but were apt to ascribe events to the actions of personalities, whether human or superhuman. We must also note that their source material included genres of very diverse kinds: records from palace or temple, chronicles official or non-official, genealogies and religious sources, but also prophet stories and what would now be called legends, ballads and songs. Not all of these would be acceptable to modern historians as evidence for historical events.

Yet at least parts of the history of Israel can be established on rather more secure foundations than can its origins, the reason being the existence of extra-biblical evidence, available now to varying extents and mainly for the later centuries. Though no inscriptions by Hebrew kings recording their deeds have come down to us, other inscriptions, ostraca (inscribed potsherds) and inscribed seals provide some evidence. Archaeological discoveries can tell us much, though they cannot often be securely linked with an exact point of time, historical event or personality. Moreover, texts found outside Israel – especially in Mesopotamia, and to a rather smaller extent in Egypt – provide both important chronological pegs and historical information. Assyrian royal records, for instance, from the ninth century onwards, followed by Babylonian texts, refer to direct contacts with Israel. They allow us (after some scrutiny) to place events referred to in the Bible in a wider context and extend our knowledge, especially when they are supported by pictorial records like the reliefs featuring Sennacherib's siege of Lachish in 701 BC. Other outside evidence is sporadic, but we should mention the works of the Jewish historian Flavius Josephus who lived in the first century AD. Though largely paraphrasing biblical accounts he sometimes drew on information not preserved elsewhere. Biblical texts may moreover receive unexpected outside support even in cases where they occur in books whose reliability is often not rated highly, such as Chronicles. Yet such favourable circumstances are largely restricted to the last three centuries of our story and obscurity tends to increase the further we go back.

Support for biblical statements about this obscure period is nevertheless on occasion offered from other directions. Thus it has recently been shown that the style of the trolleys made by King Solomon for the Temple, as described in 1 Kings (7, 27ff.), would in fact suit his period best, and the report about the golden shields made by Solomon (1 Kings 10, 16–17) need not, in the light of ancient Near Eastern evidence concerning such objects, be an invention; although in other cases – as with the list of fortresses reported in 2 Chronicles (11, 6–10) to have been built by his successor Rehoboam – there are difficulties in squaring the archaeological evidence with the biblical text. We cannot just dismiss biblical statements, however. This applies in a case like that of the description of David's reign and Solomon's succession in 2 Samuel (9–20) and 1 Kings (1–2), which has recently been labelled as a historical novel and its value as an accurate source queried. According to critical scholarship the report on the eleventh-century BC mission of the Egyptian emissary Wen-Amon to Byblos is similar in nature, but it has nevertheless been used as a historical source, if with some reservations. Nor should it be maintained that all the conversations (including some of a very private nature) contained in 2 Samuel (9–20) and 1 Kings (1–2) must be completely free inventions of the author. We cannot apply modern standards of privacy to ancient Near Eastern courts, which were full of 'non-persons', eunuchs, guards and others, who had eyes and ears – and tongues which could presumably be unlocked by suitable inducements.

The period of the Judges

Following the example set by the Bible, the early history of Israel from its first emergence down to the coming of the Monarchy is generally called the period of the Judges. Biblical tradition mentions a succession of these officials who were not only active in the legal sphere in putting things to rights (the Hebrew term *shophet*, 'judge', is cognate with the Carthaginian magistrates called *suffetes*) but were also divinely inspired when occasion demanded it to save Israel from her enemies. This period is exceptionally difficult to deal with. Much of our information (contained in the books of Judges and 1 Samuel) appears to go back to popular traditions emanating from the central hill country, which were formulated at some remove from events described and interested in the outside world only where or when there was conflict with it. There is, in particular, a curious absence of any clear reference to the Egyptian imperial presence which dominated Palestine well into the twelfth century, or to Egyptian influence thereafter. None of the persons or events mentioned in the biblical sources, on the other hand, are known from external accounts. Chronology is vague concerning both single events and the total length of the period. The Bible treats the latter as comprising several centuries, but many modern scholars, influenced by the idea of a Ramesside Exodus, would restrict it to the time between the late thirteenth and the middle of the eleventh century BC. (A number of judges referred to by the Bible in sequence may, they think, have been contemporary, repelling enemies in different localities at much the same time.)

Judges gives a general picture of an essentially rural society, linked by a common faith, but turbulent – 'every man did that which was right in his own eyes' – and on occasion the scene of some remarkable events, such as the sacrifice of Jephthah's daughter or the rape of the maidens of Shiloh (Judges 12, 30ff.; 21, 21ff.). Non-Israelite urban communities survived in its midst, and still more in the plain belt below the Israelite hill country. Archaeology has confirmed this picture to some extent. There was a steady expansion and growing differentiation of the farming communities in the hills, but also unbroken development in some towns surviving from the Canaanite Bronze Age. Shechem was destroyed in the twelfth century, perhaps by Abimelech (cf. Judges 10, 45), but Megiddo and Beth Shean fell to the Israelites only under David, apparently instances of a wider take-over. Tribal organization, like the confederation, was still developing. The Song of Deborah mentions only ten tribes, Judah and Simeon being left out of the count. Judah, indeed, separated from the central hill tribes by independent Canaanite Jerusalem, was probably not fully constituted much before David's time. The original nucleus, some think, may have only consisted of Manasseh, Ephraim, Benjamin and Gad.

Whether there was, in peacetime, much common governance is doubtful. The idea that there was a sacred confederation around the central sanctuary at Shiloh, with a common priesthood proclaiming common religious codes of action, has lost credit. There were, in any case, other, local sanctuaries (see below, p. 242). The Bible has little to say about the day-to-day activities of many judges, although it seems by implication to distinguish major judges, who freed their people from great dangers and whose deeds are related at some length, from minor figures, to whom no such deeds are attributed. Concerning the 'minor judges' mentioned in Judges 10 (1–5) and 12 (8–15) we learn little except that they officiated. Some have regarded them as a succession of pan-Israelite functionaries, but others see them simply as local worthies. Major judges, on the other hand, like Ehud, Deborah, Gideon, Jephthah and Samson, following a divine call, delivered a greater or smaller part of Israel from oppression by a remarkable variety of outsiders – Moabites, Canaanites, Midianites, Transjordanian bedouin, Ammonites and Philistines, among others.

That the Israelites should have had to contend with outside pressure is not in itself unlikely – indeed the attack repulsed by Gideon has been regarded as the first invasion by forces of cameleer raiders known to history. Significantly, however, we hear that Gideon was asked to accept permanent rulership for himself and his house (Judges 8, 22), that his son Abimelech established a local kingship over Israelites and Canaanites around Shechem (Judges 9, 1–6) and that, later again, the Israelites, beset by Philistine and Ammonite assaults, wished for a king to rule over them all (1 Samuel 8, 15). Kingship on the Canaanite model seemed to promise more efficient defence and order at home, both of which were increasingly needed in a developing social body. Tribal separatism and theological scruples could not stand against such needs, for the Ammonites were decimating the Israelites east of the Jordan, while west of it the Philistines had defeated Israel overwhelmingly, captured the Ark, probably burnt the central sanctuary at Shiloh, and extended their sway over the hill country.

The United Monarchy

Saul

Of Saul's reign we know disappointingly little – even its length is disputed, though it must have fallen late in the eleventh century. His power-base was circumscribed, his tribe, Benjamin, and his family his mainstay, but his sway was effective in the hill country from Mount Gilboa to the fringes of Judah, and he had firm allies in Gilead. The Bible pictures him mainly as a military ruler who cleared the Philistines from the central uplands, and credits him also with exploits against Israel's enemies all around (1 Samuel 14, 47–8). This he managed to do by establishing his own permanent band of picked warriors, in addition to the tribal levies who were called out when need arose. His army was organized into bodies of 100 and 1000 men, officered by Benjaminites who received grants of land for their service (1 Samuel 22, 7). He also seems to have possessed sizeable landed estates, administered by special functionaries such as Doeg the Edomite (like later kings, Saul employed foreign talent), and a royal residence of sorts at Gibeah (possibly fortified, though the identification with Tell el-Ful is uncertain and excavations there have produced no clear picture),

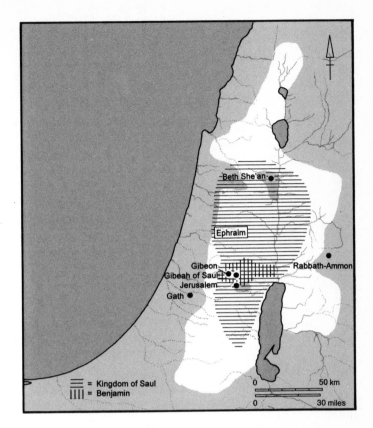

*11 Saul's kingdom according to a
maximalist view* (white area; after
Y. Aharoni) *and minimalist view*
(horizontal shading; after J. Maxwell
Miller) *respectively. More distant regions
included in the maximalist territory were
in any case probably not closely controlled.*

where he would hold court in the style of a chieftain. Saul's rule depended
largely on common consent, a fact remembered later with nostalgia.
Administrative arrangements in the country were probably rudimentary and
governmental exactions not yet oppressive. If he had any plans, as some think,
to turn the subject city of Gibeon into his capital, then nothing permanent
came of it.

Militarily effective for a time, Saul failed disastrously, however, to maintain
friendly relations with the influential religious establishment, in spite of his
zeal for the Lord (see, for example, 1 Samuel 28, 9). We are told he was disqual-
ified by Samuel, the last great judge, and that he slaughtered the priests of Nob
whose loyalty he suspected. Given increasingly to bouts of depression linked
with his vain attempt to prevent the rise of a rival supported by divine choice –
David – he finally succumbed tragically, together with most of his sons, in the
battle lost against the Philistines at Mount Gilboa. He had, however, won
lasting loyalty: his son Eshbaal (Ishboshet) ruled for some years over his
kingdom from Mahanaim in Transjordan. After Eshbaal's assassination the
men of Israel did offer David the crown, leading to the institution of the United
Monarchy under David. Yet hopes for the renewal of the rule of Saul's house
continued, and Benjaminite disaffection was still thought a danger in the time
of Solomon.

David (*c.* 1005–965 BC)

The reign of David witnesses three important events: the transfer of power from northern Israel to the south and to a new dynasty; the effective joining of Judah to the main body of Israel to the north; and significant political transformation from chieftainship towards true monarchy, though David himself to some extent still ruled as a shrewd mediator between conflicting interests and sentiments. He did, however, also build up a new and effective power-base. Though in some ways the United Monarchy remained a union of crowns, and tribal levies were not always reliable, he also created a body of mercenary troops, Cheretites, Peletites, Gittites (non-Israelites of Philistine affinities), in addition to a chosen band of Israelite retainers who were loyal to him alone. Jerusalem, which he acquired and made his capital, was his own special possession which provided neutral ground linked previously with neither Israel nor Judah. Here he built a palace and installed a central administration, recalling Egyptian prototypes (see below, pp. 106–7); to what extent there were local functionaries is unclear. He also made Jerusalem the religious centre of Israel by transferring the pan-Israelite 'palladium', the Ark (which had languished after being released by the Philistines), into a tent-shrine on Mount Moriah and he is said to have thought of constructing a temple to house it. It was served by Zadokite (and other) priests and, like the court prophet Nathan, it was closely linked with the monarch. The support of the religious establishment was a source of strength, and throughout the whole country the Levites – minor religious functionaries – may likewise have been helpful. Though David had obtained the kingship of Judah and Israel by offer and compact, religious support added a different dimension, namely that of kingship by divine grace, with the promise that this would be vested in his descendants for ever (cf. 2 Samuel 7, 12–16). Divine sonship of the monarch – an idea widespread in the ancient Near East – was thus brought in with a special Israelite meaning.

Politically and militarily the new monarch at first proved most efficient. David put a permanent end to Philistine domination, and in a remarkably short time transformed the United Monarchy into an empire. Edom, Ammon and Moab, as well as the neighbouring Aramean states including Damascus, were reportedly subjugated, and friendly relations established with Hamath and Tyre, opening a reservoir of skills in craftsmanship and commerce lacking in Israel. At home, the Canaanite and other enclaves, such as Megiddo and Beth Shean, were incorporated into the state, and, as archaeological finds testify, Israelite settlers now advanced into areas in the coastal plain and the Negeb which had previously been closed to them. Definite traces of royal buildings have not, however, yet been revealed. The gigantic pyramid-shaped stone base for a citadel on the eastern flank of the Ophel hill in Jerusalem might contain Davidic work, but the citadel itself has gone, and whether any administrative buildings at Megiddo VB or IVB–VA go back to him is a very moot point – most think them Solomonic.

Later on, though, internal strains did develop – due to tribal rivalry, strife within David's family over succession, and probably a widely shared resent-

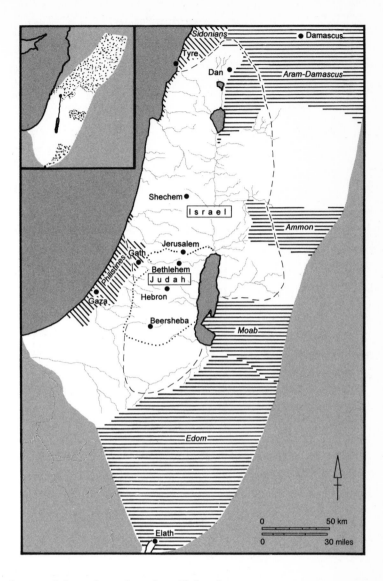

12 The Empire created by David, and inherited by Solomon. The main map shows a maximalist view of the United Monarchy (white areas), conquered territory (horizontal shading) and states in treaty-relations with David's realm (diagonal shading). A minimalist view is shown by broken lines (see also fig. 13). A maximalist view of peripheral territory is shown in the inset.

ment against new burdens in taxations and forced services, insufficiently compensated for by an efficient judicial system. Twice, indeed, rebellion nearly lost David his crown. He nevertheless left to his son and successor Solomon a kingdom of international stature, firmly governed. This was to split later, but two developments in David's reign have retained their importance to this day: Jerusalem began its transformation from a petty Canaanite capital to a holy city of international significance, while the promise that there would be a never-ending line of kings from David's family was, after the end of the rule of the dynasty, an important factor in the hope for a Messiah from the House of David.

Solomon (*c*. 965–925 BC)
Solomon succeeded David without trouble, but the later part of his reign was marked by increasing difficulties at home and loss of power abroad.

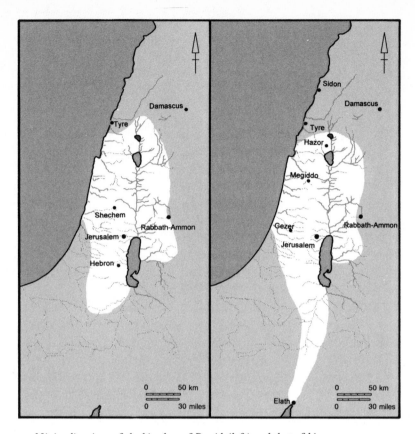

13 Minimalist views of the kingdom of David (left) and that of his successor Solomon (right), according to J. Maxwell Miller.

Nevertheless, in the eyes of Israelite historians, it marked the apex of Israelite achievement. Curiously, no reference to him or his father David, or their empire in a non-Israelite source is known, although, inscriptions from this period being scarce, this need not be significant.

The reign saw the consolidation of the structure of the state: the central bureaucracy was underpinned by a new regional administration, the country (apart from Judah, perhaps exempted as a favour) being divided into twelve districts (each with its capital), meant to support the court for one month each. In addition to income from royal estates, official building projects were funded by taxation and labour service, to which Israelites and non-Israelites were liable. Revenue was also obtained from tribute or gifts from foreign potentates, besides tolls levied on merchants crossing Israelite territory on international trunk roads, and from the proceeds of royal trading ventures – trade in horses and chariots between Egypt and Cilicia, for example, and joint expeditions by Tyrian and Israelite ships down the Red Sea to Ophir (Somalia?) in search of tropical luxury goods. The visit by the (North or South Arabian?) Queen of Sheba was perhaps in response to these, but it remains obscure.

21 An enthroned Canaanite king and his retinue, depicted on a Bronze Age ivory carving from Megiddo. He is receiving captives brought in under guard.

22 A detail from the same ivory carving from Megiddo: note the sphinxes (cherubs) supporting the king's throne, and the lyre-player in front of him.

23 The 'Black Obelisk' of Shalmaneser III, recording the submission of King Jehu of Israel (and other rulers) to Assyria.

Opposite

24 A detail of one of the registers of the 'Black Obelisk' showing King Jehu (or his envoy) prostrating himself before Shalmaneser III.

25 In this detail of the 'Black Obelisk' Israelite tribute-bearers are shown carrying various items that are listed in the accompanying inscription.

26 An aerial view of the excavated remains of Lachish: note the siege ramp (bottom right).

27 The Assyrian siege ramp, shown in section. It takes the form of a large sloping triangular mass of stony material, to the right of the mound.

28 A reconstruction of Lachish, before the siege. The zone of civilian housing is mainly to the right of the road leading in from the gate past the palace-fort.

The siege of Lachish

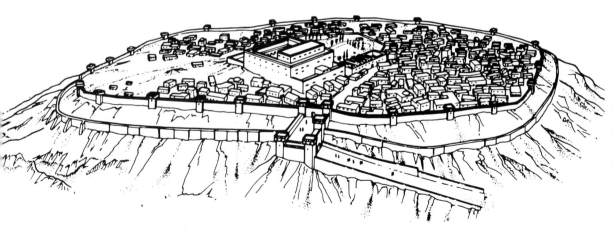

29 *(Opposite, above)* Assyrian slingers and soldiers with crested helmets, on one of the reliefs recording the siege of Lachish from Sennacherib's palace at Nineveh (detail).

30 *(Opposite, below left)* Assyrian helmet crests found at Lachish: they resemble those shown on the relief.

31 *(Opposite, below right)* Sling stones associated with Sennacherib's siege of Lachish.

32 *(Above)* Crushed storage jars sealed by Level III debris from Sennacherib's destruction of Lachish.

33 *(Below)* Deportees being led away after the fall of Lachish to the Assyrians. A woman and child are allowed to travel on a cart carrying belongings.

34 *(Above left)* The 'Israel stela' of
Egyptian pharaoh Merneptah. In it he
claims to have defeated Israel in the fifth
year of his reign (1207 BC, according to the
new widely used shortened chronology).
This is the earliest recorded mention of
Israel on a monument.

35 *(Above right)* The 'Moabite stone': a
victory monument put up in *c*. 830 BC by
King Mesha of Moab in which he describes
how he conquered and annexed Israelite
territory. This stela was for long almost the
only document giving a detailed record of a
conflict between Israel and a neighbour
referred to in the Bible.

36 Fragments of an Aramaic inscription on a
victory monument erected by King Hazael
of Damascus at Dan (found recently by A.
Biran). It contains the first mention outside
the Bible of the 'House of David'. It also
states that Hazael killed King Jehoram of
Israel and King Ahaziah of Judah though,
according to the Bible, Jehu killed them.

Foreign relations were at first satisfactory. Indeed, with Hiram, King of Tyre, they were close – he is reported to have sent materials and specialist workers for the royal building programme, including the palace complex and Temple in Jerusalem. With Egypt, relations were to begin with similarly good. An unnamed pharaoh, possibly Siamun, married his daughter to Solomon – a most unusual honour – and in addition the king received the city of Gezer, conquered by the pharaoh, as her dowry. Later, however, when a new dynasty, the 21st, came to power in Egypt, the pharaoh gave refuge to fugitive malcontents from Solomon's dominions. The overstrained Israelite monarchy was unable to maintain its rule over some of the territories under its control: Damascus made itself independent and Edom largely so. No counter-measures are mentioned. Solomon avoided wars, though he had strengthened his country militarily by erecting a number of fortresses, both garrison towns and store cities. He had, furthermore, developed chariotry into a powerful field force. Royal control over the Negeb at the time of the United Monarchy allowed an increase in Israelite settlement there according to some.

Culturally, the reign appears to have benefited from contacts engendered by enlarged horizons. History and 'wisdom' writing (works offering moral and practical advice) have been thought in the past to have begun in Solomon's reign and some have talked of 'Solomonic enlightenment', though recently there has been a tendency to ascribe these things to later times. The most important event of the reign historically, however, was probably the building of the Temple, which functioned both as a pan-Israelite sanctuary and as the royal palace chapel. It enhanced the role of Jerusalem as the religious centre of Israel and of its clerical establishment, linking the latter closely to the crown. In return, ideas of the king ruling by the grace of God were strengthened. Kingship was thus both firmly established and transformed, and the ideological consequences were long-lasting.

Archaeology has offered some possible clues about the activities attributed to this royal builder. Though in Jerusalem nothing has as yet been brought to light which can be ascribed to Solomon with certainty, many scholars assign to him the city gates and adjoining casemate walls at Megiddo, Hazor and Gezer, as well as substantial administrative buildings, like Palace 6000 at Megiddo. All are impressive and competently built, though not perhaps outstanding by later standards. Yet, as we saw, chronology is disputed. Thus the famous 'Solomonic' gate at Megiddo may date from the period of the Omrid dynasty. It is also doubtful that royal fortresses guarded the Negeb: most of the buildings there were probably the abodes of pastoralists or farmers and are of disputed age. More clearly defined information about the greatness that was Solomon's is still desirable.

The Divided Monarchy (c. 925 BC)

After Solomon's death the tensions which had built up in Israel came into the open. The northern tribes resented Judean domination and the new absolutism

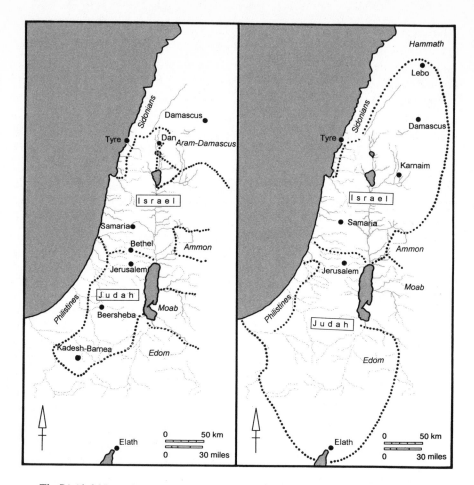

14 The Divided Monarchy. On the left are the kingdoms of Asa and Basha in Judah and northern Israel respectively, following minimalist lines, as suggested by J. Maxwell Miller. On the right are the two kingdoms at the time of Jeroboam II's rule in the north, representing maximalist views.

with its burdens; some of the religious, especially among the prophets, had also been alienated by the accommodation extended to foreign cults in the capital. When Solomon's successor Rehoboam refused to redress grievances and rule by covenant, the North revolted and proclaimed a king of its own, Jeroboam, a former Solomonic official. The revolt could not be suppressed and the division of the realm, which left only Judah and Benjamin under Jerusalem, proved permanent. It was soon underpinned by Jeroboam's promotion of official sanctuaries at Bethel and Dan, and changes in the religious calendar in his kingdom (1 Kings 1, 26ff.) – all intended to deflect religious loyalties away from Jerusalem, which regarded these innovations as heretical and maintained its claim to sole legitimacy.

The whole of the former United Monarchy was, however, before long the object of an invasion by Pharaoh Sheshonq, the Shishak of the Bible. According to 1 Kings (14, 25ff.), this happened in Rehoboam's fifth year, but chronology at this point is unclear, and it has been suggested that the event may have taken place late in Solomon's reign. Sheshonq's detailed campaign record supplements the meagre biblical data. In Judah, flying columns spread out over the Negeb, perhaps with the aim of cutting the trade route from Gaza to Elath which threatened Egyptian Red Sea trade. Jerusalem had to pay a heavy ransom for its safety. Much of Israel was traversed by the Egyptians, who even crossed the Jordan to Penuel and Mahanaim. At Megiddo, Sheshonq put up a victory stela, a fragment of which has been found. This attempt to assert Egyptian interest proved isolated, but it impoverished the country, and some destruction of (or selectively inside) settlements, from Megiddo and Beth Shean down to the Negeb, may be linked with it. In the Negeb there also followed a period of abandonment at a number of sites.

It took over another generation before Israel and Judah again attained international importance, at least as members of a system of small and medium-sized Levantine states. An Israelite empire of the rank ascribed to the realm of David and Solomon never quite occurred again. It had arisen within the political vacuum caused by the temporary absence of great power states in Egypt and Mesopotamia. Now the scene was to be transformed by the rising military might of Assyria, which soon threatened the whole region and led to greater Egyptian involvement in coalitions meant to oppose the Assyrian advance.

There were important differences in character between the two rival successor states. Judah was the smaller and poorer but at the same time less exposed, for contending armies marching along the great trunk road in the coastal plain were apt to pass it by. It was also more stable: in Jerusalem, the permanent capital, the House of David maintained its divinely appointed rule (individual kings were overthrown, but not the dynasty). It also found support at most times in the Temple and religious establishment. The northern kingdom was larger, better endowed by nature and traversed by important roads opening it up to international commerce. It was, however, more open to outside attack. There was for a time no fixed capital, and the appointment of kings by divinely sanctioned popular covenants was a destabilizing factor. Revolts caused by a combination of influential prophetic disapproval and the ambition of military leaders resulted in frequent changes of dynasties. The disaffection of religious circles looking to Jerusalem was a permanent threat to the crown.

The dynasty of Omri (c. 885–843 BC)

For some 40 years after the break-up of the United Monarchy the two successor states were weakened by recurring internal wars; they lost dependencies like Moab, Ammon and Edom, and became in turn the object of external attacks, in particular by Philistines and Damascenes. Few achievements can be credited to this time. At Mizpah (Tell en-Naṣbeh) excavations have revealed powerful fortifications built perhaps by King Asa of Judah (2 Chronicles 16, 6), but the ring of fortifications around Judah ascribed to Rehoboam (2 Chronicles 11, 5) is credited by some scholars to later rulers, especially perhaps Hezekiah.

In Israel, the accession to power of Omri (*c*. 885–873 BC) and the reign of his son Ahab (*c*. 873–851 BC) marked a turning-point. Omri built a new capital at Samaria, in a dominating strategic position. It was enlarged and embellished by Ahab, who also rebuilt and fortified Megiddo, where the famous 'Solomonic stables' were his work, and Hazor, which he also enlarged. The army was developed into one of the strongest in the Levant, especially in chariotry, with the result that Moab could be reduced once more to dependency and foreign relations conducted from a position of strength. Close links were established with Phoenicia, a ready market for Israelite farming produce and an esteemed supplier of goods made by Phoenician craftsmen or obtained by Phoenician trade. The use of international highways under Israel's control by Phoenician and other foreign traders was also financially advantageous. The alliance with Phoenicia was cemented by the marriage of Jezebel, the daughter of the king of Sidon and Tyre, to Ahab.

A daughter of either Ahab or Omri, Athaliah, was married to Joram, son of Jehoshaphat, King of Judah, so that the two kingdoms now became allies – with Israel as the dominant partner. Relations with Damascus also changed temporarily from enmity to friendship. When King Shalmaneser III invaded the Levant in 853 BC, Assyrian, though not biblical, evidence shows that the two kingdoms fought side by side against him at Karkar, as members of a coalition of twelve potentates. Israel was on this occasion the strongest power in chariotry, reportedly with 2000 chariots – many more than the 1200 attributed to Solomon – while Damascus was the stronger in infantry, boasting 20,000 soldiers as against the 10,000 provided by the Israelites.

Internally, a growing farming population was extending the cultivable area by clearing forest areas, especially in the western hill flanks, while urban life developed at the same time. Judah was similarly prospering – Jehoshaphat took an active interest in extending agricultural areas as well as developing his army and reducing Edom to dependency. There were still problems. The Israelite regime apparently attempted to satisfy both its Canaanite and Israelite subjects (the support given to Baal as well as YHWH may be linked with this) and Jezebel's worship of the Baal of Tyre (some identify him with Baal Shamen, the great sky god worshipped in Syria and elsewhere) together with her absolutist attitudes – shown in the affair of Naboth's vineyard – deepened prophetic hostility, as exemplified by Elijah's confrontation with the Baal prophets at Mount Carmel (1 Kings 18). Both Elijah and his pupil Elisha called for the overthrow of the dynasty, a call which was heeded under Ahab's second successor Joram (1 Kings 2, 1). There were in fact two contemporary kings of this name listed in Israel and Judah, and some have suspected that the same monarch was then in power in both states. Though this king still appeared powerful, it was in fact a period of decline in both kingdoms. Israel was losing territory in Transjordan to King Mesha of Moab, who had thrown off the Israelite yoke, and was making no headway in a war against Damascus. Similarly Edom, which had been a Judean dependency under Jehoshaphat, resumed its independence, and Judah lost Libnah on the Philistine border as well. With King Joram of Israel sick of wounds and the army discontented, the stage was set for revolt.

The rebellion of Jehu (843 BC)

The sequence of events involved here is described in one of the most dramatic accounts in the Bible (2 Kings 9–10). Jehu, one of the officers unsuccessfully besieging Syrian-held Ramoth Gilead in Transjordan, was designated king by Elisha. Accepted as such by his fellow officers, he moved quickly, surprised and killed the king of Israel and dowager queen Jezebel, and also the visiting king of Judah. He subsequently induced the apparently semi-autonomous city of Samaria to join him, and to butcher the whole royal family there. Next, he arranged for the Baal-worshippers to be enticed into the Baal temple in Samaria where they were all killed, and the temple pulled down. He did not, however, in spite of his professed zeal for the Lord, follow orthodox religious ideas sufficiently enthusiastically to gain wholehearted approval from that side. Asherah worship, centred probably on the sacred tree symbol of the Canaanite goddess of that name, continued under his successors.

A very different contemporary account of the overthrow of the royal houses of Israel and Judah has recently come to light, however, in the shape of a fragmentary Aramaic inscription discovered at Dan, which had apparently been set up there as a victory monument by King Hazael of Damascus. In a badly broken passage he apparently claims (if the reconstituted reading is accepted) that he killed King Jehoram of Israel and King Ahaziah of Judah. This statement is of course in direct conflict with the biblical account, though Syrian support for Jehu's rebellion, whom Hazael regarded as his instrument, may be referred to. If so, relations between Damascus and various factions in Israel may have been more complex than the biblical narration suggests. It is, however, interesting that both in the case of the Mesha stone inscription and that of this newly discovered text, the Israelite and non-Israelite accounts diverge significantly.

The consequences of the revolt were disastrous. Understandably, the alliance with Phoenicia did not survive the murder of the Phoenician-descended dowager queen. In Judah, the Omrid queen mother Athaliah seized power, and secured herself against possible rivals by slaughtering the royal princes – only the infant Joash was spirited away by the High Priest, and installed as monarch seven years later, after a coup. Isolated, Jehu had to seek safety by becoming, in 841 BC, the vassal of King Shalmaneser III of Assyria (an event figured on the 'Black Obelisk' (pls 23–5) now in the British Museum). However, some years later Assyria became preoccupied with problems nearer home, so that Jehu and his successors had to face alone the military might of Damascus, then reaching its zenith during the reign of Hazael, a usurper like Jehu. Israel's Transjordanian regions were overrun (2 Kings 10, 32), and the population suffered massacres still remembered years later by the prophet Amos (Amos 1, 3ff.). Under Jehu's son Jehoahaz, Israel's military strength was reduced to 50 horsemen, 10 chariots and 10,000 foot (2 Kings 13, 7). Accordingly, Hazael was able to cross Israelite territory and to progress down the coastal plain to take Gath in Philistia while King Joash of Judah had to buy off a threat to Jerusalem by giving him the contents of the Temple Treasury (2 Kings 12, 18). In fact, Hazael appears to have established an empire or sphere of influence not unlike that ascribed to David. Not surprisingly, material culture at this time as revealed by excavation has nothing outstanding to show. Buildings or repairs at Samaria or Megiddo attributed to the post-Omrid era are inferior to those put up before the fall of that dynasty.

Relief for Israel came only when Assyria, freed from other preoccupations, was able to turn south again. In four campaigns, Adad-Nirari III reduced Syria, including Damascus, to tributary status, after which it never quite recovered military eminence. Pressure was thus taken off Israel, whose king, Joash, paid tribute to the Assyrian ruler in 796. Thereafter, Assyria again withdrew for half a century. This allowed Israel to fill the local power vacuum left by the weakening of Damascus. Under Jeroboam II (785–745 BC) Israel is said to have reestablished her sway from 'the entry of Hamath' (perhaps the *Beqa'a* valley in Lebanon) down to the Dead Sea (2 Kings 14, 25); Amos (6, 13) indicates that much territory was also regained east of the Jordan. Indeed, Jeroboam II is even said to have reduced Hamath and Damascus to dependency (2 Kings 14, 26). At the same time Judah likewise entered a period of recovery and expansion under Azariah/Uzziah. There was economic prosperity among the urban élite in Israel, and expansion of agriculture in Judah. However, there were underlying weaknesses. Prosperity had been achieved at the price of growing division between the estate-owning rich and the poor who had lost their holdings to them; in Transjordan especially the Israelite population had been reduced; and while militarily impressive by local standards, Israel was outclassed by Assyria. Renewed Assyrian intervention was likely to prove calamitous.

The decline and fall of Israel (745–722 BC)

In 745 BC, Tiglath-Pileser III, a new and outstandingly able ruler, came to the throne in Assyria. He not only expanded the Assyrian empire but also reorganized it. An efficient, centralized state was to replace an Assyrian homeland ringed by tributary vassal states of doubtful loyalty. As part of this policy, not only were rebellious client rulers removed but significant numbers of their subjects were exiled as well, to be replaced by more reliable foreign colonists. Such policies were not inflexible. Where special circumstances made the survival of the small 'buffer states' advantageous, as near the frontier with Egypt (reviving under the 25th Dynasty, *c.* 751 BC), they might be allowed to continue. Judah was to benefit from this principle for a time.

Israel's capacity to face up to this challenge was weakened by a sequence of upheavals. Jeroboam's son Zecharia was overthrown by Shallum in 745 BC and there followed a series of seizures of power by various pretenders to the throne, accompanied by much spilling of blood. In these circumstances, resistance to the Assyrian advance may first have been headed by Judah, which was still nominally ruled by the now-incapacitated Azariah/Uzziah. If so, his death soon after may have saved him from retribution. When Tiglath-Pileser in 738 BC reduced Israel's old ally, Hamath, the Israelite king, Menahem, like neighbouring rulers, thought it prudent to pay tribute. This tribute is mentioned in Assyrian records, and its amount specified in the Bible (2 Kings 15, 19ff.). One thousand talents of silver were demanded: Menahem raised them by assessing persons of substance (probably mainly landowners) at 50 shekels each. Since the Israelite talent contained 3000 shekels there must have been some 60,000 people able to pay – a substantial element of the population. In 734, Assyria advanced further south, reducing the Philistine plain as far as Gaza to obedience. This threat gave rise to another coalition in which King Pekah of Israel joined the expansionist King Rezin (Raṣiyan) of Damascus. Since Judah, now under Ahaz, would not join it, the two rulers invaded the country in the 'Syro-Ephraimite' war, intending to put an amenable ruler of their choice on the throne in Jerusalem. Ahaz was reduced to extreme straits, especially since Edomites and Philistines joined in the attack. Against the advice of the prophet Isaiah, he became an Assyrian vassal in the hope of delivery from that quarter. This did indeed materialize – Tiglath-Pileser could in any case not allow the coalition to succeed.

In 733, Tiglath-Pileser turned against Damascus. By 732 BC Rezin had been killed, and Damascus reduced to an Assyrian province. Israel lost all her territory except the Samaritan uplands in 732: Gilead, Galilee and the northern coastal plain, all possibly previously occupied by Syria, were turned into Assyrian provinces. Provincial towns like Hazor were destroyed and many of the inhabitants exiled (cf. 2 Kings 15, 29). These events caused the replacement of Pekah by Hoshea, who paid tribute to Tiglath-Pileser in 731, and likewise to his successor Shalmaneser V (727–722 BC). Eventually, however, he rebelled, perhaps in coalition with Phoenician and Philistine rulers and apparently in expectation of Egyptian support. When this did not materialize Hoshea was somehow made captive by the Assyrians and Samaria placed under siege. It speaks for the strength of the place, and the determination of the defenders, that it took the Assyrians up to three years to reduce it. Whether Shalmaneser V lived to see the fall of the city is uncertain. Final arrangements after it succumbed were made by his successor Sargon II (722–705 BC), who in 720 had to confront one more revolt in Hamath, Damascus and Samaria – 27,290 inhabitants were exiled to Mesopotamia and Media, to be replaced by a new upper class from Babylonia and Syria (later augmented repeatedly, by, for example, Arabs). Israelite religious symbols were removed, a new Assyrian chariot corps raised from the remainder of the army, and an Assyrian governor installed in the city after its rebuilding. These arrangements were to prove enduring. Though many Israelites remained, especially in the countryside – which recovered well from the ravages of war – the upper strata in Samaria were non-Israelite and elsewhere, as at Megiddo, an Assyrian ruling class which included members of various subjected nations was also found. It was not numerous, but it has left some archaeological traces. Despite this, a certain revival of the Israelite cult was allowed (2 Kings 17, 27–33).

Other Israelites fled south to Judah, where Jerusalem saw a large influx of population. With Judah (and also Ammon, Edom and Moab) reduced to satellite status, and the coastal plain held by Sargon in spite of repeated Egyptian attempts to foment trouble, submission to Assyria seemed the wisest course and Judah withdrew in time from a revolt she had joined in 713 BC. Any weakening of Assyria might, however, seem auspicious for reviving old ambitions.

Judah and Assyria

Sargon's last years were taken up with troubles nearer home, and his death in 705 BC was followed by widespread revolts. Babylonia under Merodach-baladan in the south rebelled, as did several provinces in Anatolia. Egypt under the 25th (Ethiopian) Dynasty – which naturally opposed Assyria – now had supporters in Phoenicia and in the 'buffer states' including Judah, where pro-Assyrian, anti-Assyrian and neutralist policies all found advocates. It took Sargon's successor Sennacherib till 701 before he was free to turn his attention to Syria, Phoenicia and Palestine. King Hezekiah of Judah (727–698 BC), who had succeeded Ahaz, thought conditions opportune for re-establishing Judah as an independent power, following Davidic visions. The sequence of events arising from this is documented not only in the Bible (Kings, Chronicles and Isaiah) but also in Sennacherib's own campaign record and by the Hebrew Siloam inscription – there is even a possibly relevant passage in Herodotus (II, 140). In addition, the archaeological record at Judean sites such as Lachish, and the relief pictures illustrating Sennacherib's campaign against that city, found in the ruins of his palace at Nineveh, offer important testimony (see fig. 48). Much detail remains in doubt, but the suggestion that Sennacherib waged not one but two campaigns against Judah is now widely rejected.

Hezekiah proceeded systematically. At home, loyalties to Jerusalem as a religious centre linked with the Davidic dynasty were strengthened by the abolition of local sanctuaries – the 'high places' – which caused some perplexity among country folk. An attempt was made to enlist sympathies in Assyrian-occupied northern Israel by invitations to a great Passover feast. Fortifications in the capital and other important towns were strengthened and in Jerusalem the water supply was made inaccessible to assailants by the digging of the Siloam tunnel to deflect the flow of the Gihon spring into the urban walled perimeter. The army was provided with depots of weapons and stores (the store jars with the stamp *'la-melekh'* (see below, p. 200) may have served for the accumulation and distribution of food or wine). Diplomatic links were established with both Egypt and Babylonia, and alliances with Philistine towns such as Ashdod underpinned by the removal of the pro-Assyrian king of Ekron to Jerusalem. Judah's eastern neighbours and the Phoenician cities were also drawn in.

Yet when Sennacherib's army approached, the coalition proved ineffective.

Many members quickly changed sides and an allied army including a strong Egyptian-Ethiopic chariotry force was beaten at Eltekeh in the Palestinian plain. Recalcitrant Judah was now invaded. In the absence of effective resistance by Judean field forces, the war quickly turned into a series of sieges of Judean towns by the Assyrians. Some of these proved troublesome – Lachish, for example, as the combined evidence of excavation results and Sennacherib's descriptive reliefs shows, fell only after much effort. Jerusalem itself was surrounded but not taken by assault. Instead, harsh terms were agreed. Not only was there heavy tribute to pay, but Judah also lost much territory to the Assyrian-installed vassal kings at Ashdod, Ekron and Gaza. The fact that Sennacherib did not take Jerusalem might seem miraculous indeed and it gave rise to the conviction that the Lord would always protect His holy city and Temple if His commands were obeyed. Hezekiah thus gained credit as a pious champion of righteousness rewarded. Yet the country was terribly wasted and depopulated, while the Judean army, and especially the chariotry, never regained its standing.

After this object lesson, Hezekiah's successor Manasseh understandably became an obedient servant of Assyria. Together with any strivings for an independent political role, cultic reform was abandoned, and advocates of such unseasonable ideas were harshly persecuted. Assyrian power was in fact now reaching its zenith. Sennacherib destroyed Babylon in 689 BC (though his successor Esarhaddon (680–669 BC) inadvisedly allowed it to be rebuilt); in 671 BC Esarhaddon invaded Egypt and took Memphis, and his son Ashurbanipal (668–627 BC) looted and destroyed Thebes. In his later years, however, Ashurbanipal had to face increasing problems. Direct Assyrian control over Egypt was now replaced by agreement with princes installed with Assyrian consent, first Necho I and then Psammetichus I – the 26th Dynasty. Reports that Manasseh veered towards religious orthodoxy in his later years, and strengthened the fortifications of Jerusalem (2 Chronicles 33, 14ff.) may be linked with such changes in circumstances. Manasseh's son Amon was murdered after a two-year reign (642–640 BC), and his eight-year-old son Josiah was installed as king by the 'people of the land'. Josiah's reign (639–609 BC) was to witness momentous changes in the international scene, offering one final chance for the revival of the pan-Israelite kingdom under the House of David.

The rise of Babylon, the fall of Assyria and the revival of Egyptian power

After Ashurbanipal's death, Assyria quickly entered a disastrous phase. The succession was disputed; Scythian nomads ravaged the Levant (they are said to have got as far south as Ascalon); Babylonia, now under the Chaldean king Nabopolassar (626–605 BC) was aggressive, and so was the Median empire in Persia. Both attacked the Assyrian heartland. The Medes took the old capital Assur in 614 BC, and in 612 combined Babylonian and Median forces captured Nineveh – an event which caused an immense international tremor as reflected in the biblical book of Nahum. A last Assyrian ruler, Ashur-uballit (612–609 BC) established a precarious base at Haran. Egypt had meanwhile used the period of Assyrian decline to obtain control over Philistia and Lebanon and to extend her sway into northern Syria. Here she now supported the last Assyrian king, doubtless regarding a weak protégé as preferable to Babylonian and Median domination.

The withering of Assyrian influence was also regarded in Judah as an opportunity to revive old hopes of re-establishing the Davidic monarchy – a plan likely to lead to a clash with Egyptian domination in Palestine. Accordingly, there was another religious reform, in which the Temple was cleansed of pagan features and the 'high places' were abolished, not only in Judah but also the old northern sanctuary at Bethel. Most importantly, a 'book of the law' was discovered in the Temple in Josiah's eighteenth year (cf. 2 Kings 22–3; 2 Chronicles 34–5). With its stress on cult centralization and divine punishment for disobedience it must have aided the cause of reform considerably. There was a great Passover celebration at which northern Israelites were present. It seems likely that Josiah attempted to extend his religious and also his political sphere of influence into Samaria, Galilee and across the Jordan. A fort at Megiddo has been credited to him by some, but by others to Egypt, which was then in an expansionist phase, or to the Persians. Discoveries at the fortress of Meṣad Ḥashavyahu on the coast south of Tel Aviv, manned by Greek mercenaries but where some Hebrew ostraca have been found, may indicate that Josiah's sway extended into Philistia, perhaps again in agreement with Egypt. In 609 BC, however, he confronted Pharaoh Necho II on the latter's way to aid the last king of Assyria, at Megiddo and was killed by him, possibly in battle. All his plans perished with him.

Josiah's son Jehoahaz was installed as king by the 'people of the land' but deprived of the throne by Necho on his return from Syria, and led off to Egypt as a captive. Necho appointed his brother Eliakim to the throne instead. With the official throne-name of Jehoiakim, he ruled as an Egyptian vassal.

Judah at the time of Babylonian supremacy

Until 605 BC Egypt successfully maintained its presence in Syria, but in that year was decisively defeated at Carchemish by the Babylonians, led by the crown price Nebuchadnezzar. Syria and Palestine now fell, and Judah also submitted to Nebuchadnezzar (605–562 BC). Yet it was still not clear whether Egypt or Babylonia would prevail in the long run and the Egyptian connection attracted many. The pro-Egyptian party was, then and later, countered by a pro-Babylonian party who thought Babylon could not be effectively opposed in expectation of Egyptian help, a prominent proponent of this attitude being the prophet Jeremiah. Events were to prove this view correct. Following a Babylonian setback, Jehoiakim rebelled, in 600 BC, in hopes of Egyptian support. Nebuchadnezzar at first sent forces locally available, including Ammonites and Moabites, against him (2 Kings 24, 2). An Edomite menace to the Negeb is also implied in some of the ostraca found at Arad. Then in 597 BC, Nebuchadnezzar himself marched on Jerusalem and, after a few months' siege, took the city.

Jehoiakim possibly did not live to see the end. It was his son and successor Jehoiachin (also referred to as Jeconiah and Coniah in the Bible), who surrendered. The royal family with their retainers, together with important civilians and army men, as well as craftsmen such as smiths (including armourers) – all potentially useful in case of another rebellion – were led off as prisoners to Babylonia. The Temple treasures were also taken (cf. 2 Kings 24, 10–16). In place of Jehoiachin, his uncle Mattaniah was installed as ruler with the throne name of Zedekiah. The main events in this sequence are also briefly related in Babylonian chronicles. However, Jehoiachin was not formally deposed, and many in Jerusalem and among the exiles hoped that one day he might be allowed back as king, and continued dating by his regnal years. Zedekiah's position was thus weak from the start. Neither did he have the strength of character to prevail in a city dominated by powerful families deeply divided into pro-Egyptian and pro-Babylonian factions. Many of the former advocated another rebellion against Babylonia with Egyptian support, a course opposed in particular by Jeremiah at increasing personal risk.

After an abortive attempt in 594/3 BC, insurrection finally materialized in about 588 BC, in concert with Egypt, Ammon and Tyre. One of the 'Lachish letters' – a correspondence on ostraca found in the ruins of that city – relates how a high Judean military officer had travelled to Egypt, no doubt to coordinate military efforts. With an impoverished and divided nation behind him, Zedekiah had in fact few chances. Though relevant passages in Babylonian chronicles are missing, the Bible gives the main sequence of events. The Babylonian army quickly overran most of the country, with only two fortresses, Lachish and Azekah, managing to hold out for a time. Jerusalem was besieged and an abortive Egyptian relief expedition only temporarily drew off the Babylonians. After a two-year siege, Jerusalem fell in 586 BC, largely due to famine. The king, after an attempt to break out with his forces miscarried, was captured, blinded – after having been forced to witness the execution of his sons – and then carried off as a prisoner to Babylon.

Jerusalem, like other cities conquered by the Babylonians, was destroyed, including the palace and the Temple, all other important buildings, and the fortifications. Most of the population – two-thirds perhaps – had perished in the war or were carried off into exile in Babylonia, though a remnant was left under an administrator appointed by the Babylonians named Gedaliah, the son of Akiham, the scion of a family of distinction. He set up his headquarters at Mizpah, just north of Jerusalem – an important religious centre in pre-monarchic times which had escaped destruction – and did his best to get the fugitive population to settle down to agriculture. However, by doing this he incurred nationalist wrath as a Babylonian collaborator, and presumably also resentment for having settled people on land traditionally owned by families now exiled. His efforts were accordingly cut short by his assassination. Fearing Babylonian reprisals, most of the Judeans whom he had gathered fled to Egypt, taking an unwilling Jeremiah with them. Those who remained were largely found in small non-urban settlements, though in Benjaminite territory towns like Mizpah and Bethel survived the war, together with some in the far south. There may even have been inhabitants left in Jerusalem, including some wealthy ones, to judge by the Ketef Hinnom tombs. Yet overall, population must have fallen drastically. The southern part of Judah was gradually infiltrated by Edomites – it came to be known as Idumea – but unlike the Assyrians in northern Israel, the Babylonians did not settle foreign colonists in Judah. A chance was thus left for a 'Return to Zion'.

Archaeology mirrors and defines the sequence of events during the last stages of Judean history. Sennacherib's invasion had, as he claimed, been devastating. Revival was slow. Few buildings of distinction appear to have been put up thereafter – the palace, the building of which Jeremiah chided Jehoiakim for, (Jeremiah 22, 13ff.) seems to have been such, but if it is correctly identified with the one unearthed at Ramat Rachel then the luxury of the final structure may owe something to an earlier, ninth-century building. Yet, when the kingdom succumbed, many of its inhabitants had been living comfortably, and some were well off, even rich. The crash was felt all the more.

With the fall of the Davidic monarchy, the cessation of organized worship in the Temple and the removal of the most important part of Jerusalem's population, we are at the end of an epoch, even though culturally there was continuity. Hopes were indeed kept alive for a reconstitution of the kingdom and its society to their previous state. Some of these hopes were realized, others not. Some of the exiles did return in due course and the Temple was rebuilt, but the reinstatement of the House of David to full kingship did not take place. Moreover, when the returning exiles founded the Jerusalemite community associated with the names of Ezra and Nehemiah, theirs was a society different in outlook and temper from the one which had come to an end in 586 BC.

CHAPTER FOUR

Social Structure, Constitutional Ideas and Government

Ancient Israelite society is imperfectly known, but biblical and other sources offer an outline picture of some of its main features. It was never purely Israelite, for intermixed with free Israelites there were descendants of Canaanite and other Bronze Age town and country folk, landless alien labourers in the countryside, as well as a scattering of foreign craftsmen and traders. Slaves were apparently not a major social element, though perhaps increasing overall. From the mixed multitude of aliens, Israelites were set apart by the principles of consanguinity and assumed common descent, embodied (in descending order) in tribes, clans and families. Such a comprehensive system, and the detailed genealogical interest and recording which went with it, was unusual in the ancient Near East, though tribal societies were known there among pastoralists, judging from those referred to in documents from eighteenth-century BC Mari on the Euphrates onwards, and descent from families or clans is occasionally referred to. Such genealogical records as are known outside Israel also tend to differ in scope and method from those reported in the Bible. Israelite traditions, which embrace the ramification of a whole society, may be either linear, from father to son, sometimes over many generations, or segmented, showing how the various descendants of one ancestor spread out to form a social group. Some linear records are known among Israel's contemporaries, mainly from royal houses or other families of standing. These would have served to support claims to succession or inheritance, and would also have been used during family feasts when the good will of all departed ancestors had to be assured by commemorative sacrifices. (Such, it is now thought, were also found in Israel – see below, p. 255.) Segmentary genealogical records, however, seem to have been less popular. Overall, the best parallels to the detailed genealogical traditions covering the type of society found in Israel come from pre-Islamic Arabia.

This system based on consanguinity proved extraordinarily resilient and durable in Israel. It survived governmental pressures involving the rise of a bureaucracy, wars and social processes such as the replacement of small independent landholders by the owners of large estates, and the rise of an urban middle and upper class. The development of class divisions and religious reforms might transform society, but they left its gentilic structure in evidence. When the Jews returned to Jerusalem from their Babylonian Exile they still had documents giving details of their lineages (cf. Ezra 2, 62).

Towards foreigners around their folk groups, Israelites, according to biblical accounts, had mixed feelings. They might emulate their civilization, imitate their religion, and yet dislike them, though they might accept them if useful, or sometimes show them kindness. Towards their Canaanite neighbours they seem to have felt a special antipathy, fuelled by fears of the attractiveness of their religion to many. Some recent scholarship regards such a picture as mis-drawn, reflecting much later tensions between the embattled Jewish community in Jerusalem and its neighbours after the return from Exile when much of the Hebrew Bible received its definitive shape. The growth of hostility seems, however, to have been a gradual process, whose origins went a long way back.

Interpretations of Israelite society

Before studying this ancient society more closely, we must note that it has been viewed, in the course of time, from rather different points of view, some of which still affect our thinking now. Ancient Israelites saw it as God-given, but already the Jewish historian Flavius Josephus (first century AD) applied Graeco-Roman terms to it; later, the views of biblical as other scholars were affected by their classical training; more recently Western scholars have seen in it the interplay of forces in terms of which they explained historical events in general. Here some developments which occurred in the nineteenth and twentieth centuries were of special significance, in particular, the rise of sociology and ethnography, economics and political science. These have transformed the way in which ancient Israelite society is viewed. For example, classes and class struggle rather than ideological conflicts, and the material basis of different social groups are by now widely accepted as prime factors in the process of change.

Attempts have been made to classify the stages of Israel's evolution in categories derived from comparative ethnography. Pre-monarchical Israel, it has been suggested, can be viewed as a 'segmentary' society – a body of individuals and groupings of essentially equal standing with little overall cohesion or control living in a state of 'regulated anarchy'. The next stage would be chieftainship, exemplified by the rule of Saul, while the transition to monarchy, begun under David and completed under Solomon, transformed Israel into a social pyramid directed by officialdom forming part of an upper class. Class division would have become exacerbated by the eighth century. Such reconstructions have been subjected to criticism, however, by some scholars, both in general – our sources are mainly later narratives and we lack contemporary non-literary documentation – but also specifically, where the existence of tenth-century Statehood is concerned. This, it has been asserted, requires the existence of literacy to a degree not found in Israel then, and indeed perhaps not until the eighth century. There have been counter-arguments. The evidence available does however suggest some modifications may be needed in the evolutions proposed. It hints, for example, that quite early on there was social differentiation between wealthy and influential persons, and others of lesser significance. Such limitations on the interpretation of sparse data must be kept in mind in the attempt to present as coherent a picture as seems feasible.

Population size

To estimate the numbers of Israelites and others inhabiting the Promised Land at various periods is not easy, nor do the Israelites themselves seem to have had very clear ideas in this respect. At times of national elation they might think their numbers beyond counting (cf. 1 Kings 3, 8), but in their more sober or perhaps despondent moods they realized they were a small nation, perhaps even the smallest (cf. Amos 7, 2; Deuteronomy 7, 7). Census-taking they disliked as presumption likely to evoke divine wrath, but some figures are available nevertheless, such as the 800,000 northern Israelite warriors and 500,000 Judean ones, given as the result of the census undertaken by Joab at David's behest (2 Samuel 24, 9), or the reported strength of the army of Judah at various times (see, for example, 2 Chronicles 17, 14ff.; 26, 11ff.). These have puzzled scholars, since they seem to imply population totals of several millions, which the contemporary economy of the country could not support. Various attempts have been made to interpret such figures, for instance by assuming the 'thousands' mentioned were not absolute numbers, but kin groups or nominal 'thousandships' whose actual effective strength was small or even minute. The matter remains problematic, however.

Recent scholarship has tried to approach the question from a different angle. The inhabitants of modern Palestine before new techniques transformed agriculture there numbered about one million, a figure some thought could be taken as the upper limit which the population in Israelite times might have attained, since under traditional farming methods the country could support no more. (Even this estimate is too optimistic.) Lately, more refined methods have been used. Estimates have been based on the addition of known local data, such as the potential grain production, or the available water supply suggested by archaeological investigations, but particularly on adding up the known or estimated areas of presumed Israelite settlements and multiplying these by a coefficient representing assumed population density. The results of this latter approach have been startling. That the number of Israelites increased during the Iron Age from a comparatively small number to a respectable total had been long assumed. On the basis of such calculations, however, I. Finkelstein has recently suggested that the total settled Israelite population in western Palestine during the twelfth century BC was only c. 21,000, rising perhaps to c. 55,000 on the eve of the monarchy; if unsettled pastoralists were added the total might perhaps reach a maximum of 150,000.

Using the same methods, Broshi and Finkelstein concluded that by 734 BC the population of Judah and northern Israel including Gilead had risen to a total of 460,000–350,000 in the northern kingdom and 110,000 in Judah (including their respective capitals). Somewhat earlier, Yigal Shiloh had estimated the urban population of Israel during the period of the Monarchy as c. 150,000. Such estimates may err on the side of caution, and indeed the population estimate for eighth-century Judah has been raised somewhat recently. But Sennacherib's claim to have captured some 200,000 inhabitants of

Judah, excluding Jerusalem, in 701 BC, has mostly met with incredulity, though some regard it as possible if the gross total includes non-Judean districts annexed by Hezekiah. Later, wars probably brought a decline – the Syrian and Moabite incursions in the ninth century BC must have reduced the Israelite population drastically, as must the Assyrian wars in the eighth century in western Palestine. Such losses seem to have been made good fairly speedily in the Samarian countryside. In Judah the devastation caused by Sennacherib was not made good in the Shephelah, but during the reign of Manasseh the Judean hill country recovered well and population even expanded into the Judean desert and the Beersheba region. The final Babylonian campaign in 587–586 BC left much of the southern kingdom depopulated. Even in the early Persian period it has been estimated that the population of Judah, including Jerusalem, was only one third of what it had been in 734 BC.

It is difficult to estimate what proportion of the inhabitants of the country may have been non-Israelites, at various times. During the twelfth century BC the Israelites may well have been in the minority. Later, at the time of Solomon, we are told (in 2 Chronicles 2, 17) that 153,600 aliens were conscripted for forced labour – a much smaller number than the 1,300,000 Israelites liable to military service given in Joab's census a little earlier. We should, however, be cautious about assuming that the proportion of non-Israelites in the population had decreased drastically. The Bible contains many enactments intended to ameliorate the wretched lot of the landless resident alien – the *ger* – and this class of people may well have remained numerous. Remaining 'upper-class' Canaanites, however, will quite likely have found employment by using their special skills in the new monarchical administration.

It is difficult also to compare the size of the population in ancient Israel with that in the neighbouring states. Philistia with its important cities should have been well populated – Broshi and Finkelstein credit it with some 50,000 inhabitants – while the inhabitants of the Damascene kingdom at its peak may well have outnumbered those of Israel. There can be little doubt that the inhabitants of Egypt and Assyria vastly exceeded the Israelites in numbers, and the feeling of helplessness voiced by Amos (7, 2) would thus be founded on a very real demographic basis.

Physical types and appearance

Though skeletal remains of ancient Israelites are not numerous, it seems that a basically 'Mediterranean' stock was common. There were, however, local variations. The human remains found at Lachish in southern Judah show similarities with the inhabitants of Lower Egypt (though these do not amount to identity, or prove immigration from that region); on the other hand, the Early Iron Age people of Megiddo in the north differed in showing a tendency towards 'brachycranial' skull shape. In both cases, analogous characteristics are noticeable in the pre-Israelite Bronze Age, and there is no indication in the record of the arrival of a new human stock identifiable with the Israelites.

Interestingly, rheumatoid and arthritic effects on the bones found indicate a certain prevalence of disease, but whether this was more common in some localities or among certain social strata remains unclear.

Illustrations of ancient Israelites are very few, and do not help greatly to define what they looked like. An Egyptian carving on a temple wall at Karnak (ancient Thebes) is now thought by some to represent casualties among the Israelites whom Pharaoh Merneptah claimed to have defeated in *c*. 1207 BC. Unfortunately, the picture is schematic, and badly preserved. There is, moreover, dispute as to which group of the defeated enemies are the Israelites – some think they are the bedouin in *shosu* attire, others a group which comes within the Egyptian tradition of representing Syrians. Rather later, the 'Black Obelisk' of Shalmaneser III (pls 23–5) shows, among other tribute-bearers, some emissaries of Jehu, King of Israel, sent in 841 BC (and perhaps even Jehu himself), but anthropologically the pictures help little. More instructive are the representations of the captured inhabitants of Lachish on the reliefs illustrating Sennacherib's campaign in 701 BC. These captives are figured as somewhat stocky and round-headed, which might be due to artistic convention but agrees well with information about the population of Judea in the Roman period. There is better evidence then, indicating that they tended to be meso- to brachy-cranial, short and robust.

Ancient writers outside Israel have left no descriptions of what the Israelites looked like, and allusions in the Bible tend to be ambiguous. From the praises heaped on the beloved in the Song of Songs (the date of which is disputed) we glimpse a slender and graceful figure with wheat-coloured skin and tresses of fine, shiny black hair – a physical type known in Syria and Arabia. As against this, there are some references to men which may refer to a pinkish and white skin (1 Samuel 17, 42; Lamentations 4, 7). Physical types may have varied. Tall stature seems to have been unusual – it was especially noted in the case of Saul (1 Samuel 9, 2) and befitted his heroic character. Life expectancy was probably not high, and degenerative illnesses such as arthritis must have made the later years of many painful. Among the upper classes, who were better fed and housed than their inferiors, life-expectancy was probably greater – the known or estimated lengths of life of Judean monarchs averaged *c*. 46 years and a number reached 65 to 70. Such figures are very close to those for medieval English monarchs.

Dress and fashions

We are better informed about how the Israelites dressed than about their physical characteristics, and can even distinguish some regional and social variations, as well as modifications within our period. Basically, those traditions in vogue during the Late Bronze Age in the Levant tended to be followed. Both men and women wore nightshirt-like garments, with either long or short sleeves, which might reach down almost to the ankles; those of the well-to-do might be adorned with ornamental borders and fringes at the bottom. Tassels,

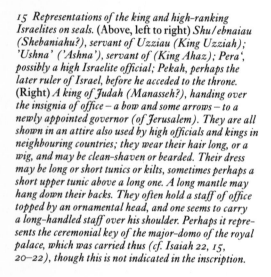

15 Representations of the king and high-ranking Israelites on seals. (Above, left to right) Shu/ebnaiau (Shebaniahu?), servant of Uzziau (King Uzziah); 'Ushna' ('Ashna'), servant of (King Ahaz); Pera', possibly a high Israelite official; Pekah, perhaps the later ruler of Israel, before he acceded to the throne. (Right) A king of Judah (Manasseh?), handing over the insignia of office – a bow and some arrows – to a newly appointed governor (of Jerusalem). They are all shown in an attire also used by high officials and kings in neighbouring countries; they wear their hair long, or a wig, and may be clean-shaven or bearded. Their dress may be long or short tunics or kilts, sometimes perhaps a short upper tunic above a long one. A long mantle may hang down their backs. They often hold a staff of office topped by an ornamental head, and one seems to carry a long-handled staff over his shoulder. Perhaps it represents the ceremonial key of the major-domo of the royal palace, which was carried thus (cf. Isaiah 22, 15, 20–22), though this is not indicated in the inscription.

which had adorned the dress of noble Canaanites, were prescribed for Israelite men (Numbers 15, 38–39), singling them out as members of a nation of distinction. When at work or on military service, Israelites made do with a short loin cloth held up by a belt, from which a knife, seals or similar might be hung; otherwise scarves served as girdles, those of priests being specially ornamented. Some have thought that the puzzling vestment worn by Joseph (Genesis 37, 3) and later sported by royal princesses (2 Samuel 13, 18) consisted of a length of cloth wrapped around the body in sari fashion – a type of dress popular in the Bronze Age, but not referred to in Israel after the time of David. Priests were ordered to wear linen drawers (shorts) under their garments (Exodus 28, 42), but we do not know if anyone else did. Upper garments included wraps and sleeveless coats (some with fringes) held together in front first by straight pins, but by safety pins from the twelfth century onwards.

For headgear, when not going bare-headed, men wore turbans. Those of the inhabitants of Lachish depicted on the reliefs representing the siege of the city by Sennacherib were wound in a special fashion with one fringed end of the cloth hanging down. Priests wrapped theirs around a high fez, and adorned it with a diadem, which was also worn by royalty and nobility. Northern Israelite fashions in headgear seem to have differed. On the 'Black Obelisk', Jehu and his retinue seem to wear 'night-caps' recalling the 'Phrygian cap' in vogue in Anatolia. They also differ in their footwear. When not walking barefoot (as they frequently did, and officiating priests had to), Israelites wore sandals, though soldiers also had boots; but the boots worn by Jehu and his attendants on the 'Black Obelisk' are of a special 'Anatolian' or North Syrian type turned up at the toes. Women in general dressed rather like men (their tunics were longer) but wore head-cloths – those of the women of Lachish reached far down their backs; veils covering the face like those worn by Muslim women are not attested, though women might hide their faces (cf. Genesis 38, 15).

Both sexes also paid much attention to their hair-styles. Men might wear theirs long, especially in the early period, and possibly in separate locks like Samson (cf. Judges 16, 19), or in a coil. Side curls are not attested in early Israel (a statue from Amman, featuring an Ammonite ruler of the ninth or eighth century BC wears them, however, and other examples are known from Tell Halaf and Zinjirli). On the other hand, the men of Lachish on Sennacherib's reliefs wear their hair in short curls. Women might similarly have long hair parted in the middle, or short fringes, or elaborate sets of curls. Both sexes may also have worn wigs on the Egyptian model. Men never went clean-shaven but trimmed their beards; they might shave the upper lip. Aromatic oils were applied to hair or beard; women also used cosmetics, especially eye paint. Both sexes wore such jewelry as they could afford – finger-rings, bracelets, armlets and necklaces, though anklets, nose-rings and toe-rings were specially feminine

16 Head of an Ammonite king or deity. His headgear, patterned on the Egyptian atef crown, resembled that worn by a number of Levantine rulers, but we do know whether the crowns of David and his successors resembled them.

adornments. Men of standing would carry a staff of office with an ornamental head, perhaps of Egyptian type. Foreign fashions in dress were in fact imitated by the upper classes more widely, in spite of prophetic disapproval (cf. Zephaniah 1, 8). In particular, neighbouring monarchs tended to wear crowns of Egyptian derivation and kings in Israel may have followed suit. Representations on seals owned by persons of high standing (intended probably as their likenesses) may also offer information: that they tended to resemble those showing kings and high officials in neighbouring countries would fit the situation.

Social structure: tribes, clans and families

From biblical sources it is clear that the lives of individual Israelites were much affected by their membership of social groups – tribes, clans and families. Information about these units is, however, somewhat patchy. The boundaries between them were apt to fluctuate and, moreover, we can only discern them in a settled state, when they tended to coincide with regions or localities.

About the tribes we know least. Their boundaries, claimed or real, as described in the Bible (as well as their kinship groups), may reflect pre-Israelite regional divisions. Whether they were based on territorial units of economic significance has been doubted, though the curiously oblong shape of the territory of Benjamin, extending from the Jordan Valley beyond the crest of the western uplands, would have offered tribesmen a useful mixture of varied environmental opportunities (see fig. 40). Such may also have been available, though less obvious, in other tribal 'inheritances'. On the human side, we know that tribes might have a pronounced sense of identity, involving sometimes special dialectal speech features (cf. Judges 12, 6), and a sense of tribal honour and jealousy. We are, however, ignorant of what kind of tribal government there may have been, especially in peacetime. In particular we do not know whether there was a regular succession of tribal chiefs, or to what extent they shared responsibility with meetings of tribal elders. Possibly such arrangements were called for only at times of emergency, and with the coming of the monarchy any tribal self-government would have been displaced by the royal administration.

Concerning clans or extended lineages (the older translation of Hebrew *mišpaha* as 'family' is misleading) we are better informed. The Bible gives a good deal of information concerning the localities and regions in which they lived, and the Samaria ostraca show that in northern Israel clans mentioned in the biblical texts were in existence as administrative units in the eighth century BC. There is also more evidence about their judicial and economic functions. It was the business of the clan rather than the tribe to pursue blood revenge for murder, or to see to the redemption of family lands which a clansman had lost. Since the clan often coincided with the township, it must also have been influential in law cases decided in the local court. Combining such legal powers with a feeling of community of descent, the clan must have had a great influence upon the lives of Israelites. In addition, the clan also functioned as a military unit, providing a nominal 'thousandship' (*'eleph*) in times of war, though the actual strength of such units must have varied considerably, in relation to the sizes of the clans which provided them (cf. Judges 6, 15). To what extent there were any regular institutions of clan government is again obscure.

The 'nuclear' family was the smallest unit of kinship. It comprised the householder with his wife or wives and offspring. Grandparents, brothers or uncles who had not set up house on their own might also live with him, thus extending the family circle. In such cases, additional rooms might be added to the standard 'four-room' house and later several houses would form a family compound. However, according to recent estimates, the number of persons in an average household was low – nearer four than eight, perhaps. High mortality among infants in particular would have tended to limit the size of families.

Over his household, the father of the family would wield patriarchal powers. He would also see to the cultivation of the family plot, which would no doubt vary in size in response to the quality of the soil and crops cultivated. An estimate of some 10 ha (25 acres) of arable land per family unit, proposed for the early Israelite village of 'Izbet Ṣarṭah, may give some idea of magnitudes involved. It is possible that land was inherited by the oldest son, only chattels perhaps being divided among all of them. In addition to farming activities, Israelite householders no doubt engaged in other tasks in the slack season, and some specialized in trades like potting or weaving which were handed on from father to son. It is, on the other hand, unclear to what extent their circumstances were affected by the actual application of biblical prescriptions about the Sabbatical year, when the land was to lie fallow, or of the 'Jubilee', when fields and houses that had been alienated were to return to their original owners.

Freemen and slaves

According to biblical law, all ordinary free Israelites were of equal standing, except for the special status accorded priests and Levites. Slaves on the other hand were of different status, being, with certain humanitarian limitations, their master's property. This applied less to Israelites who through insolvency or otherwise had been sold as slaves, than to non-Israelite slaves bought abroad or acquired as prisoners of war. The former were supposed to be released at the end of six years except in cases where they preferred the security offered by being part of their owner's household, but the latter were slaves in perpetuity, unless their master saw fit to free them. However, domestic slavery was in all likelihood usually fairly tolerable. Slaves formed part of the family and males, if circumcised, could take part in the family Passover and other religious functions. Moreover, in general there were probably only a few in each household – there is no indication, for example, that large gangs of them were toiling in deplorable conditions to cultivate big estates, as in the later Roman world. Slaves employed by the state on building projects and similar are likely to have had a much harder lot. Ordinary slaves on the other hand might become their master's trusted and influential servants (those serving the king in particular had chances of advancement) and rise above ordinary freemen; they could also own property. Slavery as an institution seems to have been accepted generally and we hear nothing of slave revolts.

The position of women

As with slaves, so in the case of women – legal and actual social status did not necessarily coincide. In biblical law, women were under perpetual wardship – first their father's and then their husband's or another responsible male's. They could be divorced by their husbands but not divorce them. Their fathers received a 'bride price' (*mohar*) from their suitors, but whether any of this or anything else went to them as a dowry or widow's portion is uncertain; it is also doubtful whether they could testify in courts, and their religious activities were restricted. Nevertheless, they enjoyed some status in their homes, particularly if they had children, who owed them respect. Similarly, while they were largely excluded from public life this exclusion was not total. For instance, Huldah and Deborah were prophetesses – the latter even a war leader – while queen mothers in Judah in particular enjoyed high standing. Lower down the scale, upper- or middle-class women might dispose of property, as seals inscribed with their names attest (cf. also Judges 17, 2–4). It seems in fact that women of character could make their weight felt: the 'great woman of Shunem' (2 Kings 4, 8ff.) may be taken as an example, and the mother of kings Jehoahaz and Zedekiah of Judah, a lady from the country gentry (2 Kings 23, 31; 24, 18), will not have been likened to a lioness for nothing (Ezekiel 19, 2).

Size of population

Having discussed the constituent members of the Israelite social body, we may venture some tentative guesses as to their respective numerical strength. Regarding nuclear families we appear to be on comparatively safe ground: if they numbered four or five persons each then, recalling the estimates of population in eighth-century BC Judah as 110,000 and in northern Israel 350,000, the number of families in Judah would have been between *c.* 22,000 and 27,500 and in Israel between 70,000 and 87,500, or perhaps somewhat less if resident aliens, of whom there were probably more in northern Israel than in Judah, are deducted. Coming to the clans the situation is less simple. According to Numbers 26, there were *c.* 60 clans in all Israel, but, it has to be pointed out, the list does not include all those additionally mentioned in later historical records. It is not clear how large a complete list would be. The size of each clan in Israel should, however, be smaller than 460,000 divided by 60 (=7666), especially as resident aliens would again have to be deducted. Regarding tribes we are faced with even greater difficulties. By 734 BC, when Reuben and Simeon had practically disappeared as independent entities, the number of tribes would have been ten, averaging 46,000 each. Actual figures would, however, have varied considerably, and while in some regions, like Lower Galilee, reasonable estimates seem possible, elsewhere, especially in Transjordan, uncertainty prevails.

What was the proportion of the élite to the rest of the population? According to one estimate, the former amounted to a mere 2 per cent of the total, which would work out as *c.* 7000 in the northern kingdom, and 2200 in Judah. Since, according to T. Ishida's estimate, as early as the tenth century BC, David's family, officials, etc. had amounted to 5600 persons, this figure is probably on the low side. There are, furthermore, indications that between rich and poor in both kingdoms there was a substantial middle class. There are archaeological indications of this (see below, p. 127), but attention should here be drawn to the ways in which King Menahem allotted the tribute imposed by Assyria in *c.* 738 BC: 60,000 landholders paid 1000 talents of silver at the rate of 50 shekels each (2 Kings 15, 20). Since there will have been heads of families, of which we saw there will have been up to *c.* 87,000 in the kingdom, this is a very substantial proportion of the total. Analogous information is lacking in Judah, but we are told (2 Kings 24, 34–35) that in 609 BC Pharaoh Necho exacted a tribute of 30 talents of silver and one talent of gold from Judah, which was taken from the 'people of the land' – here the taxable country gentry – according to their individual assessments. We are not told what the individual sum required was, but since the total tribute on Judah was less than one-twentieth of that demanded from Israel, then at a similar rate of assessment, the heads of notable country families in the southern kingdom (excluding Jerusalemites, priests, Levites and aliens) might have numbered *c.* 4000, or more if the assessment was lower, as might have been the case in an impoverished country. Beneath these heads of households there would have been a much larger number of poorer country men below assessment. Such a split within the 'people of the land' into rich and poor has indeed been assumed on other grounds also.

Social mobility and differentiation

There were, however, forces making for important transformations of this society. First of all, there appears to have been a shift in the ownership of land. Early Israel seems to have been largely a country of peasant farmers, though even by the time of the early monarchy we hear of some unusual wealth like that of Nabal (1 Samuel 25, 2ff.) or Barzillai (2 Samuel 19, 31ff.) and, conversely, there were outcasts like Jephthah (Judges 11, 1–8) or David's early war band (1 Samuel 22, 1–2). By the eighth century the scene had been transformed by the creation of large estates in the place of many individual holdings, hinted at by prophetic denunciations in Amos and Isaiah (especially 5, 8). The increase in the number of the poor (ranging from the indigent to the destitute) which went with this led to something approaching class distinction. Some of the upper class who may be called 'country gentry' were found outside the main cities. These were apparently the 'people of the land' in Judah who were apt to play a conservative role in politics. Yet, in the main, the new élite was urban, and found in particular in the capitals, where landowning nobles who profited also from engaging in the grain trade could live in style, together with the higher ranks of the royal bureaucracy, the court and the priesthood. Here also were found important concentrations of craftsmen and merchants, including a number of foreigners. Archaeology has to a limited extent supported the testimony of the biblical texts. The distinction between the 'egalitarian' planning of Tell el Far'ah (Tirzah) in the ninth century and the differentiation between rich and poor quarters there in the eighth is often referred to, but more evidence is needed. True slums are lacking so far, however.

In this new differentiated society, there were opportunities for social mobility. The decline of the small farmers was balanced by the rise of men in the royal service, including non-Israelites, who might achieve positions of wealth and influence in the administration as well as in the army. In the northern kingdom in particular a number of military commanders even aimed at the throne – and some, like Jehu, managed to seize it.

Political organization

The political development from a loose Israelite confederation, first to a united and then a divided monarchy, brought other important changes in the lives of Israelites. During the period of the Judges, governmental restrictions on individual freedom must have been very limited, for the extent to which effective supra-tribal government existed is questionable. Tribes might on occasion combine to meet a common outside threat under the leadership of judges (i.e. political and military as well as legal commanders) who felt a divine call to effect redress. However, whether common leaders existed in peacetime is unknown. That the 'minor' judges mentioned in the Bible (Judges 10, 1–5) were such has been queried. Similarly the suggestion that early Israel constituted an 'amphictyony' – a tribal group around a central sanctuary with a common priesthood and code of religious and civil laws – is now out of fashion. We simply do not know whether a sanctuary like Shiloh did in fact command more than regional adherence. Belief in the Lord who had brought Israel out of Egypt, and who demanded obedience to His commands to the exclusion of any other authority must however have been important quite early in establishing a bond of common outlook, though this was effective to a varying degree.

The advent of regular royal government transformed the situation. Safety from external attacks had to be paid for by restrictions on a man's right to do 'what was good in his eyes' and also by the acceptance both of heavy burdens in taxes and service (cf. 1 Samuel 8, 11ff.) and of the orders of royal officials not of his own tribe. In addition there loomed a basic dilemma – was it possible to combine the continued observation of a social and legal order based on the absolute supremacy of the Deity with an institution affected by Near Eastern ideas of kingship and royal mystique, and swayed by reasons of state? We shall note some of the ways in which this tension – never completely resolved – restricted royal power.

In recent years the coming of the Monarchy has been viewed from fresh points of view. While it has long been recognized that it came into being in response to external threats, in particular that posed by the Philistines, it is now pointed out that it was also meant to provide an answer to internal problems linked with the evolution of Israelite society. It has also been considered as a development conforming to more general laws governing the rise of states. This would have led by stages from the 'early state' – based on a society with little social differentiation, a tribally-based government with only a rudimentary staff involving few specialist officials – to the 'mature state' based on a fully developed class society, a division between ruler and ruled, and a fully elaborated bureaucracy and tax system. The history of kingship from Saul to Solomon would mark stages on this road.

An important aspect of the transition to monarchy was the adoption in Israel of a royal ideology which was heavily indebted to ideas current in the ancient Near East. Kingship, it was widely held, was divinely instituted, and individual kings owed their thrones to divine will, though popular acclaim and formal agreement had their part. In Israel, the king was not regarded as divine himself, as in Egypt, but divine sonship might be ascribed to him (cf. Psalm 2, 7). The king's functions, in Israel as elsewhere, were defence against threats from abroad and the maintenance of justice – especially social justice towards the weak, the poor, widows, orphans and sojourners – within the realm. If he fulfilled these duties then even nature would respond to the upholding of divinely willed order by providing plentiful sustenance. If he did not, then there was no constitutional machinery to call him to order. Kings had, however, to reckon with forces which could not be disregarded with impunity: priests, prophets and Levites, bureaucrats and rich town folk, the country gentry and the army. All needed to be watched and, up to a point, satisfied. Beyond these practical limitations on the king's freedom to act there were constitutional ones. He could not by himself legislate, and important decisions, such as the implementation of the rules laid down in the book found in the Temple at the time of Josiah (2 Kings 22; 23, 1–3) or the freeing of Hebrew slaves in the reign of Zedekiah (Jeremiah 34, 8–20) required national consent. During the late Monarchy, the king's power to act was severely circumscribed. The formal limitations imposed on him in Deuteronomy (17, 14–20) have struck some as unenforceable theories post-dating the fall of the monarchy, but they conform to the general attempt to adapt political realities to religious requirements, and they would not seem out of place in the programme followed in King Josiah's reform.

Opposition to monarchy, however, went further than attempts to control kings or even to overthrow unsatisfactory rulers. There was, in Israel, side by side with the view that regarded monarchy as a divine gift, one in direct opposition that believed kingship to be inherently evil since it breached divine sovereignty. Such a view seems quite unusual in the ancient Near East, where rebellions to overthrow individual monarchs were not unknown, but kingship itself was not condemned. In Israel, such anti-monarchical tendencies seem to have been present from the very start of the monarchy. Their actual influence varied from time to time, but their effect on later political thought in medieval and modern Europe in particular was to be considerable, together with the alternative ideal of the Just King. The Civil War in seventeenth-century England may serve as an example of their long-term consequences.

Royal officials

A central feature in the establishment of kingship was the creation of a staff of ministers and civil servants linked with the court, supported by local officials in charge of districts of the country. This process began under Saul. We are badly informed about what originally were probably somewhat rudimentary arrangements, but it appears that besides a chief-of-staff commanding a permanent picked war band as well as tribal levies, the king had some officials like Doeg the royal herdsman, a non-Israelite, though most of the king's retainers were Benjaminites rewarded with fields and vineyards (cf. 1 Samuel 21, 7; 22, 6–7). There may have been a district organization different from the later one, but there was no capital city nor was there a religious establishment linked with the crown. Religious opposition in fact constituted a serious element of weakness.

A new, far more elaborate and comprehensive administration was created during the kingships of David and Solomon. Biblical sources (2 Samuel 8 and 20; 1 Kings 4; supplemented in 1 Chronicles 18 and 27) offer detailed information both about the central government in the new capital Jerusalem and the district administration in the country, besides details about taxes in kind and labour services imposed on Israelites and non-Israelites in support of government projects. We have less information about later reigns, but enough to follow constitutional and administrative arrangements in outline.

At the top of the pyramid was the king, divinely chosen and acclaimed by the people in theory – his accession might involve a convenant between the Deity, the monarch and the nation – though less constitutional avenues to the throne were not uncommon in the northern kingdom and in Judah the 'people of the land', or country gentry, might take a hand. Women could not constitutionally become monarchs, while among sons, succession did not necessarily go to the firstborn. On accession, the king was (usually?) anointed, a ceremony known in the Bronze Age. It indicated the monarch's religious aura, which was expressed also in bracketing together as crimes worthy of death cursing God and cursing the king (cf. 1 Kings 21, 10ff.). The king was personally active as a leader in war and in dispensing justice during the early monarchy. He also supervised or regulated the religious establishment, but except perhaps during the early period he was not involved in functions which were more properly priestly. In administrative and political matters he was assisted by a 'cabinet' which included various important functionaries (who might be succeeded in their offices by their descendants), among whom were found non-Israelite specialists as well as Israelites. Apparently patterned on the Egyptian model, the list included the 'secretary of state' (*sopher*), who headed the bureaucracy which dealt with royal correspondence, including presumably missives to local officials. Communications were in writing, authenticated by the king's seal. The secretary-of-state must also have been in charge of records and responsible for the maintenance of chronicles. The 'herald' or 'recorder' (*mazkir*), controlled court ceremonial, access to the king and communications between ruler and ruled. The 'major-domo' (*ašer 'al-habayit*='he who is over the house') was in charge of the palace, an office which took on additional important functions in the course of time. There was a chief of conscripted labour and the leaders of the army and of the priesthood were included. There were in addition royal counsellors and the 'king's friend', who had somewhat uncertain functions. Also at court were men in charge of various produce from the royal estates which, in addition to taxes in kind, helped to maintain the establishment. There were also various lower officials. Royal princes might also be active in the administration. This central bureaucracy, once established, seems to have continued with little change, at least in Judah. Local administration seems to have been less centralized, and the local elders might have been asked to act.

The capital cities, and perhaps other important ones, might be placed under a city governor (*śar-ha'ir*) but elsewhere local elders remained in charge. The country as a whole was, from Solomon onwards, divided into twelve districts, presumably of similar economic importance, each of which had to support the court for one month in turn. Some of these were based on tribal divisions, but others broke with the tribal mould, especially in the case of the Joseph tribes who were dangerously separatist. Whether Judah was part of the scheme or not is unclear; it had in any case a district organization of its own, the date of which is disputed. In the northern kingdom, the Solomonic system seems to have survived, as the eighth-century Samaria ostraca indicate.

The system of government outlined above was, during good times, able to provide security and even some prosperity at home and respect abroad. It bore heavily on the people, however, especially as they were also liable to pay substantial religious dues, such as tithes. In times of famine or war the combined burden may well have been crushing for the poor, helping to depress their status. Occasionally they may have benefited from booty gained in successful wars, but this must have been rare, and foreign tribute went into the king's coffers. Criticisms by prophets were on the whole, though, not directed against the king, but against his ministers who instead of maintaining general justice were in league with the rich and powerful who oppressed the poorer people.

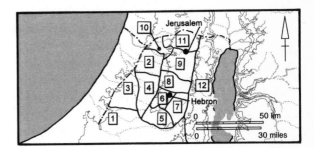

17 The administrative districts of Judah. The time when these districts were created is uncertain but the reign of Jehoshaphat, Ahab's contemporary, is favoured by some. The numbering refers to the sequence in which they appear in Joshua 15, 21–62, including the Septuagint, to which Joshua 18, 25–8 should be added.

Law and justice

While the position of the king in Israel resembled in many ways that of contemporary Near Eastern monarchs, his powers in the legal sphere as in others were, so far as we can tell, far more limited. Mesopotamian rulers promulgated law codes, though they were to a large extent reproductions of current practice, but in Israel no king or governmental institution is known to have issued laws. Divine law (as detailed in the Bible) was to be followed instead, governing matters civil, criminal and religious. It was kept in writing, and it was to be proclaimed periodically (cf. Deuteronomy 31, 10ff.). Yet we do not know to what extent biblical prescriptions governed actual legal practice – there is at present a total lack of documents illustrating individual cases. Nor is it known to what extent Israelite law differed from the preceding Canaanite, although both analogies with and differences from Mesopotamian laws and legal practice can be found.

Law suits arose from accusations by individual Israelites, for there was no public prosecutor. The rights of resident aliens to bring a suit may have been restricted (cf. 2 Samuel 21, 1–6). Ordinary courts involved the local elders, though we hear also of appointed judges and clerks of court (Deuteronomy 16, 18). The king had the right to judge cases involving him as military commander-in-chief and those not covered by standard legal tradition. In addition, the king could judge in cases of pleas made to him on grounds of denial of justice or special difficulty. Whether he could normally review verdicts of lower courts is doubtful, though there may have been instances involving stay of execution (cf. 2 Samuel 14, 5–11). Similarly, a court comprising priests, Levites and lay judges set up by Jehoshaphat in Jerusalem (2 Chronicles 19, 8–11) may have been intended to deal with cases of special difficulty, rather than the review of sentences given in lower courts (cf. Deuteronomy 17, 8–13).

Court cases, which would normally be completed within a day, consisted of pleas by the parties involved. Evidence might include testimony on oath (that of women or slaves was perhaps excluded), written or material evidence, and in some cases, like that of a woman accused of adultery, an ordeal. Penalties in civil cases might, in addition to restitution of damages caused, involve a fine payable to the injured party, but no fines were apparently payable to court or king. Justice was not a source of royal income, except perhaps in special cases like *lèse-majesté* (cf. 1 Kings 21, 8–16).

In cases of murder the criminal was handed over for execution to the 'avenger of blood' in the murdered man's family; in other cases involving the death penalty by stoning the witnesses for conviction cast the first stones, followed by the whole community. There was no publicly appointed executioner. In such cases, biblical law expressly excluded the faculty to grant a pardon which in other ancient Near Eastern monarchies was vested in the king. In judicial matters the pursuit of justice thus remained to a remarkable extent vested in the community.

Social ideas

Whatever the real circumstances, this ancient society, or at least its articulate sections, treasured certain ideals concerning social order, where due respect was paid by the young to the old, and by the humbler folk to their social betters, who in turn were expected to be proud to help the less fortunate, even if this meant a struggle. Good manners were similarly prized, and things had to be done with due ceremony, especially in matters of law. Job 29, though possibly written after our period, offers a good impression of what was valued, and others are supplied by Psalms and Proverbs. Where the social system failed, prophets might call for redress of wrongs and, if Job 30 can be taken as a guide, the wretches and outcasts from this family-dominated society might riot when it seemed safe to do so, though otherwise there seems to have been no call for social revolution. The idea that the humble and meek were specially dear to the Deity may represent a deflection of social tensions into the religious sphere – it was to become increasingly significant in the future.

Chivalrous generosity towards a defeated enemy, referred to in 1 Kings (20, 30ff.) might have been part of a social code; significantly it did not pass without criticism, but it may be noted that there is, in the Bible, no hint that Israelite kings or nobles engaged in the chase as an aristocratic pastime, as their equals did in the neighbouring lands. Though the lifestyle of the nobles of Samaria reproved by Amos bears some resemblance to that of the suitors in the *Odyssey*, a complete adoption of aristocratic ways in a country influenced by the social code enshrined in biblical commands was perhaps not possible. Thus while in many respects Israelite social ideals resembled those found in neighbouring lands, there must also have been some significant differences in outlook, and this would have been true both for those at the top and those at the bottom of the social pyramid. An Israelite king might be divinely appointed (though such appointment could be revoked by the Deity), and as we saw this conforms to current Near Eastern ideas, but that monarchy as an institution could be opposed on religious as well as other grounds is startling in terms of the contemporary Near East. The ensuing tensions worked out in Israelite history may perhaps be compared with those which led to the fall of the early Islamic Ummayad state. In both cases it proved impossible to accommodate the demands of a newly arrived religion with the adoption of the ways of the society in which it was now to play a leading role. The increasing appreciation shown to the pious poor might be similarly compared with later Christian and Islamic attitudes. It is indeed true that certain ancient Near Eastern monarchs described themselves as poor or humble (divine favour might be gained in this way) but such an attitude seems to have become more widespread and significant in Israelite society than elsewhere.

Conclusion

In its early stages Israelite society was mainly rural, fairly egalitarian, and organized on kinship lines with little interconnection between local communities.
This developed into a society divided into an urban élite – administrators, rich
landowners, the royal establishment and others – and the rural masses. The
importance of kinship groups lessened and there was a tendency towards class
division, though the split between rich and poor does not entirely conform to it
since there was, for one thing, a substantial middle class. Political centralization, which broke down local exclusiveness, became paired in Judah with religious centralization emanating from the urban political centre. This involved a
substantial transformation in the lifestyle and outlook of country folk, who
were directed to forsake old-established beliefs and to seek salvation in the doc-
trines and organized cult of the capital. Such success on the part of the religious reform party made Israel, and especially Judah, unusual among its
contemporaries.

Geographical factors clearly affected the organization of Israelite society, its
internal and external contacts in peace and war, and its outlook, but the facts
which have been reviewed do not, in the case of the Israelites, beyond a certain
point support Braudel's thesis that highland zones depend on, and tend to be
dominated by, their richer and more civilized lowland neighbours. There was
indeed very probably a steady flow of indigent highlanders seeking a living by
working in the lowlands, and there were times when the latter exercised political dominion over the upland zone. Yet at other times the exact reverse was
true – the power that had accumulated in the highland kingdoms was more
effective than lowland influences, and became politically dominant.

In the interpretation of Israelite history we saw increasing reference to social
factors, though we must not forget that our information in that, as in other
respects, is patchy. Nor must we forget that individuals could shape events
decisively: Israelite as well as non-Israelite sources point to this in cases of such
rulers as Omri or Hezekiah. Models which do not acknowledge this do not fit
Israelite history.

There is, finally, a curious postscript to our summing up. Israel, we saw, was
closely linked with its ancient Near Eastern neighbours, and its comprehensive
gentilic structure is best paralleled within the sphere of west Semitic pastoralists – the early Arabs in particular. (It is not, on present evidence, well paralleled among the Canaanites, and those who would derive Israel from a purely
Canaanite ancestry have some explaining to do in this respect.) Yet recently
Mosheh Weinfeld has pointed out an impressive number of parallels between
traditions concerning the origins of Israel, and those about early Greek settlements. Cultural contacts, possibly early, may be involved here. It is to be hoped
that more light will be thrown on this intriguing but at present tantalizing topic.

CHAPTER FIVE

Towns and Villages: Planning and Architecture

By the time Israel had become archaeologically visible, it seems to have been a mainly settled society. Nomadic pastoralists may still have been important, but most Israelites seem to have lived in houses, though some of these were perhaps occupied only seasonally, especially those on the desert fringes. And by the time the United Monarchy broke apart after Solomon's death, the cry 'to your tents, O Israel' (1 Kings 12, 16) was probably a literary archaism. Such pastoral tent-dwellers as there were in early Israel have not so far been traced archaeologically.

Similarly, very little can be made of the remains of some of the first Israelite settlements – storage and dwelling pits, post-holes and patches of floor which offer no intelligible architectural features, perhaps representing the presence of pastoral nomads settling down either temporarily or permanently.

Though some early Israelites were probably to be found in Canaanite towns such as Shechem or perhaps Megiddo, theirs was essentially a non-urban life-style. They lived mainly in small villages covering areas well below one hectare, hamlets and isolated farmsteads. Towns were at first Canaanite, survivors from the Bronze Age, most of which Israel did not manage to incorporate before the reign of David. For some Canaanite towns, incorporation brought decline, for others a change in function. Israelite settlers came to live in them in varying proportions, sometimes even replacing the Canaanite townspeople. For example, Jerusalem, from being the head of a petty kingdom, acquired the status of imperial capital, with Canaanites apparently surviving side by side with the Israelite newcomers; Megiddo found new importance as an Israelite administrative and military centre; Beth Shean, however, once a crucial Egyptian base, found no permanent new Israelite role and soon declined. Genuinely Israelite towns arose in the tenth century BC, after the establishment of the United Monarchy, followed by still more in the ninth. Government involvement in their rise has been suspected, especially since they came into being at a time when a number of villages were abandoned, and their inhabitants presumably transferred to the new strongholds. However these towns might have arisen, their existence brought about a new dependence of the countryside on urban centres, and this in turn modified the character of rural Israel.

Rural settlement: the early stages

Both the siting and character of early Israelite rural settlement has been the object of intensive investigation in recent years. During the pre-Monarchical period – Iron I – Israelites tended mostly to avoid the neighbourhood of Canaanite towns, and kept away also from main roads. They preferred more remote if sometimes less attractive but defensible locations on high ground – clearings in backwoods or on deserted mounds – in places where grain production and the keeping of livestock were feasible. Nor were their settlements always near springs. Water might have to be fetched from a distance, or rain-water stored in cisterns, dug into impermeable rock or waterproofed with lime plaster. Such techniques were known in the Bronze Age, when the digging of wells began.

Though occupation was sparse, especially on the desert fringe, some patterning is discernible. In Ephraim, villages which sometimes covered an area of a hectare or two, though mostly well below a hectare, and whose inhabitants numbered between a hundred and (very rarely) a thousand, were arranged on the principle of one main village per valley, surrounded by smaller hamlets or isolated farms. Arable land would be within a 1–2 km (½–1¼ miles) radius of the village, with pasture and rough brushwood extending perhaps to a 4–5 km (2½–3 miles) distance. This would allow the inhabitants to undertake daily tasks without lengthy travel and permit them to return to the comparative safety of their homes at night.

Early Israelite villages seem occasionally to have favoured an oval or circular plan. Houses, some of the 'four-room' type (see below), were arranged around the periphery in a continuous line which offered some defence against wild animals or raiders. The area inside this ring was left vacant, and could be used as a pound for livestock or a refuge for people in times of trouble. Sometimes, as at Ai, the rear rooms of houses were contiguous, anticipating later casemate

18 (Left) *Beersheba, a reconstruction of Stratum VII, showing a typical settlement of Iron Age I type, in which buildings were arranged around a central courtyard for defence against marauders.*

19 (Right) *The rural site of 'Izbet Sartah; plan of Stratum III (Early Iron Age). It comprises an oval ring of rooms around a central open space, a plan favoured at this time.*

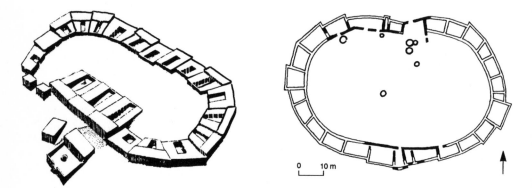

0   10 m

walls. True defence walls were exceptional at this stage though there may have been some, for example at Khirbet Dawara, northeast of Jerusalem, but walling at Giloh to the southeast may have served to keep animals inside a grazing area rather than raiders out. Some former Canaanite defence works were patched up, but proper fortresses were probably non-Israelite and some – in Galilee, at Har Adir and elsewhere – may indicate Phoenician control of Israelite territory.

Buildings of a communal nature seem to have been rare. A communal store house may have existed at Shiloh, and Khirbet Raddanah near Jerusalem had a communal building of some sort. Whether a non-domestic structure at Tel Qiri near Jokneam was Israelite, or what its functions were, is not clear. The existence there of cultic equipment does not necessarily mean that it was entirely devoted to religious ends. Settlements whose areas were largely filled up with irregularly placed buildings, like Beth Shemesh III, may have been on the way to becoming townships.

Rural settlement during the period of the Monarchy

The most striking feature of settlement during this time (Iron II) is its growth – both in northern Israel and in Judah the rural population increased dramatically. The Assyrian invasions, especially Sennacherib's campaign, caused some setback but this was later made good by the foundation of numerous small towns along lines of communication. At this time there was rarely more than 3–5 km (2–3 miles) between sites. About their architectural character it is still difficult to generalize, but the oval settlements found earlier seem no longer to have been built, though some houses might still offer a common front. Villages might have had defence walls but it was towns that now offered refuge when required.

In the countryside the agriculture practised also changed in character, becoming diversified and employing more sophisticated techniques. It was now geared to producing surpluses to go to the towns as taxes, rents (cf. Amos 5, 11) and religious dues, as well as providing income through sale. The countryside's new role was thus dependent on the urban centres. Towns lived as 'parasites' on the country, to which they gave little in return except perhaps safety in time of danger. The increased volume of traffic involved was facilitated by an improved system of roads or tracks.

The towns

While some quite important cities in the Late Bronze Age were not fortified, any locality defended by walls was, in Israelite eyes, a town. Many such places were small, covering areas of 2–3 ha (5–7½ acres) or less, and numbering perhaps some 1000–1500 inhabitants. Indeed, when Tiglath-Pileser III invaded Galilee in 732 BC he mentions that he exiled totals of only 625, 650 and 656 inhabitants respectively from three conquered localities (*ANET* 283). Such 'towns' were in reality fortified villages, with presumably only limited social differentiation between inhabitants who largely made their living from agricultural pursuits – perhaps a normal size for the more important among them may have been 3–5 ha (7½–12 acres). There were indeed larger cities with possibly several thousand inhabitants. Thus Hazor in the tenth century BC covered some 6.5 ha (16 acres), Gezer and Megiddo *c.* 10 ha (25 acres), while Lachish later occupied some 15 ha (37 acres) and Jerusalem reached an area of some 50–60 ha (124–148 acres) with *c.* 20,000 inhabitants in the seventh century BC. Samaria may have achieved a similar magnitude before its fall in 722 BC. Yet even these two capitals are only just the equal of those of medium-sized contemporary Syrian states such as Sam'al and Gozan, and perhaps Hamath and Damascus, and were vastly inferior in area and population to imperial capitals such as Nineveh. The 120,000 inhabitants credited to the latter in Jonah (4, 11) may be no exaggeration; Babylon with perhaps 50,000–80,000 inhabitants and probably also the less well-known Memphis and Thebes in Egypt were similarly much bigger.

The larger Israelite towns do show truly urban features. They subsisted to some extent on contributions from the countryside – rents, taxes and religious dues – while their inhabitants included people of varying wealth and social status, who fulfilled diversified functions such as administrators, soldiers, priests, scholars and scribes, craftsmen and traders. This functional diversity would express itself in the presence of buildings or zones devoted to special purposes – military, administrative or religious – and also in a division between the quarters inhabited by wealthier and poorer citizens. Such towns needed a more advanced infrastructure than ordinary villages – in addition to a defensible position on a hill, spur or mound, other requirements were an assured water supply of sufficient capacity to meet the needs of citizens in peacetime, good communications both inside the town and with the world outside, permitting imports and exports, and a capable administration assuring public order and a minimum level of hygiene, including some removal of rubbish and burial of the dead. With all this, towns offered a more sophisticated life than villages. Yet it seems that not all citizens participated equally in it. Officialdom and administrators were kept separate from common folk – by a wall at Lachish – and rich and poor might be located in separate quarters. Social life was probably a family and clan affair rather than being shared by the whole citizen body. There are no signs of public facilities for recreation, and it is doubtful whether the King's Gardens in Jerusalem were accessible to the public. This is still far from the comprehensive common life found in the later Greek *polis*, but we must not underrate the variety of experience offered by cities and their intellectual life, which was supported by increasing literacy in the towns.

Distribution of towns

In a country where there were many towns proper and small towns – Sennacherib claims to have taken 46, as well as numerous villages, in Judah alone (*ANET* 258), though this list may have included some in the territory annexed by Hezekiah – one would expect some system of 'ranking', with 'central places' surrounded by dependent towns and villages. This has still to be worked out, yet data do exist. Some important cities, such as Jerusalem, Hebron and Beersheba, were roughly one day's journey apart. These marked one axis, while a second (Jerusalem–Beth Shemesh–Lachish) went along the Shephelah. Smaller settlements depended on the central stations. Other cities were much closer to each other – the proximity of Shechem, Samaria and Tirzah is startling. In particular we cannot say up to what distances towns served as marketing centres, or indeed how many such market towns there were. Jerusalem and Samaria had markets, and there were shops along the street leading into Lachish from the gate and perhaps a market area in Hazor during the eighth century, but at present we cannot say that a market was a normal feature of a town as it was in medieval Europe. There would have been less need for it, for various crafts, like that of the smith and the weaver, were also carried out in villages.

Urban planning

Among Israel's neighbours, urban planning was a well-established practice. Though some cities were the irregular products of undirected growth, others were laid out according to geometric schemes – their outlines might be rectangular, square, rhomboid, oval, round or semicircular. In Assyria and Babylonia, main roads might divide up the urban territory. As early as the second millennium BC Egypt had quite sophisticated town plans embodying a regular grid of roads crossing at right angles, differentiated zones devoted to various functions and the serial repetition of identically planned dwellings.

In Israel, where most towns were built on hillocks or mounds, geometrically determined outlines for settlements were not usually attempted, their shape being largely imposed by the oblong, oval or roundish configuration of the ground on which they were placed. Where regularity does occur, as in the cases of the roundish towns of Shechem or Tell Beit Mirsim, it is a pre-Israelite configuration that is carried over. On the other hand, planning is frequently discernible inside the urban perimeter, determining both the overall arrangement and individual complexes or buildings. Accuracy in the execution of plan schemes varies, tending to be greater in the case of buildings presumed to have been put up by royal architects than those attributable to private builders. In either case, however, its quality is quite comparable to standards found in Mesopotamia or Egypt.

Different types of town

Leaving for later consideration the two capital cities of Jerusalem and Samaria, we can, following Yigal Shiloh, distinguish two main types of town plan. On the one hand there are towns with administrative or military functions, often of a fair size and characterized by the orderly disposition of a limited number of

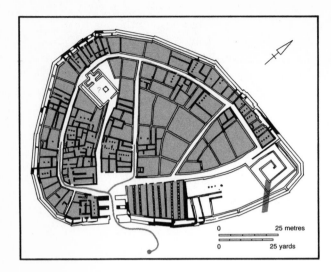

20 *Plan of Beersheba, City II (eighth century):
much of it is given over to housing but there is very
efficient planning of the street-system and there
were official buildings such as stores, a governor's
residence and, probably, in an earlier stratum, a
sanctuary (shown reconstructed).*

21 *Proto-Aeolic capital carved in stone, from Megiddo.*

impressive building complexes or individual buildings, surrounded sometimes
by large open spaces. Any purely residential quarters were kept separate here.
The quality of structures tends to be noticeably higher and there is, in particular, a preference for high-class ashlar construction with balanced design and for
architectural decoration such as proto-Aeolic capitals on pillars (pl. 17). Such
buildings were clearly meant to impress the beholder. A very different state of
affairs is found, on the other hand, in what are essentially country towns, which
are smaller in size, crowded and with only a limited regularity discernible. The
quality of construction tended to be lower; ashlar is rare and there is no architectural decoration. Houses present an unimpressive exterior, while the interior – where life was carried on – was not visible to outsiders. Needless to say, the
distinction between the two types is not absolute.

Residential towns
Residential country towns, exemplified by Tell Beit Mirsim and Tell en-
Naṣbeh (Mizpah), are characterized by a peripheral or concentric arrangement. A road running either along the city wall or parallel to it roughly at the
distance taken up by the length of a house, separates an outer circumference
zone from a central core area. The circumference zone may be taken up entirely
by dwellings backed up against the wall (and with their rear rooms possibly
taking the form of casemate rooms), or the space may be left open and used for
public cisterns, ovens or stone-lined storage pits. The core area shows no
regular road network or through roads, but access to groups of houses (the plan
of which may here as in the outer zone be distorted by crowding) is gained by
alleys or cul-de-sacs. Such groups of dwellings around a common access may
represent areas occupied by family groups or clans. A piazza inside the gate
provides the only defined public open space. There are no outstanding official
or religious buildings, nor are there many indications of a sharp division
between rich and poor – slums, in particular, are absent.

Occasionally, dwelling quarters may show greater regularity. At Tell el-Far'ah (N) (Tirzah) there is a rudimentary road grid arrangement in strata VIIb and VIId; in VIIb a quarter of respectable dwelling units just next to poor ones consists of houses very similar in plan and size, regularly aligned to the cardinal points. Effective civic planning and supervision were obviously at work.

Sometimes there are more advanced planning features, anticipating the system of a road grid around blocks of houses (*insulae*) in vogue in the later Classical world. At Tell es-Sa'idiyeh VIII (eighth century) a block of houses on an approximately identical plan (forecourt and back room), facing in opposite directions from a spine wall, is flanked by straight roads, while a more crudely executed example of a similar scheme has been pointed out at Tell en-Naṣbeh: both are at right angles to the town wall. Transjordanian links have been suggested in the former case.

Official administrative and military centres

Among cities devoted to official functions, the Israelites distinguished store cities, chariot cities and cities of horsemen, in particular (1 Kings 9, 19; 2 Chronicles 8, 4–6). Identification of any of these with towns revealed by excavation has proved difficult, so it seems sensible to present the architectural data on their own.

We may begin with the orientation of buildings. A comprehensive geometric grid plan is not found before Megiddo III in the late eighth or early seventh century BC. However, important public buildings, even if set at a distance, may

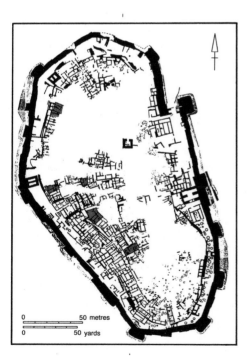

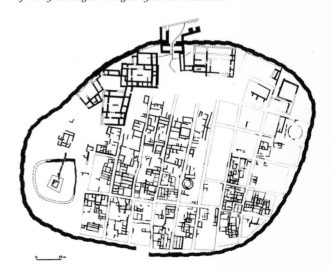

22 (Left) Tell en-Naṣbeh (Mizpah) was perhaps originally a small walled country town but was turned into a strong royal fortress by the addition of the massive outer wall (built by King Asa, 905–874 BC). Many inhabitants continued to live mainly from farming or crafts (possible workshops are shown shaded).

23 Megiddo, plan of the city in Stratum III–II (late eighth/seventh century BC). This is the earliest known example of a city arranged on a grid system in Palestine.

0   50 metres
0   50 yards

be roughly on the same alignment, as at Lachish III, though more often their orientation follows the outline of the mound on which they are built. There are nevertheless cases where either the sides or the corners of structures are approximately aligned with the points of the compass.

Where the plans of individual buildings or building complexes are concerned there seems to be a preference for the square, the square and a half, and the double square (as Helga Weippert has noted), again with some occasional lack of exactness in execution. Thus, the platform for the first residency building at Lachish and the enclosure for Palace 1723 at Megiddo VA–IVB are nearly square, complex 1576 at Megiddo – a court backed by halls in stratum IVA – covers a square and a half, while the acropolis enclosure at Samaria is laid out as a double square. It seems that the square represented some idea of perfection to Israelites – when Ezekiel had a vision of the divinely prescribed renewed commonwealth to come, some thirteen years after the fall of Jerusalem, the sacred district around the capital, the Holy City in its midst and the inner precincts of the Temple all occupied concentric square areas (Ezekiel 42, 15–20; 48, 16ff., 30ff.). We seem here to be dealing with the culmination of a tradition of some antiquity. Whether foreign models were involved in its genesis is doubtful.

The capitals: Samaria and Jerusalem

Our knowledge of both Samaria and Jerusalem is at present patchy. In Samaria, the splendid royal acropolis, set in an ashlar enclosure *c.* 178 by 89 m (584 by 292 ft), is partly known but information is almost totally lacking about the city proper. Some indeed have doubted whether there was much of a town outside the royal headquarters. On balance, there was probably a city of something like 20,000 inhabitants, occupying an area of *c.* 60 ha (148 acres) at its zenith. As for Jerusalem, the situation is the reverse – we have information about the royal acropolis only from biblical descriptions but an increasing amount is known about the city, with archaeology supplementing the fairly extensive biblical and post-biblical literary sources (among which latter Flavius Josephus ranks high). We can even discern something of the city's development, overall zoning and architectural features.

Of the two hills, once divided by a now largely filled-in valley, it was the eastern, the biblical Ophel, running south from the present *Haram* enclosure, that dominated the important spring (ancient Gihon) and which was the site of Canaanite Jerusalem. The space available for habitation was small, only *c.* 4 ha (10 acres) (though it was progressively enlarged by terraces built on the steep eastern slope, carrying houses), and crowded with official buildings. Noticeable among these is a high pyramidal stone structure backed up against the hillside which bore first the citadel of the Canaanite ruler and then David's. Since, according to Tomo Ishida's estimate, David's family, his functionaries, official establishment and their households amounted to some 5600 persons in all, it would have been impossible to accommodate more than part of them in the city – the remainder would have had to live outside.

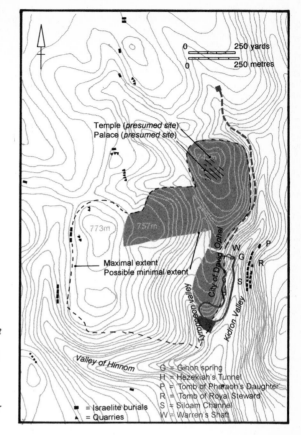

24 Plan of Iron Age Jerusalem and its stages of development. To the right, on the eastern hill, the original Canaanite and Davidic nucleus with its Solomonic extension northwards are shown. To the west of the present Haram platform there developed a limited extension of uncertain size; this became merged into the city at its greatest extension during the eighth and seventh centuries, when most if not all of the western hill was also included in the walled perimeter. The exact boundaries of these extensions require further definition.

Solomon extended the urban area northwards, establishing his royal palace complex – including the Temple – in the *Haram* area (their exact location is unknown), but overcrowding must have remained a problem. Interestingly, Josephus, who is often well informed, by implication attributes the extension of the urban perimeter to take in the western hill (long regarded as Mount Zion), and as defined by his 'first wall', to the Jewish kings right back to Solomon and David (*Wars V*, 142). This would have dealt with the problem, since there would be nothing intrinsically impossible in their having begun but not finished a wider fortified circuit. The work would have stopped when the United Monarchy broke apart and the attempt to make Jerusalem an imperial capital failed. However, there is at present no archaeological proof that this did happen. Much later, in the late eighth century, the time of King Hezekiah, the western hill, which had by then become part of the inhabited area, was taken into the defensive perimeter by a strong wall 8 m (26 ft) wide, part of which was revealed by Nahman Avigad. Whether its western side ran right along the edge of the western hill, or somewhat further to the east, remains to be determined. Since Hezekiah also deflected the waters of the Gihon spring into the widened urban territory by the construction of the Siloam Tunnel (see below), Jerusalem became almost impregnable to assault, except perhaps from the north.

This enlarged town developed definite zoning features in the seventh century. The eastern hill had long carried official buildings – Solomon's Palace and Temple – and the homes of people of rank. The western hill now developed similar characteristics, including, some think, new palaces belonging to the later kings, from Manasseh onwards, though they still have to be found. The intervening central valley, less desirable for living, became the home of traders and artisans.

It remains to say something about Jerusalemite architecture. We saw earlier that official Israelite constructions were distinguished by large-scale and spacious planning, and by the use of imposing ashlar walling. About the latter the Bible has much to say when describing Solomon's Temple and palace buildings, but no parts of these can now be identified with certainty. Impressive ashlar constructions from the ninth century BC have recently been revealed by Professor Benjamin Mazar and his granddaughter Eilat at the northeast corner of the Ophel hill. Elsewhere, as in the late urban quarters revealed by Kenyon's and Shiloh's excavations along the eastern fringe of the Ophel in particular, buildings are curiously lacking in the monumental character and regular urban planning one might have expected in the royal capital. Still, there are hints that this was not always so – fine ashlar blocks, perhaps Solomonic, have been found in secondary use in eighth-century walling, as well as a proto-Aeolic capital, hinting that splendid buildings once stood not far away, presumably forming part of more orderly schemes than the present irregular layout. Unfortunately, since much of the hilltop has been removed by later quarrying, we cannot be sure that anything remains to be retrieved.

A hint of Solomonic architectural magnificence is nevertheless offered by the *Haram* enclosure. The present platform owes its size largely to Herod's extensions, and the exact limits of Solomon's royal enclosure are not known. It is agreed, though, that it was very large: 250–275 m by 160 m (820–900 ft by 525 ft) has been suggested by Busink, or even a square area with sides 500 royal cubits long (*c.* 262.5 m/861 ft). This is considerably in excess of the area occupied by the acropolis at Samaria. The effort involved and the means required must have been enormous – no wonder we are told it took Solomon 13 years to build his residence (1 Kings 7, 1) – and the effect spectacular.

Urban requirements and organization

Civic administration

To ensure the smooth running of the affairs of a sizeable body of people the unaided efforts of a council of non-specialist elders would not have sufficed. The Bible mentions the existence of a special royal functionary known as the 'administrator of the city' (*śar ha-'ir*) in Jerusalem and probably in some important towns elsewhere, and seals of such persons have been found. The question is where the civic authorities did their work and kept their records. While periodic meetings of the elders in the gate of the settlement might be enough in small places, it would not have been suitable for more advanced towns. A chamber above the gate, for which there are medieval parallels, would have suited, or special buildings analogous to town halls in function. No special architectural arrangement is known, but buildings such as the tower-like house attached to the town wall at Tell Beit Mirsim, or large 'four-room' houses by the gate, as at Tell en-Naṣbeh, might have served for this purpose. Whether individual town quarters in larger towns like Jerusalem had their own authorities with related premises is unknown.

The maintenance of public order is another requirement, and we hear of the watchmen going their rounds especially at night (Song of Songs 3, 3; 5, 7 – perhaps a late source) though not of any police headquarters. Prisons are mentioned, and the seal of a prison has been found, but no building devoted to such purposes is known, nor are court-houses.

Communications within cities were just as important as those with the world outside. Main streets would lead through the gate or gates to a piazza and might be paved and sufficiently wide to take wheeled traffic. Only rarely, however, did they lead any distance into the built-up area, which was largely served by lanes of irregular width and layout. It must have been difficult for the chariots of the upper class, or for the carts of the peasantry, to progress along these – not to mention to pass each other – though access for pack animals would have been feasible. The amount of attention devoted to the construction and maintenance of roads varied. In some important cities there were stretches of cobble paving linking the gate with the interior, as at Dan, but elsewhere a surface of gravel, clay or pounded chalk mixed with potsherds might have to suffice. Moreover, good roads were allowed to deteriorate, as at Hazor.

Roads were also linked with drainage, especially for the violent winter rainfall. Main streets leading to the gate tended to have proper drains, lined and covered with stone slabs, which conducted the water outside the town – possibly into a cistern or well. Further inside the town, the water would have to find its own way down slopes, perhaps with curbs to deflect it from buildings. Occasionally spouts might be cut into walls lining the upper edge of a road fringing a slope: examples have been found in Jerusalem. Domestic sewage was not dealt with in this way, but was collected in individual cesspits.

Arrangements for the disposal of refuse were apparently somewhat sketchy. Householders might simply drop rubbish into the street, where scavenger dogs would deal with it, or throw it over the town wall. Refuse must, however, also have been removed from towns and taken to dumps along customary routes. In Jerusalem, the name of the Dung Gate attests that this procedure existed. Mounds of refuse, like the one on which the stricken Job is related to have sat, would thus have been generated over a period. None have been found in ancient Israel so far, though there is an example from later Nabatean Petra. Alternatively, refuse might have been spread over the fields as fertilizer.

Crafts noisome through smoke, like the potter's, or through smell, like the tanner's, were usually located at the town fringes. The fuller also worked there (Isaiah 7, 3ff.) and it appears that the production of olive oil tended to be carried on at the periphery too. People exercising the same craft might follow their trade in the same neighbourhood – the bakers' street in Jerusalem (Jeremiah 37, 21) is an example – though other occupations might be found scattered throughout the residential area.

Urban structures

Building materials

Israelite builders needed three main raw materials. Stone was used for foundations, walls and pillars, especially in the hill country. Clay went into mudbricks, of which the upper parts of walls or, in the coastal plain especially, entire walls might consist. It was also used in the top layer of the usually flat roofs, as mortar between building stones (lime mortar was not employed for this) and as plastering. Wood served many purposes: for pillars, roofing beams, as a strengthening element for walls or foundations, for door or window fittings and wall panelling. Upper storeys might be largely or exclusively made of wood, and occasionally entirely wooden buildings may have been built, both in the early period and later (cf. 2 Kings 6, 2).

Of these basic raw materials, limestone was usually obtained in open-air quarries on or near the site where it was to be used. Underground quarries like the 'royal caves' in Jerusalem were rare. If building stone of specially high quality was obtained from a distance, as for outstanding buildings like Solomon's Temple, this might rate a special mention (1 Kings 5, 17–18). It would also raise problems of transport. Pack animals or carts on bad tracks could not convey much, though teams of linked oxen might. As for timber, fairly serviceable wood of various types was usually available in the hill country. In a case of emergency or scarcity fruit trees might be used – thus at Gibeah of Saul almond-tree wood served for timber in the second phase, though cypress and pine wood had been available for the first. The amount of wood needed for construction in towns and villages must have been considerable, and there may have been some official management to ensure that resources were used sensibly (cf. 1 Chronicles 27, 28). However, for really high-class official or private buildings cedar wood might be imported from Lebanon over considerable distances. It was used for example in official buildings at Arad and Beersheba, as was cypress wood. Similarly, hard acacia wood, obtained from the Negeb, was brought to Lachish for the making of the doors in the gate of City III. Good building timber was thus perhaps a traded commodity, while cheap wood, such as tamarisk, could be obtained locally, as at Beersheba. On the other hand, though brick was conveyed over large distances in the Hellenistic period there is no sign it happened at this period. Subsidiary materials such as pebbles for good floors, lime plaster for floors, walls and cisterns, or brushwood and reeds used in roof construction were presumably usually at hand.

In their building techniques, the Israelites followed earlier Levantine traditions, even down to quarrymen's or masons' tool kits, with remarkably little impact from those of Egypt, which had ruled Palestine for several centuries and remained influential in other fields. Walls were normally given stone foundations: for private houses these might be made of poor rubble placed in shallow or non-existent foundation trenches whereas some important public buildings had massive, deeply buried foundations. Those of the acropolis of Samaria, and others at Dan or Ramat Rachel south of Jerusalem – often ascribed to Phoenician masons – were placed in deep foundation trenches penetrating down to the natural rock, which was adapted to receive each individual stone. Ashlar blocks were then laid on top, closely fitted without mortar in horizontal courses of headers hiding a rough core. To allow a tight fit, the front face of each stone was provided with marginal drafts, the centre being left as a rough quarry boss in foundation work. Where masonry was visible, the boss was removed later. An alternative method, exemplified at Lachish and at Megiddo in gate 2156 and also in gate 1567 in the enclosure wall for palace 1723 (now ascribed to VA and IVB respectively), consisted in building up the foundations on the existing land surface like an ordinary freestanding wall – spreading the load where necessary by placing foundations on a raft of logs – and burying them in a massive deep fill. This was an unsophisticated but cheap and effective method, displaying some ingenuity, and so far has been found mainly in Israel.

The walls erected on such varying foundation work differed in kind, too. While the worst were execrable, Israelite masons could do creditably when occasion demanded. Walls in ordinary dwelling houses might consist of quarry split stones more or less squared, or plain rubble, laid in good or often poor courses, possibly strengthened by ashlar quoins at corners. Walls of 'Phoenician' style at Samaria and Megiddo VA–IVB in particular were built of fine ashlar laid in horizontal courses of headers and stretchers, and given completely smooth faces by diagonal adze dressing. Alternatively, walls consisted of short pillars of ashlar between stretches of rubble masonry. This latter type of construction is attested early in Phoenicia, and the technique could have come to Israel from there. As for the splendid ashlar at Samaria and elsewhere usually attributed to Phoenician craftsmen, doubts have been raised by Yigal Shiloh about its being Phoenician work, for it is attested earlier in Israel than in Phoenicia. It is conceivable that the masonry building programmes of Solomon and his successors may have stimulated the development of ashlar masonry techniques. Yet the presence of Phoenician masons in at least some cases cannot be ruled out – they may have worked with Israelite colleagues, for example, in the building of Solomon's Temple (cf. 1 Kings 5, 18). Elsewhere, as at Lachish or Jerusalem, the massive but crude stone walls, improved by ashlar quoins at corners, must have looked well when plastered over and fulfilled their purpose admirably.

Beams, either laid singly and horizontally, were sometimes used to strengthen walls, as in the face of the towers of the Megiddo VA–IVB gate, or as timber framing for mud-brick or stone walling, as perhaps in the residency building 338 at Megiddo and in an eighth-century town wall in Jerusalem. A more complicated formation of beams in mud-brick as found in North Syria and Anatolia is represented at Tell el-Kheleifeh, but it is unusual in Israel. A stabilizing course of branches laid transversely above foundations and below mud-brick upper work, discovered at Kuntillet 'Ajrud in the Negeb, exemplifies perhaps a local tradition.

Floors might consist of earth, crushed lime, or pebble or slab paving. Though a wooden floor is said to have existed in the Temple of Solomon, a possible example, reported at Tell Deir 'Alla, is so far exceptional. Upper rooms would have clay floors spread over the ceiling of rooms below.

Houses

While there is a good deal of variety among Israelite houses, both in planning and building technique, many conform to a type with characteristic features of plan and execution – the 'four-room' or 'pillar' house. It is found in both town and country – as are houses of alternative, simpler plans, there being no distinction except that country dwellings may be more crudely built – and regional variations are not major. This kind of house is attested from the earliest times Israel is on archaeological record, namely in the late thirteenth century at Khirbet Dawara or Tel Masos in the Negeb, and in the twelfth at et-Tell (Ai) in the hill country. It continued in use unchanged except for increasing regularity and often improved technical standards throughout Israel's history. Neither technically nor in plan has it any clear forerunners in the Palestinian Bronze Age; any prototypes made from wood, which early Israelite settlers might have constructed, remain hypothetical at present. The type is occasionally found outside Israel, as at Tell Qasile XI – then a Philistine settlement – and at some sites in Transjordan. Its area of distribution as known at present coincides so closely with the area occupied by the Israelites that Yigal Shiloh had some justification in calling it the typical Israelite house, though many now oppose this identification, in view of the occurrence of the type elsewhere.

In plan the 'four-room' house consists essentially of a rectangular structure, perhaps some 12 by 8 m (40 by 26 ft), with one of the narrow sides facing the road and normally containing the centrally placed entrance. Internally, the rectangular area was divided into three longitudinal room units, the central space being often a courtyard open to the air, but sometimes roofed over, as the lateral rooms regularly were. At the back was another, transversely placed, roofed room. All the rooms around the central space might be further subdivided by cross-walls into several small chambers. Simpler types of house might have only three room units – one at the side of the courtyard and one at the back – or even only one alongside the central space; these do not appear to have preceded the four-room plan, but rather to have co-existed with it.

Inside these houses, the rooms around the courtyard are not usually wholly separated from it by walls; instead, lines of stone pillars are placed at a distance of about 1 m (3¼ ft) apart (either single monoliths, or made up from several superimposed stones) linked sometimes for part of their height by rough rubble walling. These pillars, which vary in height from *c*. 0.8 m to 2.2 m (2½ to 7 ft) would carry an entabulature on which the transverse roof beams were placed. The lower rooms thus delimited were probably intended for stores or animals, but the higher ones, where light and air could enter between pillars or through doors, would have been used as kitchens, pantries, living or working rooms – vertical looms, for example, might be placed between pillars. These rows of pillars are not found in a rarer type of well-built structure, squarish in plan. Here the central space is divided off by walls. These have been called 'court-yard' houses, and may have had official functions.

Roofs were mostly flat – though in houses provided with cisterns and also in some upper-class residences they may have been at an angle – and consisted of a layer of waterproof clay rolled level with a stone roof roller, above a packing of branches or reeds laid over the roof beams. Wooden doors, fitted in the gener-ally narrow door openings, had pivots turning in wooden hinges or in simple holes in the ground as pivot stones are not frequent. However, some doors might only have been closed by a curtain or something similar, if at all. Windows were probably small, placed fairly high up, and rare. Internally, rooms would probably have been fitted with shelves for storage of portable items, like pottery, or pegs to hang things on. Bulky staple goods such as grain, flour, wine and oil were kept in big storage jars, the bottoms of which were placed in holes in the floor. Built-up storage bins were not widespread.

A house of this kind might comprise one floor only – cellars are exceptional. In fine weather, daily life would concentrate in the courtyard, where there might be a fire place, an oven of clay (these occur within rooms, too), a hand-mill, perhaps also a cistern. Cisterns were not generally found, and Rab-Shakeh's promise to the Jerusalemites that they should, after surrender, 'drink each one from his own cistern' (2 Kings 18, 31) is somewhat utopian. In Moab somewhat earlier, King Mesha had to 'encourage' his subjects to make a cistern each in his house (*ANET* 320–1). Fairly sophisticated arrangements with clear-ing basins linked to store cisterns occur quite early, nevertheless. Lime plaster, known since the Late Bronze Age, was used to coat cisterns, but sometimes the bare rock would retain water sufficiently well. That the courtyard may have contained a trellis with vines and the occasional fig tree is hinted at by the ideal of every man sitting 'under his own vine and his own fig tree' (1 Kings 4, 25).

Israelite houses often boasted an upper storey, accessible usually by stairs or flights of steps (the lower part of which consisted of stone, the upper of wood) placed outside, more rarely inside, the building. This upper storey, whose walls might be made of wood and mud-brick rather than stone, often did not cover the whole roof, since part would be left open to serve as a living or working area, surrounded by a balustrade for safety (cf. Deuteronomy 22, 8). Upper rooms were preferred as being airier than those below, and were considered suitable to lodge an honoured guest, who might find his apartment furnished with a bed, a table, a chair and a lamp (cf. 2 Kings 4, 10). No actual examples of such furni-ture have survived, but clay models from Lachish and elsewhere indicate that they were sturdily built and serviceable. They were, however, probably used mostly by the well-to-do; poor people would sleep at best on mattresses or otherwise cloaks spread on the ground (Exodus 23, 27). For covering, both rich and poor used garments or cloaks (Exodus 23, 27; cf. 1 Samuel 19, 13–14 where

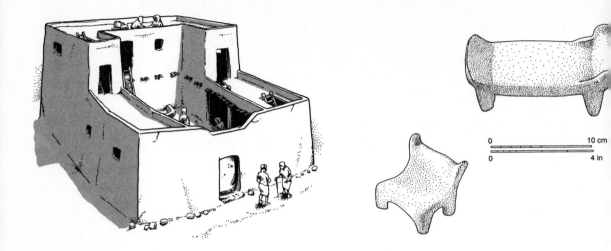

a quilt or mosquito net may be intended). Whether living and store rooms contained chests in addition to shelves is uncertain, but not improbable; they may also have been provided with mats or carpets but these are at present unattested.

Private houses had no bathrooms, though movable wash basins, bath tubs and foot baths were known. Similarly, lavatories with stone seats found in Jerusalem are exceptional (pls 8–10), though they had long been known in the Near East, and a privy is mentioned in the Ehud story as part of the palace of Eglon, King of Moab (Judges 3, 24). It is possible that fittings made of wood were more frequent but have not survived. The dwellings of the Israelite upper classes or royalty probably contained such items, but we have at present no way of telling.

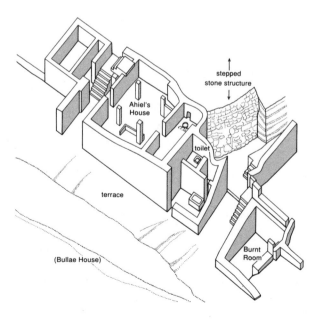

25 (Above left) A reconstruction of an Israelite house. There were also apparently houses with a complete upper storey, turning the inner courtyard into an enclosed room.

26 (Above right) Model terracotta furniture (a chair and a couch) from Lachish. They give an idea of what domestic furniture (for those who could afford it) was like – it was obviously sturdy and serviceable. The luxury furniture, such as the couches inlaid with ivory, found in the dwellings of the aristocracy, will have been more sophisticated.

27 (Right) Architectural reconstruction of the 'House of Ahiel', excavated by Y. Shiloh in the 'City of David' in Jerusalem. It was a well-made example of the 'four-room' type of house, adjusted to its position backed up against a slope. Pillars support the upper floor. See also plates 8–10.

Most houses known so far can be classified as upper- or lower middle-class dwellings. Quarters of hovels inhabited by a proletariat, such as dispossessed country folk who had drifted into the towns, have as yet not been found. At the opposite end of the scale, genuinely patrician mansions in the two capital cities are at present similarly unknown archaeologically. Larger and well-constructed mansions have, however, been found, like house 148 at Tirzah, which may have belonged to local grandees. Houses covering over 250 sq. m (2,690 sq. ft) have sometimes been classed as patrician, yet the denunciations of the prophets, Amos and Isaiah in particular, refer to something different. These seem to have been castle-like dwellings constructed of ashlar walls and cedar beams (Isaiah 9, 10; Amos 5, 11) and, like royal palaces, included special buildings adapted to summer and winter conditions as well as boasting wall panelling or furniture adorned with ivory inlays or carvings (Amos 3, 15). Imitations of recessed wall panelling are carved into the sides of tomb chambers in the St Etienne cemetery in Jerusalem, which may follow architectural traditions attested in Urartu (modern Armenia). The tendency in the ancient world for elaborate tombs to reflect the architecture of the dwellings of the living may mean that the houses of the Jerusalem aristocrats or courtiers buried in the necropolis of Siloam (Silwan) and St Etienne near the Damascus gate may also have shown other architectural features derived from Anatolia, Cyprus or Egypt, such as cornices in rooms with vaulted or pitched roofs or ceilings.

There are hints too that upper-class houses in various localities may sometimes have been adorned with architectural sculptures (cf. below, p. 279). These buildings must have been sizeable – Amos (6, 9) speaks of houses in which ten men are only a remnant of the original number who dwelt there. Such numbers are well in excess of what the normal four-room house could accommodate, and the possibility of buildings of several storeys should be considered. These existed in Phoenicia, then and later, and also in Egypt; and here a man might dwell with his sons and their families and retainers in safety. This type of building would suit the passage in Amos. Clay models found in excavations hint at the existence of tower houses in Israel. However, neither this nor any other type of aristocratic dwelling has so far been adequately documented. We have the descriptions in Amos of the aristocratic lifestyle, including sumptuous banquets consumed to the sound of the lyre (Amos 6, 4–6; Isaiah 5, 11–12), recalling that of the suitors in the *Odyssey* – except that here the ladies took an active part in the carousing (Amos 4, 1), surprisingly, in what was essentially a man's world. We also hear of the nobles engaging in pleasant sophistries, and parading an enlightened scepticism towards received theological ideas (Isaiah, 5, 19–21). Archaeology, however, does not so far provide direct support for these descriptions, where either rooms in aristocratic mansions suited for social gatherings or their fittings, like ivory couches, are concerned. Still, as we saw, funerary architecture may offer some hints as to the former and wall panelling in particular may have been fitted in the houses of the rich.

The lifestyle of most of the lower classes must have been simpler – their houses would be sparsely furnished, lamps would be sparingly used at night and their diet would have been more basic. Meat would have been rare on their tables, as would probably the fish which we now know was imported to Jerusalem from the Mediterranean and perhaps Egypt, as well as from the little rivers in the coastal plain or the Jordan (it probably travelled salted or dried).

Bread, vegetables and herbs, olives and fruit would have been staple foods; condiments and sauces would have added variety. Milk, fresh or sour, and cheese were also part of the diet. Cooked meals, it has been concluded from the rarity of sherds of the fragile cooking pots, were not part of everyday food (though the argument must not be overstated: lentils and other pulses, staple foods surely, will always have required cooking). The later deep Judean cooking pots would have been specially useful for stewing or boiling; earlier shallow forms may have been used for frying.

Israelite houses, especially the poorer ones, were not well equipped against the dampness and cold found in winter. Dripping roofs must have been familiar and damp walls affected by fungal growth (the 'leprosy' of the Bible) must have been frequent enough to have merited mention in law. Heating facilities were of limited efficiency; braziers in living rooms, cooking stoves or even the warmth generated by stabled animals would not heat a house. Such conditions must have facilitated the spread of rheumatoid and other diseases, especially in the houses of the poor who could not afford much fuel. Better housing as well as better diet would have meant that the upper strata of society had a better chance of health and survival than their poorer neighbours could hope for, and more children of the former may have reached adulthood than those of the latter.

Royal palaces

The palaces of the kings of Israel and Judah, or their local representatives in the provinces, must have been among the most impressive buildings in the country. The Bible mentions some – those in Jerusalem, Samaria, Jezreel and Tirzah – but there may have been others, for example in towns that for a while acted as royal capitals, such as Hebron, besides country residences, for instance perhaps the one at Ramat Rachel near Jerusalem. At present, however, statements in the Bible combined with available archaeological evidence offer only limited information about these buildings.

The earliest royal abode identified with some likelihood is the stronghold of Gibeah of Saul/Tell el-Ful north of Jerusalem, possibly Philistine built. Excavation has revealed part of a crudely constructed stone fortress, with an upper storey largely made of wood, arranged round a courtyard measuring 52 by 35 m (170 by 115 ft) and provided with corner bastions each 13 by 9 m (43 by 30 ft). Its plan owes nothing to the tradition of Canaanite palaces of the preceding Bronze Age; if anything, it is descended from the tower-like fortresses (*migdals*) of that period. David is reported to have built himself a house in Jerusalem with the help of Tyrian carpenters and masons, which incorporated cedar beams (2 Samuel 5, 11). The building may have been modelled on Tyrian prototypes, which are at present unknown, but presumably included a first-floor state apartment with a large window, like the palace of the ruler of Byblos

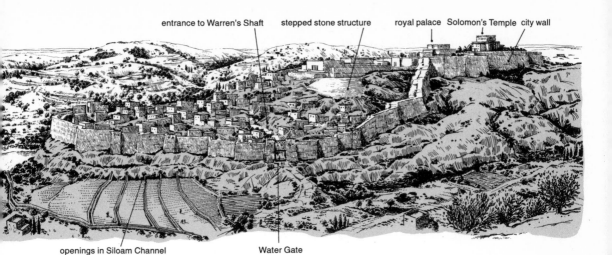

entrance to Warren's Shaft   stepped stone structure   royal palace Solomon's Temple city wall

openings in Siloam Channel   Water Gate

28 Artist's reconstruction of Jerusalem as it may have appeared in the time of Solomon. The fields in the foreground could be irrigated from openings in the Siloam channel.

in Phoenicia described by Wen–Amon about a century earlier. If so, David's palace would have been an early example of a type which we shall meet again.

More is said in the Bible about Solomon's state buildings. The description of his palace complex in 1 Kings (7, 1–9) mentions a number of individual structures. One of these, the 'House of the Forest of Lebanon', measuring *c*. 50 by 25 m (164 by 82 ft) and 15 m (50 ft) high, had three floors in all. Its ground floor was divided longitudinally into three aisles by four rows of fifteen cedar pillars each (the two outer rows backed up against the walls, presumably) supporting the ceiling beams. The three rows of windows and doors were square. A pillared hall and porch, a cedar-panelled throne room, a court, Solomon's private apartment block, and the house of pharaoh's daughter receive more summary mention. The whole complex, situated next to the Temple, was constructed of ashlar blocks laid on gigantic ashlar foundations, individual blocks of which were 4 or 5 m (13 or 16 ft) in length. The circumference walls consisted of three courses of ashlar above a course of cedar beams. However, in the absence of any archaeological information much remains unclear about the grouping of these units – not necessarily the only ones – and their character. The pillared hall has been compared with analogous buildings in Urartu (Armenia) and with the great temple of Astarte at Kiton in Cyprus, and the entire palaces with Syrian examples like those at Zinjirli/Sam'al, Tell Halaf/Gozan, Tell Ta'yinat, or Hamath/Hamah. In the latter two instances the royal temple is situated near the palace, as in Jerusalem. All these examples belong to the 'hilani' type: an oblong structure accessible by a porch centrally placed in one long side, with a monumental entry divided up by columns and sometimes approached by a flight of steps. Behind the porch is the longitudinally placed main or throne room, while a flight of steps in a side room gives access to an upper storey with state rooms lit by large windows. It has been suggested that Solomon's palace buildings are related to this type of structure, and this comparison has furthermore been made in the cases of the monumental stone buildings 6000 and 1723 in Davidic, or more probably Solomonic, Megiddo VA. A large building at Jericho is also similar in plan to Palace 6000 at Megiddo. However, the analogies are not perfect – buildings 6000 and 1723 show no sign of the typical monumental entry with columns and the entrance to the latter was adorned with proto-Aeolic pilaster capitals which are not typical of the 'hilani' but are a frequent constituent of monumental architecture in Israel during the ninth century BC in particular (cf. fig. 21). Indeed, building 1723 has been compared with Egyptian structures. We are, in fact, apparently dealing with the rise of a local tradition of monumental building, indebted in varying degrees to Syrian, Phoenician and Egyptian inspiration.

The royal acropolis at Samaria is archaeologically better known than Solomon's Jerusalem, due to excavations. However, the whole area has not been investigated, and the buildings found were much reduced by destruction and later activity; there is also some disagreement about the dating of the various phases. Essentially the acropolis (erected apparently over the emplacement of an eleventh–tenth century estate) consisted of a platform, at its largest $c.$ 200 by 100 m (656 by 328 ft). During the original Omrid stage it was retained by a simple ashlar-faced wall but later, after reconstruction and extension probably by Ahab, by splendid ashlar-faced casemate walling around much of the perimeter; the entrance was probably on the east side. Within this perimeter stood the palace proper, of which only part has been revealed: its plan is not completely known, but rooms seem to have been grouped around courtyards in an arrangement harking back to Canaanite traditions. A complex of store rooms flanking access corridors is situated west of the palace, beyond the Omrid circumference wall. This contained the famous Samaria ostraca, administrative dockets dating probably from the early eighth century (in the reigns of Jehoash and Jeroboam II). A further complex of possible stores built by Jeroboam II is located just outside the western casemate wall. North of the palace complex was a large water basin, perhaps the 'Pool of Samaria' (1 Kings 22, 38). Disturbed debris above stumps of buildings further east has furnished clay bullae, originating perhaps from a chancery, and ivory carvings which once adorned wall panelling or furniture. Whether the latter came from Ahab's 'Ivory House' (1 Kings 22, 39) or from a later royal building is disputed, and it is indeed not certain exactly where the building in question was located. (Similarly unknown is the emplacement of an official inscribed stela of which only a small fragment has turned up.)

Since nothing is preserved of the upper storeys of buildings, we cannot say whether the palace in Samaria had the kind of large window for royal public appearances, as described in the palace at Jezreel (2 Kings 9, 30ff.). However, the discovery of a number of proto-Aeolic pilaster capitals, which may have flanked doorways or fronted walls, show that royal buildings in Samaria combined ashlar construction with the use of this type of decoration – a combina-

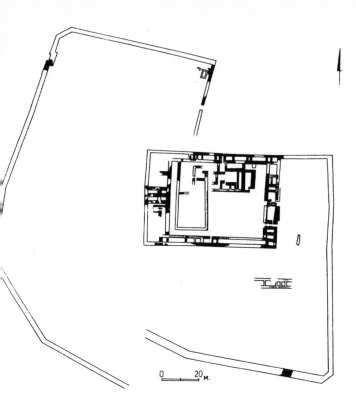

29 *Plan of the palace-complex at Ramat Rachel which comprised a large outer courtyard, delimited by a wall, and the palace proper, enclosed by casemate walling of ashlar. The architectural quality of the palace was very high; it was provided with Proto-Aeolic capitals and at least one ornamental window with a balustrade supported by dwarf columns (see pls 14 and 15). These may date to the earlier stage (ninth–eighth century) rather than the later (seventh–sixth century).*

30 *Hazor, reconstruction of the entrance to the citadel complex, which was embellished by two Proto-Aeolic capitals.*

tion which became typical of Israelite monumental architecture. This form of capital is attested only later in Phoenicia and Phoenician-influenced Cyprus, and cannot on present evidence be derived from there. Israel is for the moment its main zone of distribution, though it was known in Transjordan.

The most instructive remnants of palace architecture are perhaps those at Ramat Rachel south of Jerusalem, despite the fact that the history of the building is disputed. In addition to the foundations and remains of walling, which show that the complex was in its final stage an ashlar building arranged round a courtyard and adorned with proto-Aeolic capitals (pl. 7), excavation here has, for once, also unearthed part of the decoration of the upper storey. This included dwarf columnettes picked out in red paint, which supported the balustrade of a large window intended for the king's public appearances, and crow-step battlements. The appearance of this structure, set in a wide exercise yard surrounded by a casemate wall, must thus have been impressive. Whether this was the palace built by Jehoiakim which aroused the displeasure of Jeremiah, who, in addition to large windows, mentions a cedar ceiling and vermilion paint (Jeremiah 22, 14), or whether that building was located in Jerusalem is debated. Jointly, though, the finds of Ramat Rachel and Jeremiah's text give a fairly good picture of Israelite palace architecture in its later stages which perpetuated old customs. No significant differences seem to have existed between Judah and the northern kingdom in this respect. Foreign conquest and the fall of the Monarchy, however, put an end to this architectural tradition in both kingdoms, though it continued outside. In the northern state, official buildings derived from the Mesopotamian courtyard house served thereafter as palaces for Assyrian administrators, like buildings 1052 and 1369 at Megiddo III or in the remodelled citadel of Hazor III. This type of structure was later modified under local influence.

Fortifications

A number of Israelite cities had citadels which both controlled the towns and could serve as ultimate points of defence or refuge in case of need. Situated on commanding high ground, either near the centre of the urban area or on its periphery, they took various forms. At their largest – the royal acropolises of Jerusalem and Samaria might be counted here – they were perhaps better able to resist a sudden attack than a regular siege. A somewhat smaller defensible compound is represented by the fortress at Arad in southern Judah. During its most significant phase (strata X–VI, early eighth to sixth century BC) it was defended by a solid wall, provided with bastions 3–4 m (10–13 ft) thick and made up of slightly jagged (indented trace) short sections; this enclosed an area *c*. 50 sq. m (538 sq. ft), containing dwelling units, stores and a small temple. The slope below the defence wall was provided with a glacis resting against another, outer wall. A square fortified area within an offset-inset solid wall defending a large ashlar structure is also found at eighth-century Tell el-Kheleifeh II. However, neither at Arad nor at Tell el-Kheleifeh was there apparently any significant area of settlement outside the compound, so that they were really forts rather than citadels, as they are usually identified, the one at Arad in particular.

The headquarters building at Tell el-Kheleifeh has been viewed as a customs post with stores, yet – built in the form of an enlarged 'four-room' house, with its wall base strengthened by a small glacis – it can be compared also to the

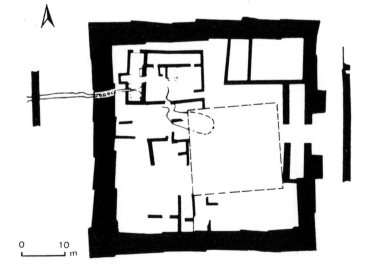

31 Plan of the fortress at Arad, Stratum X (early eighth century?). This fort, measuring roughly 50 × 50 m and surrounded by a solid wall with a saw-tooth outline, succeeded an earlier one surrounded by a casemate wall provided with towers. The solid wall appears to have existed until the final destruction of the fortress by Nebuchadnezzar. Among the internal buildings, a small temple (below, fig. 59) is of special interest.

0   10
�_____⌐ m

citadel building located at the western extremity of Hazor VIII. Only the base-ment walls of that mid-eighth-century building have survived, which are on the plan of a large 'four-room' building, complicated by various cross-walls. These, the excavator thinks, may well have been absent above ground, resulting in a more normal four-room plan. It is not known how many floors this impos-ing building – with its entrance adorned with proto-Aeolic column capitals – had, or what its upper (brick built?) stages were like. It was flanked by adminis-trative structures and surrounded on three sides by the city wall, though it was not similarly separated from the city for which it acted as a stronghold. At En Gev there was also a citadel at the northern end of the city. Little is known of it but it was apparently a much simpler building.

In addition to the outstanding citadels and fortified towns described, there are a number of lesser defence works. In the western hill region of Samaria simple enclosures placed in dominant positions controlled access roads and may also have served as lookout posts and signal stations. Similar functions can also be assigned to a number of more regular fortifications and isolated towers in Judah, especially in the Jerusalem region. Somewhat different in function were some forts and fortified settlements in the Negeb which were part of a system defending the southern approaches to the hill country, while others controlled important caravan routes, such as at Kadesh Barnea. This had a long history. After a short-lived elliptical enclosure in the tenth century, a rectangu-lar fortress, c. 40 by 60 m (131 by 197 ft) was built in the eighth century. This was surrounded by a wall 4 m (13 ft) thick provided with bastions at the corners and in the middle of the sides, held up by an earth rampart supported by a retaining wall. A reservoir inside was filled from a canal. Destroyed in the early seventh century, the fort was rebuilt somewhat later, this time with a casemate wall, and survived until the fall of Judah in 586 BC. Some 50 km (31 miles) to the south, the roadside station of Kuntillet 'Ajrud represents a simpler example of basically the same type.

The Palace Fort at Lachish was begun perhaps in the tenth century (stratum V) as an isolated fort, built of bricks and located on a nearly exactly square (32 by 32 m/105 by 105 ft) artificial platform held in by powerful stone foundation walls (in places up to 11 m (36 ft) high). Later, in strata IV and III (c. 900–701 BC), it was extended southwards and eastwards, reaching 76 by 36 m (250 by 118 ft), and served as the governor's headquarters. Store rooms or stable units placed round a square courtyard and accessible by their own gate were now attached on its northern and eastern sides, the whole complex being separated from the civilian town to the south by a strong wall. Not enough remains of the building to permit detailed analysis of its internal planning, where flights of rooms were arranged around courts, but in view of the strength of its massive foundations it was presumably several storeys high and defensible at least against civil riots or enemy raids. It is nevertheless a fortified palace rather than a citadel proper. Citadels in Israel seem generally to have been neither as impor-tant as in Mesopotamia, nor positioned astride the city wall as frequently was the case there.

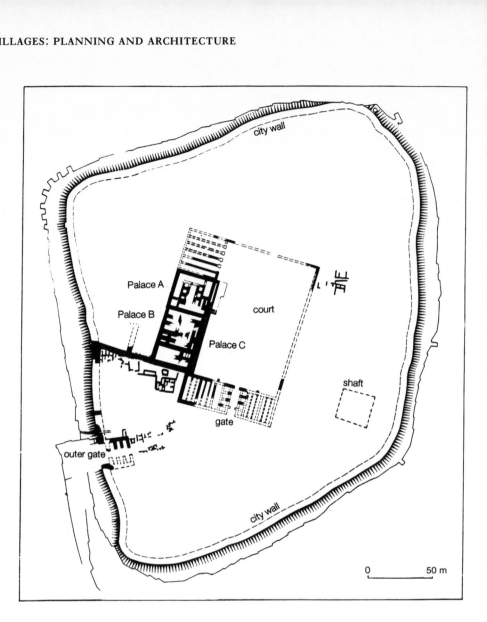

32 Lachish, Stratum III. The city is clearly dominated by the large 'Palace-fort', which will have functioned as the military and civilian headquarters. A wall linking it to the town defence wall separates the civilian residential and official sectors.

Not all buildings of this kind reached high standards in planning and execution, and it is interesting that in the northern kingdom the architectural splendours of Megiddo – and to some extent Gezer – remained somewhat unusual. Even at Hazor, ashlar was little employed. A small crowded strongpoint like Tell el 'Oreme/Kinneret II is not impressive either in planning or execution. Nor is the later citadel I there.

Town walls and gates

With few exceptions, towns were defended by walls. A single circumvallation is common, but a combination of an inner with an outer wall occurs occasionally, as at Lachish III, where the outer wall may have been low, and at Gezer. A covered way outside the defences but behind a screen wall, is an occasional refinement. A sloping glacis, meant to impede both access to the wall and sapping, found at Lachish between the inner and outer wall, is often employed, with examples at Hazor, Beersheba, Tell Halif and En Gev. Moats, always dry and rarely as substantial as the great fosses of the Middle Bronze Age, are a less common feature, but they are found at Hazor, Jezreel and Tell en-Naṣbeh for instance. It was the town wall proper, however, that was always the main element of defence. During the early period, including the reign of Solomon, casemate constructions consisting of an inner and outer wall a few metres apart and linked by cross-walls, were in fashion. The rooms thus created might be used for storage or accommodation, or alternatively filled with earth, which created at low cost a defence of considerable strength. Such cheaply produced walls continued in use especially in country towns in Judah which had not suffered from attack. However, from the ninth century onwards solid walls several metres thick tended to supersede or rival them in the case of important fortresses. Some were straight, while others consisted of short sections arranged in a broken trace in a succession of insets and offsets, slight salients and recesses, allowing a minimum of flanking fire. Still others had slight projections arranged on a saw-tooth plan. Towers, sometimes strengthened at their base by a stone glacis of their own, might be added where a weak point needed extra defence by flanking fire. They never became very frequent and a systematic arrangement of towers at set distances from each other around the urban perimeter guaranteeing intersecting fields of fire is rare. It is found in the Negeb. At Gezer the towers may be Solomonic in date, but this is disputed.

The walls themselves might consist of mud-brick above a stone base mostly several metres high, or of stone or brick only. The quality of the stonework varied from fine ashlar facings via hammer-dressed stones with ashlar corners to poor rubble work, hidden behind plaster. Where such walling was backed up against a city mound or terraces it gained additional strength. The upper parts of walls and towers are usually not known from excavations, having practically never survived to the level of the rampart walk with its parapet and battlements. Exceptionally at Lachish III a bastion of the outer wall survived to its original height of *c.* 6 m (20 ft) and the main wall was 4.60 m (15 ft) high; both were covered by the Assyrian siege mound. One piece of crow-step battlement found at Megiddo may have come from the town wall, or may have ornamented a state building. Assyrian representations of the sieges of Gezer and Lachish show that on top of the walls and towers fighting platforms were erected for the defenders, protected by round shields. Windows in towers were apparently not for archers, and there is no sign of arrow-slits anywhere.

Gates, being points of potential weakness, needed special attention. The fact that even important cities like Megiddo had only one gate may be due to this, though Jerusalem had a number of gates. Basically they followed the Levantine tradition, consisting of a tower structure, divided into a central passage flanked on both sides by a number of bays or chambers, created by piers of masonry

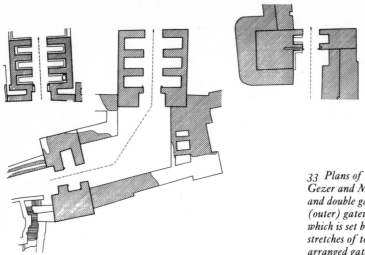

33 *Plans of Israelite gateways at Gezer and Megiddo, including single and double gates, and the plan of the (outer) gateway at Tell en-Naṣbeh, which is set between two overlapping stretches of town wall. A similarly arranged gate existed at Dan.*

projecting from the side walls. The building might be roofed – if Ussishkin's interpretation of the Assyrian reliefs depicting the siege of Lachish is accepted, the gate of that city in 701 BC carried an upper chamber topped by battlements (cf. earlier 2 Samuel 18, 33) – and the outer face of the gate might be strengthened by projecting towers. 'Solomonic' gates at Hazor, Megiddo and Gezer (their dates have been disputed, especially in the case of Megiddo), erected according to a basic plan scheme with individual modifications, had six chambers, three on each side. This type was still built later on, when two or only one lateral chamber to the right and left of the passage became the dominant fashion.

In the course of time, gates at important places increased in strength and size. Those at Lachish and the recently found gate at Dor are particularly large. The Lachish gate measured 25 m (82 ft) deep by 24.5 m (80 ft) wide, as against 19.75 by 17.5 m (65 by 57 ft) at Solomonic Megiddo. Gates entirely without lateral chambers, as at Arad or Meṣad Ḥashavyahu are rare. Unusual also is the arrangement at Dan and at Tell en-Naṣbeh, where a gate structure of normal type is fitted in a tangential rather than frontal position between overlapping walls.

Only one set of doors was normally provided in the outermost gate opening. They turned in door-socket stones, and at Lachish III they were very heavy, made of hard acacia wood brought from the Negeb, covered with arsenical bronze fittings, and could be barred. The gate and its inner and outer approaches might be paved above a main drain coming from the nearby inhabited area inside; plastered stone-built benches, or a water basin, for the use of guards, meetings of city elders or passers-by were often provided in the gate chambers, and there might be benches also in the nearby piazza. A kind of baldacchino supported on four columns placed on bases of Syro-Hittite type found in front of the main gate at Dan may have been intended to shelter a royal

34 Megiddo, reconstruction of the gate, showing the inner and outer gateways, which are linked by an approach-road across a courtyard. Here any intruder who had penetrated thus far had to turn a right-angle, offering his flank and back to the defenders.

throne used when the king sat in the gate (cf. 1 Kings 22, 10) or perhaps a statue; it is so far unique.

A number of gates in particularly important places were given the additional protection of an outer gate in front of the main, inner gate, to which they were linked by flanking walls delimiting a courtyard. Here any attackers who had broken through the outer defence would find themselves subjected to fire from all sides. Megiddo VA–IVB, Gezer, Dan, Lachish III and Beersheba V were provided with such, though this scheme was sometimes given up in later rebuildings. It is understandable that these important structures were usually well built – the 'Solomonic' gate at Megiddo consisted of beautiful ashlar with the additional refinement of a horizontal course of beam-work in its outer face. Altogether Israelite defence works fulfilled their task well. It took the Assyrians, who were past masters in siegecraft, much time and effort to take Samaria and Lachish – the attack on the latter was obviously regarded as a memorable achievement, being represented in a very prominent position in Sennacherib's palace at Nineveh – and they prudently omitted an assault on Jerusalem altogether.

Storehouses and stables

In a country where taxes were largely paid in kind, produce like grain, oil or wine delivered to the authorities had to be stored in bulk. Bulk storage was also needed for the grain trade, or to meet food requirements in time of war or famine. It is generally agreed that a special type of structure found in important administrative or military centres was intended to cope with such needs. It may also have served other purposes, and each case must be judged on its own merits. The buildings in question might be *c.* 30 m (98 ft) long and about 15 m (49 ft) wide and were internally subdivided by two rows of stone pillars into a central nave and two side aisles, each *c.* 5 m (16½ ft) across. The aisles were

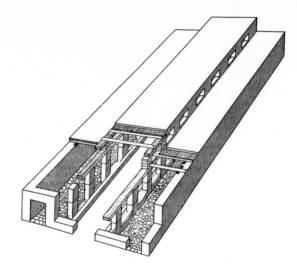

35 Beersheba II, one of the storehouses (reconstruction).

36 (Below) The 'Stables' at Megiddo (see also plate 11). These structures have also been interpreted as store buildings (compare fig. 35, above). More probably they accommodated the chariot horses of Ahab, whose army excelled in that branch of arms.

certainly roofed over, but whether the central nave always was is disputed. These structures were carefully constructed, the floors receiving special care in some cases to provide damp-proofing. Thus at Beersheba under-flooring consisted of several layers of ash, sand, charcoal and so on. Stone troughs located between pillars might serve as receptacles for storage.

Such buildings are found singly, as at Hazor VIII, but more commonly in groups – at Beersheba a number of them are located side-by-side, placed peripherally, against the town wall, while at Lachish IV–III they are arranged in groups around a central courtyard. It has to be said that other buildings, including casemate rooms in town walls, may have been used for storage too, and silos placed in a group outside the built-up area at Tell-en-Naṣbeh may have been intended for communal rather than individual storage. Possibly related to these in function is a pit, 11 m (36 ft) across at the top and 7 m (23 ft) deep, lined with rubble walling and provided with two winding flights of stairs, found in Megiddo III. If it did serve for grain storage, as has been suggested – it

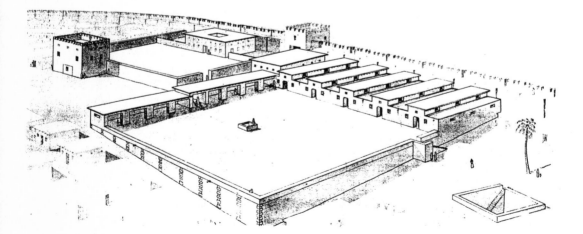

would have held 450 cu. m (15,890 cu. ft) – then some kind of covering must have been available. A smaller oval silo also occurs at Beth Shemesh II, and a rectangular stone silo measuring *c.* 12 by 12 m (39 by 39 ft) and 3–4 m (10–13 ft) deep was found somewhat earlier in Hazor VI.

Another theory is that such buildings may have been taken over as military barracks, or even served as such from the time they were built. Again, this is possible in some cases. No other buildings intended to house troops are known in ancient Israel – the commanding officers had fine residences, but troops may have had to find accommodation where possible. It has, lastly, been claimed that these structures were market halls, but this would hardly fit cases like Megiddo and Lachish.

The horses and chariots of the royal forces, on the other hand, were valuable and proper quarters would have been provided for them. Groups of buildings at Megiddo IVA were long generally regarded as stables for chariot horses (pl. 11). Attributed originally to the period of Solomon (cf. 1 Kings 9, 19), they were later dated to the period of Ahab, who is known to have possessed an impressive force of chariotry. These structures are basically of the same type as the store houses described above. They were provided with troughs between the stone pillars which have been interpreted as mangers; holes in the pillars were regarded as hitching holes for tethering the animals. Flooring in the aisles consisted of paving, which would have kept the horses' hooves dry. Recently, however, the interpretation as stables has been questioned by James Pritchard, who suggested that they were store buildings like the similar structures discussed above. This interpretation has found many followers, though it has in turn been challenged by Yigael Yadin and later, very effectively, by E.J. Holladay. Certainty cannot be had, but on balance the older interpretation has still something in its favour, especially in the case of Megiddo, where it seems likely there were Solomonic predecessors similar in character but fewer – 2 or 3. Some, it has recently been claimed, also existed near the residency at Lachish, offering accommodation for 50 chariot teams.

Flimsy shelters for horses which have sometimes been suggested as an alternative, and which would have left no recognizable trace, would hardly have been regarded as adequate for the king's beasts. That one and the same type of building might have been adapted for various functions is, on the other hand, not unthinkable. Groups of long, narrow rooms (not subdivided by pillars) attached to palaces may have served as 'treasuries' for weapons and precious metals. Lachish IV and Hazor VIII–VII may provide examples, as also the Ostraca House at Samaria. Yet this has also been regarded as a representative of another type of structure, the 'Scribes' Chambers'.

Public water supply engineering

While in the first instance a town's spring might provide water for the inhabitants, cisterns were often needed as a supplementary or alternative source of supply. Even though not every private house had a cistern, their total number in a settlement might be impressive – 53 are known at Tell en-Naṣbeh. Public cisterns might also be constructed by the government, like the one dug by King Asa at Mizpah (Jeremiah 41, 9). Wells, never frequent in Israel, were generally public, such as the one outside the city gate at Beersheba, and they might be furnished with a wheel over which the rope for the bucket was slung (cf. Ecclesiastes 12, 6). They were probably too expensive for ordinary household-ers to dig, in view of the depth required in the hill country.

Such provisions were, however, insufficient for a rising population, and moreover in times of war access to the town's spring (generally situated outside the walled perimeter) might be denied by an enemy. Measures taken in Israel by public authorities to deal with these problems in the cases of the two capitals, Jerusalem and Samaria, and of a number of important fortresses or seats of administration, are truly impressive and on present evidence go well beyond what was done for the public in neighbouring countries. In Urartu (Armenia) and Assyria substantial water engineering works were in the main intended to bring water to royal parks, gardens, fields or premises; householders were expected to look after their own needs.

In Israel, a number of methods were used to provide water for the population and to ensure a safe supply in times of war. Pools fed from springs or chanelled rain-water could store large quantities, and their construction might involve major feats of engineering. Thus a recently discovered pool located in the St Anne's (Bethzeta) Valley in Jerusalem near the later Sheep Pools involved the erection of a dam 40 m (130 ft) long, 6 m (20 ft) wide at the top and 7 m (23 ft) at the bottom to retain rain-water. It was provided with sophisticated arrange-ments to regulate the amount of water permitted to escape into a channel which led southwards along the Kidron Valley towards the northern end of the City of David. Ascribed to the late period of the Judean Monarchy, it dwarfed an earlier pool within the acropolis at Samaria. The barrage constructed to retain the water led by the Siloam Tunnel to the Pool of Siloam in Jerusalem may also have involved major building work.

While some pools were naturally situated outside the town walls, the flow of water could be directed into basins safely within the defended perimeter. Again the Siloam Tunnel provides the most impressive application of this latter method. Alternatively, a protected approach might be created to the town spring. At Megiddo VA–IVB a long, sloping, stone-built underground gallery led down from the city to the spring, which issued from a cave at the foot of the tell; the outer approach to this was defended by a guard chamber. This installa-tion, now dated by Yadin to the period of Solomon, and paralleled perhaps by a similar but earlier structure at Tell-es-Sa'idiyeh, did not prove sufficiently safe and was superseded by a third type of water passage, the construction of which demanded considerable skill as well as the application of large resources. In this scheme, fashionable during the ninth century BC, the outside approach to the spring was blocked off completely by a wall and a deep shaft was driven through the tell into the natural rock. A staircase led to a horizontal or sloping passage along which the spring could be reached in complete safety from attack. Alternatively, such shafts lacked stairs, and the passage from the bottom of the

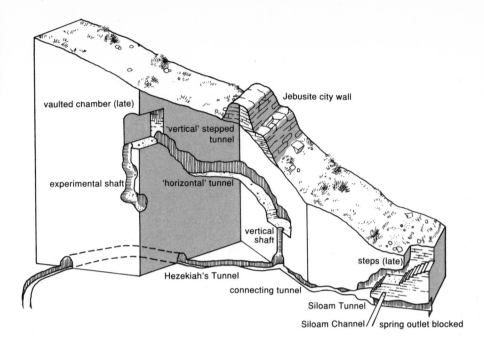

37 Diagram of the underground water systems of Jerusalem (Warren's Shaft, etc.). The different arrangements all depend on the water from the Gihon spring and were constructed at different times to ensure a safe water supply to the city.

shaft to the spring was deepened to allow the water to flow along to a point where it could be scooped up by buckets let down the shaft. Megiddo IVA provides impressive examples of both these variants. Here a shaft 35 m (115 ft) deep – the top part stone-lined, the bottom rock-cut – was linked to a horizontal gallery 63 m (207 ft) long, leading to the spring cave. In the original construction, the shaft was provided with rock-cut stairs, and the system was intended to allow water-carrying women access to the spring cave. Later, the stairs were removed and the gallery deepened so that water would flow to the bottom of the shaft, which now acted as a well. Still later, in a return to the original scheme, built-up stairs replaced the original rock-cut ones, and the water-carriers again descended on foot to the bottom of the shaft.

Yet another, fourth type of water engineering consisted of a shaft, or a shaft and passage, leading not to a spring but down to a level where the ground water could be tapped. The most impressive representative of this type was constructed at Hazor VIII during Ahab's reign. Here a shaft 19 by 15 m (62 by 50 ft) wide and 30 m (98 ft) deep (the top 10 m (33 ft) cut through the mound and lined with walling, the bottom 20 m (66 ft) rock-cut) connected with a sloping passage 22 m (72 ft) long leading down to ground water. The stairs descending along the walls of the shaft were wide enough to allow two mules loaded with water jars to pass each other. A somewhat different arrangement is met with in the 'pool' at Gibeon, where the shaft is cylindrical, with an average diameter of 11.3 m (37 ft). A rock-cut spiral staircase provided with a balustrade wound down to the flat bottom at a depth of 11.8 m (39 ft). From here a much narrower and rougher second shaft wound down another 13.6 m (45 ft) to the contemporary water level. The supply proved poor and more water was provided by an alternative system consisting of a sloping, stepped passage leading down below the city wall to the spring cave outside: the flow was improved by a so far unique gallery, 48 m (157 ft) long, cut from there back into the hill. The relative and absolute dates of these installations (presumably Iron Age) are uncertain, but the cylindrical shaft may have gone out of use following the Assyrian invasion in 701 BC. A water system analogous to the 'pool' was begun at Gezer, but left unfinished.

Several alternative methods might be used simultaneously to assure a sufficient water supply. The best example of this is provided by Jerusalem, where a number of pools stored rain-water gathered over sizeable surface areas. These supplemented the water resources offered by the intermittent Siloam spring (Gihon) which issued near the bottom of the eastern Ophel hill flank. Job's well, further south, originally a spring until covered in by the earthquake of 763/2 BC, was less important, and there is no evidence at present to support the assumption that water was channelled to Jerusalem from the region of the 'Pools of Solomon', during the Iron Age.

In peacetime, water from the Siloam spring was led from its point of issue along the lower slope of the eastern town hill in a rock-cut channel dating from the Solomonic period. This channel was partly open to the sky, partly tunnelled; window-like openings towards the up-slope admitted rain-water to augment the flow, while similar openings towards the valley served, when opened, to irrigate fields and gardens, including the king's gardens (2 Kings 25, 4) near the southern end of the eastern hill. Another water system, first investigated by Captain Charles Warren in 1867 – formerly dated to the Late Bronze Age but now attributed by Yigal Shiloh to the tenth and ninth centuries BC – would come into use in times of war. This included an underground passage sloping down from the top of the town hill towards a vertical shaft nearly 15 m (50 ft) deep, the bottom of which was linked to the spring by a horizontal tunnel bringing water to the bottom of the shaft. Buckets could be lowered down the shaft from above and hauled up in safety, so long as control of the spring cave was not lost. A third, more radical scheme to provide a safe water supply for the inhabitants of Jerusalem was engineered before Sennacherib's expected assault on Jerusalem in 701 BC. This was based on the blocking of the natural spring outlet and the deflection of the water to a reservoir (so far not certainly identified) within the walled perimeter of the city. This tunnel is a major piece of ancient water engineering. Both the laying out of its course which, for reasons still uncertain – perhaps to avoid the royal necropolis or perhaps because a natural rock fissure was followed – describes an S-shape, and the establishment of a gentle gradient of 0.06%, corresponding to modern practice, over a total length of at least 533 m (1748 ft) and perhaps originally as much as 600 m (1968 ft), imply a high degree of competence in planning and execution. Excavation began at the two ends of the tunnel, the teams of diggers meeting head-on underground after the correction of some slight errors in the direction, and level, of the two galleries. A similar procedure seems to have been followed in the making of the water passage at Megiddo.

Such tunnelling involved the cutting and removal of thousands of tons of rock, which at Siloam had to be transported over distances of up to 300 m (985 ft). Since there was room only for one quarryman at each face, who might have cut half a cubic metre in a day, some 1100 working days were perhaps required, though the use of 24-hour shifts would have helped. The pride expressed by those responsible for the construction of the Siloam Tunnel in their achievement, in the 'Siloam Inscription' (pl. 42), is thus fully justified. Once it was completed, the Jerusalemites had a number of water systems available simultaneously, and there is no hint that water shortage ever threatened the city, down to its fall to the Babylonians in 586 BC.

Israelite civil engineers and civil engineering

The public works discussed above were often substantial and demanded varied expertise. They must have been directed by people who had received specialist training and attained a high level of competence. In the Phoenician and Punic world we have evidence of such people in inscriptions, which are lacking in the case of Israel, but the remains of the structures provide eloquent testimony. Israelite water engineering must have enjoyed a high reputation outside the country. For example, King Mesha of Moab perhaps used Israelite prisoners of war for works intended to ensure safe water supplies in his country, and even in North Arabia a water shaft discovered by F.W. Winnett and W. Reed at Skaka which, as they observed, shows analogies with Israelite water works at Gibeon, may have been the work of specialists trained in Israel. We hear also of an Israelite builder or mason – probably a captive – at work in Assyria c. 701/700 BC.

The surveying and planning of major projects presumably of direct interest to the crown show a degree of competence quite comparable to that exemplified in royal projects in Egypt or Assyria. Levels of accuracy of the layout of important buildings in Israel is similar, including also the occurrence of occasional faults. Indeed, the case of the three basically analogous 'Solomonic' gates in Hazor, Megiddo and Gezer suggests the existence of central royal planning offices and plan stores, where blueprints were kept, and of a qualified royal staff. This staff must also have received training in supervising unskilled or semi-skilled conscripted work forces – the cases of Solomon's levies, (1 Kings 5, 13ff.) or of the conscription by Asa to build Geba and Mizpah (1 Kings, 15, 22) illustrate this – and arrangements must have been made to ensure the accommodation and provisioning of such large numbers of people and the watering and feeding of draught animals. Thus, a limited number of specialists might oversee the construction of town walls – at Tell en-Naṣbeh sections of walling built by separate gangs can be distinguished – or water tunnels.

Engineers in charge of large projects must, like their colleagues in neighbouring lands, have learned to estimate quantities of materials needed and food required. At work they must have known how to transport considerable amounts of soil or rock, and how to move and lift heavy weights, at a time when human and animal power alone were available, and simple mechanical devices like multiple pulleys were still unknown, though temporary ramps may have been used. Constructional fills, a simple but efficient method both of creating level or raised surfaces on which to place buildings, and of mantling foundations, were one speciality of the Israelite engineers. With this technique they achieved substantial results, such as the erection of the terraces on which some of the buildings on the eastern hill in Jerusalem were built, or the levelling operations at Megiddo preparatory to the construction of the stable or store house complexes there. Such projects involved the movement and removal of thousands of tons of fill – the making of the water passage at Hazor necessitated the removal of 5000 tons of rock and that of the cylindrical shaft (c. 10.8 m (35 ft) deep, with an average diameter of 11.9 m (39 ft)) at Gibeon the quarrying of nearly 3000 tons of limestone. Furthermore, surveying underground involved considerable problems.

Where actual buildings were concerned, a few basic models could be adapted to serve for various tasks. Thus, as we have seen, the long hall divided into nave and side aisles might be employed as storehouses, market halls or stables, while the 'four-room house' might be adapted for citadel buildings. A circular excavation provided with a winding staircase might be used as the adit to the water shaft at Gibeon, or alternatively to give access to the big round grain pit at Megiddo III. Outside the urban area the same basic construction techniques might be made to serve for yet other ends – terracing for the creation of agricultural or garden plots, tunnelling for the making of channels to irrigate fields, and sometimes perhaps in mining operations. The origins of such techniques may go back to the Canaanite period, or may owe something to outside influences, but they were handled with skill and ingenuity. In this field, the Israelites deserve more credit than they have often been given.

Outside influences

In reviewing Israelite settlements and the private and public structures found in them, we can observe a mixture of apparently local developments side by side with possible cultural borrowings. The plans of Israelite residential towns, and of the private houses in them, appear to be indigenous; similarly the overall plans of cities of an official nature, though quite different, cannot, in general, be derived from outside models. Indigenous also is the 'pillar house' building technique typical of private dwellings, though there are some analogies later in the Phoenician world. The derivation of the fine ashlar style of construction found in official buildings, often in combination with proto-Aeolic capitals, is at present unclear, but it came to be shared by Phoenicia and Israel. Where the plans of official buildings are concerned, some Israelite palaces may have been related to the North Syrian 'hilani', but whether directly or via Phoenician models cannot at present be determined. Storehouses or stables divided by two rows of pillars into a nave and two side aisles appear again to be locally derived.

Where works of defence are concerned, casemate walls may ultimately go back to Hittite prototypes, but they were known in Middle Bronze Age Palestine. They were not in fashion there during the Late Bronze Age but whether they go back to Canaanite tradition or were reintroduced from outside Palestine in the Early Iron Age remains in question. The solid walls consisting of alternatively advanced or recessed sections, typical of the time of the Divided Monarchy, are probably an Israelite invention. City gates are related both to the gates of Palestinian Bronze Age towns, and also to those found in contemporary northern Syria. Except for the late type, apparently directly inspired by Assyrian models, it is again difficult to be sure from what source the Israelites derived their inspiration. Lastly, Israelite water passages may be ultimately descended from Canaanite and Anatolian or Egyptian prototypes, but the Israelites developed their own tradition. The comparative absence of Egyptian traditions in these matters is striking, and may be deliberate.

The disposal of the dead

Having dealt with the abodes of the living, we must turn to those of the dead. While both burial and cremation were practised in the contemporary Near East, cremation was not normally used by Israelites. Burning the remains of Saul and his sons (1 Samuel 31, 12–13) was an emergency measure, while the 'great burning' at the funeral of King Asa of Judah (2 Chronicles 16, 14) was probably of spices, not of his body. The general preference for burial still allowed a number of possible variations. It could, firstly, take place within the city or outside. The former was adopted by both kings and commoners during the Bronze Age and after in the Levant – kings had stately tombs or burial crypts within the palace premises, while commoners might be placed below the floors of their houses. In Judah, the Davidic dynasty was buried for a time in the palace precincts but this tradition was later discontinued. We hear only of one example of burial within a private house, namely in the case of Joab (1 Kings 2, 34), but this was in the wilderness, and archaeology has produced no analogous examples within settlements.

In fact extramural burial was the rule, again, with several alternatives. The dead could be placed, singly or in small groups, within trenches cut into soil or rock – a small number of which have been found – or in mass burial grounds. The 'graves of the common people' in Jerusalem are referred to by scripture (2 Kings 23, 6; Jeremiah 26, 23) but these remain undiscovered. The last resting places of what was probably the majority of Israelites in fact remain unknown, and the stones – possibly sometimes inscribed – which might mark graves (cf. 2 Kings 23, 17) remain undocumented in Israel, though there are examples from Phoenician Achzib. Members of well-established families or of the élite, on the other hand, might be buried in natural caves or artificial rock-cut tombs – successors to a long-established tradition – which tended to be located around the abodes of the living, though cemeteries some distance away from settlements

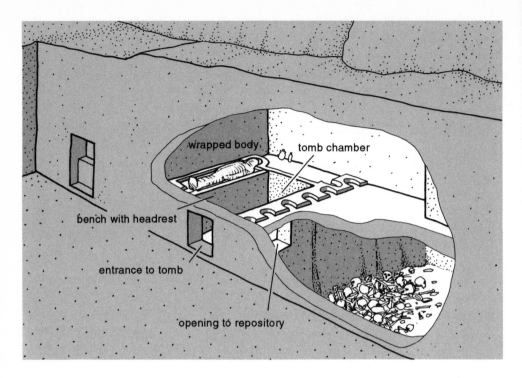

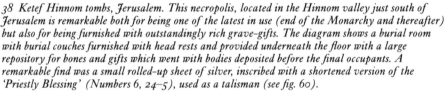

38 Ketef Hinnom tombs, Jerusalem. This necropolis, located in the Hinnom valley just south of Jerusalem is remarkable both for being one of the latest in use (end of the Monarchy and thereafter) but also for being furnished with outstandingly rich grave-gifts. The diagram shows a burial room with burial couches furnished with head rests and provided underneath the floor with a large repository for bones and gifts which went with bodies deposited before the final occupants. A remarkable find was a small rolled-up sheet of silver, inscribed with a shortened version of the 'Priestly Blessing' (Numbers 6, 24–5), used as a talisman (see fig. 60).

are known. Such family tombs, where a man was laid to rest 'with his fathers', could be in use for generations and over a time accommodate hundreds. During the eighth and seventh centuries BC, however, tombs intended for a few members of a distinguished household only became fashionable.

Israelite rock-cut tombs are best attested in Judah from *c*. 900 BC onwards. They essentially consist of a squarish room approached by a few steps, or occasionally down a shaft, through a square opening. The three sides facing the entrance were provided with rock-cut benches – hence the name 'bench tombs'. On these, the dead were deposited lying on their backs; in a number of cases, especially in Jerusalem, a rock-cut pillow or head-rest was provided. The deceased were accompanied by numerous funerary gifts including not only personal belongings like seals, weapons or ornaments, but also provender for the world to come (plates, jugs, jars etc. to contain it have alone survived) and especially lamps to lighten their darkness – a symbol of eternity. On the whole, the value of jewelry and other items deposited with the dead is moderate – ornaments of bronze predominate, and gold in particular is rare. Only at the very end of Judah's history do we find grave goods representing impressive wealth, as in the Ketef Hinnom tombs near the southwest corner of ancient Jerusalem. With the steady need to provide additional burial space in rock-cut family tombs, additional tomb chambers might be linked with the original one, but more generally the method of dealing with the problem was to sweep the remains of earlier tenants and their funerary gifts aside, or to transfer them to special repositories – sunken pits or small side chambers.

This type of tomb was in use all over Judah, including the capital, and may be intended to represent the 'four-room house' of the living. Tombs for the élite in Jerusalem were, however, different. Some shaft tombs (ninth century?) located near the southwest corner of the Temple platform may follow Phoenician prototypes. More remarkable are some groups of tombs of foreign inspiration, which perhaps offer hints concerning architectural features of upper-class dwellings. These are found in a cemetery north of the Damascus Gate, but especially in a group of rock-cut tombs in Silwan, near ancient Siloam, facing the city across the Kidron Valley. The former includes a tomb consisting of a large central room surrounded on three sides by burial chambers, each with three couches for three dead bodies. Even more remarkable are the monumental rock-cut tombs in the Kidron Valley, which served members of the court, including perhaps the Shebnah taunted by Isaiah (22, 15–16). These tombs include free-standing monoliths cut from the rock flank, once topped by a pyramid above an Egyptian-type cavetto cornice. Rooms inside have either a flat ceiling or a gabled roof. Such tombs are of non-Israelite derivation – Egyptian (via Phoenicia), Phoenician or Anatolian. Others, exceptionally fine, in the St Etienne cemetery north of Jerusalem, imitate decorative panelling found in wealthy houses. Interestingly, a few are provided with inscriptions identifying the owners, just as some houses did. Again, funerary architecture may be inspired by that of the living in this regard. Artistic embellishment is sometimes found in burial chambers. Some very crude lion-like heads in a tomb at Tell Aitun near Hebron may represent guardian spirits, or may have been intended to deter the spirits of the dead from attempting to leave the cave, since they face inwards. The tomb also contains scratched drawings.

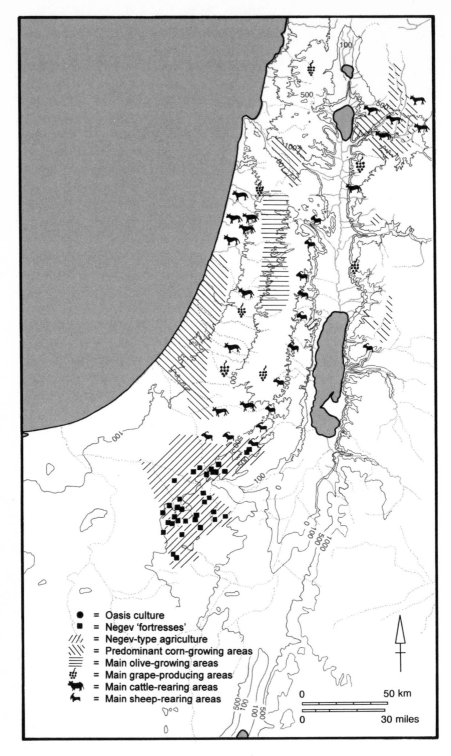

● = Oasis culture
■ = Negev 'fortresses'
//// = Negev-type agriculture
\\\\ = Predominant corn-growing areas
≡ = Main olive-growing areas
🌿 = Main grape-producing areas
🐂 = Main cattle-rearing areas
🐑 = Main sheep-rearing areas

0   50 km

0   30 miles

39 The principal types of farming and stock rearing the Israelites engaged in. Their distribution is linked to the types of climate and natural vegetation found in the various sub-regions of the country.

CHAPTER SIX

Agriculture

According to biblical accounts mixed farming and stock rearing were the foundation of Israel's existence; only among the Transjordan tribes of Reuben and Gad is pastoralism reported to have been dominant in the earliest times. Deuteronomy (8, 8ff.) extols the excellence of the Promised Land as a producer of grain, wine, oil and garden fruit – typically Mediterranean products – though by also referring to iron and copper deposits it reminds us that even a peasant society has need of certain basic industries. It was regarded as ideal that a man should work the family holding, and many scriptural passages refer to agricultural operations and conditions – some, like Isaiah (28, 24ff.), in considerable detail. Nostalgic hankerings for the times before the ills associated with a settled agricultural existence did not prove effective, and a group like the Rechabites, who refused to follow the agricultural mode of life (Jeremiah 35, 6–10), remained exceptional. Change in a different direction apparently came, however, through an increasing tendency towards the creation of large estates (against which the prophets inveighed), and which led to the dispossession of small farmers, as well as various social and moral ills.

Archaeology lends substance and differentiation to the picture offered by biblical literature, supplemented by evidence in ancient and later texts, and parallels in traditional Palestinian farming practice. According to the archaeological information available, Israel was a nation of farmers as well as pastoralists from the earliest discernible times, with no clear indications of a preceding purely pastoralist stage.

Regional variations in Israelite farming

The considerable diversity of relief and climate within Palestine meant that Israelite farmers were faced with a number of different problems and opportunities. Deuteronomy is essentially describing the agriculture of the western hill country and the adjoining coastal plain, north of the latitude of Beersheba, together with the northwestern fringe of the uplands in Transjordan, all of which enjoy a Mediterranean climatic regime. Needless to say, there are some differentiations – the plain offers better opportunities for grain growing than the hill country, and much of Judea in particular is better suited for barley than wheat, the latter being the main food grain though barley bread was made. On the other hand, fruit trees – including the olive – do better in parts of the uplands, much of which are also suited to the rearing of sheep or goats, especially on the eastern and southern desert fringes. Cattle do well in the rich valley near Samaria, and in the plain belt – Philistia, Sharon and the Jezreel–Megiddo lowlands, as well as the Bashan plateau across the Jordan. The agricultural calendar in the Mediterranean zone is governed by the climatic sequence, in which a wet winter (beginning and ending with heavy showers, known in the Bible as the 'former' and 'latter' rains) is followed by a hot, dry summer. Farming operations correspondingly begin with ploughing and sowing in about November, when the first rains have softened the hard-baked ground. There may be a second ploughing, and perhaps a third, at the end of the rainy season. The barley harvest is in about May (earlier or later, in places) and the wheat harvest roughly a month later, followed in turn by the harvesting of grapes, fruit and olives. That ancient Israelite agriculture was geared to this rhythm is shown by the tenth-century 'Gezer Calendar' (pl. 41) – a limestone tablet, possibly a writing exercise, unearthed by Macalister in his Gezer excavations. This lists the agricultural operations of the year in pre-standard Hebrew, written in an archaic Hebrew-Phoenician script. Translation presents some difficulties but, beginning its sequence with the harvest season, it may read: 'Two months of ingathering [of olives, etc.], two months of sowing, two months of spring herbage [late grass, or late sowing?], a month of hoeing [or pulling up] flax, a month of barley harvest, a month of [wheat] harvest and measuring out, two months of pruning [or harvesting?] grapes, a month of [ingathering] summer fruit.' The presence of flax (if referred to) is linked with the position of Gezer in the coastal plain, for the crop does best in moist or irrigated ground. The list is not exhaustive – it does not, for example, specify the tree fruit, vegetables or condiments grown. Fortunately archaeology has, to a limited extent, supplemented biblical references.

Different conditions prevail in the drier steppe belt fringing the Mediterranean region to the south and east. Here climatic factors impede the cultivation of fruit trees, including the olive, but grain and livestock do well. This is particularly true for the parts of the Bashan region east of the lake of Tiberias, transitional from the Mediterranean region, which was famous for both. However, on the fringes of steppe and desert, especially in the Negeb, where rainfall is limited to irregular downpours which may fail altogether in some years, stock rearing and farming is restricted and intermittent – overgrazing has to be avoided – unless special measures to conserve and use the rain-water are employed. Even so, a dry year might be disastrous. Yet overall the wilderness was economically useful and was carefully apportioned to clans or localities.

The southern Jordan Valley, Dead Sea fringes and Arabah offered yet another type of environment. Warm in winter but extremely hot in summer, this region is suited to the cultivation of warmth-loving plants such as date palms, where irrigation from springs or wadis is possible. It can also offer garden and other produce at times when the cold season elsewhere precludes this.

Obviously, these different constituent regions are economically complementary, and for a tribe or individual it would be advantageous to own land in more than one of them. Tribal territories, that of Benjamin in particular, combine various zones, and before 1948 farmers in the Samaritan hill country similarly had holdings in the adjoining Sharon Plain. Seasonal migration of

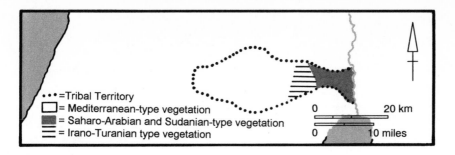

40 *The tribal territory of Benjamin, showing the various zones of vegetation, which were suited to different types of farming and stock rearing.*

labour, but also in particular of livestock, is therefore often necessary. Animals could pasture on harvested fields in the plain in autumn, or crop the new growth in the steppe fringe in winter, but they would have to retire to the hills when the summer heat dried out the latter and the growing cornfields in the plain were out of bounds to the herdsman and his animals. Such movement – and the transport of surplus produce to consumers in Israel or abroad – pre-supposed the existence of a suitable network of roads or tracks, such as apparently did exist, for example, near Jerusalem and in Samaria. The maintenance of public safety for the farming community, their produce, flocks, fields and gardens was another essential.

Surplus produce may have been exchanged by barter very early on. 'Izbet Ṣarṭah, in the thirteenth to tenth centuries BC, probably exchanged grain for oil and so on. Later, agricultural surpluses became objects of trade, taxes or rent.

Farming in the hill country

One basic requirement for Israelite farmers was the availability of sufficient cultivable land and water. Part of the hill country was still covered by forests, and in Galilee Israelite settlement began in clearings and backwoods. Forests there and further south could gradually be removed, though they also had their uses as providers of timber, fuel and rough grazing. In some places, as near Ai, they had already been replaced by open ground by the time the Israelites appeared. However, such early forest clearance had locally been followed by the erosion and leaching out of soil, and a population well in excess of the number of inhabitants in the hill country during the Bronze Age needed additional acreage. The Israelite solution to the problem consisted of very large-scale building of agricultural terraces, a technique occasionally used in the Bronze Age, and applied by the Israelites as early as the thirteenth century BC, as near Ai. They were not found everywhere – frequent in Judah, Samaria and the Negeb, they were not in fashion in Galilee, and on the hill-plain edge other methods prevailed, as at Tell Qiri near Jokneam. Their construction, usually as parts of larger complexes, and maintenance required means and efforts beyond the capacity of individual farmers. Co-operative enterprise, and in particular governmental directions and planning, were probably needed here. Isolated terraces, however, might be the fruit of individual efforts: such do occur. Generally, nevertheless, such terraces were arranged tier above tier up the hillsides, especially on slopes facing north, where moisture would be conserved longer and soil generation accordingly favoured. Essentially they consisted of a retaining wall holding in layers of gravel and cultivable soil, topped by imported humus. In this manner hillsides previously at best useful for grazing were transformed into a succession of cultivable plots. The lowest might be suited for vines; figs, nuts and pomegranate trees might be planted higher up; while the exposed upper reaches and plateaux could support grain or pulses. Below the hills, terraces and valley bottoms might be watered from springs tapped by short runnels, and irrigated ground there would serve for herb gardens or rich water meadows. Elsewhere, in the absence of springs, large cisterns might provide water for irrigated gardens. Channels and tunnels to distribute rain-water might also be constructed on high ground. These terrace systems naturally developed first and most completely near villages, getting sparser as distance increased. However, by the eighth century BC, isolated farms sited among their own terraced units appeared, for example near Jerusalem, catering for the increased food requirements of the growing population in the capital. Approached by lanes bordered by high boundary walls accessible most easily to beasts of burden rather than to carts (cf. Numbers 22, 24ff.), a dwelling house of 'four-room' type with its own cistern might be surrounded by terraces supporting gardens and fields and include such facilities as a wine- or, more rarely, an oil-press. Khirbet er-Ras, investigated by S. Gibson and G. Edelstein, offers a good example.

Individual farms of another type have been noted in the western hill border country near the head-waters of the Yarkon river. These consist essentially of enclosures with a few rooms and a cistern attached, intended for temporary occupation by the inhabitants of villages to the east when they came to work in their vineyards or olive groves. That they may also have had fields in the fertile lowlands nearby seems quite likely. Not far to the north, Israelite farmers were permanently established in the Sharon Plain. Here they might even have undertaken some drainage to reclaim swampy soil for agriculture, though clear evidence is needed.

Farming in the Negeb and in the Judean desert fringe

Very different procedures were required in the Negeb, where security had to be established and maintained if agricultural projects were to have a chance of success. Understandably, Israelite expansion southwards into the belt of land along the Beersheba Wadi and beyond in the eleventh century (previously loosely settled by a mixture of Judeans, Kenites and Amalekites) was based on what are now seen as village strongholds. Houses were built side by side – or linked by short stretches of wall – around an open central area to present a defensive outline determined by local topography. A single opening or gate allowed access. Later, perhaps in the tenth century, a network of 'fortresses' was established, covering not only the southern flank of Judah but also protecting the caravan roads between the Mediterranean and the Gulf of Aqabah, well to the south. These 'fortresses' were mostly constructed of roughly shaped blocks of stone, topped sometimes by mud-brick. Casemate walls (and later occasionally solid walling) surrounded an irregular oval or sometimes square or rectangular courtyard. Projecting towers at the corners of rectangular forts and in the middle of their sides became fashionable in the eighth and seventh centuries BC.

It was mainly in the vicinity of such strongholds that cultivation was undertaken, leading to a network of agricultural areas along tributaries of the main wadis, which were worked from isolated or loosely grouped individual farms. The basic technique employed in land reclamation for 'run-off' farming (borrowed perhaps, rather than invented locally, from those occasionally attested in the hill country where continuous occupation has largely obliterated them) consisted in subdividing the valleys into a sequence of terraces by the construction of stone walls across the wadi beds. These walls held back the flood-water generated by the winter rains, causing it to deposit the silt it carried, and to seep into the ground gradually instead of running to waste. In the wet ground grain or other crops could then be planted, and the moisture retained in the soil would maintain them till ready for harvesting. Animal husbandry, especially sheep rearing, was another mainstay. To cater for the water requirements of livestock, the rare springs or wells were supplemented by cisterns. These were often round, flat-bottomed pits up to 8 m (26 ft) across and 4 m (13 ft) deep, dug into impermeable loamy marl with the sides lined with rough stone walling. Water from hillside catchment areas was channelled to them over distances of as much as 1 km (over ½ mile) or even more. There is no indication they could be covered over, however, and so many would dry out in summer, obliging the farmers and their stock to leave for the hills, sometimes travelling considerable distances (cf. Genesis 37, 12–17) when the supply ran out. Many of the farmhouses intended for such seasonal occupation were mere shacks, though better ones of the 'four-room' type are also encountered. Individual farm areas are surrounded by boundary walls delimiting sometimes quite sizeable areas. The immense effort implied in the creation of these cultivable areas makes it possible they owe their existence to royal decree, especially perhaps Solomon's.

Many of these agricultural settlements, like the fortresses on which they depended, did not survive the late tenth or early ninth century. Some think their demise may be linked with the havoc wrought by the invasion of the pharaoh Sheshonq (Shishak of the Bible). Although later monarchs, especially Uzziah (2 Chronicles 26, 10), took an interest in establishing strong-points in the desert and promoting agriculture there, such activity was apparently on a lesser scale. On the other hand, agriculture was introduced during the eighth and seventh centuries in the biblical Vale of Achor (the Buqei'ah Plain) fringing the Judean desert near the Dead Sea, in the wake of military outposts established to control access to the deposits of sulphur, salt and bitumen found nearby, as well as the roads leading to Jerusalem. Individual farms established there cultivated not only grain but also palm trees, grapes and perhaps olives; we do not know to what extent grapes or dates were then also grown in the Negeb, though it seems likely that they were. The Babylonian conquest in 586 BC led in any case to the abandonment of cultivation in both regions.

As yet we have only patchy information about the use made of the subtropical Jordan–Arabah rift valley. Balsam was cultivated and processed at En Gedi, and date palms no doubt near Jericho, the 'city of the Palm Trees', but there is nothing to indicate that the dates grown there were of the outstanding quality which was to assure them a world market during the Roman period (cf. Pliny, *Natural History*, XIII, ix, 44).

41 A traditional Palestinian plough from Beit Jala. The plough-tip, with its iron sheathing, scratches the soil but does not turn it as a plough-share would.

Farming implements and techniques

Where agricultural techniques are concerned archaeology has so far brought only limited information, and biblical references combined with observations made from traditional Palestinian Arab methods are still our main source. Unlike some other early nations, especially the Egyptians, the Israelites have left no relevant drawings or models, and much still remains obscure.

The Israelite farmer, it has been thought, owned a holding of *c.* 200 dunam (20 ha or 50 acres) of ploughland, and used a similar amount of pasture. To plough his fields, which were probably mostly oblong or nearly square, and of moderate size, he used a wooden plough with a share provided with a metal tip. This was pulled by two yoked oxen (guided by means of a metal-tipped ox goad), or by donkeys. Camels are not mentioned as traction animals, and the reference to horses in an agricultural context in Isaiah 28, 28 is puzzling. The plough scratched but did not turn the soil. This method is in fact suited to Mediterranean conditions, for the surface layer of clods thus generated prevents undue evaporation of water retained in the ground during the hot summers. Hoes with metal heads as well as metal-headed picks were also used, but we know nothing of spades. Such tools might also be employed in olive groves or vineyards in order to turn, air and weed the soil; in vineyards, short metal pruning or harvesting knives would also be standard equipment. Iron tended to supersede bronze in farming tools from the tenth century BC onwards, though it was in more occasional use a century or two before. Alongside metal sickles, the cheaper model consisting of toothed flint blades slotted into a wooden or bone haft remained in use throughout the period, and perhaps stone was similarly employed as a cheaper alternative for other tools.

After the ploughing, seed would be scattered broadcast over the fields. For harrowing, branches may have been dragged over the ground – no harrows are known. Grain when ripe would be cut with a sickle just below the ears; straw might be cut and gathered separately. The harvested grain was tied into sheaves, which would then be taken to the settlement. In suitable conditions a cart was used (cf. Amos 2, 13), probably the two-wheeled type shown on one of the relief slabs representing the siege of Lachish by Sennacherib. Threshing was normally done on a public or privately owned threshing floor, a number of which have been found, consisting of a piece of hard level ground exposed to the westerly winds and located in the village or township, or on a piece of (preferably) elevated ground nearby (cf. 2 Samuel 24, 18 ff.), or perhaps in front of a city gate. For information about the actual threshing process we have to rely largely on biblical texts, supplemented by recent observations. From these it appears that the grain was first spread out, and then animals would be made to walk round on it, perhaps pulling a threshing-plough, a sledge-like contraption with its lower side studded with pieces of sharp flint or iron. The mixture of grain, chaff and chopped straw would then be tossed into the air with a winnowing fork – the wind would blow the chaff and straw some distance, the light chaff being caught in screens of wicker hurdles, while the heavier grain would fall straight down. Grain, chaff and straw could then be gathered into separate heaps and the grain guarded until removed for storage. Stone-lined pits, or silos, sometimes of considerable capacity, were used for this. Store buildings were rare, especially early on. A grain pit at Ai is said to have had room for 7000 litres – sufficient to feed ten persons for a year. Later, there were even bigger store pits, such as the very large round pit at Megiddo III, provided with a spiral staircase and capable of holding up to 450 cu. m (15,890 cu. ft) belonging to the Israelite or the Assyrian period. The chaff might serve for fuel, while chopped straw might be fed to animals or mixed in brick, plaster or potter's clay. After sieving, corn could be eaten parched, or possibly serve in the manufacture of simple beer (perhaps the 'strong drink' of the Bible) or, more commonly, might be ground into flour. This would be done in individual homes with a hand-mill, the sound of which was regarded as typical of normal domesticity (cf. Jeremiah 25, 10). In its simplest form, a hand-mill consisted of a bun-shaped upper millstone which was moved forward and backward over a cushion-shaped lower one. Both stones consisted usually of basalt. During Iron Age II a more sophisticated model came into use. This had a frame-shaped upper stone and the grain could be poured into the central hollow, making for steadier operation. Flour was sieved after the grinding, but some of it remained very gritty, leading to badly abraded teeth.

Where the pressing of grapes and olives is concerned, archaeological information is more abundant. Grapes (so far as they were not eaten fresh or dried) were occasionally pressed in beam presses like those used for olives, but more commonly they were trodden in square wine presses, many of which have been found. Essentially they consisted of an upper and a lower rock-cut basin linked by a channel. The grapes were crushed in the upper basin and the juice ran into the lower one, where it could be collected. It might then be drunk as fresh grape juice or boiled down into grape treacle. The same Hebrew word was

42 A reconstruction of an Iron Age olive press. The olives are first crushed in a crushing-basin and then put into fibre baskets, which are squeezed by the beam of the press brought down on them by means of stone weights attached to the beam.

used for this and for bees' honey – both served as sweeteners. Finally, it could be kept in pottery jars to ferment into wine (and perhaps, later, vinegar). Whether bell-shaped cavities cut into the chalky rock at Gibeon and elsewhere served as cellars in which wine could mature at an even temperature is uncertain.

Olives, if they were not consumed fresh or preserved salted, might be pounded in a mortar to extract oil of high quality, but greater, sometimes considerable, quantities of oil were obtained in oil presses. The operative part of these was a horizontal beam, one end of which was lodged in a hole in a wall or rock face. The free end was brought down by heavy weights, exerting pressure on a pile of rope baskets containing olives previously ground into a paste by rotating stones in a stone basin. The oil squeezed out would collect in a basin – either a cavity in the rock, or a stone or pottery container. Round stone vats found in a number of settlements or agricultural contexts, once regarded as dye vats, are now considered parts of oil presses. There might be more than one pressing, the first oil being the best. Once purified, the oil might serve for cosmetic or pharmaceutical purposes, or otherwise in the preparation of food. Such presses (known in the Bronze Age) underwent some limited improvements in our period.

In other respects some very basic information is still lacking. We do not know, for instance, to what extent farming practice included a regular alternation between fallow and cultivation (fallowing alternate halves of estates every second year has been suggested), or a rotation between grain and pulse crops; whether biblical references to dung on the fields refer to manuring, or simply to the droppings of animals pasturing on the stubble; or whether there was any regular haymaking (Amos 7, 1 might hint at this). There is nothing to tell us how far villages regulated their farming communally. Biblical texts, including Isaiah (28, 24ff.), indicate the variety of crops produced by Israelite farmers. Archaeological discoveries indicate that pistachios, pot herbs and other vegetable food were collected, but we do not know how significant this was apart from in times of famine. Lastly, we are unsure whether farming procedure was still entirely a matter of rustic tradition. The Carthaginian descendants of Israel's Phoenician neighbours some centuries later had farming manuals, such as the treatise by Mago which the Romans thought worth translating into Latin. Passages like Isaiah 5, 1–2 and 28, 24–29, addressed by a highly educated townsman to sophisticated urban audiences, may hint that agricultural topics were included in wisdom literature. There would be nothing impossible in this, but hard facts are lacking.

Concerning animal husbandry our information is likewise limited. Cattle, if the relief slabs showing Sennacherib's siege of Lachish can be trusted, were of a humped breed here, and perhaps elsewhere, but short-horned cattle bones have also been found at Lachish. Royal stables for all manner of beasts, referred to in 2 Chronicles (32, 28), are archaeologically unattested, but the low rooms often found in houses may have done duty as stalls for the fattening of calves, and may also have accommodated the occasional sheep or goat. For much of the time, however, the animals were probably kept in the open. Stone-built enclosures next to farmhouses would serve as pens, but folds made of perishable materials have not been identified. Sheep were fat-tailed and wool-bearing. Goats had spiral shaped horns and some probably had the glossy black hair still commonly found in the region. The animals provided meat, milk (from which cheese was made), leather, horn, goat's hair and wool. Sheep were dipped before the spring shearing, but no clippers have been preserved. They might be slaughtered young for their meat, but cattle tended to be kept for a number of years. Cattle and donkeys also provided traction, while donkeys and mules could carry loads in addition to being ridden. Camels were used more rarely – they seem to have been most frequent near Lachish but were perhaps not bred there, being imported rather from Arabia. Dogs were kept, but little esteemed – unlike the early Greeks and Arabs, the Israelites are not known to have kept prized breeds for hunting. Domestic cats were unknown. Chicken were probably found occasionally from the eighth century onwards, when representations of cockerels appear on seals, but whether geese, ducks or pigeons were included among farm animals is not known, nor whether bees were kept, or whether the honey of wild bees was the only type available. Hunting – of deer in particular – contributed to the limited meat ration, especially in times of emergency.

We also cannot at present discern whether in Israel stock breeding was gradually overtaken by grain production as the leading form of agriculture, as it was in early Greece. However that may be, stock raising and the keeping of goats in particular permanently affected the face of the country, since overgrazing destroyed vegetation and prevented the regeneration of forest cover. Other permanent signs of early stock keeping, such as the walls, ditches or dykes known to have delimited divisions of pasture in early Europe have still to be discovered in Israel.

Social structure

It remains to say something about the social structure of the rural population. While prophetic strictures like those found in Amos (8, 4–6), Micah (2, 2) and Isaiah (5, 8) refer to the growing tendency during the eighth and seventh centuries BC for large landowners to reduce small farmers to an oppressive tenant status, or to drive them out – though there are at present no indications that such dispossessed people went to live in new slum quarters in the towns – other biblical texts hint that fairly large landowners were present quite early. Such apparently included not only the family of Saul, whose descendant Mephibosheth employed a steward to administer the estate, and that of David, whose son Absalom was obviously a sheep farmer of some importance (2 Samuel 13, 23), but also individuals like Nabal (1 Samuel 25, 2ff.) or Barzillai (2 Samuel 19, 31ff.). Later, after the division of the United Monarchy, Elisha's father must have been a man of considerable substance if he owned 12 teams of plough oxen (1 Kings 19, 19–21). In the eighth century BC, the Samaria ostraca, according to recent interpretation, indicate that a number of important people held multiple estates in various clan territories around the northern capital, whether as fiefs, or in their own right. Some of the constituent parts of these might specialize in different produce (wine, fine oil).

Later, during the reign of Menahem in northern Israel, there must, as we saw, have been some 60,000 important estate owners or holders, from whom the king could extract contributions of 50 shekels each (2 Kings 15, 19ff.). Such people would have at least a proportion of their land tilled by day labourers. A band of these on harvest work is attested in the sister kingdom of Judah in the seventh century ostracon of Meṣad Ḥashavyahu; perhaps they were conscripted to work on the king's harvest (1 Samuel 8, 12). However, it is difficult to guess how large a proportion of the rural labour force consisted of Israelite hired hands, or non-Israelites of 'sojourner' (Hebrew *ger*) status, or impressed labour doing service, or of slaves. There is no special type of rural building denoting the residence of a large landowner, analogous to the Roman villa. Better houses of 'four-room' type interspersed among hovels, in the Negeb in particular, may indicate the abode of the proprietor or his steward among his dependants. Whether there was any distinction between domain land farmed from a manorial centre and the individual holdings of dependent peasants we have at present no information.

By the eighth century, Israelite agriculture was, at least in parts, geared to the production of crops both surplus to local requirements and marketable – grain, wine and, in particular, oil. A comparison of settlement plans offers some hints of how this came about. Iron I settlements like 'Izbet Ṣarṭah, Tell Beit Mirsim and Ai, have a profusion of grain storage pits, but other installations, such as oil presses, are not prominent. By the ninth century, the remainders of 'Shemer's estate' below the later acropolis of Samaria may have had a number of oil presses sufficient to supply the needs of a population of *c.* 150 (who may have lived nearby); by the eighth century, the village of Ḥirbet Jem'ein in the western Samarian uplands boasted a public oil press capable of producing far more oil than could be consumed locally, and it was not unique – Beth Shemesh may have functioned as a major oil production centre up until Sennacherib's invasion.

Local mass production of wine is less easy to establish – not everybody agrees that the 63 rock-hewn bell-shaped cisterns found by J.B. Pritchard at Gibeon are part of a 'winery' where thousands of gallons of locally produced wine could be stored. Wine production, though massive in the aggregate, may have been based on numerous small units instead, and the same is probably true to some extent for grain. Camel caravans may then, as fairly recently, have brought grain from Hauran and Bashan (the latter Israelite at times) to the coast for shipment – though also from Moab to Judah.

After the Assyrian invasions, especially Sennacherib's, there was a change. During the seventh century, the oil producing industry was located mainly in Philistia. Here Ekron and Timnah, which probably attracted much of Israel's olive harvest (in return for grain?), became production centres of international importance. Some 100 double oil presses are known from Ekron alone. Interestingly, this important industry was still based on presses located in individual homes.

All told, Israelite farming was efficient. In normal years it provided food for the bulk of the population – sufficiently if not amply. The amount of meat and dairy products consumed by ordinary people may have been small, their diet being based largely on grain with the addition of a certain amount of fruit, wine, olives or olive oil and some vegetables. In regions given over to cattle rearing, such as the Sharon, the consumption of beef even by common people may have been larger, and that of rich townspeople was great enough to give offence. In good years in particular, there would have been substantial surplus available for marketing and export. In moderately poor years supplies stored from the previous harvest, together with the ability to spread the danger through the availability of harvests in less affected parts of the country, would have done something to limit the poverty which could lead to debt slavery or emigration. However, the system was powerless to deal with catastrophes like prolonged periods of drought or plagues of locusts, though in this respect neighbouring lands were no better placed. Some imported food might be available, but its cost would be far too high for the common people.

Technically the level of agricultural equipment and operations was similar to that found in other Levantine countries. It also presents analogies with Iron Age Greece, and, interestingly, with parts of contemporary Europe and North Africa further west. Where agriculture was concerned Israel was in fact largely a Mediterranean country, even though it had links with Mesopotamia and Egypt.

CHAPTER SEVEN

Industries and Crafts

While ancient Israel did not develop industries and crafts to the same level as neighbouring Phoenicia, whose products found ready acceptance in international markets, they were not absent. Even farming folk, who can put their hands to many things, need the services of specialist craftsmen such as the smith, and the more sophisticated requirements of the urban élite in particular would involve the products of a great range of artisans. The Bible does in fact refer to a variety of craftsmen, headed by the versatile *ḥaraš*, who was competent both as a smith and a woodworker and perhaps also in the making of high-class textiles; such people might even be remembered by name. A number of specialized tradesmen are also mentioned – the activities of some of them, like those of the potter and the metal refiner, are described in detail and were obviously regarded as suitable subjects for literary comparisons, but others, like the lowly tanner, receive no mention. In general, craftsmen remained anonymous. Their numbers must have been quite substantial by the sixth century, for after the surrender of Jehoiachin to Nebuchadnezzar in 597 BC, a thousand craftsmen and smiths were reportedly carried away from Jerusalem (2 Kings 24, 16), a high proportion of a total population of perhaps 25,000. It seems quite likely the total number of artisans in the capital was greater than this, for those of no military interest may well have been allowed to stay.

Yet how many of the craftsmen working in Israel were Israelites? Some have thought only a few, and those not very efficient. This may have been true at first, but by the ninth or eighth century a proportion of the craftsmen active in Israel were probably Israelite (some perhaps of Canaanite descent), including those working in crafts requiring considerable skill, like ivory and bone carving. Other needs were probably met by resident aliens or by imports. Within their various fields of activity, Israelite artisans (whether itinerant, working in their own homes, or in groups) did not differ significantly from their non-Israelite colleagues in their methods and equipment; like them they carried on the traditions current during the Bronze Age. Living, furthermore, in the fully developed metal age they were also basically dependent on metal for their tools as well as some of their products – both on the long-familiar copper and bronze, and on the recently developed hardened iron or steel.

Metal

Terrestrial and meteoritic iron had long been known in the Near East, but unimproved iron was of little practical use, though its rarity and perhaps its supposed magical qualities led to its occasional employment for ceremonial weapons or jewelry. However, by *c.* 1200 BC the art of turning iron into hardened steel through carburization, quenching and forging had been discovered, and implements such as knives made from improved iron or steel were in use by the twelfth century. Palestine began to use this new improved iron fairly quickly. Some 20 iron items – weapons and ornaments – dating from the twelfth century have been found in the Philistine or Canaanite inhabited plain belt, and some steel jewelry at Umm ed-Dananir and Medeba in Transjordan might even be a little earlier.

The eleventh century witnessed an increase in the quantity of iron used – though iron items were still outnumbered by those made of bronze where tools or weapons were concerned – and also the Israelite hill country was now involved, as finds from Ai and neighbouring Khirbet Raddanah, and also from Beth Zur show. Iron technology seems to have advanced early especially in northern Palestine, perhaps under the influence of 'Sea People' elements. A pickaxe of excellent steel was found in an eleventh-century (Phoenician?) fortress at Har Adir in Galilee, and Tel Qiri near Jokneam has furnished a well-carburized axe head of similar date; Taanach (after 1020 probably in Israelite hands), has provided finds of iron or steel ranging down to *c.* 926 BC. By the tenth century iron tools and weapons became fairly frequent in Israel and Philistia, and by the ninth–eighth centuries they were almost exclusively used for such purposes. Bronze remained predominant, however, for the making of jewelry, vases and ornamental fittings, and more of it was probably produced now than during the Bronze Age, though of the latter little has survived plundering and resmelting.

How this change-over came about, or why, is still unclear. The new technology probably reached Israel via the Philistine–Esdraelon–Beth Shean plain, but whether a shortage of tin, or of charcoal fuel needed in greater quantities for bronze than iron working, promoted its application in Palestine and perhaps elsewhere is not certain. Nor would iron always at first have been technically superior to hardened bronze, or cheaper. Taken overall, metalworking in Philistia did not produce iron markedly superior to that found in Israel, or in noticeably greater amounts; the craftsmen may in any case have come from further afield. Nor does present information support the interpretation of the much-quoted passage in 1 Samuel (13, 19–22) as indicating that the Philistines kept iron weapons for themselves, allowing the Israelites only agricultural tools. Iron weapons (two lance heads and perhaps a dagger blade) have been found at Ai in eleventh-century contexts. The biblical passage may refer to a later and temporary rather than a permanent ban; it does not mention iron specifically in any case. The speedy acceptance of improved iron technology by Israel, then a society of simple farmers, contrasts interestingly with the slower change-over in, for example, Assyria and especially in Egypt.

When we ask, however, whether the copper and iron used in Israel were produced from ore in Israelite territory the answers are at present somewhat equivocal. Copper and iron ores do exist (as Deuteronomy 8, 9 hints) – the former in the Arabah rift valley, especially near Timnah (Wadi Mene'iyeh) north of Elath, and at Feinan (biblical Punon) and south of Petra, on the Edomite side, the latter especially in 'Ajlun (ancient Gilead). Traces of copper-mining and smelting in the Arabah were first observed in the 1930s by Fritz Frank and then by Nelson Glueck. The latter thought operations were initiated by Solomon, and he interpreted a building at Tell el-Kheleifeh as a large smelting plant, a hypothesis now rejected.

More recently, mining and smelting in the region have been systematically investigated over many years by Beno Rothenberg, most recently in collaboration with German and other mining specialists. Copper, it now appears, was mined and smelted near Timnah under Egyptian auspices and by local (Midianite and perhaps Amalekite) labour from the late fourteenth to the mid-twelfth centuries BC. The labourers were housed in camps of simple huts while site supervisors might live in better constructed, isolated buildings. Mining was carried out in galleries and shafts. Ore nodules thus obtained were crushed and concentrated on site, and the crushed ore was transferred to special smelting camps, which might contain store buildings and workshops, to be smelted in simple pits or more complicated furnaces partly sunk into the ground. Charcoal obtained mainly from local acacias was used for fuel; the flux material perhaps included some locally mined iron ore. In addition to the natural wind, artificial draught produced by bellows or blow pipes helped to create the necessary heat for smelting: some clay tuyère nozzles have been found. Metal chisels and occasionally picks were used in the mining and crushing operations, but also many stone implements – mining hammers, anvils, mortars, pestles and so on. (Such stone tools have also been found, for example, at Rio Tinto in southern Spain where the Phoenicians were associated with mining operations during the eighth century BC.) Safety for the installations, probably active only during the cool season, was provided by strategically placed blockhouses.

Even though Israelites must have been in Palestine while these Egyptian-directed operations went on, a more interesting question is whether the short period of operations which took place in the tenth century had anything to do with the Israelites. In 1962, Rothenberg still agreed that mining and smelting took place near Timnah for a short while at the behest of Solomon (though it would not have produced much copper) and the late Professor Yohanan Aharoni had no doubt in classifying the wheelmade pottery found in the supervisors' dwellings as tenth-century Israelite. (The workmen's huts were stocked with crude 'Negeb ware', some apparently made on the spot by itinerant potters.) However, Rothenberg now assumes the late phase was due to the initiative of the 22nd Egyptian dynasty, probably in the wake of Sheshonq's invasion; operations thereafter ceased for centuries. This would mean that there never was any Israelite mining or smelting activity in the Timnah region. There have indeed been some dissenting voices, but on present evidence there is no unequivocal indication of Israelite mining or smelting here.

Elsewhere, the picture is also patchy and often uncertain. Copper smelting from imported (Negeb?) ore took place on a small scale at Tell Masos II in the Negeb fringe during the twelfth and eleventh centuries. In addition, copper seems to have been smelted seasonally to the north of the Dead Sea at Tell Deir

'Alla, apparently by itinerant metalworkers of unknown origin. A number of furnaces have been discovered here but it is more likely that they were used to resmelt copper rather than to smelt it from ore (which would have had to be imported). The situation is similar at Beth Shemesh in the Shephelah, where several furnaces were in use during the period of Philistine occupation and operations continued during the immediately following Israelite period, and perhaps also at Khirbet Raddanah near Ai, where a small smelting installation was found. However, all the installations referred to date from the period before the Divided Monarchy. On present evidence foreign copper imports may have driven copper producers in Israel out of business thereafter. That production ceased because the supply of acacias from which charcoal was made was exhausted seems less likely, since acacia wood was still used by Israelite carpenters for various purposes much later.

The tin needed for the production of bronze certainly had to be imported, since tin is lacking in Palestine. Some may have arrived via Assyria from as yet unidentified sources further east, but tin in bar shape reached Palestinian ports in the Late Bronze Age, as shown by finds in the sea near Haifa, which may have come from Spain via Cyprus. This traffic continued in all likelihood during the Iron Age, especially since Ezekiel (27, 12) mentions tin, together with iron, lead and silver, in a list of goods carried by the Tyrians from Tarshish (probably located in the Guadalquivir region of southern Spain), and since a similar bar from the same marine context has been attributed to the fifth century BC. As for iron, there are at present no clear indications that iron ore was mined and processed in Israelite territory, but it was perhaps mined and smelted at or near Mugharet el-Wardeh near Rajib in 'Ajlun – ancient Gilead – and some iron was smelted at Tulul edh-Dhahab very early in Iron I. Iron produced here may have partly supplied Israelite requirements, but apparently not entirely so, for we hear in particular of imported 'northern' iron of high quality (Jeremiah 15, 12) which probably reached Israel from Anatolia via the metalworking centre of Damascus. The iron from Uzal mentioned in Ezekiel (27, 19) may also have come from North Syrian Izalla rather than from Ṣanʿa in the Yemen. Western iron shipped by the Tyrians from Tarshish was presumably also available.

Both western and northern (Anatolian) supplies must also have been drawn on in the cases of silver and lead, both absent in Palestine. The separation of silver from lead and other metals by refining was familiar to Jerusalemites in particular, to judge by the graphic descriptions in Jeremiah (6, 29–30) and Ezekiel (22, 20–22). Gold also had to be imported to meet the goldsmiths' and other requirements. It may have come in particular from Egypt, Arabia and from the mysterious Ophir (located variously in Arabah or in Africa, India and even Sri Lanka). Gold from Ophir, repeatedly referred to in the Bible, is in fact mentioned in a Hebrew ostracon of the eighth century BC found at the river port site of Tell Qasile just north of Tel Aviv. Imports of Ophir gold were thus apparently not restricted to the time of Solomon.

These different metals were used by a variety of craftsmen. Agricultural and other tools and implements (of common Levantine types) were made or repaired by smiths proficient in dealing both with iron and bronze. Such men were to be found in towns and sometimes even in villages, though they may not always have been resident there. Hoards of tools and weapons of various kinds found, for example, in Taanach and Megiddo may have been in store, awaiting the coming of an itinerant smith, unless they were to be transported to another place for repair, or destined for the scrap merchant. More advanced craftsmen knew how to cast bronze or other ornaments, and even statuettes either in one- or two-piece moulds or perhaps by the 'lost-wax' process. They also knew how to hammer out dishes or jugs from metal sheets, as shown by a tenth-century bronze juglet found at Gezer, and perhaps even how to make a composite statue consisting of metal sheeting over a wooden core (cf. Jeremiah 10, 8–9). The craftsmen concerned with more basic tasks may have included Israelites in their ranks, but more sophisticated items were almost certainly made by non-Israelites, such as Canaanites, Sea Peoples and, later on, Phoenicians. Thus valuable objects, which date from the twelfth and eleventh centuries BC, such as wine-drinking services comprising bowls, strainers and jugs discovered at Beth Shean, Megiddo and Tell es-Sa'idiyeh, are in the Canaanite tradition, though there are links with the Aegean – as in the case of a bronze cauldron from the latter site, or double axes. The central Jordan Valley was then an important bronze-working region, as it was in the time of Solomon. These localities were at that time not in Israelite hands, but a lugged axe in Canaanite style was found at Tell Masos, and another in a hoard at an Israelite 'high place' at Hazor XI.

Phoenician influence became marked later, during the reign of Solomon. In particular, the metal equipment of the Temple in Jerusalem, referred to in 1 Kings 7, was fabricated by Hiram, a craftsman of mixed Tyrian and Israelite descent. Such contacts may have helped to introduce Israelites to higher craftsmanship. The Temple equipment included major castings, such as the two massive bronze columns, Jachin and Boaz, in the Phoenician style (regarded by some as solid, by others as hollow, or alternatively as consisting of a thin metal covering over cores of wood or stone); or the 'Molten Sea'. Items like the trolleys supporting lavers with their figurative décor, the bronze altar and smaller objects were probably mostly in the Levantine tradition, combining local Canaanite with Aegean, Cypriot or Syrian features. Outside Jerusalem, a probably Phoenician metal bowl has been found at Megiddo IV.

After the break-up of the United Monarchy, courts and nobility in the successor states of Israel and Judah presumably commissioned metal luxury goods of various kinds. Here we may refer to metal bowls found, not indeed in Palestine but in Assyria, but which were probably part of booty or tribute taken from Israelite or, more likely, Judean kings, in particular Ahaz or Hezekiah. Some of these bowls are decorated with simple 'marsh patterns', while others show the scarab beetle, probably a royal symbol in the eighth century BC, and a number have Hebrew names written on their sides. In their décor they differ from normal Phoenician bowls in the absence of figurative representations, but whether they were made by Judean craftsmen or by Phoenicians working to local specifications is hard to decide.

Goldsmiths or jewelers producing ornaments such as rings, ear-rings or armlets (pl. 56) by casting or by more complicated methods may again have been partly local, partly foreign. Some personal ornaments, like fibulae, may well have been largely imports, but amulets inscribed with the divine name on a tiny rolled-up sheet of silver, found in a Jerusalem tomb of the early sixth century, were surely made by local craftsmen.

Stone

Stone of various types provided the raw material for a range of objects. Tripod bowls, made mostly from basalt but sometimes of limestone, including some sophisticated ones, served as mortars in which various substances, for instance paints or spices, could be pounded with pestles. Examples of such bowls may even have been exported, to the Aegean in particular. Alabaster vessels inspired by Egyptian imports and intended as containers for aromatic oil seem to have been less frequently manufactured in Palestine in the Iron Age than in the preceding Bronze Age. Round cosmetic palettes intended for face- or eye-paint and made mostly from fine-grained limestone are probably a typical Israelite product. Often elaborately decorated with incised patterns, and sometimes even adorned with small inlays of coloured paste, they are frequently found from the eighth century onwards within Israel, but rarely outside. Such objects were probably turned on a simple lathe, the use of which was also known, it seems, to the carpenter.

Mineral substances

In addition to ores, the land of Israel contained other potentially useful minerals. Salt could be obtained near the Dead Sea, either as rock salt or from salt pans (cf. Zephaniah 2, 9); whether sea salt was also collected at this time is not known. Whatever the source, salt was much in demand, not only as an ingredient in the preparation of food or for ceremonial uses but also for industrial purposes, as probably in tanning. Sulphur from the Dead Sea region was perhaps less important; Dead Sea asphalt, later an important export article, was occasionally used – some has been found at Tell Beit Mirsim – but it was not regularly employed as a binding or waterproofing agent in building, as in Mesopotamia, or in mummification. The encasing of linen-wrapped dead bodies in blocks of asphalt, encountered in a twelfth-century non-Israelite grave at Tell es-Sa'idiyeh, is exceptional. Other industrially useful substances like alum (for tanning) were perhaps imported, but the widely found mountain limestone was burnt into lime in some quantities near Jerusalem. It might have been used for whitewash, but not yet in mortar for building purposes.

Pottery making

As scriptural references show, potters and their craft were both familiar and yet fascinating to the Israelites. We hear only of male professionals; there is no sign that women assisted them, or made pottery themselves in their spare time. Some potters were organized as family groups or guilds, like those referred to in 1 Chronicles 4, 23 who worked for the crown, others may have set up on their own, and yet others may have been itinerant. Their wares were required in simple villages as well as the more affluent towns, satisfying a variety of domestic, industrial and other needs, and overall production must have been considerable. Workshops might be found in, or near, big towns like Jerusalem, but also in small localities in the countryside, as in the case of the potters in the Shephelah referred to in Chronicles. Since this was a partly wooded region with limited agricultural land the Shephelah potters may have belonged to the well-known type of backwoods craftsmen seasonally supplementing an otherwise insufficient livelihood. Overall, ceramic studies show that the number of production centres was large at first and few types of pottery were made, but within these there was little standardization. Later, during Iron Age II, the number of production centres decreased and a wider range of pottery types was produced, within which standardization increased considerably.

Recent studies, including petrographic and neutron analyses, suggest that potteries tended sometimes to serve fairly large areas and their products travelled quite far afield – thus Judean bowls might be retailed in the northern kingdom, while 'bichrome' ware and 'Samaria ware' produced there (if not in Phoenicia) went to the far south of Judah. Diffusion might also result from governmental activity. In particular, store jars with handles provided with royal *la-melekh* stamps (see below), produced in royal Judean potteries in the

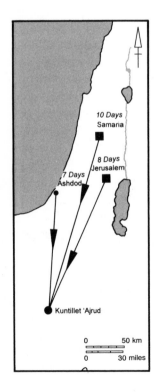

43 The regions of origin of some types of pottery found at Kuntillet 'Ajrud, and the time it would have taken to transport them to the site. Different types of pottery (manufactured in various districts inside Israel or imported from abroad) were widely distributed all over the country.

Shephelah, were distributed all over the southern monarchy, while another type of stamped jar made in Jerusalem reached Lachish. Yet regional production led only to limited regional differentiation; differences in repertoire and style developed rather between the territories of Israel and Judah. The border between the two ceramic territories can indeed be drawn locally with some precision, though some pottery products did cross it. What impeded the sale in one kingdom of ceramics made in the other is not clear. Mutual antipathy may have been to blame or perhaps customs barriers – we do not know.

The materials needed for making pottery were widely available, in particular clays of varying composition and plasticity. When high-quality clay was needed, potters might get it from some distance. Those working in Jerusalem, for example, obtained it from Mozah about 8 km (5 miles) away. For temper, crushed local limestone was preferred in the hill country. This was not ideal, for under prolonged exposure to temperatures above 900°C (1652°F) it disintegrates, and the resulting gas bubbles damage the fabric. Much Israelite pottery is thus not fired to the point where the core is of the same colour as the surface. However, lower firing temperatures meant a smaller fuel consumption, and this in turn would facilitate the establishment of potteries, for a mixture of fuels – lopped-off branches, thorns, grass, olive waste, dung (to go by recent Palestinian practice) – in sufficient quantities was probably widely obtainable. Firing at a modest temperature would also leave vessels porous, which was no disadvantage for water jars or bottles, since evaporation would keep the liquid in them cool, but where impermeability was desirable it might be achieved by a coating of pitch, or by a highly burnished slip. In the latter case, red hematite containing clay was most commonly used, organic substances like milk or oil more rarely. During Iron I burnish was irregularly applied by hand, but from the eighth century BC onwards it was increasingly applied by wheel in regularly spaced ring or spiral fashion. The popularity of burnished surfaces meant in turn that there was less scope for painted decoration, and this was in fact much rarer now than during the Late Bronze Age. Much of what does occur consisted of simple black or red bands, though motifs such as stylized palm trees or ibexes, inherited from Canaanite repertoire, are met occasionally, as are Egyptian-derived lotus flower and bud designs. A rare representation of cattle on a sherd may be inspired by Phoenician zoomorphic friezes or metal bowls. True glazes were not normally used by Israelite potters and the glazed vessels referred to in Proverbs (26, 23) may have been imports.

In the early period the quality of Israelite ceramics tended to be poor, with bad paste and firing; vessels were then mostly made by hand or in a mould, though finished off on a slow wheel. From *c.* 1000 BC onwards improvement is noticeable, and by the eighth century the fast wheel was increasingly used. From then onwards, potters showed a high standard of competence, and their throwing and turning might, indeed, come close to good Greek standards. They were familiar with methods suited for quick mass production, such as the repeated pinching or string cutting of vessels from a high rotating cone of clay, or the thinning down of large bowls thrown with thick walls by turning. The best of their products are not only practical, but also truly beautiful.

Archaeological discoveries allow us to say more about potters' workshops and production methods than biblical texts by themselves afford. In view of the unpleasant smoke they tended to generate – and of the attendant fire risk – potters' kilns and workshops were usually located either on the fringes of settlements, as at Tell en-Naṣbeh, or outside them – at Lachish in a cave, at Megiddo in former cave tombs. Such working areas contained cavities for storing clay or leather-hard vessels, bowls or jars for water, and simple implements of pottery, bone and shell for use in shaping, turning and burnishing. At Lachish and Megiddo the cave floors also had circular depressions with deeper holes in the centre, which might have accommodated potters' wheels pivoted on socket stones placed in the central cavity. The exact shape of these wheels is still in doubt, though. Some ring-shaped basalt disks, found at a number of sites, might have supported wooden tournettes or slow wheels. A somewhat improved version consists of two superimposed stone disks, the upper one rotating on a pivot-like projection on the lower. However, no example of the true fast-wheel in use during Iron IIC has yet been found. It may have consisted of one pivoted disk only. A more advanced type comprising a massive lower wheel driven by the potter's foot and intended to provide momentum, linked by a vertical axle to a smaller upper disk on which the clay is centred, is attested by the Hellenistic period (cf. Ecclesiasticus 38, 29), but whether it existed earlier is not known.

We are somewhat better informed about the installations in which pottery was fired. The primitive method of finishing pottery in bonfires does not seem to have been used. Proper kilns were employed throughout the period, and excavations have uncovered the lower part of a number of these. They were partly dug into the ground, partly free-standing. Early examples consist of two oblong clay-lined chambers, branching off from a common stoke hole, and separated by a wall projecting like a tongue from the rear, in a bilobate plan, resembling a 'U'. Originally there would have been flooring above on which pottery to be fired would have been placed, and temporary vaulted roofing above this. Vases would thus have been fired in an enclosed space by the heat provided by the updraught from the lower storey. A fairly well-preserved kiln found in Cave 37 at Megiddo shows a sophisticated variant of this basic scheme, in which the combustion gases passed from the lateral chambers through vents into rooms linked by a central duct above; from there they would have been carried away by a superstructure now lost. Later kilns were more omega-shaped in plan, but worked on much the same basic principle as the U-shaped ones. Parallels to both are found in the Phoenician world, and ultimately this family of kilns goes back to eastern Mediterranean prototypes of the Late Bronze Age.

The Israelite potter's repertoire was, by Iron II at least, a wide one, ranging from large store jars for corn, oil and wine to tiny perfume bottles and pyxides. Early store jars, usually provided with two handles, are sometimes distinguished by a long 'collared' rim (a variety of which with a short neck

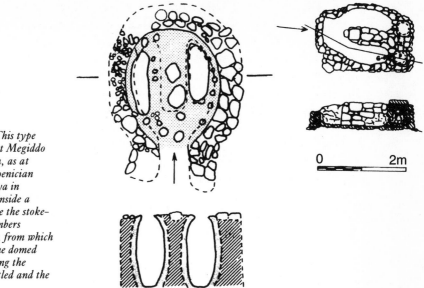

44 Iron Age potter's kilns. This type was found in ancient Israel at Megiddo (right), but also at Phoenicia, as at Sarepta (left) and in the Phoenician colonies overseas (as at Motya in Sicily). The pots were fired inside a temporary dome placed above the stoke-hole and two connecting chambers covered by a perforated floor, from which the hot gases travelled into the domed chamber above. After the firing the temporary dome was dismantled and the finished pots were extracted.

survived into the developed Iron Age). This type has often been found in early Israelite settlements, and was once thought to serve as proof of Israelite character, but it is also known elsewhere. Ovoid jar shapes, sometimes wider below the middle of the body and with a pronounced shoulder, were popular between *c.* 1000 and 800 BC, especially in the north; the eighth to sixth centuries BC witnessed the development of long 'sausage' or 'torpedo' shaped jars with low rims, as well as the popularity of holemouth jars, in Judah in particular.

One particular store jar, with ovoid body and four-ridged handles, found in the southern kingdom during the late eighth century, was sometimes impressed on the handles with government stamp seals, figuring either a four-winged scarab beetle (perhaps a royal symbol) or a 'flying scroll' (possibly a simplified form of another official emblem, the winged sun disk). Above the design the letters *lmlk* (i.e. *la-melekh* – 'belonging to the king') were written, below it the names of four towns – Hebron, Ziph, Sochoh and an as yet uncertain *Mmšt* (pls 45–49). The date and purpose of the jars bearing these stamps has been much debated (see p. 200). Recent excavations at Lachish and Tell Batash have shown they were in use at both during the reign of King Hezekiah. Since neutron activation analysis has now shown that the jars were all produced in the Shephelah, the names of the towns on them cannot indicate the locations of royal potteries. The varying capacity of the vessels seems to preclude their use as standard measures for public reference, or for delivery of taxes in kind. Most probably they were intended for the storing of provisions in royal army depots or taxation centres from where the administration perhaps would have conveyed them to military strongholds in border regions most likely to be attacked. The four towns mentioned on the stamps may then have been the centres of royal estates from where the stores were drawn. Though the scarab beetle design is found mostly in western Judean cities and the 'flying scroll' more in the north they seem to have been freely exchanged between various localities within the kingdom. To what extent they remained in use after Hezekiah is uncertain; jars stamped on the handles with concentric circles may be later parallels, possibly dating from the reign of Josiah.

Craters, or large mixing bowls, were another type thought diagnostic of early Israelite settlement and early on included, in addition to Late Bronze survivals, a shape with multiple handles and frequently rope or incised décor. They occur in early Israelite sites, but also elsewhere. Cooking pots, certain shapes of which are likewise often regarded as indicative of early Israelite settlement, tend at first to come in shallow basin shapes without handles, and with turned-out rims triangular in section. These were replaced by more oblong and sometimes ridged rims which have been regarded by some as Israelite 'type fossils', though they are again found also in definitely Canaanite milieux. Handles became popular on cooking pots from the tenth century BC onwards, and after c. 800 BC high-ridged rims were fashionable in the north, while squat two-handled cookers with a high and sometimes ridged neck became a specially Judean variety. Bowls, at first poorly made and sometimes decorated with horizontal bands of paint in the north, but with Canaanite-derived motifs such as the simplified palm tree in the south, attained a much better standard of craftsmanship after 1000 BC, being then made of well-mixed, smooth clay, and well finished and fired. There was a large repertoire of shapes – straight-sided, rounded and carinated types all varied in popularity during the period.

From c. 1000 BC onwards, red slip – at first plain, then burnished by hand and increasingly by wheel – also became fashionable on bowls, and bar handles, imitating metal prototypes, were popular, though by Iron IIC they had been reduced to vestigial ornamental ledges which sometimes surrounded the whole vase. Deep bowls with fine spiral wheel burnish were then common in Judah; some may have been exported from there to the northern kingdom. The best of these were handsome, but they could not rival the 'Samaria ware' found from the tenth to the sixth century in northern Israel and in neighbouring Phoenicia. This came in two variants, one eggshell thin with a red core, the other thicker and made from creamy clay; both are covered with brilliantly polished slip. Shallow bowls decorated inside with concentric zones of yellow and red slip are typical of the thin ware; the thicker ware, likewise mostly used for bowls, is given two shapes with increasingly high ring or stepped bases, covered inside and out with red, yellow, or black burnished slip. Samaria ware was probably produced in the hill country of Samaria, as well as in Phoenicia, but no kiln sites have yet been found in the northern kingdom.

Chalices with a high trumpet-shaped foot, on the other hand, were popular throughout Israel during Iron I and II, though again they may be found also in non-Israelite sites. Southern shapes were distinguished by a stepped base, and they might be elaborately painted. Other shapes are goblets, jugs and dipper vessels used to ladle liquids out of jars. Small perfume juglets, mostly black-slipped and burnished, are a typical Israelite shape after *c.* 1000 BC; at first long-necked, they became short-necked and tiny after *c.* 800 BC. Decanters, derived from metal shapes and intended to contain liquids, were sometimes beautifully finished. They were a typical Iron IIC shape in both north and south, though showing some differences between the two regions, especially in the preference for a grooved rim in the northern kingdom. Another common shape intended to contain liquids, the 'pilgrim bottle' or travelling flask was descended from Canaanite prototypes – late variants include a large asymmetrical shape with one flat and one convex side. Pyxides, ultimately of Mycenaean derivation, underwent a steady deterioration and decrease in size. Finally, saucer lamps, usually with one spout (a seven-spouted variant is rare) and with increasingly wide turned-over rims, developed during Iron IIC into a specially Judean form with a high solid foot. In addition to this considerable variety of ceramics, the Israelite potter could meet more specialized requirements of varied kinds, ranging from footbaths to crucibles, clay rattles, toy animals or furniture models, as well as figurines or plaques of deities.

The Israelite potter did not, however, rule his market undisputed. Excavations have shown that ceramics entered the country from a surprising number of directions at various times. In the thirteenth and twelfth centuries BC, Midianite painted pottery spread from northern Arabia not only to the mining region in the Arabah but to the Negeb fringe and the adjoining southern coastal plain (see fig. 46). Crude handmade 'Negeb ware', which it is sometimes found in association with, continued to be produced in the zone fringing Judah on the south for several centuries thereafter, perhaps the work of Amalekite or other non-Israelite potters. Later, during Iron II, Moabite and Edomite pottery is found in much the same general neighbourhood, and spread as far northwest as Timnah (Tell Batash) in the central coastal plain. These eastern imports may have arrived via trade routes along with other goods travelling towards the Mediterranean. In the opposite direction Philistine pottery, incorporating both local Canaanite traditions and imported Aegean traits, spread from the southern coastal plain – the location of the Philistine 'cities' – into the hill country, either in the wake of Philistine military expansion or through commerce. Ceramics of a similar style, found at Tel Deir 'Alla in the Jordan Valley and at Beth Shean in the Esdraelon, may be the work of kindred groups such as the Tjeker who settled near Dor in the northern coastal zone; whether it was trade or folk movements that carried them there is uncertain. A number of fabrics reached the country from the north and northwest. Bichrome jugs and bowls from Phoenicia as well as northern Israel spread south into Judah during Iron I and Iron II, decreasing in Iron IIB. An early example has turned up as far south as Tell Masos. Cypro-Phoenician Black on Red I (III) and II (IV) vases, especially small perfume bottles with a ridged neck, are found from *c.* 1000 BC onwards in many localities in both the northern and southern kingdoms; other Cypriot wares such as White Painted I are found more occasionally. Phoenician pottery, either red-slipped and burnished or painted, including in particular jars with trefoil mouths or jugs with mushroom lips, occur in both Israel and Judah during Iron II A–B–C, on sites as far apart as Hazor and Lachish. Greek imports, on the other hand, are sparse. There are a few Middle Geometric vase fragments at Megiddo VA–IVB and Samaria III, possibly dating from the mid-ninth and eighth centuries. Among the few earlier pieces there is one which may even go back to *c.* 1100 BC. A somewhat larger number of seventh-century products, especially East Greek ceramics, were found in particular at Meṣad Ḥashavyahu in the coastal plain and may be linked with the presence of Greek mercenaries and traders there, though there is no sign that Greek traders or others who might have brought Greek pottery entered Israel in any significant numbers. Greek pottery imports became substantial only during the Persian period.

These various kinds of foreign pottery are connected mainly with peaceful trade. Another type of foreign pottery, Assyrian and Babylonian, is linked with the advance of the Assyrian empire from the late eighth century onwards. It is found mainly in seventh-century contexts, largely in northern Israel as well as the neighbouring countries to the east and west. Luxury vases ('palace ware') figure conspicuously and local potters not unnaturally imitated such desirable goods.

Faience, frit and glass

While pottery was on the whole utilitarian, vessels made from glazed faience or unglazed frit were luxury goods. They had long been produced in the Levant, together with smaller objects such as amulets, scarabs and beads in which Egypt and Phoenicia specialized, and they continued to be imported into Palestine during the Iron Age. A small amount of faience may have been made in Israel. Megiddo has furnished a number of faience or frit vessels, some plain, some involving animal representations, such as duck vases or a lion holding a pot between his forepaws, all inspired by Egyptian models. The late Professor Carl Watzinger ascribed them to a local workshop active from the eleventh up to the eighth century and continuing Late Bronze Age traditions. More recently, however, they have been classified as Phoenician. Little if any glass was produced in the country. A few items, like a cosmetic palette made of glass found in Megiddo, and pins with glass heads found there were executed to local orders, but in general glass seems to have been imported. Megiddo has also furnished a seventh-century cosmetic palette made from faience; other palettes found up and down the country, made from stone in the normal manner, show possible traces of faience or frit inlays. They may well have been produced in the country, for a Phoenician derivation seems unlikely, since cosmetic palettes were not in vogue in the Phoenician world. Yet even if this is accepted, faience and frit production in Israel must have been very small.

Woodworking

One of the basic requirements for civilized life was wood, building timber included. The forest and woodlands in the country provided a variety of suitable trees, such as pines, oaks, sycamores and acacias. Olive wood was preferred for some purposes, and more valuable wood like cedar or boxwood might be imported, especially from the north. Isaiah (44, 14) hints that timber might be raised in plantations as a private venture; it would appear that the Crown likewise provided for its own needs. There is a reference to an official at the court of David in charge of the sycamores in the Shephelah in 1 Chronicles (27, 28). Villages and towns probably did not allow uncontrolled exploitation of woodland, which was after all a valuable communal asset. Workers in wood are mentioned repeatedly in the Bible, and textual references as well as actual finds are instructive about their tool-kits. Axes and adzes, saws (some still of flint) for cutting planks, planers, borers, chisels and knives are all of Near Eastern, and more particularly Levantine types. It seems there were also simple lathes for turning wood. For design and control there were marking-out tools or stylos, measuring strings and callipers. Jointing would be done with nails, especially of copper, probably also by dovetailing.

The carpenter was employed in building projects for making doors, gates and windows with their frames, cross-staves, balustrades and grilles; he might make columns, panelling, ceiling and roof beams and indeed much of the upper storeys. Objects of daily use like bowls or boxes, and furniture such as beds or couches, chairs, footstools and tables were also produced by the carpenter. Pottery models found at Lachish, Tel Masos and Tell en-Naṣbeh show them to have been sturdily made and serviceable, but the chair, perhaps the governor's, shown being carried off as booty by Assyrian soldiers on one of the Lachish reliefs presumably belonged to the class of luxury furniture. In the making of luxury items the carpenter would collaborate with ivory-carvers producing inlays, or goldsmiths producing gold leaf covering. Artisans engaged on such tasks would probably include a high percentage of non-Israelites, Phoenicians in particular, and no doubt they followed foreign models. Significantly some fragments of ornate woodwork found in recent excavations in Jerusalem, made from imported boxwood, were carved with Phoenician-type palmetto ornaments. Idols consisting of a wooden core overlaid by metal also required similar co-operation (cf. Isaiah 44, 10; 13–17; Jeremiah 10, 3–4). It is likely that some of the woodwork would also have been stained or painted. However, compared with the Middle Bronze Age woodwork that has survived at Jericho we are still poorly off for actual specimens from the Israelite period.

Industries dependent on farming

Agriculture and stock rearing produced a number of commodities which, properly processed, were of potential market interest. Grain was one of these, but there is no sign that flour milling ever became an 'industry'. Wine seems to have been produced individually by vineyard proprietors. Some writings on clay bottles, like the *smdr* (*semadar*) attested at Hazor, or the *ḵḥl* brand from the Hebron region (the letters may indicate either 'bluish' wine, or the name of the locality where it was produced), hint that some local brands were marketable.

However, the interpretation of rock-cut beehive shaped pits near Gibeon as cool deposit rooms for wine jars in a large 'winery', as well as the reading of graffiti on wine jar sherds found there as indicating the particular enclosed vineyards from where the grapes had come, have not escaped criticism. On the other hand, olive-crushing plants with a number of presses may have served for market production rather than home or estate consumption. Perfume-producing plants, like the one discovered at En Gedi, quite possibly had a similar function. Animal husbandry, in addition to offering meat supplies to the big towns (on the hoof – there is no sign meat was sold dried or salted), also provided raw materials for leather manufacture and textiles.

Tanning and leather working

Leather was employed for a wide range of objects, from tent covers to bags, wineskins and bottles, belts, armour and shoes. The Bible, however, while mentioning these does not refer either to tanners or to leather-workers, or to their activities. Furthermore, no tanneries from the Israelite period are known and very little leather has survived. Some guesses as to the methods used can nevertheless be ventured by comparison with contemporary practice in the neighbouring countries, combined with the evidence offered by the finds of leather from the Dead Sea caves and Masada from the Roman period. Skins of cattle, sheep, goats and sometimes gazelles – *tahash* (dolphin?) skins were a rare luxury import – would be separated from the flesh and de-haired. Minerals like alum and salt, or organic agents such as oak galls, pomegranate skins, tree bark and flour would have been employed in tanning them. They would then have been dried, stretched and preened with milk or fat. Whether the men following this malodorous and probably despised trade were locals or foreigners we cannot tell; their products, while satisfying the needs of the home market, do not seem to have enjoyed international standing. Leather-workers seem to have been active in a number of localities, as finds of leather-cutting knives of a special shape indicate.

Spinning and weaving

We are better informed about the production of textiles. Biblical texts are supplemented by archaeological finds, including a number of fragments of fabrics or their imprints. Egyptian tomb pictures also offer valuable comparative data. Nevertheless much detail, particularly concerning the actual looms used, still remains unknown.

The wool shorn from the numerous sheep in the country, probably by means of a knife – whether clippers were in use remains doubtful – was the main raw material used for textiles in ancient Israel. Wool plucked in the older way may still have been used for making felt, about which details are lacking. Goats' hair was employed mainly for coarser fabrics for use as tent covers or sacking. Home-grown flax was available only in limited quantities, and much of the highly prized flax, linen thread or actual linen must have been imported, especially from Egypt, though 1 Chronicles (4, 21) mentions weavers of fine linen in

Judah. Cotton was becoming known in Mesopotamia by the eighth century, but it was still a rarity – Sennacherib specially mentions 'trees bearing wool' in his garden – and one may doubt it was used to any significant extent in Israel before the Exile.

Spinning was mainly an occupation for women – it was dishonouring for a man to engage in it (cf. 2 Samuel 3, 29) but brought credit to a housewife (cf. Proverbs 31, 19). A distaff with one or more spindle whorls made from pottery, bone, ivory, stone or even glass, assuring even rotation of the spindle, was employed. The variety in the material, shapes and weights of the whorls may hint at the production of various thicknesses and qualities of thread. Specially strong and thin twisted thread made up from more than one strand could be produced in 'spinning bowls'. These were provided on the inside with two or three loops to prevent the threads tangling and to keep them tense. Such twisted thread might also combine several colours. The quality of both plain and twisted thread was good, to judge by the finds of textiles made from simple yarn, and of twisted sewing thread, all of mid–ninth century date, at Kuntillet 'Ajrud in the Negeb. Much woollen and, in particular, linen cloth was probably left plain, but for the making of coloured cloth, a number of vegetable- and animal-derived dyes were available, though the valuable purple dye was probably a Phoenician speciality. It seems to have been the unwoven thread, rather than the finished cloth, that was dyed. Dyeing took place in round stone vats some 70 cm (27½ in) wide and of similar depth, either excavated into the rock or more commonly taking the form of solid stone drums placed on the floors of buildings. The vats contained a central cavity accessible from a narrower opening at the top; the balls of thread to be dyed would be immersed in the liquid dye in the cavity, any overflow being caught by a groove surrounding the opening and returned to the cavity by a hole drilled from the groove. Some such installations may have functioned as part of oil presses, but this interpretation is unlikely to fit all cases, especially where such drums have turned up in or near weaving establishments like the structure H.15:1003 at Lachish; dual use at varying seasons is a possibility. With the dyes available, linen could only be dyed blue, while wool would take red (and other) colours. Cloth containing both blue and red threads could thus most easily be made from linen and wool combined. The use of such fabrics was expressly forbidden to Israelites (Leviticus 19, 19; Deuteronomy 22, 11) though the rich apparel of the high priests may have included them. Some specimens of variegated cloth made from blue linen and red wool threads have been found at Kuntillet 'Ajrud.

Weaving was undertaken by both men and women. Housewives might weave linen for sale (Proverbs 31, 24); male professionals included specialists in the production of fine linen (1 Chronicles 4, 21). Two types of loom were in use, one horizontal, the other vertical. The horizontal loom, mentioned in the story of Samson and Delilah (Judges 16, 13–14) was probably basically analogous to the loom still used by bedouin women now. The vertical loom consisted of two wooden uprights supporting a horizontal beam from which were suspended the warp threads, groups of which would be held taut by a clay loom weight. Many

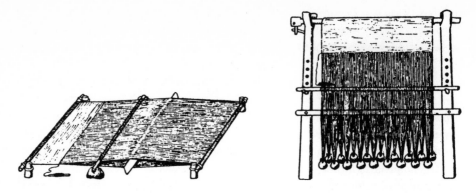

45 *Two types of ancient Palestinian looms still familiar to Palestinian farmers and Bedouin. In the upright loom* (right) *which might be fixed up between two stone pillars in Israelite houses, the warp threads were suspended from a horizontal beam, and kept taut by loom-weights. The horizontal loom* (left) *may have been of the type used by Delilah to entangle her husband's locks of hair (Judges 16, 13–14).*

of these have come to light in various Israelite sites, and also some pieces of upright posts which may have formed part of vertical looms, attesting that weaving was practised widely. For pattern weaving, bone rods, also found in a number of localities, were perhaps employed as 'pattern sticks', used to pick up threads and hold them apart while intricate designs were executed.

Fulling would have been the final stage in the preparation of the cloth. According to biblical references, it appears to have been carried on outside the settlements, but no actual remains of the installations concerned have been discovered so far.

Finds of textile fragments (or imprints on pottery and so on) at Kuntillet 'Ajrud and elsewhere now permit us to discover something about the technical characteristics and quality of products of this industry. (Though a Phoenician origin cannot be entirely ruled out, the textiles found at Kuntillet 'Ajrud in particular are more likely to have been made by Israelites.) In linen cloth, the number of warp and weft threads per square centimetre tended to be similar – a Palestinian peculiarity of long standing – but woollen fabrics show a much higher weft than warp count – again a style which was, and remained, traditional in the country. Stitched hemming has been found on linen fragments, and knotted, sometimes double-knotted, fringes on woollen cloth. The seams of hemming were neatly made, and where patches were joined by sewing this was done very skilfully with a fine needle, stitches being so close set that the work resembles 'invisible mending'. In textiles, as in other branches of industry, high quality was thus achieved in ancient Israel, though lack of archaeological finds has long hampered knowledge of this. We still have no examples of embroidery, or any of cloth containing threads of gold, mentioned for example in Psalm 45, 13, or purple, and must hope for future finds to inform us about such luxuries.

Bone and ivory

In a farming country, bone from cattle, sheep and particularly goats was a widely available and cheap material. It was used from the earliest times to make a wide range of objects, from needles to arrowheads and even bone flutes, but was specially popular during the period of the Monarchy (Iron Age II). Bone spatulae, often made from ribs, pointed at one end and rounded at the other, are frequent finds in settlements. Among their many possible uses they served particularly as tools in pattern weaving – probably a popular cottage industry. Ornaments, such as beads, might also be made from bone; among these a variety shaped like small clubs and often decorated with straight lines or circles around a central dot, were popular especially during Iron Age I. One possible explanation is that they were used in divination. Bone was also used as a cheap substitute for ivory – for furniture inlays and fittings, luxuries like toilet spoons, or small containers (pyxides). Such objects were often decorated with incision or carved in relief. The best items were probably of foreign – Phoenician or Syrian – origin; in cases where technical competence is not achieved to the same degree, it may be evidence of Israelite attempts.

Ivory was an expensive luxury, imported in the raw, or already carved, from Syria – where herds of elephants survived until they were hunted to extinction – Africa and just possibly India. Hippopotamus ivory may also have been obtained from animals still surviving in Iron Age II within the Palestinian coastal plain area and perhaps the upper Jordan Valley. Considering its expensive nature, it was surprisingly widely used, though mostly for small items like disks for furniture inlays, handles and similar. More sophisticated, and, no doubt, more expensive items were ivory fittings for furniture, sometimes carved in the round, or wall panelling in the form of flat plaques carved in relief, openwork, or cloisonné work with coloured paste or glass, or gold leaf inlays. As with bone work, the best was no doubt produced by Phoenician or Syrian craftsmen working from a widely appreciated repertoire. Some more clumsily executed items were possibly produced by Israelites. The extravagant furniture which adorned the palaces of royalty or the nobility, like the ivory couches of which Amos disapproved so strongly (Amos 6, 4), or the ivory which Hezekiah had to deliver as tribute to Sennacherib, have yet to be discovered, though fragments hint at their splendour. They may well have rivalled the magnificence attested from Nimrud in Mesopotamia or Salamis in contemporary Cyprus.

The question of productivity

There are no ancient statistics or other texts permitting an estimate of Israel's industrial output. While actual figures are unobtainable it is possible, nevertheless, to venture some guesses as to the magnitude – thousands, ten thousands or hundred thousands – of units in question. The likely requirements of the population and the size of output feasible using contemporary methods, are factors which may guide us, and it is clear from the outset that the kind of production figures made possible by the Industrial Revolution are not to be expected.

We may begin with iron and steel production. Local output would probably largely have covered ordinary demand – high-quality 'northern iron' would not have been needed much by the masses and the annual needs of ordinary family units would have been very limited. Consumables would have included nails, arrowheads and similar, while items like knives and agricultural implements such as plough tips and hoes would not have been replaced annually, though some would need repairs requiring some metal. About 3–4 kg (7–9 lb) per family would probably have covered annual needs over a period, a figure which had indeed been arrived at on other grounds as appropriate for an estate in early Greece. With about 100,000 family units, 300–400 tons of iron would have covered the annual needs of Israel's population. Industry would have found it a hard task to supply this quantity, since the output achieved in an iron production operation was measured in single kilograms. However, we have yet to add to this the requirements of the state and in particular of the army, which were no doubt substantial, especially before impending major wars. The weight of metal needed for a single fully equipped warrior seems quite surprising. A helmet might need as much as 3 kg (7 lb) of iron, scale armour 18.6–26.6 kg (41–58 lb) and an iron sword c. 0.3–1 kg (0.6–2.2 lb), thus arriving at a total weight per warrior of perhaps c. 25–30 kg (55–66 lb) – up to 3 tons for 100 men. This is to say nothing of armour for horses and chariots, or arrow, javelin and lance heads needed in large amounts. The quantities of iron drawn by the Assyrians from subject nations as tribute – mostly 3–9 tons – would thus represent quite reasonable stocks held by small or medium-sized states against military emergencies.

It is, on the other hand, difficult to quantify bronze production. Bronze vessels and ornaments were no doubt used by those who could afford them but we cannot say just how frequent they were in ordinary or upper-class households. The state and especially the army used bronze in quantity but more specific clues are lacking. Much high-quality bronze would not anyhow have been produced by Israelites, as we noted. It is even less possible to quantify the amounts of silver and gold worked in the country.

We are on somewhat firmer ground with other industries, pottery production being one. We may start with the estimate that in eighth-century Jerusalem five vessels were perhaps broken annually per household.

This figure seems high, and less affluent people outside the capital may have been more careful. Country-wide, a lower average – say three – may be nearer the mark. With c. 100,000 families in Israel this would mean a replacement market of c. 300,000 items, most of which would not be imports. An ancient Israelite kiln could fire over 200 large jars at a time; a mixed fill of large, medium and small vessels would comprise many more – over a thousand, perhaps (a somewhat larger modern Lebanese kiln can take c. 1500 items at a firing). With kiln fills of over 1000 items, about 300 firings would therefore suffice to produce 300,000 items. If we assume 15 firings per kiln annually (some would have been worked seasonally only) then around 20 kilns could have supplied home consumption. There may have been some production of large jars for shipping Israelite oil, and perhaps wine, but this cannot be quantified. We must in any case again add production to meet the requirements of the state, especially store jars to accommodate taxes in kind and military supplies held in store cities and fortresses. Yet even if we double or triple the number of kilns in Israel and assume less intensive working, the number of pottery-producing centres in the country would remain small. Megiddo alone may have had a dozen or so kilns, a substantial percentage of the total required.

It is harder to reach conclusions about woodwork and carpentry. Its products were long lasting, woodworking for building and carpentry included, and this must have restricted market demand and production, except at times of population expansion and prosperity. As for stone, we know that certain types of stonework, like mortars or cosmetic palettes, were popular, but we do not know how long they stayed in use or how many women owned them, or perhaps passed them on.

Olive oil was one of the staple foods in Israel, and we know also that some of it was exported, for example to Egypt. To estimate the amount produced, it again seems best to start with the likely demand for home consumption. Here we are confronted with a number of varying estimates of consumption per person in ancient and modern times. Among these, M. Heltzer's figures, based on a study of records from ancient Ugarit, seem specially relevant. Oil assigned to various personages there averaged 2.3 jars, each holding 22 litres (4.8 gallons), per year, that is 51 litres (11 gallons) per year. The oil was presumably intended also for a man's family: dividing the total by a notional five, we arrive at a ration of c. 10 litres (2.2 gallons) yearly, or 27 cu. cm (1.6 cu. in) per day, per person. For 460,000 people in Israel, c. 4,600,000 litres (1,012,000 gallons) of oil would be needed on this estimation. To this should be added exported oil. We do not know what percentage of home consumption it amounted to but it must have been substantial in order have merited reference to it. Total Israelite production must thus have been substantial, even though it was not concentrated in a few major production centres as it was in Philistia in the seventh century BC.

Wine production in the country must also have been considerable. As in the case of oil, though, the daily consumption of the average Israelite was presumably modest – well below a litre per day. The total consumed by the nation may not have been very different from that of oil. Much oil and wine will have been required by the state – to what extent it also produced and perhaps sold them we cannot estimate.

In a simple society an accepted figure for the amount of wool fibre a person required annually for clothing is 1.5–3 kg (3.3–6.7 lb) which, for a population of c. 460,000 equals 690,000–1,380,000 kg (1,521,450–3,042,900 lb). We are also told that a caprovine produced c. 0.5–1 kg (1.1–2.2 lb) of cloth-grade fibre per year. This means that somewhere between 690,000 and 1,380,000 sheep or goats – mainly the former – would be needed to clothe the population. But how many such animals could there have been in the country? In the early Iron Age village of 'Izbet Ṣarṭah there were an estimated 6–7 caprovines per family. This would work out at between 600,000 and 700,000 for all Israel, which would just supply the basic clothing needs to be met, but leave no surplus for possible export. Of course, flocks held by large landowners and the crown might well have augmented the total considerably, but it is perhaps relevant that the Israelites demanded from King Mesha of Moab a very substantial tribute of wool-bearing lambs and sheep (2 Kings 3, 4). Home production, it seems, was sometimes not sufficient to cover needs. Figures based on an early British Mandatory census of western Palestine confirm the impression: in 1925 there were 290,503 sheep and 537,904 goats there, to which we may add half these figures again for the estimated ancient Israelite territory in Transjordan – some 1,200,000 in all. This would again cover only basic needs, and leave little room for exports.

There must have been plentiful raw materials for leather production of various kinds, and no doubt varied requirements, but it seems impossible to quantify supply or demand satisfactorily. We cannot be sure, for one thing, whether all available animal skins were tanned.

All told, such figures, admittedly hypothetical, are interesting. A feature worth noting is the important part which the state played in the economy. The Temple in Jerusalem was not of the same economic importance, even though it attracted considerable quantities of animals and of commodities like oil, salt, flour and spices for use in the sacrificial system. There is no indication, though, it was involved in production, as some other ancient Near Eastern temples were.

CHAPTER EIGHT

Trade and the Economic System

Quite early on in the period of the Judges, in the twelfth century BC perhaps, the stoppage through general insecurity of caravan trade along the high roads was, as the Song of Deborah (Judges 5, 6) indicates, regarded as an intolerable evil from which Israel had to be delivered. Trade was obviously important for the Israelites even then, and during the period of the United and Divided Monarchy it must have become crucial. The economy could not function without the distribution of commodities available or produced within the country, such as salt, grain, millstones or pottery and was, moreover, dependent on basic raw materials like iron, copper, tin, lead, alum, natron or antimony coming from outside. In addition, the lifestyle of the upper classes relied on imports of luxury goods of the most varied kinds – metal vessels, textiles, glass, faience or frit, unguents and perfumes, incense, spices, ivory, choice timber and, of course, gold and silver – obtained from neighbouring countries or even further away. Certain of the ritual and ceremonial needs of the priesthood and monarchy could only be met by imports. The gold and precious stones used in the high priestly apparel and breastplate (Exodus 28) and no doubt in royal robes, the sacrificial incense and the fragrant substances mixed with it (Exodus 30, 34), the holy anointing oil blended with myrrh, cinnamon, aromatic cane and cassia (Exodus 30, 22ff.) or the myrrh and aloes giving fragrance to royal robes (Psalm 45, 8) could none of them have been prepared without imports from Africa, Arabia, India, Sri Lanka or from even more distant lands. Internal, Levantine regional, and international long-distance trade were thus all necessary to maintain the Israelite fabric of life. How they operated is the next question we shall turn to, examining the limited textual and archaeological evidence available.

Israelite exports

These varied imports were sometimes obtained for cash, as in the deals undertaken by Solomon's merchants (1 Kings, 10), but in other cases barter deals might also be arranged. Thus we are told that in return for Lebanon cedar and fir trees, Solomon gave King Hiram of Tyre large quantities of wheat and oil (1 Kings 5, 8–11), to which the parallel account in 2 Chronicles (2, 10) adds barley and wine. Agricultural products were in fact the main commodities Israel could offer for export, on whatever terms, then and later. Ezekiel (27, 17) lists wheat, oil, possibly rice, honey, oil and balm as objects of Tyrian trade with the northern kingdom and Judah; oil was also exported to Egypt according to Hosea (12, 1). The territory of Manasseh in northern Israel in particular produced large supplies of this valuable commodity. In addition, Ezekiel (27, 6) mentions the oaks from Bashan (which was sometimes under Israelite control) as being sought by Tyrian shipbuilders for making oars. Presumably the pistachio nuts and almonds mentioned in the story of Joseph as choice products of the land (Genesis 43, 11) were esteemed in our period (the gum tragacanth and myrrh also referred to were probably imports from the east). Livestock notably does not feature in any of these lists (Ezekiel tells us the sheep and goats of Kedar and Arabia were preferred by the Tyrians (27, 21)). Nor does wine feature after Solomon – in discriminating markets, the competition of the internationally famous vintages from Helbon in Syria and of the Lebanese vineyards could not be matched. However, it seems that wine produced in Israel did find customers in Egypt, which was not a wine-producing country and would take cheaper brands. Evidence of this is offered by finds of Israelite and Judean amphorae of the eighth and seventh centuries BC in the sea near the coast of Israel. Some of these had been made impermeable by a lining of pitch, a common practice among ancient wine-shippers, and the wine is likely to have been intended for Egypt. Other amphorae may have contained oil, while grain was probably shipped either in the hold or in sacks. Grain from Israel or Judah, perhaps re-exported from Philistia or Phoenicia, appears to have been sold as far away as Assyria. A seventh-century BC clay tablet found in Nineveh mentions grain measured by the Judean *sutu* measure; the merchants concerned may have been Philistines. The most likely explanation is that the consignment concerned originated in Judah and was certified there in the local standard. During the seventh century BC in particular, Philistine cities seem to have processed Israelite raw materials and marketed the products internationally. The oil production at Ekron is an outstanding example.

Israelite industrial goods, on the other hand, feature little among exports. Most textiles produced in Israel do not seem to have appealed to foreign customers, though the sheets and sashes produced by housewives found foreign buyers (Proverbs 31, 24). Israelite pottery is only occasionally met in foreign countries. Certain store jars produced in Galilee and useful as shipping containers may have found a market in Tyre, while stone tripod vessels and similar were a minor export. Israel did feature, however, on occasion at least, as a possible supplier of slaves for foreign buyers, especially after catastrophes like war or famine. Tyre in particular had an interest in this nefarious trade (cf. Amos 1, 9).

The infrastructure of trade

Such trafficking, involving both fragile and bulky goods, required first of all an efficient system of internal and external communications. To some considerable extent this seems to have survived from the preceding Bronze Age. Some roads could even take wheeled traffic during the period of the Judges and soon after, when the cart carrying the Ark could travel by stages from the Philistine plain to Jerusalem, if with some local difficulties (cf. 1 Samuel 6; 7, 1–3; 2 Samuel 6, 1–16). Moreover, the chaotic conditions during the late thirteenth and early twelfth centuries BC did not permanently put out of commission the important international trunk roads which crossed Israelite territory. The first of these, the 'Way of the Sea', went from Egypt along the coast and through the Esdraelon valley, and so across the Jordan, on to Damascus and finally Mesopotamia, and the second, the 'King's Highway' in Transjordan, linked up with the great caravan road along which incense and spices were conveyed from Arabia, and crossed Israelite territory north of the Arnon on its way to Damascus (an important branch route going westwards across the Negeb to the port city of Gaza). We must not forget, either, that inland Israel was well connected by a number of tracks to Mediterranean harbour towns with international commerce (see pp. 43–6).

With the coming of the monarchy, the maintenance and improvement of the road system was likely to be of interest to the crown. Solomon is credited by Josephus (*Antiquities* VIII, 187) with having paved roads near Jerusalem with black stone, an assertion not so far substantiated. No road building by later kings is reported in the Bible, but they are hardly likely to have been less active in that direction than King Mesha of Moab who, according to his Inscription, made a high road by the Arnon (*ANET*, 230), and made-up and unmade roads are mentioned repeatedly in the Old Testament, for instance in Isaiah (35, 2) and Jeremiah (18, 15).

Archaeology has up till now supplied only limited information about the manner in which highways were engineered, but we do have some examples of roads constructed in different types of terrain. In the Beth Lidd region of Samaria secondary as well as local rural roads are built on natural rock foundations and are bordered near villages by stone fences; locally, there are signs of rough paving or quarrying. Unfortunately these roads, which were constructed apparently during Iron II, remained in use into the Roman period, and so may have received their present shape then. In rocky terrain in the south of the country, road cuttings and steps on tricky slopes were also provided, as well as the bordering stone walls. Both archaeological findings and biblical texts like Judges (19, 10–12) show that main roads often bypassed settled places. Though travellers could turn off to seek lodgings in the nearest village or town, as Judges shows, places where traders could stay, analogous to later caravanserais, were desirable, and a seventh-century building near the road from Jericho to Michmash may have served such a purpose. Rectangular in shape it comprised a large courtyard surrounded by rooms, with mangers for animals. In the Negeb somewhat earlier, Kuntillet 'Ajrud may have similarly sheltered wayfarers along the trade route from the Mediterranean to Elath. In the north, the existence of an Iron II caravanserai close to the medieval one at Khan et-Tujjar near Mount Tabor has been suggested. Wells or cisterns near roads were also provided for travellers; we hear too in the Bible (Jeremiah 31, 21) of road markers and perhaps cairns, to assist in lonely and difficult country. There may also have been customs post buildings – Tell el-Kheleifeh has been interpreted as such.

For the conveyance of goods, pack animals were probably more commonly used than carts. In long-distance trade, for instance to Syria and Mesopotamia, and especially on the roads to Arabia and Egypt which went through arid country, strings of baggage camels would no doubt have been used. The region around Lachish probably provided a ready supply of these beasts, as it did in more recent times. For small loads, on the other hand, human porterage would have sufficed. Wayfarers would have been travelling for many different reasons, ranging from itinerant cooking pot sellers, offering their wares by the roadside or at markets, to messengers and letter-carriers.

Israel was also linked with sea-borne trade and controlled a number of harbours on the Mediterranean coast south of Mount Carmel, including for a time the important port city of Dor, which even in the Bronze age was provided with proper quays of masonry. Further south there were a number of anchorages, stretching down to the riverside harbour at Tell Qasile on the Yarkon ('Auja) just north of present-day Tel Aviv. Non-Israelite ports would also have handled trade with Israel, like Akko (which comparatively recently still dealt with grain brought there by camel train across Galilee from the Hauran region), Jaffa, the natural port for north Judah and Jerusalem, and the Philistine harbours down to Gaza. All these were available to coasters plying between Phoenicia and Egypt, but also for traffic with Cyprus, the Aegean and regions further west. On the Gulf of Aqabah Solomon developed Ezion Geber as a base for the seaborne trade with Ophir. This was probably the small island of Jeziret Far'aun some 11.25 km (7 miles) south of Elath, equipped with a (pre-Solomonic?) enclosed inner harbour of Phoenician *cothon* type. Its later use is obscure, but trade up the Gulf must have continued, as shown by the discovery of a sherd with a South Arabian (Minaean) graffito from the seventh or sixth century BC, found at the administrative centre of Tell el-Kheleifeh near the head of the gulf.

In addition to benefiting from this system of internal and external communications, trade was also facilitated by two other factors. Firstly, the Israelite system of weights and measures was analogous, with some local and temporal variations, to the one in use in neighbouring countries in Asia, Mesopotamia in particular, and some of the Israelite standards also corresponded to Egyptian ones, while others could be easily related to them, thus four Israelite shekel weights corresponded to five Egyptian *qedets* (tenths of the *deben*-weight). Secondly, the common standard of value in Israel as in the nearby Asiatic countries was the shekel weight of silver. For common use, silver tended to be cut into small fragments ('*Hacksilber*') which could be weighed out, tested for purity by scratching or refining, and tied up in bundles for safe keeping or transport. However, in the late eighth century BC Sennacherib referred in an inscription to the casting of half-shekels as something obviously familiar (fractions of shekels may indeed have been usual even in the Bronze Age, as a Ugaritic text hints). Yet many doubt that such castings were real predecessors of coins. Whether Israelite monarchs went in for such casting is not known, nor whether the Temple issued silver of proper purity, like some foreign sanctuaries perhaps. The not infrequent discovery of weights corresponding to the shekel standard, or fractions or multiples of this unit, may indicate that in common practice silver had to be weighed out for payment. The abundance of such weights in certain excavated sites may hint at their importance as centres of payment, whether commercial or for other purposes, such as taxation or sacred dues. The invention of proper coined money in seventh-century BC Lydia does not seem to have affected ancient Israel significantly before the end of the Monarchy.

Our information about the legal framework within which trade in Israel operated, including such matters as association between traders and their suppliers, and their liabilities, is rather sparse. This is partly because no commercial documents clarifying actual practice have come down to us (as so many have in Mesopotamia, especially from the period before papyrus tended to supersede clay tablets during the first millennium BC). Certain ostraca may be commercial credit or delivery chits, like two eighth-century Hebrew notes from Tell Qasile, referring respectively to 1100 measures of oil and 30 shekels of Ophir gold, or an Aramaic one of similar or later date found at Tell es-Sa'idiyeh east of the Jordan, where someone is credited with 30 *Kor* (*c.* 150 bushels?) of barley, or ostraca referring to grain and oil from Jerusalem. We also know very little about prices or their overall movements during the period. Temporary glut or scarcity understandably depressed or raised them, as the example of the fall in wheat and flour prices after the relief of Samaria, described in Kings (2: 7, 1, 18–20), shows. We have no instance of the authorities trying to regulate them, or trying to maintain what was regarded as a fair price (like the price of 50 shekels of silver for a homer of barley, referred to in Leviticus 27, 16), though conservative public opinion may to some extent have counteracted market forces. While the open spaces near city gates served as market areas, we do not know whether they did so daily, or at fixed intervals, as in medieval Europe.

Foreign merchants

It is clear that among the merchants connected with Israelite trade there were, in addition to Israelites, a considerable number of foreigners of very diverse origins, with Phoenicians and especially the Tyrians enjoying a predominant position. The Bible is probably referring to the Phoenicians, rather than to the descendants of the pre-Israelite inhabitants of the country, when it speaks of 'Canaanites' (with the meaning of 'merchants' or 'traffickers') – Palestinian 'Canaanites' are not otherwise known to have specialized in commerce, while the Phoenicians called their country Canaan and their Carthaginian colonists referred to themselves as Canaanites. Assisted by the friendly relations which prevailed between Israel and Phoenicia from the time of David and Solomon up to the revolution headed by Jehu, they seized their opportunity with remarkable energy, if perhaps not always with scrupulous honesty (Hosea 12, 7 alludes to deceitful balances associated with 'Canaanites'), recalling the doubtful reputation the Phoenicians enjoyed in Homer.

Finds of ostraca and graffiti as well as the occasional formal inscription show that the Phoenicians were active all over the country, even as far south as Kuntillet 'Ajrud in the Negeb. They imported a host of necessary or desirable things – metals, timber, textiles (especially purple garments), luxury vessels in metal, glass, frit and faience, tridacna shells, aromatic ointments, pottery and no doubt many other commodities of varied origin. Their ranks seem to have included itinerant craftsmen, executing commissions from royalty or private individuals – ivory-carvers, seal-cutters, skilled masons and carpenters, workers in metal, glass and faience. Some had probably taken up residence in the commercial centres of the country, as the Tyrians did in Jerusalem after the Exile (Nehemiah 13, 16). The 'Canaanites' lodging in the Maktesh quarter of Jerusalem (Zephaniah 1, 11) may have been such, and they quite likely brought their families too. From such favourable positions they handled much of the exports of both northern Israel and Judah, but also roamed the country to pick up goods locally. We hear, for instance, of the 'Canaanite' who buys from Israelite housewives the fruits of their domestic industry, like sheets and sashes (Proverbs 31, 24).

Damascene merchants had, at least temporarily, a quarter in Samaria. They probably handled goods which reached Syria in transit, like metals from Anatolia, in addition to Syrian products such as wine from Helbon, white wool and luxury goods like faience vessels. Some Aramean graffiti and seals may be related to their activities; but they are far fewer than corresponding Phoenician ones. Yet in spite of the Damascene ascendancy during the second half of the ninth century, Syria does not appear to have reached the commercial rank attained by Phoenicia.

Assyria also developed commercial interests in Israel, especially after her military advance in the region from the mid-eighth century onwards. If Nahum (3, 16) does indeed refer to Assyrian merchants (and not to their intelligence officers) then it seems they were not much liked by the Israelites, being regarded as comparable to a host of locusts. Valuable Assyrian glass, found sporadically in strata pre-dating the Assyrian conquest, may have been imported by them. However, Assyria was probably more interested in trade with Egypt, on the border of which Sargon II established a trading settlement. In spite of her dislike for Assyria, Israel may have derived some advantage from her presence there.

More significant for Israel were merchants from Arabia and bordering lands. Ishmaelites and Midianites acted, early in the Iron Age as before, as carriers of spices, incense and similar goods. If the distribution of Midianite pottery is a guide then their trade reached a fairly wide belt of southern Judah and the coastal plain. Later on, Edomites and Samarians appear to have followed similar routes, to judge from pottery evidence. South Arabian traders may have had dealings at Samaria and Bethel, though a seal from South Arabia found at the latter site has been the object of controversy. They certainly came to Jerusalem and apparently some of them stayed there, as indicated by graffiti in the South Arabian script on local potsherds found in the recent excavations.

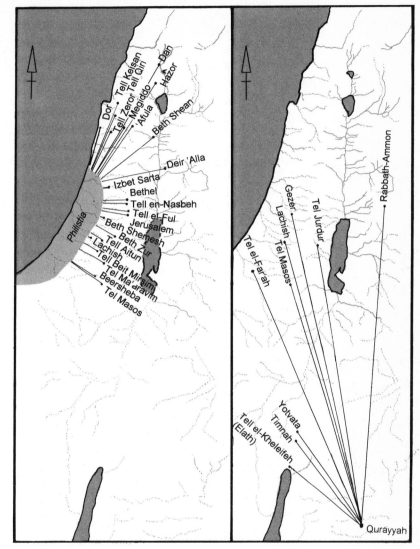

46 *Two maps showing the distribution of, respectively, Philistine (left) and Midianite (right) pottery imports into Israel. The Philistine wares obviously spread out from the coastal plain, perhaps in the wake of political domination, while the Midianite ones apparently accompanied the import of incense and spices from Arabia. The distribution of these wares was restricted, but others (like Cypriot and Phoenician products) became almost ubiquitous.*

The spices, incense and gold they dealt with were in demand at the Judean court, and were stored in the royal treasury (cf. 2 Kings 20, 13).

There is little sign of merchants from Philistia being active in Israel after the establishment of the Monarchy put an end to Philistine political predominance. Before then, the distribution of Philistine and related pottery may be an indicator of wider activity on the part of traders from that quarter. Israelite farming produce, on the other hand, seems to have been processed and marketed by Philistine industry and trade, especially in the seventh century BC. Judah and Philistia became economically integrated.

By the eighth century or before, Greek pottery had begun to arrive in the country in small quantities, which increased during the seventh and sixth centuries. There is no definite indication, though, that it was brought by Greek traders, except perhaps in coastal sites like Meṣad Ḥashavyahu, for Phoenician traders may have imported Greek pottery and other goods, like so much else. The same may also be largely true of the much more numerous Egyptian imports. There is nothing to show that these were carried by Egyptian merchants; in Egypt proper, the Egyptians preferred to leave their foreign commerce to licensed alien traders, Phoenicians and Greeks in particular, who were made to reside in special settlements.

Israelite merchants

Evidence about Israelite traders and their activities is tantalizingly incomplete. To what extent they were active in the internal market is unclear. Between the huckstering of goods of little intrinsic value by their producers and the trade in valuable commodities which attracted foreigners, there is likely to have been a field of commerce open to local enterprise. Somewhat more can be said about Israelite trade outside the country. The Bible mentions in particular royal merchants – not necessarily of Israelite descent – who were engaged in it during the reigns of Solomon and Ahab. According to a traditional but now less accepted translation, Solomon's merchants were concerned with obtaining linen yarn from Egypt. More certainly, they had a hand in the international trade in horses and chariots mentioned in the same context (1 Kings 10, 28–29) and in the royal expeditions undertaken jointly with the men of King Hiram of Tyre to Ophir, which resulted in the import of Ophir gold, 'almug' trees and jewels (1 Kings 9, 28; 10, 11), and in the joint journeys to Tarshish which brought in gold, silver, ivory, apes and possibly peacocks (or baboons) (1 Kings 10, 22).

The list of commodities imported appears to be geared strictly to the needs of the king and the royal establishment, including perhaps a royal 'zoo' showing off strange creatures, as is known with other ancient oriental monarchs. There is no sign that the royal merchants were concerned with meeting the requirements of the population in general. We are given no hint about what the merchants sponsored by Ahab dealt in, or whether they worked under similar narrow directives, and are told only that they were, by treaty, given special precincts in Damascus equivalent to those enjoyed by Damascene merchants in Samaria (1 Kings 20, 34). Neither the extent of the institution of royal merchants nor its importance in other reigns are known. Overall, royal trade seems to have been of limited scope and there is no sign of royal monopolies such as existed in Bronze Age Ugarit. On the other hand, there are indications that Israelite traders who perhaps did not have official status were, in limited numbers at least, active outside Israel from the ninth century BC onwards, either in association with others – Phoenicians, for instance – or on their own account, and that they were quite likely engaged in the import and export business in general.

Attention has been given some time ago to the discovery of Israelite or Israelite-type seals in Phoenician contexts. These, it was suggested, were due to the presence of a limited number of Israelite visitors or residents – perhaps as merchants active among their Phoenician colleagues. Such an argument can be extended, especially if we add to the seals finds of typically Israelite objects, such as pottery or cosmetic palettes, or the occurrence of Israelite names outside Palestine. In the Phoenician sphere, Israelite seals have been reported both in the homeland, as at Beirut and Tarsus, and in the overseas Phoenician colonies at Carthage. They have also turned up in Cyrene and Egypt. In Syria they occurred in Damascus and in Aleppo; in Mesopotamia some few in Babylonia and Assyria. In addition, Israelite pottery has been recognized at Nimrud in Assyria. Similarly, cosmetic palettes of Israelite type are known from Byblos and Aradus in Phoenicia, and from Nineveh in Mesopotamia. Such items may be due to the presence of Israelites as visitors or residents, most probably for the purpose of trade. While some of the objects found in Mesopotamia may be connected with exiles, it is worth remembering that Babylonia and Assyria became the domicile of a good number of foreign artisans and traders, Phoenicians and others, so that the presence there of a small number of Israelites for similar reasons would not be surprising. A representation of a trading ship on an eighth-century Israelite seal impression is suggestive of Israelite commercial activity in the Mediterranean. It shows familiarity with seafaring, but whether this was acquired by sharing in Phoenician commercial voyages (hinted at quite early, in Judges 5, 17), or whether the Israelites had trading ships of their own remains uncertain.

Such cases are, however, few. If they point to Israelite traders' affairs outside Israel then such trade cannot have been massive. Furthermore, none of these indications of possible external activities have so far been reported from Arabia, or points further east. The Arabs, it seems, kept the profitable incense and spice route to South Arabia strictly to themselves, and goods from there, or countries like India and Somalia, were available to Israelites only through intermediaries. The joint Ophir expeditions by Solomon and Hiram of Tyre represent the only real attempt to breach this monopoly during our period. The ships concerned may have been transported to their port of departure at Ezion Geber by camels, in sections, either from the region of Kerak in Moab where there was good timber, or even from the Palestinian coastal plain. The Crusaders used this method when they launched a fleet on the Red Sea in AD 1182/3. Prefabrication may have been known to the Phoenicians – their Carthaginian colonists certainly used it some centuries later.

Whatever the scope of the external activities of Israelite traders may have been, there are signs that Samaria, and later on Jerusalem in the final years of the Monarchy, had become centres of international trade of some importance. Benefiting from their position between the 'Way of the Sea' and the 'King's Highway' they, Jerusalem in particular, were able to attract trade from both east and west, making serious inroads on the Phoenician trading network. Ezekiel's pronouncement (26, 1–2) that Tyre hoped that the breaking of Jerusalem – this 'gate of the peoples' – would turn trade back to her, and that she would be replenished when Jerusalem was laid waste, sums up the position succinctly.

The Israelite economic system: comparative aspects

Scholars dealing with the economy of the ancient Near East, and that of Mesopotamia in particular, have often classified it as a temple- and state-dominated system, in which kings and sanctuaries not only owned much of the land and regulated its use, but craftsmanship and trade also depended on them. This classification (which has been under criticism in recent years, stress being laid on the existence of a sometimes important private sector) has also been thought by some to include ancient Israel. It would thus have formed part of the 'Asiatic' system which differed fundamentally from that of contemporary Greece, where the private sector was dominant and temples and state possessed only limited property or influence. Such a picture, however, does not seem to fit ancient Israel's economy very closely, even allowing for a lack of information about the economic aspects of Israelite sanctuaries in general, and of the Temple in Jerusalem in particular. There is no indication in the Bible that they were permanently endowed with land. According to Leviticus (27, 16ff.), any property – including real estate – vowed to the Sanctuary could be redeemed by money; land not so redeemed might revert to the donor in the Jubilee, and otherwise it became the property not of the Temple but of the priests. Neither is there any sign the Temple acted as a bank, lending money to traders or other entrepreneurs to finance their ventures, as Mesopotamian temples did. Nor did it direct the economy in general – religious law might affect economic practices, but there is no instance of it being promulgated *ad hoc* outside pentateuchal legislation. Economically, the Temple was a centre of 'conspicuous consumption' but not, it seems, of production or exchange.

The case of the monarchy is different, but not completely. It likewise acted as a centre of conspicuous consumption, but this was partly supported by probably fairly substantial royal estates, subjected to royal management. Though schemes of land amelioration like those undertaken by King Uzziah (2 Chronicles 26, 10) may have extended the royal domain or its tenantry, private or family holdings were probably always much more extensive, and there is nothing to show that the Crown interfered with private management there. Similarly craftsmen working for the Crown must have been part of a larger total, and we do not know how much direction was extended to them. Lastly, where trade is concerned, we saw that the scope of the activities of royal merchants was strictly limited, and that they were part of a probably much greater total number. Finally, there is no sign at present that the Crown regulated economic activities in general, whether by fixing prices or laying down conditions for economic activity, such as those governing liability, credit and so on as Mesopotamian rulers did. All told, the Israelite economic system may be regarded as a 'mixed' one, bearing some partial relation to the 'Asiatic' type but not so different in other respects from the one prevailing in early Greece. On grounds of geography and history this is perhaps not entirely surprising. Both Israel and Greece were part of the same eastern Mediterranean region, and they had been interconnected from early times onwards.

Within the predominant private sector, the profit motive found, in the eighth century, increasing scope in the growth of large estates geared to production for sale at market. This tendency conflicted with the traditional agricultural ideal of an independent peasantry, and was sharply attacked by the prophets for the social upheavals it caused. Money-lending to farmers faced with calamities such as failing harvests was another facet of 'pre-capitalism' which brought about undesirable consequences. However, Israelite society as a whole was not dominated by the profit motive. The ideal expressed in Proverbs (30, 8), that a man should ask to be preserved from riches as well as poverty, conforms in fact with the 'middle-class' existence which, with some variations upwards or downwards, seems according to the archaeological record to have been the lot of a large part of the population. There is no sign they were discontented with it. Genuine wealth was probably found mainly in the two capital cities; wretched poverty no doubt existed widely, but archaeological findings do not hint it was predominant.

At the lower end of the social scale, simple villagers might afford small luxuries like pottery brought from a distance. Higher up, we hear indeed of conspicuous wealth, especially among the élite in the capitals. However, it is worth noting that imported articles of considerable value, Phoenician or other, were less frequent in Israel than in neighbouring countries to the west or east. Objects made from gold are particularly rare, both as tomb gifts and as stray finds in stratified sites – gold has in fact been more frequently encountered in Bronze Age contexts. It would seem that the Israelite upper class had less to spend than the aristocracies of, for example, early Greece or of the Ammonite realm. No burials enclosing riches comparable to some from those regions have yet been found in Israel, except, curiously, in a few from the very end of the period or just after. However, the inscription on the tomb of Shebna in Jerusalem, which states no gold or silver was to be found in it, indicates treasure might reasonably have been expected in the sepulchres of the court aristocracy. At least some of the northern and southern monarchs seem to have possessed appreciable wealth. Their incomes derived not only from taxation and the revenue of crown estates, but also from confiscation, tolls levied on merchants, gains from mercantile enterprise they promoted and, on occasion, tribute or booty. This wealth is shown by the amounts of tribute Israelite and Judean rulers were made to pay to the Assyrian kings in particular. The sums listed show that their economic strength was quite comparable to that of contemporary Levantine rulers, and indeed a visit to Hezekiah's royal treasury was expected to impress envoys from Babylonia (2 Kings 20, 12–13). It must also be said that, while the confrontations with the Assyrians during the eighth century caused much devastation, this was apparently fairly quickly made good in the northern kingdom, once it had passed under Assyrian administration, and Judah was beginning to recover from the havoc caused by Sennacherib's invasion at the time when the kingdom came to its end. With some fluctuations up or down, the Israelite economy was able to provide the bulk of the population with a tolerable or better existence, throughout most of Israel's history.

CHAPTER NINE

Warfare

Wars occurred frequently in the ancient Near East, sometimes almost annually – indeed in Samuel (2: 11, 1) the 'turn of the year' (spring) is referred to as 'the time when kings go out to battle'. Israel was often involved in warfare, and the effects not only on the lives of individuals but on the whole social fabric were apparently considerable. Our information on the subject is, as usual, patchy. Scattered references in the Bible are to a limited extent supplemented by enemy campaign accounts – Assyrian, Egyptian and Moabite – and by epigraphic discoveries in Israel, while Judean ostraca from the late eighth to the early sixth centuries are informative about army dispositions and supply arrangements. Excavations have cast light on fortresses and defensive arrangements in both northern Israel and the southern kingdom, but little on arms and equipment. Assyrian reliefs illustrating the campaigns of various monarchs (but especially those featuring the siege of Lachish by Sennacherib in 701 BC) offer most valuable detail. There are unfortunately no similar ones from Egypt, nor are there Israelite visual records illustrating their own campaigns.

Since the military history of Israel extended over some six centuries at least, it is only to be expected that both development within the country and changes in the external threats facing it would have led to modifications in the armed forces during that period. Those that took place between the time before and after the institution of the Monarchy were apparently fundamental, but there were changes right up to the end.

Israelite military organization during the period of the Judges

According to biblical sources, the fighting strength of early Israel was made up largely from levies raised among one or more tribes, to counter local or more general threats. Judges (5, 8) envisages a grand total of 40,000 warriors, but numbers actually involved in combat tended to be much smaller. Equipment was often inadequate – the host of Deborah and Barak is said to have lacked shields and spears. Daggers and especially swords were rare at this stage, and so probably were helmets and the coats of mail made up from bronze or iron armour scales stitched on leather or linen jerkins. Slings allowed attacks on enemy forces from a distance, but bows and arrows were at first infrequent among Israelites (composite bows were costly, and perhaps the preserve of foreign mercenary archers). At the battle of Gilboa Saul's forces still had nothing to counter the devastating effect of enemy archery (1 Samuel 31, 3), even though we hear of some archery training at court. Chariots, sophisticated and expensive, were lacking at this period, as were effective fortifications of settlements. Israelite armies could thus not normally stand up to Canaanite or

Philistine forces equipped with chariots in the plains, and if faced with sudden overwhelming threats in the hill country they might have to seek safety where they could find it (cf. Judges 6, 2). They nevertheless prevailed on occasions over superior enemy forces, either by clever use of ground and weather conditions – as when the army of Deborah and Barak overwhelmed enemy chariotry bogged down in treacherous ground by a sudden flood of the Kishon river (Judges 5, 21) – or by surprise and the creation of panic. This latter was the method reportedly used by Gideon against the Midianites, an enemy enjoying the potentially devastating advantage of high mobility, and able to bring overwhelming numbers to bear where least expected (Judges 6–7).

In addition to tribal levies, the period witnessed the formation of personal war bands by a number of individuals, like Abimelech (Judges 9, 4) or Jephthah (Judges 11, 3); unlike the former, which were called out only rarely, these bands were permanent. With the coming of the Monarchy, Saul similarly drew to himself a permanent body of picked warriors (1 Samuel 14, 52), and later when David was outlawed he likewise collected a war band (1 Samuel 22, 1–2). This was to become the nucleus of his standing army, augmented after his accession to kingship by forces of foreign professional soldiers – Gittites, Kerethites and Pelethites, of Philistine or allied descent and with military training. The combination of a permanent force of professional warriors dependent on the king and of the tribal levies called out only when necessary was to become a basic feature of Israelite military arrangements thereafter.

The period of the Monarchy

Even if the puzzlingly high figures given in the Bible about Israelite fighting strength during the United and Divided Monarchy are disregarded, it is clear from other evidence that the armed forces of David and Solomon were powerful, as well as those of the successor kingdoms, and at times of international importance. In the ninth century, Ahab was able to send a contingent of 2000 chariots and 10,000 foot to join the allied force confronting Shalmaneser III at Karkar in 853 BC – one of the biggest groups and the strongest in chariotry. The Judean army at the time of Jehoshaphat and Azariah/Uzziah seems likewise to have been respectable. In the early eighth century Jeroboam II for a while made the army of northern Israel a redoubtable force, while later Hezekiah built up the military strength of Judah to such a degree that he felt (mistakenly, it proved) he could confront Assyria. However, such periods of strength were interspersed with others of weakness, and in the end the armed forces of neither country were able to defend their independence.

The administrative framework

An efficient bureaucracy was behind the military organization during the period of the Monarchy. There are brief references to it in the Bible and the ostraca found at Lachish and Arad give us a glimpse of how it worked, at least in

Judah during the late period. Written documents, differing in style and mode of address according to the superior or inferior standing of the recipient, passed between the capital and local units; registers were kept both centrally and locally. Recruitment to the forces was based on data compiled in writing – under David, we hear of a census of the number of fighting men in the country begun, but not completed, by Joab (2 Samuel 24, 1–9). At the time of Uzziah there is a reference to a record of the fighters in the Judean army kept by clerical officials (2 Chronicles 26, 11ff.); when Jerusalem finally fell to Nebuchadnezzar a minister of war and a chief scribe in charge of mustering the people were among the most important prisoners taken (2 Kings 25, 18). Regional drafts were probably organized by district recruiting officers (cf. Deuteronomy 20, 5–9); contingents from more than one tribe were perhaps combined to make up units of predetermined size and combining a mixture of local skills. Sudden local emergencies might result in written orders from the capital to the nearest unit command to send men (recruits?) where needed, under pain of death (cf. Arad letter No. 24). Records were kept of stores and equipment, issues authorized, acknowledged and booked; combat orders, field and intelligence reports, signals and other matters were all subjects of correspondence. There are occasional human touches: a curt 'Can't you read a letter?' addressed to a subordinate is countered by 'Nobody has ever tried to read anything out to *me*!' (Lachish letter 3). With this system of bureaucratic backing for military organization, ancient Israel continued traditions in existence in the Bronze Age, developed especially in Assyria and Egypt, quite possibly beyond what was found in other contemporary medium-sized or small Levantine states.

Army organization

From early times onwards the Israelite forces knew units of 10, 50, 100 and 1000 men (as did neighbouring countries), though these will not always have been up to nominal strength. From divisions of stores of food issued at Arad into individual rations it has been suggested that a nominal unit of 50 might only consist of 35–40 men, and that 75 might have been the actual strength of a unit of 100. Larger bodies of troops might be created by the combination of these basic units – groups of 600 men are mentioned repeatedly early on. Correspondingly, officers included captains of 50, 100 and 1000 but we also hear of Zimri leading half the chariotry of northern Israel (1 Kings 16, 9) and a whole army might be under one field commander, when the king did not command personally (cf. for instance 2 Samuel 11, 1). A 'chief of the army' (a title held by Abner and Joab in their days) is mentioned in Lachish letter 3 (*c.* 588 BC) but we do not know whether it refers there to a field or administrative officer. Nor do we know about staff arrangements – the groups of three officers mentioned under David (2 Samuel 23, 8ff.), inspired perhaps by Aegean models, are not heard of later and may not have had advisory functions.

Troops were of various kinds. Infantry (divided perhaps into heavy and light) armed now with swords, lances and shields – some perhaps also with helmets and body armour – predominated. They were assisted by slingmen, and from David's time onwards archers became important (cf. 2 Samuel 1, 18). Some guard units seem to have been trained in fast movement, and were called 'runners' (2 Kings 11, 4). Foreign mercenaries were probably also mainly in infantry formations. After those employed by David we hear of Carians serving in Judah when Athaliah was overthrown (2 Kings 11, 4); later, at, or after, the time of Josiah, Greek mercenaries may have served at Meṣad Ḥashavyahu on the coast, and Greek or related troops – the *Kittim* mentioned in the Arad ostraca – were subsequently stationed in the Beersheba region.

Chariotry, then the 'queen of battles', was important in the United Monarchy and in the north under the House of Omri, but declined later. Yet when Samaria fell to Sargon II Israelite chariotry was still sufficiently pre-stigious for him to incorporate a unit of it in his army. Cavalry co-existed with it fairly early on, however, as a recently found Aramaic inscription from Dan shows. In Judah, chariotry was probably never quite as significant – the country is less suited for horse rearing – and after Sennacherib's invasion it is no longer in evidence. Horsemen were known, but still mainly employed for scouting, the conveyance of news and harassment. Assyrian reliefs show that mounted archers were important for military operations by the time of Sargon II. Better control of horses by means of improved reins and bits permitted independent cavalry, but proper cavalry charges were a thing of the future for, before the invention of saddles and stirrups centuries later, horsemen were insecurely seated and found it difficult to control their mounts and use their weapons at the same time. This disadvantage was obviated for a time in the Assyrian army by employing horsemen in pairs, one of whom controlled both horses while the other used his lance or bow. According to one translation of Sennacherib's cam-paign account, Hezekiah's forces included Arabs; if so, it is perhaps possible they were cameleers, like those brought by Gindibu the Arab chief to the battle of Karkar some 150 years earlier. They would in any case have been useful for surveillance in the Negeb.

We have no direct reference to pioneers for road clearance, camp construc-tion or siege operations being employed in Israel's armed forces, but since there is occasional reference to the breaching of enemy town walls (2 Chronicles 26, 6, for instance) they may have existed. Similarly we hear nothing about arms manufacture or repair shops, fixed or mobile, or medical facilities.

Equipment

Our information about equipment is in some aspects deficient. The exact connotation of biblical references is rarely clear, archaeological finds are scarce and partly from marginal locations, while Assyrian pictorial representations offer only limited help.

Among offensive weapons, lances or pikes, and javelins seem to have been dominant at first; later, their importance decreased. The length of shafts may have varied from *c.* 1.25 to 1.8 m (4 to 6 ft); heads were of iron or bronze, and either tanged (especially for javelins, in which case it is hard to distinguish them from large arrowheads) or with a cast or folded-over socket; there might be a metal spear butt – itself a potential weapon (cf. 2 Samuel 2, 23). Whether Goliath's javelin (1 Samuel 17, 7) was of a special Aegean type provided with a cord ending in a loop wrapped round the shaft, which would impart a rotary motion to the weapon when thrown, is disputed; there is in any case no other evidence of this type.

Swords and dirks, of bronze at first and then of iron, were rare early on (see p. 161). When Israel appeared on the scene, swords were superseding the earlier rapiers. Biblical references indicate that they were intended for slashing as well as stabbing (contrast Judges 3, 16ff.; 2 Samuel 2, 16; 20, 10 with 1 Samuel 17, 51; 2 Samuel 16, 9). Though not from Israelite contexts, fragments of a Late Bronze Age weapon from Gezer and a (short) Early Iron one from Megiddo, both of bronze and in the Naue 2 tradition, together with a fine sword with horned projections found in Tomb 102 at Tell es-Sa'idiyeh, hint at what early Israel may have aimed to obtain. During the period of the Monarchy swords

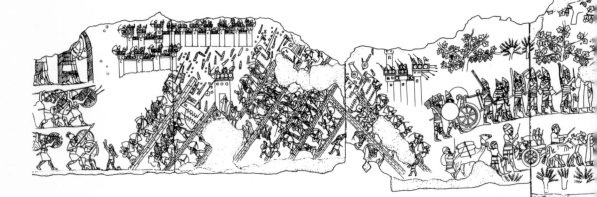

47 Arrowheads found at el-Khadr, near Bethlehem, bearing the name of their owners (eleventh-century BC). They may have belonged to members of a guild of archers, Canaanite or possibly Israelite. Arrowheads are more frequently found in later contexts, showing that archery was becoming more widely practised then.

48 (below) Drawing of part of the reliefs from Sennacherib's palace at Nineveh, recording and celebrating his siege and capture of Lachish.

became standard army equipment according to the Bible, but evidence from finds is scarce. The best example known is a recently discovered straight iron sword, 1.04 m (3 ft 4 in) long, from Vered Jericho, found in a seventh-century context. Such swords would be kept in a scabbard suspended from a belt. A slightly curved iron slashing sword, *c.* 62.5 cm (24.6 in) long and with one (inner) cutting edge, found in a late context (*c.* 588 BC) at Tell Beit Mirsim belongs to an alternative fighting tradition – curved swords, found earlier in Assyria, were developed contemporaneously as infantry equipment in Greece. A bundle of such weapons besides the commander's own weapon may be shown among the booty taken by the Assyrians at Lachish. Daggers, presumably tucked in the belt, are difficult to distinguish from knives.

Among weapons for long-distance fighting, slings were popular in Israel from the earliest times. They were used in battle, in attacks on towns (2 Kings 3, 25) and are shown in the Assyrian reliefs being used by the defenders of Lachish against Sennacherib's assault troops. None have survived, but slingstones the size of tennis balls have been found in fortresses such as Lachish where they were stored. Bows were probably generally of the 'composite' type made of an inner core of horn slotted into the wood, and an outer layer of sinews; being delicate they were kept in a combined bow case and quiver. Such bows are very effective, allowing direct aim at 100 m (328 ft) range or more, and random shooting at several times that distance. None have been found – nor bow cases or quivers – but though there are also no complete arrows with their shafts of reed or wood and feathers, arrowheads are plentiful. They were more often made from iron than bronze (the proportions varied in time and locally), usually tanged rather than socketed, often ogival, leaf-shaped, or triangular in outline and mostly flat, though some have a slight midrib. A stem or swelling between the blade and the tang would sometimes be added to prevent the head

being driven into the shaft on impact. Specially heavy models, or heads with a round or square cross-section, were for piercing armour. Socketed three-bladed 'Scythian' arrowheads, triangular in section, came in about 600 BC.

For defence, Israelite soldiers had shields, helmets and body armour. Shields would be of the hand-grip type, made of leather (which needed oiling to keep it in condition) backed by wood or wickerwork. They were of two types, the large tower shield carried by a bearer, and the smaller round shield carried by the warrior himself and perhaps having metal surfacings or a shield boss. Both varieties are common in the Near East. Again none survive, but on the reliefs showing Sennacherib's attack on Lachish round shields are represented hung on the battlements to protect the defending Judeans. These reliefs also show that conical helmets (of leather or bronze) were worn by them; at present there is no other direct information on Israelite helmets of any period. Armed collars would defend the neck above the body armour. The latter consisted of bronze or iron scales, flat or with a midrib, stitched on a leather or cloth jerkin. It was very heavy, impeding quick movement (cf. 1 Samuel 17, 39), and thus suited charioteers better than foot soldiers (cf. 1 Kings 22, 34), who needed special training. Though Greeks and other Aegean mercenaries served in the forces, no bronze corselets of Greek type have so far been found, neither have any greaves (which are mentioned only in the Goliath story) – high leather boots may have offered leg protection instead (cf. Isaiah 9, 5).

Among non-personal army equipment, chariots were of prime importance. Our information about these comes once again mainly from the Lachish reliefs. These give a detailed representation of a large chariot with high, eight-spoked wheels and a square body, fitted for four horses – probably the governor's personal vehicle, resembling chariots used by Assyrian monarchs. There are more summary pictures of smaller chariots with six-spoked wheels being flung down on the attacking Assyrians from the battlements, probably some of the Judean battle chariots stationed at Lachish. Few actual remains of chariots or horse trappings have been recovered. At Tell el-Far'ah (N) an iron armour scale from stratum VIIB (tenth century?) had particles of wood adhering to its back and must have come from an armoured ('iron') chariot. A cheek-piece for a chariot or cavalry horse was found in Lachish, a doubtful one comes from Meggido.

There is so far no concrete indication of siege engines, such as moveable battering rams, being used by Israelite forces. Something must be said, however, about the 'engines invented by cunning men' for King Uzziah, 'to shoot arrows and great stones' (2 Chronicles 26, 15). Some have thought of these as predecessors of the later catapults, but Yadin preferred to see in them fighting platforms erected on the bastions. Though the latter certainly existed, the question remains open.

Training and army dispositions

Warfare had to be learnt (cf. for instance 2 Samuel 1, 18; Micah 4, 3), and troops were instructed in simple or complicated evolutions, from drawing up in lines

(2 Kings 11, 8) to facing adversaries in two directions (2 Samuel 10, 9). There are hints of a special Hebrew command vocabulary. Large open spaces like the courtyard around the palace at Ramat Rachel may have served as an exercise and parade ground; there was weapons training, for instance in archery (2 Samuel 1, 17), and trumpet or horn signals, for initiating or breaking off action, must also have been taught. Discipline seems at times to have been strict (cf. 2 Kings 18, 36).

The capital cities of the United and later of the Divided Monarchy, together with a system of strong fortresses guarding the frontier approaches, formed the backbone of military organization, and the main bodies of troops were stationed there. Chariotry was based on special 'chariot cities' located in positions controlling important roads. If the 'stables' at Megiddo IV really were such then that city, which dominated vital north–south and east–west roads, may have accommodated 150 chariots. Military stores and food were correspondingly located in the capitals, and also in special 'store cities'. Elite army formations including foreign mercenaries might be found in the capitals (like the Carians in Jerusalem in Athaliah's time) but small detachments of them were also placed in exposed regions. Thus some Greeks apparently served in the coastal fort of Meṣad Ḥashavyahu in the time of Josiah or later, and 'Kittim' were stationed in the Beersheba region threatened by the Edomites during the last years of the Judean monarchy. Such troops formed part of the back-up force for a chain of forts, comparable to the later Roman *limes* system, in the southern and eastern Judean desert frontiers, and in the advanced Judean Negeb zone in particular. These were located along important roads or tracks, but placed at varying distances from each other, near watering points. If Judah had armed cameleers they would have been ideal here. Communications between fortresses and forts, and with headquarters in the capital, including the conveyance of orders and intelligence reports and the handing over of sensitive correspondence, were maintained by messengers carrying letters. Examples are offered by the Lachish and Arad letters. A fast horseman or cameleer could probably link most frontier points and the capital in a day. Simple, but more urgent, messages such as alarm signals could be relayed faster

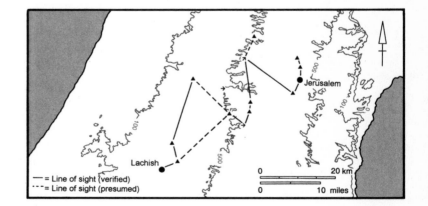

49 Diagram showing some of the stations which carried signals by smoke or fire quickly across the kingdom of Judah, according to textual references and archaeological indications (see also pl. 43).

Jerusalem

Lachish

— = Line of sight (verified)
--- = Line of sight (presumed)

0   20 km

0   10 miles

by coded optical means, including smoke signals, between chains of mutually visible signalling stations. These are mentioned in the Lachish letters (pl. 43) and part of the stations have been tentatively identified. Signals could also be sent from outposts surrounding border fortresses, giving advance notice of suspicious movements near the frontier.

Supply arrangements

Though advancing armies in enemy territory could to some extent 'live on the country', and individuals might be supported by food sent from their families, such basic arrangements were clearly insufficient to maintain an army for long. At present we are not well informed about how Israelite troops were maintained in mobile warfare (a question with which the Assyrians dealt remarkably successfully) but archaeological and especially epigraphic finds offer interesting details concerning the Judean 'static' supply system for the eighth to the sixth centuries BC, which can be combined with biblical information. At the time of King Hezekiah it is possible that the so-called *la-melekh* store jars with the royal stamps (see pls 45–9) were sent to four supply centres at Hebron, Ziph, Sochoh and *Mmšt* (the identity of which is unknown) to be filled with oil, wine or grain. Thereafter they may have been sent to depots in the frontier districts to support troops stationed there. An ostracon found at Beersheba shows how supplies were also drawn regionally. To what extent this system survived Sennacherib's crushing invasion in 701 BC is doubtful. However, the Arad letters of the late seventh and early sixth centuries show how, after the demise of Beersheba as a store city, Arad functioned as a supply centre for the Beersheba region. Barley and perhaps other foodstuffs were delivered to it from villages south of Hebron. Supplies were 'booked in', and issued on orders sent from a superior authority by ostracon vouchers directed to the local commander. Amounts and quality of goods to be issued to individuals or groups are carefully itemized: grain, flour (fine or coarse), dough or bread, wine (table quality or poor sour) and oil. If travel was involved, issues were varied according to distances to be traversed before arrival at the destination, and if the journey took more than four days, flour or dough were substituted for bread, which did not keep well. When orders had been complied with, the date on which stores were issued might be noted by a local scribe on the back of the ostracon; the 'chits' were kept and, it seems, the total of all issues was booked once a month in a master register which has not come down to us. From somewhat tentative calculations, which have recently been queried, it appears individual daily rations were about 1.2 kg (2.2 lb) of bread or equivalent (perhaps sometimes less), *c.* 0.17 (or 0.3) litre of wine and possibly *c.* 0.1 litre (3 fl. oz) of oil. The bread ration is comparable to that of a Roman soldier, but the oil issue is smaller, and the wine ration startlingly so – even if, following the alternative calculations by some authorities, a *bath* measure of twice the capacity assumed here were to be substituted. No mention is made in the Judean documents of meat, which was a regular ingredient in Roman military diet.

The army at war: the religious aspect

Turning now to actual fighting, we must first note that in ancient Israel as in the neighbouring countries war was not simply 'the continuation of diplomacy by other means'. It involved the national deity, the Lord of Hosts, whose will had to be ascertained by priestly oracles or prophetic utterance before campaigns or battles so that there would be hope of his decisive intervention with over-powering might. He could overwhelm Israel's enemies by calling up the forces of nature or letting loose on them a divine panic. Victory was his and he could achieve it without human effort; indeed the prophets frowned on reliance on human rather than divine power. Warriors had thus to be in a state of ritual purity and to be consecrated; religious prescriptions also affected campaigning. In certain conditions an enemy might be put under the 'ban' that is to say, if defeated, every living soul and even domestic animals on his side would be devoted to destruction. The same treatment was on occasion meted out to the Israelites – King Mesha 'devoted' Israelite prisoners as a sacrifice to his national deity Kemosh, as his inscription tells us. After the coming of the Monarchy such rigorous treatment became rarer, for the kings of Israel were known as merciful (or 'to be trusted', cf. 1 Kings 20, 31) but such a chivalrous, or polit-ically profitable, attitude met with religious condemnation (2 Kings 20, 35ff.).

Strategy and tactics

Israelite armies might be involved in mobile or static warfare. In a war of move-ment they showed some sophistication and might apply pincer movements in an indirect approach to their objective so as to reap the advantage of surprise. Similarly, they might trap their enemies in difficult terrain, attack when not expected or lure them to disaster by feigned flight. For operations at some dis-tance from home, advanced bases might be used. David may have employed the Transjordanian Succoth region for this purpose in his war against the Ammonites. Later, at the time of Sargon II's campaign in Philistia (712 BC), we hear of a (Judean and allied?) base camp in the Shephelah, tucked away 'in a thicket where the sun never shines, and surrounded by a moat'. For battles involving chariots, level ground accessible by roads was required. There they could operate as mobile firing platforms, harassing the enemy with volleys, and attacking them on the march or when in flight. It does not seem that more mobile forces of mounted archers, used so successfully by the Assyrians, were employed to any extent by the Israelites, whose main strength lay in heavy and light infantry. Actions would be opened and broken off by trumpet or horn signals, troops would operate in several bodies – perhaps three, rallied round their standards – and charges would be opened by war cries, but details of the tactics used elude us.

Israelite forces fought with varying degrees of success against neighbouring states but they could not face Assyrian or later Babylonian field armies, who seem to have swept them off the open country. They were more successful in

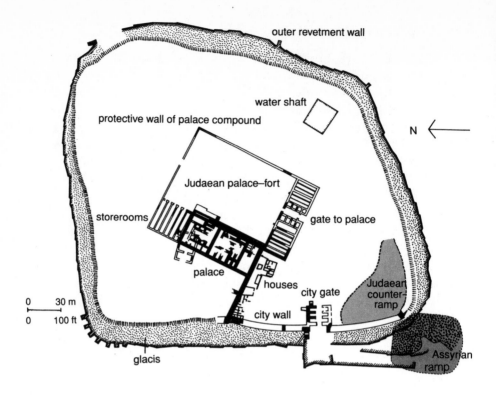

50 Plan of Lachish, showing the Assyrian siege ramp and the Judean counter ramp. Both involved very considerable efforts.

wars of position, defending their fortresses. Indeed the major sieges seem to have caused severe difficulties to the Assyrians, past masters in siegecraft as they were. In 712 BC Sargon II described Azekah as 'an eagle's nest, inaccessible to ramps and battering rams'. In 701 BC, Sennacherib did indeed take Lachish (pls 26–8), but he seems to have regarded this as an outstanding achievement worthy of a specially detailed visual record prominently displayed in his palace at Nineveh. He never took Jerusalem. The siege of Samaria lasted three years before the city fell and there, as in the later Babylonian siege of Jerusalem in 586 BC, famine may have been a determining factor. The Lachish reliefs give us some insight into Israelite and especially Judean methods of defence – enemy scaling parties and engineers were subjected to a hail of slingstones and arrows from troops stationed on the special fighting platforms erected on the towers and bastions, and siege engines were attacked with flaming torches thrown from above, together with anything heavy which might come in handy, even whole chariots. Finally, the Assyrian siege ramp was opposed by a counter-ramp thrown up just inside the city wall under attack. A less determined and formidable enemy might have been seen off by such skill.

The consequences of war

An army with banners might be an impressive sight and dominion, the exaction of tribute or the taking of booty and prisoners might be an occasion of joy to king or commoner – yet even if successful, war led to sinister consequences. The absence or death of husbands and sons needed to ensure family livelihoods led to debt and debt to slavery, while the rise of ambitious and ruthless troop commanders offered opportunities for revolts and the extermination of dynasties, attended by much bloodshed and horror. Defeat brought about even worse catastrophes. The Syrian and Moabite advance in the ninth century seems to have led to the annihilation of much of the Israelite population across the Jordan. The Assyrian and later the Babylonian invasions led to massive destruction of towns and villages and the exiling of important sectors of the population. While the countryside in the former northern kingdom recovered somewhat under Assyrian administration, town life did not, and in the south the Babylonian conquest resulted in long-lasting desertion of those parts of Judah which had been most directly involved in warfare. Peace, longed for by the prophets, remained a distant ideal and the animosities between the Israelites and their neighbours, kindled in past débâcles, long survived the occasions which had given rise to them.

CHAPTER TEN

Language, Writing and Texts

Hebrew, the language the ancient Israelites spoke and wrote, has long enjoyed a very special appeal. As the language of the Hebrew Bible it has been regarded as sacred among both Jews and Christians. Ancient scholars considered it to have been the original language of mankind, and the tongue in which the Words of Creation were spoken. Its influence has been felt world-wide: Hebrew words like Sabbath and Messiah are known internationally, and phrases found in the Bible have been transferred into many languages. Hebrew can, nevertheless, be described and analysed in the same way as any other language.

Language

We may begin with a surprising fact. Though 'Hebrew' might sometimes denote 'Israelite', the language spoken by the Israelites is not known to have been called Hebrew before the use of that term in the prologue to Ecclesiasticus (*c.* 130 BC). Instead, the Israelite language is called the 'language of Canaan' in Isaiah (19, 18), while Jerusalemite speech is referred to as 'Judean' in Isaiah (36, 12–13). There are good grounds both for the general and the special designation. On the one hand the language the Israelites spoke is closely linked to the one used by the Canaanites during the Late Bronze Age and the related speech of Ugarit, the former known from grammatical aberrations and explanatory glosses in the Akkadian Tell el-Amarna diplomatic correspondence, as well as from Canaanite loan-words and names transcribed by the Egyptians, the latter from a multitude of documents written in alphabetic cuneiform script, discovered at Ugarit and elsewhere. Hebrew thus belongs to the Northwest Semitic language group. Moreover, Israelite Hebrew in the Iron Age remained closely linked to other languages descended from Canaanite, especially Phoenician and Literary Moabite, and the linguistic influence of the Canaanites within Israelite territory whom, the Bible tells us, the Israelites never managed to dispossess, must also have made itself felt. Jerusalemite and Judean Hebrew, on the other hand, had definite characteristics of their own; and our sources show that in some respects the distinction is of considerable antiquity.

Antecedents and early development
By the thirteenth century BC, when the Israelites were present in the Promised Land, they found themselves in a basically Canaanite-speaking environment.

The linguistic effects of Egyptian imperial domination, of the presence of originally Hurrian- or Indo-European-descended urban aristocracies and of international connections, including trade, were all limited. Whether the Israelites affected the linguistic situation by bringing with them their own form of speech, related to later Aramaic and Arabic, is unclear. Some scholars have pointed to the presence of some Aramaizing vocabulary in the very early Song of Deborah (Judges 5), and more generally to the fact that Hebrew includes words akin to Aramaic and Arabic paralleling in meaning others related to Canaanite, as in the case of *zahab* and *ḥarūs*, both meaning 'gold'. The Aramaizing features would reflect the early kinship between Israel and Aram depicted in Genesis, or indeed Israel's Aramean ancestry as proclaimed in Deuteronomy (26, 5). Comprising elements drawn from two distinct traditions Hebrew would thus be a 'mixed language' (like English, which combines Anglo-Saxon and Norman French features). At present, however, direct (non-biblical) information about a suitable early non-Canaanite source language is lacking. In any case Hebrew throughout its history showed many irregularities and cantonal divisions of its linguistic territory: to what extent a common 'high' language bridged local dialects in spoken Hebrew even at a later stage remains doubtful.

The progression from Canaanite to Hebrew can, however, be documented in terms of an interplay of conservatism and simplification, the latter perhaps not unconnected with the social and ethnic changes during the final stages of the Bronze Age, which did not favour the maintenance of accepted standards. For instance, the number of Canaanite consonantal speech sounds was reduced by fusions, so that by *c.* 1200 BC *ṯ* and *š* were both realized as *š*. Particularly instructive are the relations between the Canaanite and Hebrew verbal systems. In Canaanite as in all Semitic languages, meaning was, in verbs like nouns, mainly linked with the root consonants (usually three – vowels were mostly of secondary importance). Meaning could be modified by prefixes (such as *h-* for causative), doubling of the second root letter (for intensification), or the infixion (insertion) of *t* (for the reflexive). The passive could be indicated by internal vowel changes. The system survived into Hebrew, but in an impoverished fashion. Thus reflexive forms with infixed *t* went out of use (they survived in neighbouring Moabite), and passives indicated by internal vowel changes occur only selectively. Even more significant, though rather complicated, is the relation between tense and aspect markers in Canaanite and Hebrew.

Early Hebrew: the period of the Judges

From the thirteenth century down to the tenth information about the Israelites' language remains limited. The few available graffiti offer little help and we are thrown back on the Hebrew Bible. From this, regrettably, few clear facts concerning very early Hebrew prose language can be obtained, but some scholars have suggested (not without contradiction by others) that a number of biblical poetic texts may be assigned to the twelfth, eleventh and tenth centuries BC.

These include in particular the Song of the Sea (Exodus 15), the Song of Deborah (Judges 5), the Testament of Jacob (Genesis 49), the Oracles of Balaam (Numbers 23–24), the Blessing of Moses (Deuteronomy 33) and the Song of Moses (Deuteronomy 32) – perhaps in that order. David's lament for Jonathan (2 Samuel 1, 17–27) and a number of psalms, including Psalm 18 (cf. 2 Samuel 22) and the allegedly very early Psalm 113, would be other relevant texts. Linguistically these poems show a number of special features. They make use of uncommon or archaic grammatical forms and tend to make rather restricted use of items absent or exceptional in Canaanite speech but regularly employed in later Biblical Hebrew, especially prose, namely the definite article *ha-*, the sign of the direct object *'et*, and the relative pronoun *'ªšer* ('who/which').

The origin of this type of poetry remains doubtful, though an Ephraimite descent for some of it has been suggested. To what extent a super-tribal common poetic diction or, on the other hand, local linguistic features may be involved is unclear. What normal non-poetic and, especially, dialectal Hebrew were like at this time remains obscure. Though the *Shibboleth* story in Judges (12, 6) hints at regional differences in pronunciation there is no agreement as to what was involved. Varying and substantial deviations from the later standard language may have to be considered, for the cryptic text of the tenth-century Gezer Calendar (cf. p. 150) hints that these still occurred after the rise of the Monarchy, when linguistic levelling must have begun.

Standard Hebrew in the period of the United and Divided Monarchy
The rise of the United Monarchy brought about far-reaching social and political changes, including not only the creation of a powerful, prestigious and culturally active court supported by a substantial bureaucracy but also the establishment of wide-ranging and varied external connections. A Canaanite element was also incorporated within the fabric of the united country. All this appears to have affected Israel's language significantly. The diction used in court and Temple in Jerusalem must have enjoyed prestige, and set and perpetuated linguistic standards to be imitated. Schools and the royal bureaucracy would have helped to spread this Jerusalemite Hebrew widely within the country. Being employed by a sophisticated court with cultural and especially literary interests as well as multifarious technical needs, the language had to be enriched and differentiated. Local Canaanite as well as foreign prototypes would naturally provide sources for an extended vocabulary and models for suitable styles. Once in place, the literary language which grew up in such circumstances was remarkably long lasting.

Our sources now are twofold. A large part of the Hebrew Bible, comprising both poetry and prose, originated during the period of the Monarchy. In addition, from the eighth century BC onwards epigraphy provides increasingly significant evidence, though for the moment largely from Judah and chiefly from the seventh and sixth centuries. Except for the eighth-century Samaria ostraca – brief and stereotyped administrative dockets – the northern kingdom has so far supplied little epigraphic material, so that we are left badly informed about the important question of to what extent northern Israelite 'standard' Hebrew diverged from Jerusalemite Hebrew after the political split. Some dialectal features appear in the Samaria ostraca, and where literary texts are concerned scholars have suggested the occurrence of northern Israelite peculiarities both in the narrative prose developed in the northern kingdom (such as the pentateuchal 'E' source) and in the poetic diction of Hosea in particular. There is as yet no epigraphic backing for such wider assumptions. Northern and southern 'standard' Hebrew must in any case have remained close and mutually intelligible, as shown by the ministry of Amos.

At the same time other restrictions on our information must be kept in mind. Biblical Hebrew is essentially a literary language, and the ostraca offer mainly educated scribal style with a bureaucratic slant. However, as a result of the mainly religious interests of the biblical texts preserved, wide sectors of social and technical activity find no representation in biblical vocabulary. This amounts in fact only to *c*. 8000 words, whereas a full range covering normal semantic fields might require some 20,000. Epigraphy has so far made only limited additions to the corpus. Non-literary Hebrew as spoken by the middle and lower classes is not well documented. There are hints about some styles of speech. Clipped military speech, as reported in 2 Kings 1, 9–11 or 9, 27 ('Him too – smite him!') is paralleled in Arad ostracon 24, lines 18–19 '[Get] the men to Elisha!'. Lower-class Hebrew is perhaps illustrated by a so far unique ostracon from seventh-century Meṣad Ḥashavyahu (Yavneh-Yam) containing the petition of a harvest-worker for the return of an impounded garment (though not everyone views it that way). Confused sentence structure and repetitive diction are found together with a preference for the so-called *waw consecutive* constructions (whereby an imperfect or jussive preceded by 'and' indicates the past, but a perfect preceded by 'and' the future) whether as an archaic feature in the petitioner's dialect, or due to his (not very successful) attempt to couch his missive in acceptable literary prose. To what extent the speech of simple people in biblical narratives reflects actual popular speech, or is affected by literary conventions, we are unable to assess.

Within such limits it is nevertheless possible to say something about the language used now in poetry and prose. The former – unattested so far outside the Bible, except perhaps for an ambiguous graffito in a tomb cave at Khirbet Beit Lei – continues earlier diction; in particular, archaic grammatical forms may be used, and the three 'prose markers' *ha-*, *'et-*, *'ᵃšer* (see above, p. 206) are employed comparatively rarely, though the distinction between poetic and prose language tends to diminish. Prose on the other hand employs these three 'markers' regularly, and for narrative the *waw consecutive* constructions are found fairly consistently. In syntax, several levels of sophistication are observable. The simplest style favours the bald juxtaposition of clauses linked by 'and', of which good examples are found in Genesis 1. Temporal or conditional clauses may also find expression in this fashion (cf. English 'Easy come, easy go'); even Deuteronomy, the prose of which is in some respects the most rhetorical in the Hebrew Bible, at times operates in this way. Still, the means for greater flexibility and precision were at hand and were employed, for instance, in official epigraphic texts such as Lachish ostraca. Thus, gerundial constructions might be used, like 'since your sending' for 'since you sent' or 'at his going' for 'as he went'. Particles and prepositions, either simple or composite, were often used (though some of these became 'overloaded' with a number of possible different meanings).

The development of such syntactical aids remains unfortunately undated, and it is indeed altogether difficult to trace developments within standard Hebrew with any precision. There was apparently not only a tendency towards linguistic conservatism but few biblical texts can be dated at all accurately by scholarly agreement. Limiting factors include the possibility of linguistically 'updating' older texts, so that they might remain intelligible for religious instruction or worship, and of the modification of non-Jerusalemite (and especially perhaps northern Israelite) writings to make them conform to Jerusalemite linguistic standards. A number of linguistic changes can nevertheless be noticed. Some of these can be interpreted as manifestations of general tendencies making for change, widely observable in many languages. One such is the tendency to avoid difficulties (in pronunciation or construction) and to simplify without regard for 'correctness'. Another is the introduction of new features to satisfy needs arising from new material or spiritual developments. Again, a wish to supersede worn-out or debased terms by fresh and striking ones may lead to change. In Hebrew, we may mention, under the headings of simplification or avoidance of effort, certain consonant changes and the replacement of infrequently used feminine plural forms of pronouns, pronominal suffixes and verbal forms by the more commonly used masculine forms, as well as the fact that the complicated *waw consecutive* constructions tend to become rarer towards the end of the period; the Judean ostraca do not use them much. Instead, there was increasing employment of the simple perfect to indicate the past, and of the imperfect to signify the future. In vocabulary, too, some changes have been noticed. Thus in the religious sphere the terms for 'congregation' or for the washing of sacrificial meat differ between the early and later periods. (Little can be said at present about datable semantic changes within the field covered by single terms over the course of time.) The tendency towards linguistic change seems to have become accentuated not long before the end of the Judean monarchy and late writers like Jeremiah and Ezekiel provide a number of good examples. It seems arguable that the events after the death of Josiah, leading up to the removal of a large proportion of the upper classes of Jerusalemite society following the defeat of King Jehoiachin in 597 BC (cf. 2 Kings 24, 10ff.), may have some bearing on the question. Circumstances did not favour the preservation of 'correct' speech or writing, and substandard popular forms so far banished from polite style now surfaced. The future, in post-Exilic Hebrew, was to be increasingly theirs, balanced by efforts to maintain a prestigious but outmoded type of language.

a & b *(Right)* Seal of Amoṣ the ṣribe (eighth–seventh century BC). he script is Moabite. Scribes were ten important functionaries and eir seals are known from both Israel d neighbouring countries.

a & b *(Below)* Seal of Eliashib, son Eshyahu (late seventh century BC). iashib was the commander of the yal fortress of Arad and in charge the stores there. He may have been command at Arad up to the struction of the town by buchadnezzar.

Seals and seal impressions

39 a & b *(Left)* Seal of Gedaliah, 'who is over the house' (from Lachish, sixth century BC), apparently belonging to Gedaliah who was appointed governor of Judah after the Babylonian conquest and the fall of the monarchy. This seal shows he had been a high official before this.

40 *(Above)* Bulla with seal impression of Gemariahu, son of Shaphan (from the City of David, Jerusalem). Bullae were blobs of moist clay intended to receive a seal imprint, much like the more recent sealing-wax. The building in which this was found, the so-called 'House of the Bullae', was burnt in the destruction of Jerusalem (586 BC) but the sealed bullae were baked hard and survived. Gemariahu was an important official at the time of Jeremiah (cf. Jeremiah 36, 10–12).

41 *(Left)* The 'Gezer Calendar', possibly a writing exercise, listing agricultural operations by months of the year. It is scratched on the flat surface of a limestone tablet.

42 *(Below)* The Siloam Tunnel inscription describes tunnelling undertaken to lead the Gihon Spring waters under the City of David to a pool inside the walled perimeter of Jerusalem, safeguarding the city's water-supply from expected Assyrian attack in 701 BC.

43 *(Opposite above)* The famous Lachish Letter no. IV (obverse), one of a collection of ostraca found in the ruins of the gate destroyed by Nebuchadnezzar. It mentions attempts to pass signals (by fire or smoke) between three points: Lachish, the writer's unknown abode and Azekah.

44 *(Opposite below)* Ostracon from Tell Qasile mentioning 30 shekels of gold from Ophir (possibly in Arabia, where Solomon is said to have obtained it) destined for Beth-Horon (*or* the temple of the god Horon). Ophir gold was obviously highly esteemed. Eighth century BC.

Writing and inscriptions

45, 46 *(Above)* Storage jar from Lachish, of the type which received the royal *lmlk*– 'belonging to the king' – stamp on the handles. The stamp may have indicated that the contents were destined for royal supply depots. Altogether four names of towns appear on the *lmlk* stamps: Hebron, Sochoh, Zif and an as yet unidentified Mmšt (the name of a place or perhaps an abbreviation for *Mmšlt*; *Mamshelet* = government = the capital, i.e. Jerusalem). *(Below)* Two jar handles with *lmlk* stamps, destined for supply depots at Sochoh and Hebron respectively.

La-melekh stamps

47, 48, 49 *(Top left)* One of two private seal impressions *mšlm 'ḥmlk* (Meshullam (son of) 'Aḥimelek') found in combination with two *lmlk* stamp impressions (on the other two handles of the same four-handled royal storage jar). Other seal impressions of this Meshullam are known at Lachish: he must have been an official involved in the manufacture, filling or distribution of the jars. *(Top right)* Royal stamp impression on a storage jar handle from Lachish with the legend *lmlk ḥbrn* ('belonging to the king, Hebron'), combined with a four-winged scarab beetle – probably a government symbol at the time of Hezekiah. *(Above)* Impression of a two-winged royal stamp seal, showing a symbol often called a 'flying scroll' (actually a very simplified flying sun disk) on a storage jar handle. The legend is *lmlk śkh* ('belonging to the king, Sochoh').

50 Bronze statuette of Baal covered with gold, from Late Bronze Age Megiddo. The crude statue of a seated deity, found at Early Iron Age Israelite Hazor (see also fig. 53) is derived from this type of image.

51 *(Above right)* Bronze statuette of a bull from the 'Bull Sanctuary' near Jenin in the Samarian uplands. It may have been intended for either Israelite or Canaanite worshippers.

52 *(Right)* Stone altar from Megiddo. Such horned altars were in common public and private use in Israel from the time of Solomon onwards.

53 *(Opposite)* Pottery cult stand from Taanach, with decoration in high relief. The imagery (sphinxes, lions etc.) is of non-Israelite derivation but was influential in the decoration of Solomon's Temple.

54 The Late Bronze Age (thirteenth century BC) 'Lachish Ewer', a ritual gift to the Fosse Temple III at Lachish. It carries a dedication to the goddess Elath in early alphabetic (proto-Canaanite) writing.

55 A miniature bronze incense stand, showing votaries making offerings to seated deities.

Non-standard and dialectal Hebrew during the period of the Divided Monarchy

Though the scribes' efforts to maintain 'correct' standards allowed only few deviations to creep into the texts they wrote, there are some hints of popular or regional usages, in addition to those referred to above. Scholars have indeed attempted to trace the beginning of linguistic features appearing in post-Exilic and even later Mishnaic Hebrew back to non-literary or spoken Hebrew in the period of the Monarchy, which occasionally influenced biblical and other writing. As one might expect, there seem to have been different styles of language even within Jerusalem – the non-official or semi-official Siloam Tunnel inscription (*c.* 703/702 BC) includes a few deviant forms. Additional impetus towards the use of non-standard Hebrew in Jerusalem may have come from the influx of large numbers of refugees from the north, especially after the fall of Samaria in 722, which some think is also connected with the increase in the size of the city about that time. There may perhaps be a link between the presence in biblical texts of features regarded as northern by scholars and that event. Since such features developed and spread further after the Exile it is likely that they entered popular Jerusalemite speech before that event, adding an additional twist to the linguistic situation in the Judean capital.

As for regional dialects outside Jerusalem, we have limited but significant guidance from epigraphy. Regarding the north, the eighth-century Samaria ostraca show us that in that city at least diphthongs became simple vowels, differing from Jerusalemite standards. This shows that northern Israel continued a Canaanite tradition which was not shared in Judah, but was found in the contemporary Phoenician and Moabite languages. In Gilead, the Deir 'Alla plaster inscription, datable possibly to before the Assyrian conquest of the region, reveals a linguistically complicated situation in which local speech appears to have been basically derived from Canaanite, but affected by Aramaic and linked with Hebrew and Moabite, for instance in the extensive use of *waw consecutive* constructions. Turning to the south, ostracon 24 from Arad on the Negeb fringe twice shows the replacement of *p* by *b*, which occurs occasionally in Phoenician and Aramaic, but is unexpected in Hebrew. All told, our information is still patchy – the language Israelites spoke and wrote must have been mutually intelligible, but where and when a Hebrew roughly of Jerusalemite type prevailed, and what deviations from this were found in various regions and at various times, is a question which remains to be elucidated by future epigraphic discoveries.

Foreign influences on Hebrew

Since the Israelites had active contacts with the neighbouring countries, and were moreover the heirs of Canaanite civilization – which had itself been extensively affected by outside influences – reflections of this situation are to be expected in the language. Loan-words designating objects, activities or weights and measures connected with trade (including international long-distance trade), besides craftsmanship and architecture, the arts, administration and warfare are one example. Such loan-words do indeed occur in some numbers, but it is usually difficult to say when they came into the language. A good many had been incorporated into Canaanite and are presumably linguistic heirlooms.

Nothing is known to have been borrowed by Hebrew from Moabite, Ammonite or Edomite, and hardly anything from early Arabic, except a few terms connected with the commerce along the incense trade route, such as the word *lebonah* ('incense') itself. Philistia to the west also contributed little, except for the term *seren* ('ruler'), perhaps cognate with Greek *tyrannos*, and it is possible that the (originally Anatolian?) words *k/qoba'* ('helmet') and *širyon* ('armour') entered from that side. More significant are loans from Egyptian, which include words for export goods like *neter* ('natron') and *šeš* ('fine linen'), the names of some precious stones, terms for writing instruments, and a few weights and measures, as well as terms for natural features found in Egypt. In view of the imperial sway Egypt held in Palestine up to the twelfth century more might perhaps have been expected. Most significant are loans from Akkadian, which include terms related to practically all spheres of human activity. Many had been taken over already by the Canaanites and some, like *pehah* ('governor') may be linked with the advance of Assyria in the first millennium BC, while others probably reached Israel indirectly after having been taken over by the Arameans. A number of words for precious goods such as jewels, spices and aromatics also reached Israel in an Akkadianized form (the trade routes concerned went through Mesopotamia). Such are the (Hurrian?) term for jasper (Hebrew *yašpeh*, Akkadian *(i)ašpu*) and the Sanskrit-derived word for emerald (Hebrew *bareqet*, Akkadian *barraqtu*); the stones came from Armenia and India respectively. Other terms seem to have entered Hebrew without such modification in forms taken more directly from their source language (Sanskrit, Tamil-Malaysian, Dravidian or other), like *'ahalot* ('aloes'), *piṭedah* ('topaz' or 'chrysolite') or *tukkiym* ('peacocks'). In a few cases, loans can be more closely linked with special circumstances – thus the Egyptian-derived Hebrew term for fine linen, *šeš*, is in later biblical texts superseded by northern-derived *buṣ* ('byssus'), possibly reflecting a change in Israel's external trade. Again, the fact that while many Hebrew terms for weights and measures are linked with Akkadian, but the measure for liquids, *hin*, with Egyptian, may be linked with the long-standing oil export from Palestine to Egypt in particular. On the other hand it is interesting to note that in spite of the fact that Hebrew shekel weights were so calibrated that they could easily be converted into Egyptian *qedet* units, that term was not apparently taken over and the long-established *shekel* maintained its popularity.

In the case of Phoenician it is difficult to isolate Hebrew loan-words from that source, to which it is so closely related, but it has been suggested that Phoenician style and diction influenced Hebrew writers. Thus the tendency in some late pre-Exilic, and still more in certain post-Exilic, biblical books to favour the use of the infinitive absolute instead of a finite tense has been traced to Phoenician models. Parallels have also been noticed in phraseology – the early coupling of 'kings' and 'princes' in Judges (5, 3) can be matched in a

Phoenician inscription, as can the phrase 'under the sun' in (post-Exilic) Ecclesiastes (1, 3).

Relations between Hebrew and Aramaic are specially intriguing. That vocabulary akin to Aramaic appears already in the Song of Deborah we have noted, and isolated words are also to be found scattered in the Hebrew Bible, where they appear to become more frequent in late writers such as Jeremiah and Ezekiel. More significant, however, is the presence in the Hebrew Bible of grammatical forms related to Aramaic which seem to indicate a more profound linguistic influence. Such Aramaic traits may be partly due to increasing Aramean importance in politics, war and trade in the ninth and eighth centuries setting a fashion in speech, and partly to the presence of Aramaic population elements. The latter is reflected in place-names like *Hazor Hadatta* (Joshua 15, 25), personal names like *Adriel* (1 Samuel 18, 19) and later by Aramaic ostraca, as well as Aramaic influence in the plaster inscription at Tell Deir 'Alla in Gilead. However, Aramaic apparently never achieved before the fall of the Monarchy the increasingly dominating influence on Hebrew that it was to gain in the post-Exilic period.

Writing

The antecedents

When Israel made its appearance on the stage of history, writing had long been known in the Near East. The earliest systems – those of Mesopotamia and Egypt – were very complicated. Neither were alphabetic but were based on a mixture of logographic and syllabic signs; they could thus only be learnt slowly by a limited scribal class through prolonged schooling. Apart from these common fundamentals, Egyptian and Mesopotamian writing differed entirely. Moreover, Mesopotamian scribes wrote their signs by impressing wedge-shaped (*cuneiform*) stabs on clay tablets with a stylus, while their Egyptian colleagues wrote with a brush-pen and ink on papyrus or sometimes leather for important work, but on potsherds (ostraca), wood or stone splinters for notes of only temporary importance. During the second millennium BC both systems were to a limited extent used by official circles in Palestine. Cuneiform texts in the Akkadian language were written and read by trained local scribes employed in the international correspondence of Canaanite kings, but were also used as a medium for the acquisition of Mesopotamian religious and secular literature. Egyptian writing, both in the formal hieroglyphic and in the cursive hieratic styles, was used particularly by the Egyptian administration established in Palestine after its incorporation into the Egyptian empire.

By the side of these official foreign scripts, however, alphabetic writing was developing – mainly among the Canaanites – during the second half of the first millennium BC in the Levant, where it is attested particularly in Palestine and Sinai. By the thirteenth century a limited repertoire of perhaps up to 27 conventional rather than pictographic signs had evolved. Each of these functioned as a letter standing for a definite consonant (followed by some, or no, vowel). This system was suitable for expressing the consonantal structure (of more significance in the conveying of meaning than vowels) of contemporary Canaanite speech. Later, when a number of consonants fused, a smaller number of signs (22) would suffice for this purpose. This new writing was adaptable – it could be written vertically, or horizontally (from right to left, or left to right) or *boustrophedon* (right to left then left to right on alternate lines) with pen and ink in the Egyptian fashion or scratched or incised on stone, metal or pottery. Being easy to learn, it seems soon to have been used by persons outside official and scribal circles. The alphabetic idea was even applied to cuneiform writing, resulting in the creation of alphabetic cuneiform scripts, best-known from the north Syrian city of Ugarit but attested also in Palestine. The idea of a fixed order of the alphabet and perhaps letter names often similar to those still used for the Hebrew alphabet also made their appearance during the Late Bronze Age.

The turbulent times during which the old political and social order in the Levant were overturned also affected writing. During the twelfth century BC alphabetic cuneiform vanished and Mesopotamian-derived cuneiform went out of use in Palestine, returning only in the wake of the Assyrian conquest in the eighth century, when some Assyrian victory monuments were put up in Samaria, Ashdod and elsewhere, and a few administrative and commercial tablets were used at Gezer and Samaria. With the withdrawal of the Egyptian empire, Egyptian writing similarly became a rarity. Pharaoh Sheshonq put up a victory stela at Megiddo, of which a fragment has survived; some imported articles bore Egyptian hieroglyphs, and hieratic was written occasionally (as at Arad and Kadesh Barnea in Judah) in transactions connected with Egyptians, or as school exercises, during the seventh or sixth century. Egyptian numeral signs were however used in the northern and southern kingdoms from the eighth century onwards, though the Phoenician system was also employed sporadically. Canaanite-derived alphabetic writing held the field, and the Israelites came to use it almost exclusively.

The beginnings of Israelite literacy

When did Israelite literacy begin? According to biblical records, it began quite early, even before the conquest during which Joshua is said to have written a copy of the Law of Moses on the stones of an altar he built on Mount Ebal (Joshua 8, 32) – presumably for all to see. Scholars, however, have hesitated to accept an early date. Writing, it has been held by some, was the preserve of the scribal class in the ancient Near East, and it was too recondite an art for members of a simple society like early Israel to learn. Yet, as numerous graffiti in and near Arabia show, dating perhaps from the sixth or possibly eighth century BC onwards, even members of the yet simpler bedouin society were able to scribble quite trivial messages in alphabetic writing. Moreover, a number of graffiti of possibly thirteenth- to eleventh-century date, found in the Palestinian highland belt, come from settlements possibly Israelite in character, such as Khirbet Raddanah (twelfth century BC), or from localities at some distance from Canaanite towns, as in the cases of Khirbet Tannin in Mount Ephraim (late eleventh century) and Manahat some miles south of Jerusalem. It cannot be proved these were written by Israelites, but neither can it be proved they were not. The same applies to an ostracon from Beth Shemesh on the hill border (c. 1200 BC?) which possibly contains the name Hanan, used later by Israelites. The striking incident reported in Judges (8, 13), where Gideon asks a young man encountered in the town of Succoth to write down the names of the city elders, does not necessarily have to be explained by assuming the young man must have been an official, and the town Canaanite. For the present, the issue of early Israelite literacy remains open.

51 Inscription (including a nearly complete alphabet) found at 'Izbet Sartah (twelfth–eleventh century BC). It may have served as a writing exercise, and illustrates the adoption of alphabetic writing by the Israelites.

By the beginning of the Iron Age, a 22-letter alphabet had become predominant, and the Phoenician variety of this – developed in the Lebanese trading towns – gained general acceptance in the Levant by c. 1000 BC. Two finds illustrate how this process affected Palestine. A remarkable text scratched on a potsherd, ascribed to the twelfth or eleventh century BC and found at 'Izbet Sartah near Aphek (Ras el-'Ain), east of Tel Aviv, shows a mixture of sometimes rather idiosyncratic letter shapes. It includes an (incomplete) alphabet mostly in the standard order, written from left to right (but the letter *p* precedes ',
reversing the normal sequence as in some alphabetic psalms). It may be a school exercise, and coming from what is usually regarded as an Israelite village near the Canaanite town of Aphek it may illustrate the transference of the art of writing from Canaanites to Israelites. Whether a group of inscribed arrowheads found at el-Khadr near Bethlehem and dated to the eleventh century has any links with early Israel is doubtful. The tenth-century Gezer tablet on the other hand, perhaps also a writing exercise, shows letter shapes of Phoenician derivation, written in what thereafter remained the standard direction of right to left (pl. 41). This text is mostly (though not universally) regarded as Israelite, and Hebrew epigraphy may for the present begin with it.

Characteristic features of Hebrew writing
The Phoenician alphabet had been evolved to represent the Phoenician speech sounds, which did not entirely correspond to those used by the Arameans and Hebrews. Nevertheless most Hebrew consonants could be satisfactorily covered by Phoenician letters, though the script did not distinguish *š* (*Shin*),

representing the *sh* sound, and *ś* (*Śin*), later pronounced '*s*', but originally perhaps a 'lateral' sound similar to Welsh '*ll*', which were separate phonemes in Jerusalemite speech. Vowels were not expressed in Phoenician writing when the Israelites took it over. Following possible Aramaic devices, ways to indicate long vowels by consonants ('vowel letters') were gradually introduced in Hebrew writing, however, from the ninth century onwards: final -*h* could stand for -āh, -ēh or -ōh, final -*w* for -ū, final -*y* for -ī, and final ' might also indicate -ā. With the reduction of diphthongs into simple long vowels, y̱ also came to express ē, and w̱, ō. These vowel letters were also to a limited extent introduced to indicate long vowels inside words, though standardized spellings were never quite achieved; short vowels remained unexpressed throughout. Consonants were usually written separately, though ligatures developed to a limited extent in later scribal practice. Words were divided, first by short vertical strokes and later by dots or spaces; the latter might also separate phrases, sentences or clauses.

Styles of developed Hebrew writing

Up to the ninth century there was little distinction between the scripts used in Syria, Phoenicia and Israel (and it is correspondingly difficult sometimes to be certain to which category a short piece of writing belongs). However, the development of important dynastic states in Israel and Syria, with their own scribal establishments, led to the development of separate Aramaic and Palestinian styles of writing, distinct from those used in Phoenicia; in addition, a tendency to develop cursive scripts by the side of the original monumental or lapidary shapes occurred in all three regions. In Palestine this is evident particularly in a tendency to lengthen vertical downstrokes, and to curve those of certain letters forward to the left, in the direction of writing. This came to dominate Hebrew and especially Judean but also official Moabite letter shapes. By the eighth century, cursive writing had superseded monumental styles in Israel and Judah almost completely. Even public inscriptions like the Siloam Tunnel text (pl. 42) were expressed in this way, though more old-fashioned letter forms might occasionally be used, as on seals. At the same time, several styles of cursive developed. A 'formal' cursive was used by highly proficient scribes for important or official texts; less formal, 'free' cursive writing was employed by the educated, while 'vulgar' cursive with badly formed letters was the style of those who wrote only occasionally. The best scribal styles achieved high calligraphic standards – marked by a feeling for flowing line and balance they remained unequalled in elegance in the Near East until the rise of developed Arabic writing many centuries later. From the eighth century onwards, Hebrew writing is occasionally found in the Philistine coastal plain, probably in the wake of commercial interchange or Israelite cultural and political influence, which were probably involved earlier in the linkage between the official Moabite (and Edomite) and the Israelite scripts.

The best writing was no doubt the work of professional scribes, some of whom would be employed by the administrative or religious authorities, and others by prominent individuals, like Baruch, the son of Neriah, who took down Jeremiah's dictated words (cf. Jeremiah 36, 4, 32). Still others may have made a living by writing out or reading documents for the illiterate on demand, as was customary in the Near East until fairly recently. Notes might be taken down on special writing tablets of wood or even ivory which had raised margins and a recessed interior filled with a wax mixture. Several such tablets could be hinged together like a folding screen. The writing would be inscribed on the waxed surface with a stylus, and when the tablets were folded up it would be protected by the raised margins until it was no longer needed and was erased. Actual specimens have been found – one in a wreck discovered at Uluburun (Kaş) off the south Turkish coast, dated *c.* 1400 BC, and another in a late eighth-century well at Nimrud in Assyria (though none have yet been found in Israel). Alternatively, texts of only temporary importance might be scratched, or more frequently written in ink, on potsherds. A pen-case containing recesses for the pens and others for black or red ink tablets (diluted before use), besides a special knife for trimming pens, cutting papyrus, or erasing were also part of a scribe's equipment.

Important documents or literary texts would be written in ink on papyrus (imported from Egypt) or perhaps on locally produced leather. No pre-Exilic specimens of the latter are known at present to have survived and only one fragment of a letter on papyrus, later erased to make room for a list, has come to light in a cave in the Wadi Murabba'at, near the Dead Sea. Indirect evidence for the existence of documents on papyrus is however available in the shape of clay *bullae*, pellets of clay which were once affixed to documents to fasten them and which were impressed with the validating seals. Often they still bear on the reverse the imprints left by the fibres of the papyrus sheets. As for books (which consisted of several sheets fastened together side by side to form a scroll), none of pre-Exilic date have yet been found, but an idea as to what they looked like may be gained from the eighth-century Deir 'Alla inscription written in ink on plaster and apparently copied from a formal manuscript. Its text was arranged in carefully spaced columns, framed by horizontal and vertical lines; important passages, such as the beginning, were written in red ink but the remainder in black. Whether any Hebrew books were illustrated with pictures or drawings, as was the case in contemporary Egypt, is at present unknown. For storage, books and documents might be placed in specially shaped jars or chests, or perhaps accommodated on shelves. An archive room, identified by finds of clay *bullae* and two special jars, has recently been discovered in the City of David in Jerusalem. It contained four limestone stands (possibly cultic?) but also some domestic pottery, and so perhaps served more than one purpose.

Schooling and the spread of literacy

Schools may have been established to pass on the scribal arts and traditions. That such existed in Israel as in Egypt or Mesopotamia is a reasonable assumption. It has even been suggested that there were schools with different curricula, geared to the varying needs of centres of government and religious sanctuaries, in the capital and in the more important towns, and perhaps else-where. Reading and writing would be taught (including on occasion Egyptian hieratic numerals and other symbols, as at Kadesh Barnea), presumably also basic mathematics and other subjects of practical value, besides the study of texts suited to the type of institution to which the schools were attached. No certain traces of school buildings or classrooms have been found, though some think the ninth- to eighth-century structure found at Kuntillet 'Ajrud also functioned as a school, in view of the numerous scribblings on jars found there. There are also a number of possible school exercises. The early tablet from 'Izbet Ṣarṭah may have been such, and later the first five letters of the alphabet scribbled on the steps of the residency at Lachish may represent an eighth-century schoolboy's attempt to practise his ABC. More advanced textual study may be illustrated by the tenth-century Gezer tablet (pl. 41), while an incom-plete seventh-century ostracon found at Arad (no. 88), announcing the acces-sion of a king, may have been used as a model for literary composition. Schooling cannot, however, have been entirely restricted to the scribal class. To what extent the commission reportedly sent out by King Jehoshaphat to teach the people of Judah (2 Chronicles 17, 7–9) was interested in spreading general (as against religious) instruction is not clear, but from the eighth century a considerable and growing percentage of a wider public was somehow acquiring at least a basic literacy. Indeed, by that time the assumptions in Deuteronomy (6, 9; 11, 20) that ordinary householders could write a set text on the doorposts of their houses, and that the king could copy out and read his own scroll of the Law (Deuteronomy 17, 18–19) were probably not far removed from the truth.

The existence of formal, free and vulgar scripts indicate that writing was practised over a wide social spectrum, and closer study of the location and char-acter of texts discovered makes this even clearer. Writing has been found not only in towns or fortresses, but also in rural contexts (some quite early) as at Wadi Dilbeh in the Samaritan hills, in farmsteads in the Buqei'ah Valley near the Dead Sea or at Manahat near Jerusalem. Producers or dealers in various sorts of wine or grain, and craftsmen like potters or ivory-workers, might have marked their products or recorded their transactions. Moreover, indications of ownership or content on ordinary household containers, or warnings addressed to potential tomb robbers make sense only if those concerned could read them. There seems also to have been some literacy among women, not only among society ladies or women of substance who, like their menfolk, owned seals inscribed with their names, which they could use in mercantile or legal transac-tions (cf. Proverbs 31, 16), but also among women of humbler status, if an inscribed spindle-whorl from near Beth Shean may be taken as a guide – spin-ning was women's work.

Monumental or display inscriptions

We must now take a closer look at the various types of inscriptions involved. Monumental texts for public display are not numerous, and they do not at present include any in Hebrew written on a plastered surface, as demanded in Deuteronomy 27, 2–3, and exemplified by the non-Hebrew text from Tell Deir 'Alla, with the exception of some Hebrew graffiti written in the Phoenician script at Kuntillet 'Ajrud in the Negeb. Nor are there any early examples. For the ninth century, the only monumental public text is still the inscription of King Mesha of Moab, written in a language dialectally different from Hebrew. Even the number of display inscriptions on stone from the eighth century is limited. Only one small fragment of what was presumably a victory stela has so far been found (at Samaria, none being known from Judah). The apparent paucity of such texts may have influenced the decline of the monumental script. The famous Siloam Tunnel inscription (possibly semi-official) is written in formal cursive, describing the construction of that tunnel in Jerusalem (701 BC) by two gangs of men working inwards from opposite ends (pl. 42). The text well conveys the exciting finish of the operation: 'While there were still three cubits to be cut through, a man's voice was heard calling to his mate – for there was a fissure [?] in the rock . . . so on the day the breach was made, the stone cutters struck, one gang towards the other, pick against pick; and the water flowed from the spring to the pool, a distance of 1200 cubits, and 100 cubits was the height of the rock above the stone cutters.'

A fragment of another official inscription was found on the Ophel hill in Jerusalem during recent excavations along with a stone plaque apparently giving the names of the owners of the house to which it was presumably affixed like a modern name-plate. This is a strikingly novel type of find, but should perhaps cause no surprise, for inscriptions on monumental tombs – the abodes of the dead – similarly indicated the occupiers, especially in the prestigious necropolis of Siloam/Silwan across the Kidron Valley. The best-known of these is that of (Sheban)iahu the royal steward, possibly the very person who attracted an unfavourable mention from Isaiah (22, 15–16): 'This is the tomb of [Sheban]iahu who is over the house [=the royal steward]. There is no silver or gold here, only [his bones] and the bones of his maidservant with him. Cursed be the man who will open this!' Other tomb inscriptions have been found at Khirbet el-Qom near Hebron, belonging to less exalted persons than those of the élite buried at Silwan. Here, one text curses whoever may efface the writing; two others express religious sentiments in which Asherah may be linked with Yahweh (see p. 236). More orthodox monotheistic sentiments are expressed in a graffito on rock found in the Judean desert, and in another at Khirbet Beit Lei in the Shephelah; concern for Jerusalem is also voiced in the letter, which may date from the time before or after the fall of the city in 586 BC, or *c.* 700 BC.

A fragment of an eighth-century ivory plaque found at Nimrud in Mesopotamia, containing part of a beautifully written Hebrew inscription and mentioning a 'great king', represents a special type of display text. It may have come to Assyria from northern Israel, either as booty or tribute.

Ostraca
More numerous and enlightening are texts written on potsherds, mostly in ink. There are now sizeable collections of these – Samaria has furnished some 70

legible texts, Arad a similar number, Lachish some 18, and smaller numbers or single specimens have turned up in several other sites.

The Samaria ostraca, now dated to the first part of the eighth century BC, are tax dockets recording the delivery of commodities (mainly wine and oil) from various localities in the territory of the tribe of Manasseh to the capitals. They also give the names of persons (tax gatherers, landowners or recipients of royal bounty) concerned in the transactions. In Judah, two ostraca found at Tell Qasile, one of which mentions Ophir gold (pl. 44), may similarly involve official payments linked with what was then a river port settlement. The Arad ostraca (tenth to sixth century, though there is some question as to the stratigraphy) likewise include a number of administrative texts, mainly orders addressed to a local official called Eliashib to hand out rations – some to *Kittim* (perhaps Greek mercenaries), others to persons travelling in the king's service. Such payments were apparently periodically booked in ledgers. There is also a mention of religious functionaries and of the 'house of YHWH' (the Temple in Jerusalem?), and of danger from the Edomites. The Lachish letters (dated 588 BC) may make up the correspondence of a local garrison commander with outlying stations; a somewhat stilted and florid style is typical of some of them. One begins, 'To my lord Ya'osh. May YHWH give my lord peaceable tidings even this day, even this day. Who is your servant – a dog – that my lord should remember his servant?' Various matters are dealt with in this correspondence, such as the passing of a military mission to Egypt, the sequestration of dangerous correspondence and the activities of an unnamed prophet whose pronouncements are thought to be likely to affect public morale unfavourably.

Where non-official correspondence is concerned our documentation is much poorer. Except for the fragmentary text from Murabba'at we have no private letters, though there is a petition by a field worker on corvee service to have his garment, impounded by the officer in charge of the gang, returned. This text, found at Meṣad Ḥashavyahu near Yavneh Yam, some distance southwest of Tel Aviv, is, in the opinion of some, unusual in apparently not having been drafted by a scribe; it rather reflects the dictation of the petitioner, whose disjointed speech shows both his anxiety and a lack of stylistic training (though others view it differently). Texts connected with the administration of justice, or with marriage and divorce, inheritance or other family matters remain to be discovered.

Seals

All documents of any significance were sealed, and seals or seal impressions (especially on clay *bullae* once affixed to papyrus sheets) form an important part of our epigraphic repertoire, for they are usually inscribed with the name of the seal's owner and his (or her) father, sometimes also with some additional details. Israelites used stamp rather than cylinder seals, shaped mostly like the Egyptian scarab. Many were made of limestone; the wealthy went in for semi-precious stones, and occasionally faience, glass, copper, silver or gold; the poor probably made do with ones carved from bone. Seals were pierced lengthways so they could be strung in a necklace, or worn round the wrist; alternatively they might form part of signet rings. The text was normally engraved on the flat, lower side; writing on the top of the seal, or top and bottom, is rare. Early specimens from the ninth century onwards mostly have decorative motifs in addition to the lettering (which was sometimes added to ready-made seals where room could be found). Egyptian-derived motifs favoured by Phoenician seal-cutters, or others derived from the art of Syria, were common – sphinxes, griffins, lions, Egyptian deities like Horus, and purely decorative palmettos and pseudo-hieroglyphs. Unusual themes like a lyre or a ship also appear, as well as family crests such as locusts or cockerels. Later, from the seventh century onwards, seals without such decoration became fashionable, especially in Judah. On these the text, mostly of type 'X, son (or daughter) of Y', is usually arranged in two superimposed lines divided by two parallel horizontal strokes. Though angular letter forms occur occasionally, scribal cursive, of great elegance in the best specimens, is predominant. The writing on bone seals, executed perhaps by indigent owners themselves, tends to be poor. The seals and seal imprints offer valuable information about Hebrew names in current use, including some borne also by prominent biblical persons, like Ahab and Jeremiah. They also mention a number of functionaries known from the Bible, such as the governor of the city, the royal steward and the servant (minister) of the king (pls 39, 40). No seals belonging to an Israelite or Judean monarch have been identified with certainty, though one which perhaps belonged to Jezebel is known. On the other hand there are a number of seals or *bullae* which may have belonged to prominent people mentioned in the Bible, like Baruch the son of Neriah, Jeremiah's scribe, Haggai son of Shebniah or Gedaliah son of Ahikam whom Nebuchadnezzar made governor of Judah after the fall of the Monarchy. At Arad, three very similar seals, all inscribed with the name of Eliashib, a high local official, have been found – they were probably used by his subordinates to validate documents at his orders. On the other hand, imprints of the same seal have turned up in a number of localities, possibly indicating that the same royal official performed duties in more than one place, or perhaps that rich land-owners had multiple estates under their control.

Seal imprints are also found on store jars, perhaps to identify either the private owner or the official who had to deal with the contents of the vessel. This is especially likely in the rare cases where such imprints are found together with special stamp sealings attributable to the royal administration in Judah (pls 45–9). In essence these show either a more or less simplified scarab beetle design or a 'flying scroll' – actually a much modified winged sun disk – both usually superscribed with the Hebrew letters *lmlk* (i.e. *la-melekh*: 'belonging to the king') and with the name of one of four towns, Hebron, Ziph, Sochoh and an unidentified *Mmšt* (perhaps located in northwestern Judah), written beneath. The sealings, always placed on one or more of the jar's handles, were made by over 20 stone or wooden stamps. The scarab beetle and 'flying scroll' designs are official symbols of the Judean monarchy, and are related to the iconography of the contemporary neighbouring countries. The scripts vary a little. Those on the most detailed scarab beetle designs are comparable to inscriptions on seals or on stone some time before *c*. 700, the more simplified ones are a little later, while those with the 'flying scroll' are typologically later still. According to recent excavation results at Lachish and Tell Batash both the main types existed in the reign of King Hezekiah and were found in the stratum destroyed in the siege by Sennacherib in 701 BC, though it is not known how much earlier the scarab beetle type was produced. The 'flying scroll' stamps may have remained in vogue later, especially perhaps during the reign of Josiah in the seventh century. The exact dating and purpose of these jars has been much debated.

Inscribed weights and measures

Israelite and especially Judean monarchs did, however, provide standard weights and measures (which would ensure that taxes in kind were paid in due measure), and others were no doubt produced by private initiative as occasion demanded. These would often have an indication of the measuring unit in writing, with multiples or fractions in words or figures. Our data are very incomplete, and in particular no measuring rods showing standards of length have so far been discovered. Where capacity for liquids is concerned there are two instances of writing on incomplete store jars, both of the eighth century, indicating that these each held one *bath*. One from Tell Beit Mirsim simply has the letters *bt* ('bath') but another from Lachish specifies royal measure by the words *bt lmlk* (*bath la-melekh*, 'royal bath'). Yet another, complete jar from Lachish simply uses the abbreviation *b*. No other pre-Exilic vessels indicating units of wet or dry measure are known at present.

Inscribed weights on the other hand are fairly frequent. They are mostly of stone and spheroid shaped, more rarely rectangular; weights made of metal are few. The standard indicated is the shekel or related units, and multiples or fractions of them. The shekel could simply be indicated by the (Egyptian-derived?) symbol, $\eth$, by itself. The earliest instances come from the northern kingdom and are dated to the eighth century, before the Assyrian conquest. In the south the letters *š* or *šl* were sometimes used as an abbreviation in texts. 'Royal' weight might be indicated by the additional word *lmlk* (*la-melekh*). Other units, named in writing on weights, are the *neṣeph* (written *nṣp*=⅚ of a shekel) the *beqaʿ* (written *bqʿ*=½ shekel) and the *pym* (written *pym*=⅔ shekel). The *gerah* (1/24, later 1/20 shekel) is recognizable indirectly by figures on weights though no case where *gerah* was written on a weight is known at present. The numerals used on weights and elsewhere are Egyptian hieratic – the occurrence of Phoenician numerals on an ostracon found at the river port site of Tell Qasile is exceptional – and they express the number of Egyptian *qedet* weights concerned. Since these corresponded to Hebrew shekels at the ratio of 4 shekels to 5 qedets, figures 5, 10, 20, 30 and 50 on weights refer respectively to 4, 8, 16, 20 and 40 shekel units. For other purposes, like the numbering of days or years, Egyptian numerals were used by the Israelites at their normal face value. Among the abbreviations found in texts, some symbols for measures or for commodities are likewise taken from Egyptian writing.

Writing was, lastly, occasionally employed to indicate ownership of various items, or, in the case of pottery vessels, the type or origin of their contents. Such writing was sometimes incised or chiselled after firing on the complete containers. Jars and decanters in particular might specify the type or origin of wine they held. Several came from the Hebron region. Some pottery bottles found at Gibeon have texts incised in vulgar cursive script on their handles, mostly beginning with the name of the place in Hebrew letters, followed by *gdr* or *gdd* and finally one of several personal names. These texts were first interpreted as indicating particular enclosed vineyards at Gibeon or Gedor nearby and their owners, but they are now often regarded as referring to persons linked with military detachments stationed at the place. They probably date from the very end of the Hebrew monarchy, or from the Exilic period thereafter.

Texts and literature

Ancient Hebrew literature does not become a tangible reality for us before the twelfth century BC, the period of the Judges, at the earliest, and the bulk of it is much later. The Hebrew Bible is still almost our only source. Epigraphic discoveries offer some information about the styles of writing used by official and semi-official circles (mainly during the eighth to sixth centuries), and the tenth-century Gezer Calendar (pl. 41), which was not written in standard Hebrew, may possibly reproduce an archaic farmer's mnemonic saw. None of these can be regarded as literature proper. Biblical texts are usually classed as either poetry or prose, following European tradition, but it has been pointed out that such a division fits Hebrew literature only imperfectly. 'High' prose may at times blend into poetry or 'poetic prose', and prophetic admonitions often take an intermediate position between the two. The existence of literary prose by the side of poetry in ancient Israel deserves comment, however. While ancient Israelite poetry was closely linked with that of its neighbours, and especially that of Late Bronze Age Ugarit, no literary prose texts are known from there at present. Epic verse compositions in Ugarit took the place of prose narratives as met in Israel, for which literary predecessors have still to be found. Epic works, on the other hand, are unknown in Israel, perhaps because of the non-Israelite religious association of that genre. While we are thus thrown back on the Hebrew Bible, we must remember that this contains only such writings as were selected for their religious content or relevance, from a much larger body of texts available to the reading or listening public, a number of which were either excerpted or referred to. Some were probably mainly poetical, like the Book of Jashar (Joshua 10, 13; 2 Samuel 1, 18) and the Book of the Wars of the Lord (Numbers 21, 14). Others, like the Chronicles of the Kings of Israel and Judah, to which frequent reference was made, were presumably in prose; still others, like the works ascribed to Nathan the Prophet, Gad the Seer, Ahijah of Shiloh, and Iddo the Seer (1 Chronicles 29, 29; 2 Chronicles 9, 29) may have contained elements of both prose and poetry. Still others seem to be lost without trace, in particular any works of a utilitarian character, such as texts dealing with mathematical or chemical problems. Such writings were produced in Egypt and Mesopotamia and used there for scribal education, and writings of this kind would also have been desirable in Israel for similar purposes. That something of this kind was known in pre-Israelite Canaan is hinted at by veterinary texts for horses at Ugarit – the health of humans presumably received no less attention, nor their technical needs.

Not all literature was written, though, or restricted to a literate audience. Some texts, like alphabetic psalms, are indeed best appreciated by a literate public and composed by literate authors, yet there will always have been wide circles relying on listening to recitals who would have provided an audience for oral compositions based on traditional techniques. It has been suggested that bards carrying on traditions of oral composition were found in Israel as elsewhere, but we must note that where a bard might have been expected in the social scene described in Amos 6, 4–6, he is absent. Similarly, there is no evidence that oral literature was recited around a campfire or by a well in the evening in either town or country – as Shakespeare knew, weary ploughmen snore at night, leaving literary entertainments to their social betters. We must wait for more precise evidence concerning literary production, and its reception.

Poetry

Ever since the eighteenth century, when Lowth published a revolutionary study of Hebrew poetry, parallelism has been recognized as a basic feature of Hebrew versification: the first part (colon) of a verse is apt to be echoed in the second, either repeating, or strengthening its meaning or contrasting it with an opposite; the second colon may lead on to the next verse. Instead of two there may be three or more linked cola. Meaning often crystallizes around key words in these sections (which occur mostly in traditional word pairs, like 'be glad' 'rejoice', 'silver' 'gold', 'Heaven' 'Earth'). These are often called A and B words: A words being more ordinary and B words more unusual terms with a stronger impact. The order of A and B words may be reversed in the second colon (chiasmus); A words may also be repeated in successive verses, linking them together – this feature is regarded as typical of early poems, as is the use of numbers in ascending order, like 3–4 in the first and second colon, respectively. There are other refinements too, like alliteration and rhyme or word sound effects. A number of verses may make up a stanza, of which there may be several in a poem; terminated on occasion by a refrain, they tend to be of quite different length.

A question which has aroused much discussion is whether ancient Hebrew poetry knew metre. Here opinions have varied widely, from those who held there was none, and that all one could do was to count the number of syllables (or syllable-making consonants) in cola, which may be fairly regular but on occasion subject to considerable deviation, to those who discern the presence of regular stress patterns, such as three word stresses in each colon, or 3–2 (the elegy (*qinah*) scheme). Again there are difficulties, such as our ignorance of original pronunciation, the question of whether several words could form a group with only one joint accent (or, vice versa, whether subsidiary stresses in a long word could be counted), and of course the often quite irregular length of some cola. It has also been pointed out that stress alone may not be significant – it is linked with semantic and syntactic aspects when meaningful.

More recently, Hebrew poetry has been shown to possess close links with that of other ancient Near Eastern nations, in particular Akkadian and still more Ugaritic poetry, of which latter a good deal is known because the surviving texts written in alphabetic cuneiform on clay tablets have revealed a considerable body of literary as well as other texts. In spite of the great distance in space and time, Ugaritic literature is astonishingly close to that of ancient Israel. Not only is verse structure based on parallelism (found also in Akkadian and other poetry) but Ugaritic pairs of *A* and *B* words are also met in Hebrew literature, as indeed are whole phrases which recur with little modification on the Hebrew side. Though regrettably little is known about ancient Canaanite literature outside Ugarit and its Phoenician successor, it appears that Hebrew poetry is part of a continuum covering the Late Bronze Age and Iron Age Levant. This does not mean that it is entirely derivative, for it posesses features of its own, skilfully interwoven with inherited tradition. On the formal side, we may point to the presence in Israelite odes of introductory invocations, such as 'Hear, O ye kings; give ear, O ye princes' (Judges 5, 3) or 'Give ear, O ye heavens . . . and hear, O earth' (Deuteronomy 32, 1), or a dedication like 'I will sing unto the Lord' (Exodus 15). Such seem, on present evidence, to have been a specially Israelite feature. Another such, concerning content, is a strong tendency in ancient Hebrew poetry to use imagery, often based on close observation of nature. We may give Jeremiah 14, 5–6 as an example: 'The hind calves in the open country and forsakes her young because there is no grass; for lack of herbage, wild asses stand on the high bare places and snuff the wind for moisture, as jackals do, and their eyes begin to fail.' Sometimes the mode of expression is very terse, though contemporaries would have known what was meant: when, in Psalm 126, the exiled Judeans ask for their captivity to be turned like streams in the dry Negeb, the image evoked is that of a wadi in sudden spate, overpowering and terrifying but life-giving in the end. Such imagery has sometimes been compared with that of the ancient desert Arabs who had a similarly keen eye for nature, and indeed the image of the wadi in flood is used with somewhat similar implications at the end of the great ode of Imru'l-Qays. Not all Hebrew poetry is of the same literary quality, but the best is outstanding.

Prose

Hebrew prose preserved in the Bible is mostly either legal, or narrative including historical; or hortatory including prophetic. Epigraphic finds have added a limited corpus of administrative and related texts, which show few stylistically distinctive features. Hardly any of the legal texts outside Deuteronomy can rate as literary prose but it is of interest that in their formulation (as well as in their concepts) they show some analogies with other ancient Near Eastern laws.

Casuistic formulae of the type 'If . . . then . . .' are matched especially in Mesopotamian law codes; apodictic enactments of the type 'Thou shalt . . ./ thou shalt not . . .' have been compared with Egyptian, Hittite and Assyrian laws and enactments. Deuteronomy holds a place of its own stylistically. It is drafted in high rhetorical prose showing links with the hortatory prose of Jeremiah; while foreign stylistic analogies with late Assyrian texts, especially of the time of Esarhaddon (seventh century BC), have been pointed out.

To the Israelites who traced the very birth of their nation back to a historical event – the Exodus from Egypt and the Covenant entered into at Mount Sinai – historical traditions obviously mattered greatly and they are indeed unmatched among ancient Near Eastern nations in their comprehensive sweep. Some may go back to oral accounts transferred to writing, others to written sources. Scholarly analysis has pointed out the existence of a number of literary genres here, and also of greatly varying external parallels, especially among the motifs found in folklore. Some such external analogies are widely found, others only within limited regions. Thus, the Hebrew Flood story is best matched in the Babylonian story of the deluge; similarly, while stories about the marvellous birth and early history of a hero are known in various regions, the closest analogy to the account of the birth and miraculous rescue of Moses (Exodus 2, 1–10) occurs in the Babylonian story about the birth, exposure and marvellous rescue of Sargon of Akkad. Analogies with the Aegean area have also been suggested, which could go back to early contacts. Some Hebrew motifs are perhaps 'home-grown', like that of the hero's acquisition of a bride by a well found in the story of Jacob (Genesis 29), and Moses (Exodus 2), but with a significant modification in the case of Isaac (Genesis 24) – the wooing for this withdrawn character has to be done for him. In the presentation of events, some standard techniques may be used which also have external analogies. Thus, events may be reported by the watchman in the gate, a method used in the case of Absalom's rebellion (2 Samuel 18, 24ff.), Jehu's *coup d'état* (2 Kings 9, 17ff.) but also in the 'beacon speech' in Aeschylos' *Agamemnon*.

It is, however, the overall structure of ancient Hebrew narratives which has received special attention in recent years. Three elements may be said to be involved here: the narrator, the personages in the story, and the plot. The (usually anonymous) narrator is omniscient, he can tell us the most secret, innermost thoughts and feelings of the characters involved in the story, or their conversations in secret places. He only occasionally discloses his judgment on them, however. That emerges through comments made by other characters, or by the turn events take in the story. By such means the reader's approval or disapproval will be gained.

Characters in the story tend to be few in number, with perhaps two protagonists and a limited number of supporting characters. Their nature emerges mainly through what they say or do rather than from the narrator's comments. Direct physical description is rare, and usually brought in only if it is relevant to the course of events. Thus Saul is outstandingly tall (1 Samuel 9, 2), an impressive figure suited for leadership; Esau is hairy but Jacob smooth

(Genesis 27, 11) – we all know how this fact was used to obtain Isaac's blessing for Jacob by deceit. Items of apparel are similarly mentioned only when they matter, and features of scenery where the narrative requires them. Indeterminate background may in fact lend atmosphere to a story, as E. Auerbach pointed out in his famous discussion of the account of the Sacrifice of Isaac (Genesis 22).

Language tends to be simpler in narrative than in poetry, with fewer stylistic embellishments, which might slow down the flow of the story. Imagery, based on facts of everyday experience, may nevertheless be strikingly applied. Thus pathetically small bodies of Israelite troops are compared to two little flocks of kids (1 Kings 20, 27). Other stylistic means may also be employed. Hebrew narrative in such respects may use simple methods, but its achievements can be outstanding. The depiction of David's development from lusty youth to failing old age (2 Samuel 9–20; 1 Kings 1–4) is not only quite unlike the glorification of rulers found in neighbouring lands, but unique also in its psychological insight. The characterization of Jehu (2 Kings 9–10) is on a similarly high literary level.

Plots are apt to be reduced to essentials – a chain of significant events, excluding side issues (though they may involve subplots). There may be a short exposition at the start; thereafter, the action, centred on the contact between a few protagonists, two perhaps, develops to a climax, sometimes a startling denouement, which may yet bear in itself the seeds of future events. Here moral and theological aspects may be involved: do the deeds related meet with divine approval or disapproval, reward or punishment? The narrator may give us a direct answer, but in the best Hebrew stories the moral is derived from the characters involved without being expressly pointed out. We may use two examples to illustrate the point. King Ahab has incurred blood-guilt through the judicial murder of Naboth (1 Kings 21). He desperately tries to avoid his doom, even asking his ally, the king of Judah, to wear the apparel of the king of Israel instead of his own, thus making him the main object of enemy attention. Yet in spite of all this he is killed – by an arrow shot at random: his doom could not be averted (1 Kings 22). To take an example of the opposite kind, Ruth the Moabitess, who deserves a reward for her fidelity to her mother-in-law, comes by chance to the field of Boaz who will marry her (Ruth 2, 3). Such working of a divine hand for hidden ends through apparent chance is perhaps a feature found especially in Israelite literature.

All told, Israelite narrative art, like Israelite poetry, could at its best be outstanding. This presupposes not only literary practitioners who were able to make fresh and impressive use of long-standing literary traditions, but also a sophisticated public able to appreciate their work. That the spread of Judaism and Christianity made the best of Israelite literature available to the wider world, at least in translation, is not the least contribution which this small nation made to world civilization.

CHAPTER ELEVEN

Religion

Ever since archaeological activity in the Holy Land began, attempts have been made to find in the relics discovered there evidence about ancient Israelite religious beliefs and practices, in order to 'illustrate' scriptural texts. However, a good many of the interpretations put forward have not stood the test of time. Archaeology, it appears, can offer only partial documentation of a limited number of aspects of Israelite religion. Some of its discoveries, moreover, point in directions in which a study of the Bible would not have led us to look. The paucity of relevant epigraphic discoveries in Palestine is a particular handicap in this field; nor can textual and other evidence from the neighbouring countries go as far as might be wished to fill the gaps, though it has proved very valuable in some respects.

Israelite religion according to the biblical record

The religious situation itself is anyway very complex. According to the biblical record, Israel's national existence was, from the earliest times, bound up with the Covenant into which it had entered at Mount Sinai with the Lord (whose name, written in Hebrew with the consonants YHWH, was according to scholars pronounced Yahweh, shorter forms being Yeho/Yahu and Yo). He had freed them from bondage in Egypt and given them their inheritance of the Promised Land, on condition of entire and exclusive allegiance. The Bible contains much detail about the worship due to him, or offered. It describes, or mentions, central all-Israelite sanctuaries, beginning with the Tabernacle and ending with Solomon's Temple in Jerusalem; other cult centres are also referred to, in particular the 'high places'. These latter were regarded as legitimate up to the building of the Temple, but as illicit thereafter, standing accused at that time of being contaminated by non-Israelite cult practices. Much is written also about religious functionaries – priests, Levites and prophets; sacrifices and sacrificial procedures, questions of religious purity and impurity, and other matters are legislated about at considerable length.

Yet, according to Scripture, religious prescriptions were too often honoured in the breach – Israel was almost throughout its history inclined to serve other gods. Israelites worshipped, in particular, the Baals, Ashtaroth (Astartes) and Asherah. These were local manifestations of major Canaanite deities, as we now know from the alphabetic cuneiform texts found at Ras Shamrah (ancient Ugarit) on the Syrian coast, which seem to reflect beliefs and traditions held throughout the Canaanite world during the Late Bronze Age and thereafter. In the Canaanite pantheon, Asherah was the wife of the wise and kindly, if at times lascivious, chief god El. She was the great mother goddess, though her image might at times be affected by features ascribed to the goddesses Anath and Astarte – deities of war, love and fertility. Baal, El's grand(?)-son (the name means 'master', his true name was Hadad), was the ruler of the storms and life-giving rain-clouds on which vegetation and thus human and animal existence depended. He is thought by many to have been an annually dying and rising god, slain by the deity Mot at the season of all-shrivelling summer heat, but reviving at the time of the autumn rains and disposing of Mot, ushering in the revival of nature on which humans relied.

Baal and Astarte were worshipped, following Canaanite precedent, particularly 'on the high mountains, upon the hills, and under every green tree' (Deuteronomy 12, 2), in sacred precincts provided with stone pillars (*massebahs*), wooden poles which might be carved (*asherahs*), altars or offering platforms, sacred trees, chapels or buildings for worshippers and perhaps images of deities. Such sanctuaries were part of popular, and especially rural, religion, but the Bible tells us that the Canaanite deities at times received also the official support of Israelite and Judean rulers in or near their capital cities. Thus, in northern Israel, Jezebel maintained 400 prophets of Asherah and 450 prophets of Baal – probably the Tyrian Baal worshipped in Phoenicia (1 Kings 18, 19). The well-appointed Baal temple at Samaria built by Ahab was destroyed by Jehu, but an *asherah* again stood in Samaria at the time of his son (2 Kings 13, 6). Similarly, a temple of Baal with its own priest existed in Jerusalem at the time of Athaliah and an *asherah* was repeatedly placed in Solomon's Temple – possibly even a cult image of the deity for whom – before Josiah's reform – women wove garments (2 Kings 23, 7).

How the 'queen of heaven' worshipped in Judah at the time of Jeremiah may be related to Canaanite goddesses is uncertain. She may have been derived from Asherah or Astarte. In Iron Age Palestine Anath seems to have lost the favour she had enjoyed in the Bronze Age. The extent to which minor deities like Resheph and Horon retained theirs is doubtful, but Jerusalemite attachment to Shalem, perhaps the original city god of Jerusalem, is thought by some to have been influential still when David named two of his sons Absalom and Solomon. Ṣedek may have been another Jerusalemite deity. In contrast to these minor divine figures, the high god El occupied a special position. The Israelites had been wont to call their deity El Shadday before they knew the name Yahweh (Exodus 6, 3); Abraham, who received his divine call from him, accepted a blessing from El Elyon ('God Most High') (Genesis 14, 19–20) who was worshipped by the Canaanite priest-king of Salem. In view of such early common associations some think that El worship would have fused easily with Yahwism, lending it various features.

In addition to deities worshipped in pre-Israelite Canaan, others were introduced later from foreign countries. Solomon built sanctuaries for his wives dedicated to the Sidonian Astarte, Kemosh, the deity of Moab, and Milkom – perhaps the same deity as Moloch, who received infant sacrifices at the site called the 'tophet' in Jerusalem in the Phoenician fashion – the Ammonite god (1 Kings 11, 5–7); later there are references to Tammuz worship and the cult of the sun, and of the 'host of heaven'. Assyrian religious influence in the wake of its imperial expansion has been assumed by some to explain the popularity of Assyrian cults and perhaps also the worship of Sakkuth and Kaiwan, if it is these who are referred to in Amos (5, 26) – though this is doubtful. Baal Shamem, as well as Baal of Tyre, was perhaps esteemed in Israel as in Phoenicia and Syria. Faced with such local and outside pressures it is not surprising that many would have tended to combine Yahwist and foreign religious practices, 'halting between two opinions' (1 Kings 18, 21). Even the state sanctuaries of northern Israel contained the 'calves' – bull images meant perhaps to allude to old Israelite religious metaphors, but which were of course rank heresy to the orthodoxy of Jerusalem.

Biblical evidence thus confronts us with a bewildering variety of beliefs and practices. The situation is further complicated by the fact that, according to some scholars, the biblical assumption that orthodox Israelite monotheism co-existed from the start with Canaanite and other polytheistic aberrations represents a late and theoretical reconstruction of Israelite religious development. Israelite religion, some maintain, developed out of Canaanite religion. Pure monotheism, according to them, only evolved gradually from henotheism – the worship of one god while the existence of others is not denied – or even polytheism, and had not been fully reached before the Exile, except by a minority. Such assumptions are linked with the belief that the text of the accounts referring to Israel's early religion is many centuries later than the period referred to, and thus unlikely to offer accurate facts: the aim of the writers, it is thought, was not to give a strictly correct history of Israelite religion, but rather a picture significant for their contemporaries and likely to promote what were then considered orthodox beliefs and practices.

This raises the question of whether we have any means of estimating the relative numbers of YHWH and non-YHWH worshippers in Israel at various times, and to what extent YHWH was worshipped to the exclusion of other deities at each stage. Information concerning the comparative strengths of Israelite belief in YHWH as opposed to that in other gods has been obtained by recent studies of Israelite personal names. These, as in other ancient Near Eastern countries, frequently contained the name of a deity combined with a verbal or nominal sentence element, expressing either a statement of fact – 'Yehonathan' (Jonathan), 'YHWH has given' – or perhaps a wish – 'Yehezqel', 'May El strengthen'. J. Tigay's recent study of the names on Hebrew inscribed seals from the period of the monarchy (mainly from the eighth to sixth centuries) has shown that the overwhelming majority contain the divine name YHWH, with the names of pagan deities in a small minority. It is striking that among these latter, the names of those deities specifically denounced in the Bible, such as Astarte and Asherah, do not occur at all. Baal is represented, but the name may have been used with reference to YHWH (cf. Hosea 2, 16 – 2, 18 in the Hebrew). It would thus appear that at this time the overwhelming majority among the seal-owning upper and middle classes were devotees of YHWH, though some may have recognized other deities in other sources, especially Asherah, if it is

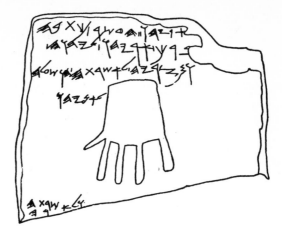

52 *Funerary inscription from Khirbet el-Qom, near Hebron. Late eighth century BC. It includes a blessing by YHWH and his Asherah. The drawing of the hand accompanying the text may be intended to ward off evil. This inscription illustrates a type of traditional piety branded as heretical by the prophets and which was left behind after the Exile.*

she to whom reference is made in the Kuntillet 'Ajrud and Khirbet el-Qom inscriptions, rather than her cult symbol.

For the period before the eighth century, we have to rely on biblical data. YHWH-names are few, but El-names more frequent. Again, however, the meaning of names containing the elements El and Baal is ambiguous, for they could refer either to YHWH or to the Canaanite deity. There appears, though, to be no significant number of Israelites named after clearly foreign gods. The question of foreign associations within Yahwism will occupy us below. As for origins, the name YHWH is not attested in pre-Israelite Palestine, but is found apparently to the southeast, in Midian, Mount Seir, Paran and so on, from where it would have been introduced. Yahwism cannot thus be simply described as a development within Canaanite religion. The embodiment of such beliefs in architecture or movable objects should help us to understand further how the two worlds were related.

Canaanite sanctuaries

We should start our review at the period when the roots of later Israelite society can first be discerned, that is, with the final stages of the Bronze Age and the beginning of the Iron Age. According to biblical accounts, the Israelite tribes were then – at the time of the Judges – living in uneasy juxtaposition with the Canaanite city states whom they had failed to conquer. Canaanite religious influences on Israel might perhaps be looked for in such a situation. Cultural transfers could of course have taken place even earlier, especially if (as some propose, see p. 58) discontented or displaced Canaanite peasantry were a substantial element in Israel's ancestry; and common Near Eastern religious traditions might furthermore have formed part of the inheritance of both groups even if their origins differed.

'High places'
Since much biblical reproof is directed at Canaanite features in Israelite high places we may begin by looking at possible Canaanite antecedents for such

mainly rural cult sites. The best example of a Canaanite extra-urban sanctuary, at Nahariyah, dates from the Middle Bronze Age. In its final stages, it included, within an open area, a roundish platform, 14 m (46 ft) wide, roughly made from small rubble heaped up above the foundations of an earlier cult building. Three steps led up towards its centre while at the back were some stone stelae. This platform apparently was the scene of (oil) libations and sacrifices. Between its stones and in the surrounding area was found a multitude of offerings, including pottery, both ordinary and special – with ritual vessels like incense-stands, bowls containing seven cups and seven-spouted lamps – besides beads, metal weapons, both full-size and miniature, trinkets and figurines of silver and bronze. Moulds for the casting of miniature weapons, and one for the statuette of a nude goddess with horns on her head, hint that such items were made on the spot for devotees. In the courtyard were the remains of hearths, together with many fragments of cooking pots and animal bones, showing that food was prepared here. A rectangular hall nearby served for the consumption of meals, the accumulated remains of which necessitated regular heightening of the floor level. In addition to the faithful, the building may have accommodated cult officials and perhaps the resident metalworkers who cast the offerings for the devout. With its platform for sacrifices and its dining hall, the whole sanctuary anticipates by some centuries the *bamah* mentioned in 1 Samuel (9, 12–19), though there is no mention there or in other relevant biblical texts of the dedication of votive offerings or their manufacture on the premises.

Open-air sanctuaries comparable to this one have been revealed by excavation in a number of places in the Levant, as at Mishrifen (ancient Qatna) in Syria (where the Middle Bronze Age 'high place' included a tree trunk erected as an *asherah*), or to some extent in Cyprus during the Late Bronze Age.

Temples

Temples are the predominant type of religious structure found in Late Bronze Age Palestine and Syria, especially within towns. They can be divided into three basic types according to their plans. One is the 'long-room' structure – the building is essentially an oblong rectangle with its entrance in one narrow side, and the worshipper faces axially down the length of the building, as in many modern churches. The second type is the 'broad-room' building, where the main cult room or the whole structure is arranged with its longer side at right angles to the direction in which the worshipper faces. Lastly, there are a few temples with a square plan.

Long-room structures were sometimes longitudinally subdivided by two rows of columns into three aisles with an entrance flanked by towers – the whole building was thus fortress-like in character (a *migdal* temple). Alternatively the side walls might project beyond the façade as piers or *antae*, forming a porch (a *megaron* temple). Broad-room temples might have a cult niche in the centre of the rear wall; this would sometimes project backwards to form a special small 'holy of holies' or *adyton*. The cult room (*cella*) might itself be fronted by a porch, with lateral towers flanking the entrance. A podium or dais might occupy the rear wall to accommodate cult symbols or statues, with steps leading up to it, particularly if it was placed inside a niche projecting rearwards. Benches made of mud-brick or plastered stone would sometimes line the walls (especially in smaller or more rustic temples) – these were probably not for worshippers to sit on, but for the placing of offerings or images of deities. Altars for incense might be found inside temples but sacrificial altars would normally be located outside in courtyards, where sacred pillars (*massebah's*) were occasionally located, too. The ritual furnishings of temples included cult stands and incense-burners of pottery, and ring-shaped *kernoi* (vessels with multiple receptacles for offerings), metal stands for ritual vessels, lamps, and ordinary pottery used for ritual meals; valuable offerings of various kinds would also be deposited there. Egyptian influence made itself felt sometimes, both in temple planning (for instance, the influence of the chapel plan as found at el-Amarna in Egypt, with a raised broad-room *cella* approached by steps) and architecture (clerestory lighting, Egyptian-type columns and capitals) as well as in furnishings and ritual gifts.

Certain Canaanite temples appear to have had special significance for early Israel. One of these was the Baal or El Berith temple at Shechem – a city which seems to have come to some kind of accommodation with the Israelites. Joshua (24) tells us about the great covenant ceremony which was arranged there, while later, under Abimelech, there was (according to Judges 9) an uneasy Israelite–Canaanite condominium here. The Baal/El Berith temple which Abimelech destroyed is often identified with the Late Bronze Age (?) broad-room temple (2 a b) uncovered above an earlier *migdal* temple. Only the outline of the structure, measuring 16 by 12.5 m (53 by 41 ft or *c.* 30 by 24 long cubits) and constructed of trimmed stones is known, but nothing of its interior fittings or cult vessels. A broken stone pillar set in a stone base, connected by some with the pillar mentioned in Joshua (24, 26–7), and a stone altar replacing an earlier one made of mud-brick, were placed axially in the court before the entrance, and two earlier pillars flanking the door were also still visible. The temple, like the town, was destroyed late in the twelfth century BC, and the area where it had stood was used for storage pits; an Israelite 'four-room' building erected above these in the eighth century has been considered by some as a possible cult structure, but it was more likely just a public store house.

Nothing is known about religious buildings in Jerusalem before its capture by David. There is, however, evidence from another city which long remained a non-Israelite enclave – Beth Shean. This was apparently still an Egyptian base in the early twelfth century and then came under Philistine sway until incorporated into the United Monarchy at an uncertain date – perhaps under David or Solomon or, according to one view, only after the invasion by Sheshonq. Excavations here revealed two edifices in stratum V (now dated *c.* 1100–910 BC by Frances James), which the excavators regarded as temples: the 'Northern Temple' they identified as the temple of Ashtoreth mentioned in 1 Samuel (31, 10); the 'Southern Temple' as that of Dagon (cf. 1 Chronicles 10, 10). Both buildings are on an east–west alignment, facing west and both have an ante-room in front of the main structure. The 'Northern Temple' consists of a single room in which four widely spaced pillars (the basalt bases of three survived) supported the roof; the 'Southern Temple' comprised a long hall, longitudinally subdivided by two parallel rows of originally three pillars each, linked by low walls. According to one view the whole hall was roofed and had a clerestory for lighting, but according to another the pillars are secondary and the room was originally open to the sky. Disturbance by a Hellenistic cistern makes it uncertain whether there was originally a transverse cult room at the eastern end. If so, the structure would bear some resemblance to the Phoenician Astarte temple at Kition in Cyprus. Two groups of three rooms each flank the hall on its northern and southern sides.

Some doubts have been expressed concerning the sacral nature of the two buildings. Magnus Ottosson thought the 'Southern Temple' was a palace, the northern one its palace chapel. In neither building have altars or podia for statues been found, though their original presence has been postulated. In view of the disturbed stratification, ritual objects found may in some cases have belonged to the underlying temples of earlier strata, though certain pottery cult stands with a special style of snake decoration are typical of stratum V only. It is not clear either just when the buildings were finally converted to purely secular uses. Frances James thought this happened only after the raid by Sheshonq but an earlier date has been assumed by others.

No trace has so far been found of the sanctuaries erected for alien deities by Solomon, or by later kings in northern Israel or Judah. However, two other non-Israelite sanctuaries of later date are known. At Tell Deir 'Alla east of the Jordan and near the lower Zerqa river, excavations by H.J. Franken have brought to light parts of a building probably dating from the late eighth century BC. It contained two groups of fragments of text written in red and black ink on plaster, which may originally have covered a mud-brick stela or the two sides of a door. Though the correct reassembly of the fragments has caused problems, the text clearly offers an otherwise unattested story about the prophet Balaam mentioned in Numbers (22–24), including a prophecy. This sanctuary may have belonged to Transjordanians – Ammonites or perhaps Midianites – active in formerly Gileadite territory. An Edomite sanctuary has been found quite recently at Horvat Qitmit south of Arad. It appears to date from the time of the Edomite incursions into Judah a short time before that kingdom fell.

In addition to non-Israelite sanctuaries on Israelite soil, others in neighbouring countries are of interest. None of Early Iron Age date are known at present in Phoenicia, but relevant information comes from the Philistine region in the southern Palestinian coastal plain, which might have exerted cultural as well as military influence over early Israel. At Ashdod, one of the five Philistine capital cities, what may have been a 'high place' has been revealed by Moshe Dothan in the twelfth–century stratum XIII (area G). This was an open space provided with a brick altar and a stone base, presumably intended for the statue of a god. An apsidal building in area H may also have had cultic significance.

Rather more information is, however, available from Amihai Mazar's excava-

tions at the small river port site of Tell Qasile north of Tel Aviv. Here, in strata
XII–X (*c.* 1150–980 BC) he found a succession of three superimposed small
temples. The first two were roughly square in plan; the third was a 'long-room'
building, aligned east–west and measuring 14.5 by 8 m (48 by 26 ft). It was
divided into an eastern ante-room, entered laterally and leading thus by indirect 'bent axis' approach to the oblong western cult room. The central feature
in this (as in the previous level) was a podium, approached by two steps, placed
in front of a partition wall which created a small corner room (perhaps a treasury) in the northwestern end of the hall. Plaster-covered benches lined the
walls of both this and the ante-room – there had been similar benches also in
the two earlier temples. The roof of the main hall was supported by two axially
placed wooden (cedar?) columns on round stone bases. A miniature temple
4.18 by 2.2 m (14 by 7 ft) was attached to the western side of the last two structures, likewise containing a podium and benches. A courtyard outside was
covered with much ash, animal bones and potsherds in each phase; in stratum
XI there was also a *favissa* – a pit for receiving ritual objects – while in stratum
X the base of an altar, 1.2 m (4 ft) long and made of stones was found, presumably having once carried a mud-brick top. The temple of stratum X is to some
extent analogous in plan both to certain Palestinian temples of the Late Bronze
Age (like the 'Fosse Temple' at Lachish) and also to others in the Aegean world,
as at Mycenae.

These Philistine sanctuaries were richly endowed with a multitude of cult
objects, vessels and votive items including pottery in the Philistine, Canaanite,
Aegean and Egyptian traditions. Of particular interest are a special abstract
rendering of a goddess of Aegean derivation seated on a throne, found at
Ashdod, an anthropomorphic vessel with Mycenaean parallels probably representing a female deity from the *favissa* at Tell Qasile and a pottery tablet imitating the front of an Egyptian *naiskos* within which two goddesses figured in
relief had once faced the worshipper – this may have stood on the podium of
the last temple at Tell Qasile. Pottery includes cylindrical cult stands (three
found in the 'miniature temple' at that site supported bowls fixed by pro-
truding pegs). Pottery *kernoi*, comparable to others in Cyprus, and a one-
handled lion-headed *rhyton* cup descended from Mycenaean and Minoan
prototypes are also of significance. This religious equipment seems to have
found limited imitation in early Israel: such analogies as there are seem to be
derived from common Canaanite ground.

There is at present little to say about religious buildings in Israel's eastern
neighbours, but something must be said briefly about a sanctuary erected by
Midianites at Timnah in the Arabah in the twelfth century BC, before Israel
gained control there. It was a crude, broad-room structure with a semicircular
cult niche at its rear, cut into the cliff against which the building was backed up.
In plan it resembles the Late Bronze Age 'stelae temple' at Hazor, but it was
provided with a tent roof above the stone walling adapted from a preceding
Egyptian shrine. The ritual objects found include a copper snake with a gilded
head which recalls the brass snake made by Moses (2 Kings 18, 4).

Israelite sanctuaries

'High places'

According to the Bible, a 'high place' (*bamah* in Hebrew) might be found inside an Israelite settlement or outside in the country, and this type of holy place continued from the earliest times down to Josiah's reform. They must have been numerous, but we know little about their locations and distribution. Archaeological investigations have, however, now revealed a number of possible sites. The earliest known at present is extra-urban, located on a high hill some distance from Israelite sites in the territory of Manasseh, about 6 km (3¾ miles) southeast of Jenin. Founded *c.* 1200 BC and in use only for a short time, it consisted of an elliptical enclosure averaging perhaps 21 m (70 ft) across, surrounded by a crude wall. Within it there was a large stone (possibly a fallen pillar or altar) fronted by a stone pavement and perhaps also a tree. Fragments of cooking pots hint that food was consumed here. Finds include, besides part of an incense-burner shaped like a house or temple, a remarkable bronze statuette of a bull (pl. 51), a miniature forerunner of the 'calves' set up by Jeroboam at Bethel and Dan, but inspired perhaps by earlier concepts, as witnessed by, for instance, the title 'the bull' for El, the Canaanite 'high god', not to mention the Golden Calf.

It is difficult to say whether a so-far unique structure located some 150 m (490 ft) below the peak of Mount Ebal, and dating from *c.* 1240 to 1140 BC was a 'high place'. This site comprised a large outer enclosure and a smaller internal one with a rectangular stone building set within the latter. This went through two stages, a flimsy structure being replaced by a more solid one. The original plan has been compared to the later 'four-room' house type. Around the building there were abundant deposits of ashes and animal bones, sheep and other: the remainders of meals consumed here. There are also various finds of a possibly ritual character, including a pottery jar handle with a bull's head attached (resembling one found in an eleventh-century context at Shiloh). Pottery includes some 'collared rim' store jars, one of which was found inside the building. During the second stage, access to the inner enclosure was across a flight of monumental steps. The building was finally put out of commission by being filled with stones, soil and ashes scooped up from the courtyard, and thereafter covered by a pavement. The excavator, A. Zertal, suggested that the final shape of the building was like the altar built by Joshua on Mount Ebal (cf. Joshua 8, 30; Deuteronomy 11, 29); others prefer to regard it as a tower. The plentiful presence of the remainders of meals makes it likely in any case that communal feasting went on here, which would suit a complex of 'high place' type.

Three early 'high places' inside settlements are also known, involving both northern Israel (Hazor stratum XI) and Judah (Arad stratum XII and Lachish stratum V). The former two date from the eleventh century, the latter from the tenth. The sanctuary at Arad was placed on the hilltop overlooking the houses on the slopes below; the *bamah* at Hazor stood likewise on dominating high ground. Our knowledge of all three is fragmentary, but the high places at Arad and Lachish again seem to have comprised pebble-paved sacral areas surrounded by a circumference wall; areas of pebble paving were also found at Hazor around a 'chapel' building. A similar building, but located along the circumference wall, existed at Lachish. Both were provided with stone and clay benches for the deposition of offerings and ritual objects (a custom known in Bronze Age Palestine but not mentioned in the Bible). Those discovered at Lachish included, besides domestic pottery, four incense-burners and a chalice stand on which a juglet and a lamp had originally been placed, besides a limestone altar 45 cm (18 in) high which probably once had four horns. Incense-burners were also found in areas around the chapel at Hazor, and an altar built of stone as well as a crescent-shaped offering platform of brick surrounded by stone walling existed at Arad. Many pits near it contained burnt bones, including the headless skeleton of a young lamb, probably remainders of offerings or ritual meals. Another common feature are stone pillars (*massebahs*). The Lachish cult area may have had one, besides an olive tree *asherah*; at Hazor four pillars stood in line near the chapel. Also at Hazor Yigael Yadin discovered what he thought was a foundation deposit – a buried jar containing votive bronze objects (these might alternatively have formed a hoard hidden by a metalworker for later resmelting). The contents included, besides weapons such as a sword and a lugged axe, the bronze figurine of a seated deity of Canaanite type, helmeted and originally holding a weapon. Whether this 'war god' expressed Israelite religious ideas must in the circumstances remain uncertain.

53 *Bronze figurine of a deity found in the 'high place' at Hazor, Stratum XI (approx. 14 cm (5½ in high). Whether it was meant to carry religious significance for Israelites is not clear.*

While this type of cult area shows similarities to certain Canaanite sanctuaries of the Middle Bronze Age, like those at Nahariyah and Gezer, such 'high places' were not in fashion during the Late Bronze Age (when temples were preferred), and especially not within cities. To that extent they mark a new departure. They are not known either to have been constructed by the Israelites during later centuries.

Finally, what appears to have been a *bamah* located in the country but linked with a nearby settlement has been revealed by excavation at Machmish near Herzliah, north of Tel Aviv. This consists of a rectangular area, *c.* 10 by 10 m (33 by 33 ft), surrounded by a brick wall on rough stone foundations and provided with a flooring of red earth. It contained a simple platform, possibly an altar; fragments of pottery and bones nearby show that meals were cooked here. Some flat stones may have served as tables. This site, dating from the tenth century when the region was apparently under Israelite control, may have depended on the settlement at Tel Michal some 400 m (1312 ft) away.

In addition to such local or regional 'high places', there were some of national importance. One was the great 'high place' at Gibeon, where, we are told, the Tabernacle and the bronze altar made by Bezalel were placed, and where King Solomon after his accession had his famous dream vision (1 Kings 3, 4ff.; 2 Chronicles 1, 3–5). No trace of it has been detected so far. Later, Jeroboam I put up two schismatic shrines at Bethel and Dan (1 Kings 12, 29); the former is likewise archaeologically unknown, but we are now fairly well informed about the one at Dan, owing to the large-scale excavations there by A. Biran, who identified massive remains as the high place founded by Jeroboam I.

What survives consists essentially of an enormous podium set in a large court measuring *c.* 60 by 45 m (197 by 148 ft), delimited on three sides by rooms or plain ashlar walls, and provided with a huge altar, the base of which survives. The podium went through three constructional phases. Founded in the tenth century as a rectangular building 18.5 by 7 m (60 by 23 ft), it was enlarged in the ninth century by Ahab to cover an almost square area measuring *c.* 18.5 by 19 m (59 by 62 ft). It was then given facings of splendid ashlar, laid as headers and stretchers, and dressed with bosses and margins in the fashion exemplified in contemporary Samaria; there was a course of beams near the bottom. The centre of the podium, which stood to a maximum height of 3 m (10 ft), consisted of a stone fill. A monumental flight of steps 7 m (23 ft) wide was added on the south side by Jeroboam II in the eighth century. While it is not known what, if anything, was on the first ashlar platform – possibly a light structure of wood and curtains evoking the Tabernacle – a large building of somewhat unusual plan was positioned on the northern part of the second. In front of the platform there was again a courtyard with a monumental altar, this time approached by steps, provided with horns in a style also known from faraway Beersheba, and set within a square paved area surrounded by a circumference wall. A small horned altar, made from a single stone, also stood in this enclosure. Rooms around the courtyard served various purposes. One, an oblong room with a pedestal, may have been intended for assemblies. Another contained three

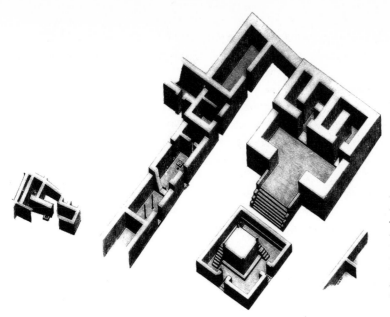

54 Dan: reconstruction of the 'high place' as refashioned by Ahab and by Jeroboam II. The earlier ashlar podium was much enlarged and approached by a monumental flight of stairs. In addition there are traces of a very substantial structure on the podium but these are not easy to analyse.

altars – two were set against a wall and one was free-standing – near the latter were found three iron shovels for removing sacrificial ash and a silver and bronze sceptre had been placed underneath it. Nearby was an oil-pressing plant, intended perhaps to produce first-class olive oil for religious ceremonies, while a somewhat puzzling installation intended for lustration (and possibly ablution) was fed with water from the spring near the tell.

Gate sanctuaries

The occurrence of sanctuaries of *bamah* type in a gate is referred to in passing in 2 Kings (23, 8). Attempts to identify such sanctuaries have not met with general agreement. One suggested example is a complex comprising a stone basin and pillar(?) placed in the open area inside the gate of the tenth-century stratum VIIB at Tell el-Far'ah (N). This has, however, now been interpreted as an olive-crushing plant. Another type of possibly religious structure has been found in the open space between the inner and outer gates at Dan (pl. 18). Here four columns set on bases of Syro-Hittite type (of which three survive) originally supported a canopy above a pedestal; a sacred pillar or statue may have

55 Ornamental column base in the North Syrian style, attached to the fixture in front of the inner gate at Dan (pl. 18).

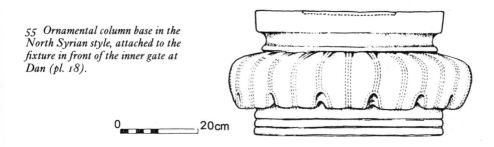

0   20cm

stood on this, or a throne for the king when 'sitting in the entrance of the gate' (cf. 1 Kings 22, 10). Lastly, the discovery of an hour-glass shaped limestone altar (perhaps for incense) in the gate area at Beersheba has suggested to some that ritual acts were carried out there also.

None of the above is entirely convincing. The best candidate for a gate sanctuary of *bamah* type is probably a structure found in the outer gate at Dan. This comprises five standing stones, against the wall, in front of which is a stone bench or table apparently intended for offerings; incense-burning dishes and oil lamps, as well as pottery bowls, were found nearby.

Cult rooms and cult corners in secular buildings

Some buildings regarded in the past as religious were probably in fact devoted essentially to secular ends with perhaps only a room or corner dedicated to cultic purposes.

At Megiddo, in stratum VA (tenth century BC), a large building of 'four-room' house type was excavated, which featured the addition of side rooms and a courtyard (Locus 2081) in front. Two stone pillars in the doorway of the building have been regarded by some as ritual, but others interpret them simply as doorposts. However, in the forecourt two projecting walls delimited a niche containing one large and one small horned limestone altar, which originally may have flanked the entrance, and one stone and one pottery incense-burner, besides various pottery vessels. A flat stone in front of the door may have been an offering table. This may then have been a cult niche or domestic chapel. Another cult niche may have existed at Megiddo, Building 338. It had been suggested that the whole building was a sanctuary, but on balance it seems that it was probably a sumptuous building intended either for administration or for residence.

It also seems doubtful whether a tenth-century building at Taanach, near which a supposedly cultic stone basin and stela were found, was a cult structure, even though two remarkable terracotta stands adorned with sphinxes, lions and other motifs – perhaps stands for incense-burners – were discovered there. The architecture and many of the finds suggest a secular building and incense might also have served to lend distinction to official or social gatherings as it did in ancient Egypt and in recent Arabian society.

Other cult sites

A so far unique building, dating from the mid-ninth to the mid-eighth century, at Kuntillet 'Ajrud (Horvat Teiman) on the southern fringe of the Judean Negeb apparently served religious as well as other functions. In plan it resembles a rectangular fort with a central courtyard and corner bastions, though it lacks the casemate rooms expected in such a building. It may in fact have functioned both as a defensible watering point and resting station for travellers, and also as a religious centre sacred to both Israelites and others. Access to it was gained by an entrance court provided with benches; immediately behind was a narrow room also lined with benches, destined for offerings. Both these rooms

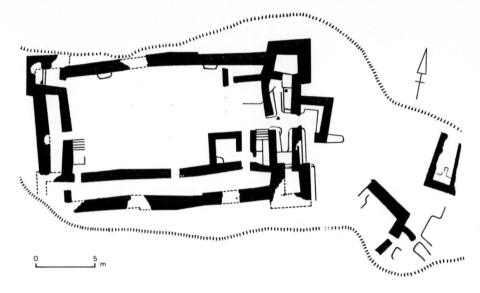

56 Plan of the wayside station at Kuntillet 'Ajrud. Though it resembled a fortress with corner bastions, its main functions were only to give travellers shelter, and a chance to offer wayside prayers.

were distinguished by fine white wall plaster not used in other parts of the structure. In the entrance court the plaster was adorned with floral and geometric paintings. The bench room contained two large broken pithoi (jars) covered with drawings and Hebrew inscriptions in red ink. The drawings include such items as a female lyre-player, the Egyptian god Bes, a lion, a cow and calf and a tree of life, in addition to rather crudely drawn human figures. These pictures may have had cultic significance. The inscriptions include two texts mentioning Yahweh (in one case perhaps qualified as Yahweh of Samaria) jointly with 'his (?) Asherah'. There were also two stone bowls, one weighing *c.* 180 kg (400 lb) and inscribed on the rim with an invocation of Yahweh's blessing on the owner. An inscription on a piece of fallen wall plaster in the bench room likewise refers to Yahweh's favour, but another fragmentary text in Phoenician writing on the door from a store room to the courtyard mentions El and Baal. Another Phoenician inscription, now illegible, was written on the door from the bench room to the court. The position of these texts on doorposts recalls the command in Deuteronomy (6, 9), but their pagan character, and indeed the whole mixture of Israelite and foreign religious professions at Kuntillet 'Ajrud, helps illuminate biblical strictures against syncretism. No altars or incense-burners were reported in this building. Whether a much ruined second structure nearby served religious purposes there is no way of telling. Fragments of wall paintings found there show secular motifs. The suggestion that Kuntillet 'Ajrud was used for *marzeah* meetings remains speculative (see p. 255).

There are other apparently sacred sites that are not easily classified. Samaria Locus E 207 is a very puzzling site. Essentially it consists of a large trench 6 m

(19 ft) wide at the top but narrowing downwards and nearly encircling a rock-cut trapezoidal island *c.* 30 by 26 by 26 m (98 by 85 by 85 ft) wide. The ground had been much disturbed by later quarrying, burials etc. and no trace of an ancient structure could be identified. However, the trench contained a large quantity of pottery, female figurines, horse-and-rider figurines, several baskets full of lamps, and other items. These may be fills which perhaps originated in some sacred site where activities were carried out at night, but whether this was located here or elsewhere cannot be determined at present.

In Jerusalem, Cave 1 is a man-made cave, some 8.12 m (27 ft) deep and up to 4.2 m (14 ft) wide. It is divided by a wall extending backwards from a central rock pillar. The cave contained more than 1200 pottery vessels, as well as solid or hollow-bodied female figurines, animal figurines, horse-and-rider figurines, bird models and other items. Some complete bowls left near the entrance contained the remains of animal bones. Much of this resembles the finds from the site at Samaria, and the cave has been regarded as a repository of ritual gifts. That it was a cave sanctuary seems less likely.

It is also difficult to be sure about the character of certain large cairn monuments found mainly, but not exclusively, in groups near Malḥa, southwest of Jerusalem. Located in prominent positions, they resemble in their unexcavated state high cones with flattened tops, and it was originally and not unnaturally assumed that these covered burials. However, excavation of one monument by Ruth Amiran has shown that the cairn, made from heaped-up rubble, covered a small platform comprising a short stretch of paving, a pit, a place for burning, and an area full of burnt debris, charcoal, and pieces of local Judean ware dating from the seventh century BC. Other sherds of the same date occurred in the cairn. The whole area was surrounded at some distance by a roughly circular, polygonal drystone wall consisting of sections *c.* 5 m (16 ft) long, set at angles to each other; short flights of steps gave access in two places to the area inside. Some peripheral outer walling was added later, and it seems the whole complex was covered by the cairn soon after its construction. No traces of a burial were discovered, and some have proposed that this is a 'high place' cult area, linked possibly with a hypothetical grave, and covered by the cairn when 'high places' were abolished (some scholars indeed assume all 'high places' were connected with burials). According to yet another opinion the cult area might have served for a memorial feast honouring a deceased family head or chieftain. The close juxtaposition of a number of such monuments and the short duration of their use argues against their interpretation as *bamahs*, but further investigation is needed to establish their true character.

Temples

In the biblical accounts the Israelites had a tent sanctuary, the Tabernacle, dating from the time of Moses, and this they carried with them into the Promised Land where it was erected at various places in the course of time. In addition to this central sanctuary a number of other holy places, situated mostly in western Palestine, are referred to early on, and certain scholars have sus-

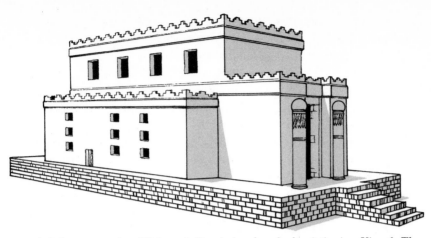

57 Artist's reconstruction of Solomon's Temple, based on the description in 1 Kings 6. The porch is fronted by the two columns Jachin and Boaz.

pected that some of these had temple buildings, though nothing is known about them archaeologically. Furthermore, we hear of a private venture, the temple which Micah the Danite built and which boasted divine images and an *ephod* (a priestly vestment), and to which he attracted the services of a Levite as priest (Judges 17). Again we have no archaeological attestation of this.

The Tabernacle likewise remains a shadowy entity, in spite of the detailed description of the tent shrine and its furnishings given in Exodus (26–27 and 36, 8ff.), which have repeatedly been made the basis of theoretical reconstructions. Comparative scholarship has pointed out that tent shrines were known elsewhere in the Semitic-speaking world, and the discovery of a twelfth-century BC Midianite shrine at Timnah in the Arabah rift, which combined a tent covering with stone foundations may be relevant for the sanctuary at Shiloh, where scholars have detected traces of features belonging to a temple building together with those of a tent structure. It is not clear how the tent erected by David to house the Ark in the precincts where Solomon later built his Temple was related to the Tabernacle (which, 30 1 Kings 8, 4 tells us, was in due course transported into the Temple), or whether either served as the basis for the descriptions in Exodus. Many scholars have regarded that account as based on late theories, projecting features of the Temple back into the time of the desert wanderings, though others have pointed out the differences between Tent and Temple and believe the story about the Tent has a historical core. Some of the measurements of the Tabernacle and its furnishings have, moreover, been regarded as relevant in a later context, as we shall see.

Solomon's Temple in Jerusalem combined the functions of palace sanctuary and central national shrine, succeeding the Tabernacle in that latter capacity, Scripture tells us. We still have to rely for our information mainly on the description (neither complete nor always intelligible) of the building given in 1 Kings (6–7), supported to some extent by 2 Chronicles (3–4) and Ezekiel

(40–43). Archaeologically the building remains largely unknown; the suggestion that some walling near the southeast corner of the present *Haram* enclosure is Israelite or even Solomonic has not met with general agreement, and attempts to connect fragmentary walling or rock cuttings on the esplanade with Solomon's sanctuary and courts cannot be substantiated in the absence of proper excavations. Even the location of the building remains in doubt. Traditional views that either the altar or the Holy of Holies was located above the 'sacred rock' (*sakhra*) inside the Dome of the Rock are now rivalled by the view that Herod's Temple, and thus presumably Solomon's, lay further to the north, with the Holy of Holies perhaps around the present 'Dome of the Tables'. Yet the biblical text, supported by archaeological and textual evidence from elsewhere, allows us to grasp some essential features of this important ancient building. It combined, in particular, a number of traditions derived from different regions, due probably to the predilections of its royal founder.

Its foundations were of large blocks of ashlar – a technique known, but only sparingly used, in rich Late Bronze Age cities like Ugarit; its widespread employment now in this and other Solomonic buildings, together with much valuable cedar wood, meant expenditure on a large scale and ushered in a new era. Whether the upper work also consisted of hewn stone or of mud-brick in timber framing is disputed. In plan, the Temple was essentially a 'long-room' structure facing east, surrounded at the sides and rear by three superimposed rows of side chambers. We are given only internal measurements for the Temple, but counting in the thickness of the walls the total length of the structure may have been approximately 50 m (165 ft) and its width 25 m (82 ft). The main building consisted of a hall, 40 (large) cubits long, 20 wide and 30 high (*c.* 20 by 10 by 15 m or 65 by 33 by 50 ft); it was fronted by a porch, 10 cubits (5 m or 16 ft) long and 20 cubits (10 m/33 ft) wide, possibly formed by the prolongation of the side walls as *antae*, and backed by the Holy of Holies or *adyton*, a cubic wooden structure with sides of 20 cubits (10 m/33 ft). Whether the porch was the same height as the main building, or less, or considerably more (as 2 Chronicles 3, 4 suggests) is unclear; in the latter case towers flanking the entrance of *migdal* temples, or Egyptian pylons may have served as inspiration. The wooden *adyton*, which may have contained the Tabernacle and served to shelter the Ark flanked by the Cherubim, has Egyptian parallels, though it had a specifically Israelite purpose. Whether it stood on a podium or whether a room above made up the difference in height against the main hall we do not know. The long-room structure itself is, however, of North Syrian derivation, though the recurrence of simple arithmetic progressions such as 2–3–4 in its measurements is a special feature. The origin of the side chambers is more problematic. The 'Southern Temple' at Beth Shean probably had, as we saw, store rooms flanking its main hall. The example of casemate walls has also been invoked, but none of these are known to have had superimposed floors.

As for the two columns Jachin and Boaz, there has been much discussion as to whether they stood in front of the porch, or helped to support its roof. In the (more likely) former case they had antecedents in a Late Bronze Age sanctuary

58 (Left) *A reconstruction of one of the bronze 'lavers' from Solomon's Temple. The rich decoration applied to the basic structure was indebted to Canaanite, Phoenician, Cypriot and other influences.* (Right) *A related laver found in Bronze Age Cyprus; note the ornamentation.*

at Kamid el-Loz in Lebanon, and parallels in the temple of Heracles/Melqart at Tyre, to which Herodotus (*Histories*, II, 44) refers. Bridging the very large roof-span in porch and temple must have presented problems. The Bible does not mention rows of internal columns to support the load of the (probably flat) roof as found in, for example, the much narrower hall of the 'Southern Temple' at Beth Shean; supporting struts like medieval hammer beams may conceivably have been used, together perhaps with engaged pillars. The ceiling was apparently coffered. Clerestory windows were located below it, but above the level of the side chambers, which had their own windows, in a basilica-like arrangement.

The interior of the main hall was, we are told, completely covered with cedar panelling adorned with carvings of cherubim (sphinxes), palm trees, and jewel and flower ornaments. Here Phoenician decorative traditions of Egyptian derivation were apparently applied – the ivory carvings found at Samaria offer some hints as to shapes, and the gold covering on the ornamented panelling would suit such a style. A similar stylistic background seems likely also for the two cherubim carved in olive wood and overlaid with gold which sheltered the Ark in the Holy of Holies. Other traditions may be discerned in the temple furnishings. The ornamented trolleys supporting basins (1 Kings 7, 27ff.) are ultimately of Aegean, and more especially Cypriot, origin, acclimatized in the Canaanite–Phoenician world; related cult stands without wheels seem to have been known in Iron Age Palestine, if a model from Megiddo V is a guide. Stylistically, their tenth-century date fits well. It is less easy to be sure of proto-types for the 'Molten Sea' with its support of twelve oxen, but it was a piece of Phoenician craftsmanship, executed by the same Hiram of Tyre who cast the other bronze fittings. Solomon's Temple was thus a building outstanding in its unique blending of traditions and the splendour of its architecture and fittings, rather than its size. Still, in being inaccessible to lay worshippers, who were kept in an outer court area (an inner court contained the altar), it conformed to

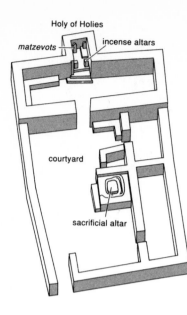

Holy of Holies

matzevots

incense altars

courtyard

sacrificial altar

59 Reconstruction of the shrine at Arad (Stratum IX) as interpreted by the excavator, Y. Aharoni. The cult building – intended to serve the garrison but probably accessible to the neighbourhood – consisted of a building set behind a courtyard containing an altar of 'unhewn stone' (cf. Exodus 20, 25). The building was a broad-room structure, backed by a central raised cult niche jutting out from the rear wall. Its equipment originally included two stone pillars of different sizes (perhaps symbolizing YHWH and his consort), prefixed by two small stone incense altars. Aharoni assumed the altar in the courtyard was suppressed by Hezekiah, and the whole temple abolished by Josiah. More recently, Aharoni's interpretation has been questioned. The cult niche at the back of the temple may have extended further to one side; the building only existed from the eighth or seventh century onwards; and change supposedly linked with reforming activities by Hezekiah and Josiah does not fit the new chronology.

ideas found widely in the Semitic world, and the juxtaposition of temple and palace may be found elsewhere in the Levant in the Iron Age, as at Hamath and Tell Ta'yinat.

While Solomon's Temple remains unexcavated, at least one sacred building which is architecturally of temple type (though regarded as a *bamah* by some) has been revealed in Israel by archaeology. This is the sanctuary located within the citadel of Arad in southern Judah, excavated and summarily described by the late Yohanan Aharoni (his collaborators have now published fuller details), and which has been much discussed since. According to him, it was founded in Solomon's reign (in stratum XI) and finally abolished at the time of Josiah's reform (stratum VII), though it was deprived of its altar and truncated during the earlier cult reform of Hezekiah (stratum VIII). The chronology has been queried by some but the essential architectural features of the complex, which underwent one major rebuilding, are fairly clear. Like Solomon's Temple in Jerusalem it faced east, but unlike it it consisted of a broad rather than long cult room, the rear and sides of which were flanked by benches for offerings, fronted by a court and backed by a centrally positioned small raised cult niche approached by three steps. During the first phase the main cult room or *cella* measured 9 by 2.7 m (30 by 9 ft), corresponding, in Aharoni's opinion, to 20 by 6 early royal cubits of 44.5 cm (17½ in). As he pointed out, 20 cubits is also the width of Solomon's Temple; he also thought the dimensions of the room were related to those of the Tabernacle. The cult niche measured only 1.5 by .75 m (5 by 2½ ft) internally, but the courtyard, paved with wadi stones, was roughly 10 by 10 m (33 by 33 ft). It contained an altar made from 'earth' (mud-brick) and field stones (cf. Exodus 20, 24–25), but later remodelling has left only a few foundation stones of the original structure which was located near the centre of the court. The whole complex was flanked by oblong rooms, at the sides and at the back. The temple was rebuilt after the destruction of stratum XI by Sheshonq in stratum X (ninth century?). This modified building was fairly well preserved, with its main ritual equipment. The width of the cult room (*cella*) had increased to 10.5 m (34 ft) – this, Aharoni thought, represented 20 large royal cubits of 52 cm (20 in) which now superseded the old shorter cubit measure (cf. 2 Chronicles 3, 3) – and the depth of the room became 3.15 m (10 ft), or 6 new cubits. An increase in the length of the sides of the altar to 2.3 m (7½ ft), he interpreted similarly. The size of the cult niche (*adyton*) was like-wise increased, as was the length of the courtyard, which also became narrower since its northern section up to the altar was turned into a room. Two column bases, supporting either free-standing columns or supports for a penthouse roof, were placed in front of the entrance to the *cella*, whose walls were lined with benches for offerings. Two small stone altars (perhaps for animal fat or incense) may originally have flanked the steps leading up to the *adyton*, and a flat cult stela with rounded top, 80 cm (31 in) high, and still bearing traces of red paint may once have stood in the cult niche (an earlier stela of flint, perhaps belonging to stratum XI, was found walled up, and some others may have stood in the courtyard).

The transformation of the northern part of the court into a store room had left the altar placed off-centre next to a wall. Made of unworked stone with mud mortar, this altar was now *c.* 5 cubits long and broad, and 3 cubits in height (cf. Exodus 27, 1). It was topped by a flint slab furnished with plastered channels to drain away blood and fat; a metal rack above may once have held the coals on which the burnt offerings were laid. No horns at the corners have survived and whether any made of perishable materials were originally fitted is doubtful. A water basin was later placed in the southeastern corner of the court and an incense-burner and an unusually large oil lamp were found in a small room, attached to the altar. Two plates found near the latter bore incised letters which will be discussed below.

Views have varied concerning the derivation of this type of structure. Late Bronze Age temples in Palestine with broad *cellas* and cult niches, modified Israelite 'four-room' houses with broad and shallow end rooms, as well as old Judean traditions linked somehow with the Tabernacle have all been invoked. There might be a connection with the broad and shallow end room in the 'four-room' structure but, as Ottosson points out, temples and dwelling houses had long followed separate architectural traditions and the very broad and shallow *cella* occurred also in the roughly contemporary Phoenician Astarte temple at Kition in Cyprus. Perhaps influences from more than one direction affected the shape of this sanctuary. Whether its location made it a 'border sanctuary' is also disputed.

The interpretation of the excavation results at Arad by Aharoni and his col-laborators, summarized above, has not escaped criticism. It has, in particular, been suggested that the sanctuary was founded, not in the tenth century BC but rather in the late eighth or even the early seventh. The plan of the building pub-lished by Aharoni would also need modification: the southern wall of the cult niche is regarded as spurious, and in fact the niche continued southwards for some distance. Until the final report is published, however, such matters will remain conjectural.

There may have been another temple at Beersheba not far from Arad. This was assumed by Aharoni and his fellow excavators, on the strength of the discovery of parts of a dismantled ashlar altar with high horns. Being of hewn rather than unworked stone and earth, it may be of non-Israelite derivation. This altar supposedly belonged to a temple analogous to the one in Arad, located in a place on the tell where a deep pit now interrupts the town plan. The pit itself would then represent the root-and-branch removal of the sanctuary by Hezekiah. Yadin, on the other hand, linked the altar with a *bamah* located, he thought, near the city gate. His views have not met with much agreement, however, and as the alternative view is not susceptible to proof, the problem remains to be resolved.

No other Hebrew sanctuaries of temple type are archaeologically known at present. Terracotta models of one-room buildings with an ornamental front preceded by columns with ornamental capitals (free-standing or supporting the architrave) may represent chapels or small temples. Examples found at Tel Far'ah (N) range in date apparently from the tenth to the eighth centuries BC. Whether the buildings they imitate were located within towns or outside, and whether they were linked with Israelite or other cults, cannot be determined. The purpose of buildings which inspired ornamental pottery stands like one from Megiddo is even more in doubt. We should not in any case forget that excavations both in residential and government towns have revealed a striking paucity of cult buildings. None were found at Tell Beit Mirsim, Beth Shemesh or Tell en-Naṣbeh, in all of which considerable residential areas have been revealed (the suggestion by Thiersch that large 'four-room' buildings at the latter site were sanctuaries is no longer in favour), and in Megiddo no cult building has been recognized with certainty.

This state of affairs differs strikingly from the multiplicity of temples, or chapels, and street altars found elsewhere in cities of the ancient world and may be connected with Yahwist ideas restricting the number of places where public worship was acceptable.

Jerusalem may have conformed more to common pattern, at least in times of apostasy. Ahaz, the Bible tells us, erected altars at every street corner (2 Chronicles 28, 24; cf. Jeremiah 12, 13), and Ezekiel (16, 24–25) refers similarly to high places in every street. It is not clear whether we are dealing with late innovations; nor can the textual references be matched by archaeological discoveries at present. To what extent there may have been buildings used for simple prayer meetings – forerunners of the later synagogues – cannot be determined.

Religious ceremonies

Cult features linked with social life

Meetings of social groups might involve religious ceremonies not necessarily linked with public sanctuaries. Family or clan meetings such as the one referred to in 1 Samuel (20, 28–29), where David's family is said to have met at the new moon in Bethlehem to sacrifice, might have involved an as yet undocumented local shrine, or other premises. Such premises may have been the location of social gatherings with an unorthodox religious aspect celebrated by the upper classes of society – the *marzeahs*. Sources such as Amos (6, 4) and Jeremiah (16, 8), combined with relevant information from outside Israel, show that at these meetings men and women feasted and drank to excess, and that commemoration of the dead was involved. The luxurious 'ivory couches' used on such occasions (Amos, 6, 4) may have been decorated with the type of ivory carvings found at Samaria. Whether any other cultic apparel was involved we do not know, nor have any special premises devoted to such feasts been identified, though Kuntillet 'Ajrud has been considered. Public business, involving the conclusion of binding engagements, was probably also accompanied by religious ceremonies. The cult stands shown being carried off from conquered Lachish by Assyrian soldiers on one of the reliefs from Sennacherib's palace, which may have come from the governor's palace there, may have featured on these occasions. The same is possibly true of the altars, incense-burners and cult stands from government centres like Jerusalem, Taanach and Megiddo – decorated pottery stands like those from tenth-century contexts there were surely not meant for everyday purposes.

Domestic cult practices

Religious ceremonies seem also to have been carried out in private houses. While these did not involve altars intended for animal sacrifices, incense must have been burnt there fairly often. This is attested by finds of incense cups, usually with perforations near the rim, found in northern Israel from *c.* 1000 BC onwards, and in Judah from *c.* 800 BC onwards in smaller numbers. There were also special small incense altars; some are of stone and perhaps provided with rudimentary horns, others of terracotta. A cuboid type with a concave top and small legs came into fashion in Israel, as in neighbouring countries, from the seventh century BC onwards though it really became popular only in the sixth and fifth centuries.

The function of a distinctive type of ladle is less clear. These are made mostly of stone, especially steatite, with the bowl usually supported below by a hand, though one example from Tell Beit Mirsim was shaped like the head of a lion with an open mouth and projecting lower jaw covered with volutes and palmettes. Where the handle should be there is instead a pipe, which has given rise to different explanations. According to some, these spoons served for blowing or inhaling incense smoke. Not all of them, however, show signs of burning, and an example made of ivory, found at Megiddo, could not have been used thus. A better explanation is that the spoons were affixed to the containers of aromatic liquids which could be poured into them, though steatite bowls are rather heavy for this. If indeed cultic, these ladles belong to domestic rather than public ritual. They were popular in Israel especially during the eighth and seventh centuries and are related to North Syrian types.

Burning incense is a practice that may well have been unacceptable to strict Yahwists, especially when directed to strange deities such as the 'Host of Heaven' to whom Jerusalemites offered incense on the roof-tops (Jeremiah 19, 13). Archaeology offers indications of other unacceptable cults. There have indeed been no finds in Israelite houses of figures which might correspond to the *teraphim*, especially life-size male ones like the one used by David's wife Michal to impersonate him (1 Samuel 19, 13). However, small mould-made plaques in the shape of female images, and solid three-dimensional female figurines might be either representations of goddesses or, in some cases, charms. The plaques descend from a series popular in the Late Bronze Age, though the type showing a standing nude female deity with 'Hathor' coiffure, represented frontally and holding divine symbols – Astarte, Qudshu or Anath perhaps – did not survive into the Iron Age. Representations of a woman lying on a couch or bed, mould-made and hand-finished, also known in the Bronze Age, continued to be made in Iron I in a number of varieties. Some are shown totally naked, some wear armlets or a necklace; the hair usually hangs down at the sides of the head, but a high hat (*polos*) occurs occasionally. In some cases there are indications of advanced pregnancy, and such images may have been intended as charms helping to obtain pregnancy or easy childbirth. Such plaques went out of fashion in Judah during the period of the United Monarchy, but a somewhat different variant, in the form of a woman clasping a round object (perhaps a tambourine) to her chest, is found in northern Israel during Iron II. This may owe something to Phoenician inspiration, and perhaps hints at fertility rites linked with music. Solid figurines (some of which might have been toys) include a female figure seated on a stool holding a child, possibly derived from Isis and Hathor images.

During Iron II, solid 'pillar Astarte' figurines became increasingly popular. They occur in houses and tombs, so frequently in some residential areas that almost every household appears to have had one. These figurines consist of a hand- or wheel-made, bell-shaped body splaying towards the base, on to which crude arms holding the prominent breasts were fixed. The heads were made separately in a mould, perhaps at a single production centre, and pegged into the body. The backs of the heads were left rough, implying that the statuettes were put up looking at the beholder. Faces are well modelled, sometimes whitened and with cheeks painted red; a coiffure of several rows of small set curls, plus some side locks, is standard; high caps or veils occur occasionally. Whether such figurines were intended to represent a deity – perhaps the 'Queen of Heaven' – or were simply charms is uncertain. Stylistically, they are again linked with Phoenician examples. No remains of statues made from other materials, especially composite ones, are known.

Models of beds, birds (doves?) and terracotta horsemen, found in houses or tombs, besides clay rattles, are all somewhat doubtfully connected with religious rites. Pottery moulds probably intended for sacred cakes of a type found in the Phoenician world, and mentioned in Jeremiah (7, 18 and 44, 19), are exceptional so far. Pottery phalloi are probably simply charms. Whether small faience ornaments of Egyptian manufacture, representing deities such as Harpocrates, Sekhmet, Bes and sacred animals like the lion and the cat, or the 'eye of Horus', had religious significance to the Israelites – among whom they were popular especially in Iron I as charms or otherwise – or whether they were simply exotic trinkets, we cannot tell.

Such milieux did not conform to orthodox Yahwist ideas, which were apparently often disregarded in other respects, too. Thus pig bones found at Lachish indicate contravention of the dietary laws, though on the whole such finds are rare, and where ritual cleanliness is concerned it seems significant that only one possible example of the ritual bath, so frequent in later post-Exilic contexts, has been identified at Tel Masos. The later form of Judaism, it seems, was only nascent when the period ended.

Religious practices connected with the dead and folk religion

That ideas about a rather shadowy afterlife for the dead were widespread in biblical times is undisputed, and indeed the practice of putting objects of daily use, food and ornament with the dead indicates that they were regarded as capable of deriving some benefit from such gifts. However, beyond this we are in some doubt. Funerary meals may have been held by the relatives of the deceased, and libations to the dead may have been offered at the meetings of *marzeah* societies, but there is little sign of regular food or drink offerings or sacrifices at burial places. We do not know either whether the fires which were sometimes lit at solemn burials had some special, purificatory religious meaning. They are mentioned in connection with the funerals of Judean kings, and the rite seems attested in a tomb at Tel Eton in Judah, but this occurrence remains exceptional. Similarly, while biblical prohibitions against 'calling up the spirits of the dead' in order to receive oracles, together with the story of the Witch of Endor, suggest that such practices existed, there are so far no archaeological indications of them, or of other modes of divination. We may, however, note that diviners, magicians and enchanters are mentioned in Isaiah (3–4) among people of high social standing.

Thus a review of the information we have about folk religion – as opposed to high religion – in ancient Israel reveals that some features that might be expected are found rarely, or even not at all. A prominent element in the folk religion of Arab Palestine and elsewhere has been the presence of shrines over the tombs of local holy men with their name prefixed by the title Sheikh, where help or information might be requested. It has been suggested that the graves of some lesser judges in ancient Israel were used in a similar fashion, but that remains hypothetical. Also notable is the rarity of sacred mountains and caves. None seem discernible apart from the few which form part of official religious tradition – Mount Zion and, in the Samaritan tradition, Mount Gerizim on the one hand, the cave of Machpelah on the other. Perhaps most striking of all is the absence of sacred springs and waters, and of the spirits found associated with them in the folk religion of many lands. No cult places or ritual deposits have been found near any, and if there were ever any cult legends associated with prominent springs, like the Gihon at Jerusalem, they are lost. As for the mysterious stranger with whom Jacob wrestled by the Jabbok ford (Genesis 32, 24ff.), his identity remains a secret.

The testimony of epigraphy

We must now consider to what extent inscriptions found in Palestine add to the testimony offered by the monuments. Where expressions of foreign beliefs and cults found in ancient Israel are concerned we can be brief. The only significant epigraphic discovery illustrating non-Israelite religious traditions is the text from Tell Deir 'Alla, mentioned earlier, with its Balaam story. To what extent this foreign-derived text reflected beliefs shared by Israelites we cannot tell.

In any assessment of the extent to which orthodox Yahwism and its scriptures did indeed go back to the very beginnings of Israel we are again hampered by a lack of relevant epigraphic evidence. No complete or even fragmentary examples either of biblical texts or of works quoted in the Bible and dating from the Israelite period – like the later Dead Sea manuscripts – have so far been found. The earliest example of a biblical quotation known at present is a text of the 'priestly blessing' (Numbers 6, 24–26) scratched on a tiny sheet of silver placed inside an amulet container and found in a rich tomb in Jerusalem, dating from the very end of the Monarchy or even later. Indirect evidence for the existence of biblical passages forbidding the retention of a garment taken in pledge overnight (Exodus 22, 25–26, cf. Deuteronomy 24, 12–13) may be contained in a late seventh-century ostracon from Meṣad Ḥashavyahu, where a harvest-worker asks for his garment taken in pledge to be returned. Furthermore, no distinguishing religious symbol was used to denote the deity of the Israelites, like those representing contemporary pagan deities, and there was no symbol for Israelite religion like the later cross or crescent. It cannot be shown that the rare examples of the six-pointed 'star of David' so far discovered were used in the modern way. As we saw, there is nevertheless no doubt that by the seventh and sixth centuries BC official and scribal circles in Judah among others were Yahwists. In the Arad and Lachish letters they used introductory formulae like 'May YHWH show concern for your welfare', 'I bless you by YHWH', 'May YHWH let my lord hear tidings of peace' and the oath 'as YHWH liveth'. Significantly, no other deities are mentioned. Very orthodox sentiments were also scribbled on the walls of a burial cave at Khirbet Beit Lei northeast of

60 (Left) *Incised inscription from Ketef Hinnom containing a modified text of the 'Priestly Blessing', written on a small sheet of silver. It contains the earliest approximation to a text in the Bible which was to become so important in the future. Seventh century BC.*

Lachish; according to Frank Moore Cross they even included a lost prophecy of salvation, but the reading is doubtful. These texts may again date to the last days of the kingdom of Judah, or perhaps earlier.

Yet even the acceptance of the God of Israel to the exclusion of all others might entail problems. In Canaanite popular religion there had been a tendency to personify the representations of the great deities at local sanctuaries – Baal and Astarte had thus given rise to a multitude of local Baals and Astartes. Amos (8, 14) offers a hint that the same process may have begun in Israelite popular belief – Israelites were swearing *inter alia* by the God of Dan. Excavations there have now brought to light a Greek inscription dedicated 'to the god who is in Dan', which might indicate the persistence of such beliefs over some centuries. Somewhat earlier, the inscriptions at Kuntillet 'Ajrud may have referred to YHWH of Samaria, perhaps also to YHWH of Teman, referring perhaps to 'the south land' in general rather than to the specific region of that name in Edom. Any such separatist tendencies were cut short, as far as mainstream Israelite faith was concerned, by the fall of Israel and Judah and the Exile. However, among the Jewish group living in the fifth century at Elephantine near Aswan in Egypt there is evidence of the survival of yet another curious localization. Bethel in northern Israel was a place hallowed by its associations with the Patriarchs, as well as the presence of one of the two main sanctuaries created by Jeroboam. Sacred stones 'inhabited' by deities were known in the ancient Near East as Bait-Il (=Bethel) – 'house of the deity' and this led to the recognition of a god of that name. In the minds of some Israelites this word Bethel may have evoked the same deity – perhaps hinted at in Jeremiah (48, 13). At Elephantine 'Bethel' is in any case used as a divine name element in the same way as 'Yahu'. The decline of the colony put an end to this aberrant theology.

Where the practice of religion, and the organization and personnel of the cult in particular, are concerned, epigraphy offers only limited information. At Arad, ostraca – perhaps for casting lots to assign duties in the temple – include the names of the two priestly families of Meremoth and Pahshur, known from the post-Exilic period (cf. Nehemiah 7, 41, Ezra 2, 38, and Nehemiah 3, 4, Ezra 8, 33 respectively). Another ostracon from Arad mentions the sons of Korah – quite possibly the well-known family of Levitical singers. On the other hand the identity of a 'priest of Dor' mentioned on a seal remains doubtful; perhaps he was not an Israelite. At Kuntillet 'Ajrud finds of variegated cloth made of both linen and woollen threads – a fabric forbidden to laymen – suggest the presence of priests there, but there is no epigraphic confirmation. About the prophets who played such an important part in Israelite religion epigraphy offers no insight, except for a reference to an unnamed prophet in the Lachish letters, just as archaeology has so far unearthed no evidence either about groups of prophets and their communal abodes (cf. 2 Kings 6, 2) or prominent individ-ual 'writing' prophets. Whether a 'servant of YHWH' mentioned on an early eighth-century seal was a temple singer is not certain.

Set ceremonies and rituals in public worship, such as the 'pilgrim festivals', or forms of prayer, whether communal or individual, are so far unattested by epigraphy. There is, however, some material which has been interpreted as referring to religious dues. The letters *qr* on jars found at Kuntillet 'Ajrud may be an abbreviation for *qorban* ('sacrifice') and *y* (numerical value 10) on a jar there may indicate that this contained priestly tithe. Similarly the letters *qk* (or *qs*?) on two eighth-century(?) bowls discovered near the altar at Arad may stand for *qodesh kohanim* ('sacred/set apart for the priests' or alternatively for *qdš* – ? with the same meaning); a similar inscription was found on an ivory pomegranate which once topped a ceremonial staff or sceptre, possibly belonging to a priest in the Temple in Jerusalem. It is unclear what it may have served for. *Qdš* (*qadosh* – 'holy') on vases found at Beersheba and Hazor may indicate that these vessels were used for religious purposes (cf., Zechariah 14, 21). Except perhaps for the sceptre-head none of the above are linked with Jerusalem and its Temple; for the present, the Bible remains our sole source of evidence concerning the personnel and practices found there.

Israelite religion: dependence or independence

From what has been said it will be clear that Israelite religion had, from beginning to end, much in common with Canaanite religion or even depended on Canaanite models. There are indeed wider analogies in the ancient Near East in general, but links with other neighbouring countries take second place to those with regions with a Canaanite background. In particular, there seem to be remarkably few affinities with the Philistine zone which cannot be explained as due to common Canaanite heritage, while to the east links are even more tenuous. The Midianite sanctuary at Timnah springs to mind, and the copper snake found there, which recalls the 'brass serpent' Nehushtan in the Temple at Jerusalem, but there are antecedents for the latter in the Canaanite world. Yet there are some differences. For instance, the tradition of producing metal figurines of deities in the Canaanite Late Bronze Age fashion ceased soon after the Israelites established themselves. In particular, there is no definite example then, or later, of a statue meant to represent YHWH. Cult stands adorned with representations of motifs inherited from the Canaanite religious repertoire, like lions, sphinxes or deities, went out of fashion during the period of the Monarchy. Ideology may well have something to do with this – Israel was increasingly to go her own way, which in the end distinguished her sharply from the traditions of her neighbours.

CHAPTER TWELVE

Israelite Art

Any attempt to discuss the evidence of Israelite visual – and especially representational – art is likely to encounter incredulity. How could such art possibly exist when the Ten Commandments include a clear and detailed prohibition of making a 'likeness of anything that is in the heaven above, or in the earth beneath, or in the waters under the earth' (Exodus 20, 4, cf. Deuteronomy 5, 8)? Yet since the passage goes on to forbid bowing down to such images and serving them, it perhaps should be interpreted as concerning objects of worship only, while some other forms of artistic representation would be permissible. Post-Exilic Judaism has in fact at times allowed representational art, even in synagogues.

Where pre-Exilic Israel is concerned, archaeological discoveries have increasingly shown that 'images' did exist then, and the make-up of such art, its stylistic features, relations with the art found in contemporary Near Eastern countries, the possible religious significance of Israelite art and the extent to which it was restricted by religious considerations have all been given increasing attention.

Obviously, we should begin at the point where an Israelite presence in the Promised Land is attested. Objects ascribed by Israelite tradition to the period before the settlement like the Tabernacle with its appurtenances such as the Ark of the Covenant (Exodus 36–38) remain hypothetical, even though recent research has shown that the biblical description can be matched with evidence from the general period concerned. On the other hand, when Israel entered into the light of history she found herself in a land whose Canaanite inhabitants possessed highly developed artistic traditions, to which must also be added the art imported under Egyptian domination. Since early Israel was liable to be influenced by its neighbours – and the Canaanites continued to dwell in the land for a long time – something must be said about the art found in Palestine during the Late Bronze Age, the time when the Israelites are first known to have lived there.

The art of Canaan at the time of the Israelite emergence

In an age when Palestine was much affected by international contacts, art there understandably reflected this situation. Domination by Egypt brought some direct transplantation of Egyptian architectural features, of sculpture both religious and secular (in the round or in relief), and of various *objets d'art*, in particular some made from ivory or faience. More significantly, Egyptian art forms affected local traditions, which were fairly mixed. Syrian and Phoenician, Aegean and Hittite contacts all left their mark. As a result, there was a stock of motifs of varied derivation, apt to be treated in set ways, but with an eye to decorative effect involving sometimes repetitive use of patterns with no effort to reproduce their prototypes correctly. Griffins and sphinxes combined traditions derived from regions as far apart as Anatolia and Egypt, and also the Aegean; representations of cattle might follow Aegean models, while lions were shown in an Egyptian or Syro-Mesopotamian mode (the lion attacking a bull or other prey was a long-established subject in the latter region). The 'tree of life' flanked by two caprids – goats, ibexes or gazelles – was popular over much of the Levant, but the lotus flower and bud came from Egypt. Such motifs, together with others, were used most skilfully in the carving of ivory objects in the round, or engraved or carved on plaques which once adorned furniture, wooden panelling, boxes or other objects. Lachish and Megiddo (pls 67–9) have yielded outstanding examples: the best from the latter site show a combination of skilful execution together with sensitivity which raises them to the level of true art.

In other branches of artistic production the level of accomplishment was varied. The limited amount of stone statuary tended to simplification, sometimes excessively so. Metal statuettes representing male deities (seated and holding an object in one hand, or standing and brandishing a weapon) are often crude, with a flat body topped by a rounded head. This was apparently regarded as adequate for them to be acceptable as votive gifts to some deity. A few, however, show both greater naturalism and artistic feeling. Relief plaques representing the naked female form – goddesses or mortal women – made from metal or reproduced from moulds in terracotta, show a similar range. Just which deities were represented is doubtful, but one type is commonly known as the 'Qudshu' goddess, and takes the form of a frontal view of a nude female figure wearing a 'Hathor' wig and holding a lily in each hand. Other representations of women without the Hathor coiffure or flowers, with their hands by their sides or supporting their breasts, may have been charms and were mass produced. Derived from Egyptian prototypes representing women lying on a couch, the best are of some artistic merit.

Pottery was also sometimes painted, though mostly rather modestly. The 'tree of life' flanked by caprids was a favourite motif, but growing simplification towards the end of the period reduced designs to an increasingly abstract style. The same tendency can be observed on stamp seals of the period. Artistic merit here is the exception, though a feeling for movement is sometimes discernible.

The coming of the Philistines and allied Sea Peoples early in the twelfth century added another component – itself of mixed ancestry – to the artistic repertoire. Cypro-Mycenaean traditions (noticeable particularly on painted pottery) are combined with Egyptian and Canaanite features. Rhytons (large drinking cups) shaped like lion-heads can perhaps be traced back to Egyptian prototypes copied in Canaan; small terracotta figures representing stylized seated goddesses, or wailing women with raised arms, reflect Aegean traditions. Other items are purely Egyptian or Canaanite. The artistic level of this mixed tradition is mostly low, and the style was shortlived.

The period of the Judges: Canaanite and Israelite art

Canaanite art, like Canaanite urban civilization in general, survived the turbulent twelfth century BC in an impoverished form. By *c.* 1000 BC the Canaanites had mostly been incorporated into Israel, but even before then relations with the Israelite hill country led to the early acquisition of Canaanite artistic products by Israelites. Products of Canaanite representational art were apparently even used in religious contexts. A bronze figurine representing a seated deity has been found in the early Israelite sanctuary at Hazor XI, while another, representing a standing 'smiting god', comes from Megiddo VB – an early Israelite stratum. Again, a bull image of Canaanite (or Cypriot) derivation was discovered at a rustic sanctuary, probably Israelite, not far from Jenin (pl. 51). Such images could carry religious meanings for both Israelites and Canaanites.

Pictures on seals or seal impressions, a potential source of information about art, are few in this period. They are found on stamp seals, either Egyptian scarabs or their imitations, or more rarely conical or pyramidal seals made from cheap materials like clay or stone. The former may show pharaoh or royal symbols, badly represented in very simplified designs; the latter vegetable motifs or geometric shapes as flat surfaces. High or low relief on the impressions is absent. Some of the pictures are not displeasing; none are artistically advanced. Though some were found in possibly Israelite places it is not clear who their makers were and they are not specially Israelite.

Early Israelite folk art

The question arises whether in addition to such foreign imports the Israelites had any art of their own. It appears that they did, though its products tended to be crude, if often vigorous. Terracotta versions of Canaanite bronze figurines found in the hill country may well be Israelite work, like a 'smiting god' image found at Bethel and bull images, or parts of them, discovered at the sacred sites of Shiloh and Mount Ebal. More frequently, however, Israelites decorated pottery vessels with three-dimensional representations. Craters from Khirbet Raddanah and Dothan have, respectively, spouts or excrescences shaped like bulls' heads and handles terminating in crude lions' heads. At 'Izbet Ṣarṭah a pot was decorated with schematic appliqué representations of an ibex and palm tree. There are other related but undated fragments of appliqué décor on vases from Tell en-Naṣbeh. A jar handle shaped in part as a human head, crude but expressive, comes from Bethel. Also, a remarkable collection of pieces of decorated pottery was discovered at the sacred site of Shiloh. In addition to part of a store jar decorated with impressed rosettes there were two sherds bearing animal figures in relief – a cooking pot with the head of a lioness on its rim and a crater with a ram's head at the base of the handle. Parts of a terracotta cult stand adorned with applied images of a horse, a lioness and a leopard attacking a deer were also found.

Though this style of embellishment is not exclusively found at Israelite sites, it seems most at home there, and I. Finkelstein has indeed called it 'the only surviving artistic expression of the Israelites in the Iron I period'. The Khirbet Raddanah crater has Anatolian (Hittite) parallels, and the deer figured on the cult stand fragments from Shiloh recalls the occurrence of cervids in North Syrian and Hittite art. We must, however, remember that many deer bones have been found in the sacred premises on Mount Ebal, showing that the animal was of some relevance to Israelite visitors there. Painted designs on pottery were apparently not popular among early Israelites and where they do occur they may betoken Canaanite survivals. A tendency towards abstraction is evident in the plastic examples too, with occasional naturalism and a striving for overall decorative effect.

Israelite art in the period of the Monarchy

'Imperial art'
The coming of the United Monarchy, and more particularly the empire of David and Solomon, also left its imprint in the sphere of art. Considerable new opportunities for artistic activity were now provided by the building programmes of David and especially Solomon, requiring the expertise of foreign specialists in architectural design, décor and fittings. Much of these great programmes has remained archaeologically unattested, or elucidated only indirectly by analogies elsewhere. We know nothing about David's residence in Hebron, or about the royal seat he later constructed in Jerusalem with Tyrian help (2 Samuel 5, 11), and for information about Solomon's religious and secular buildings we have to rely chiefly on biblical information (1 Kings 4–7; 2 Chronicles 2–4).

As discussed earlier, a general Canaanite tradition as well as its special Phoenician offshoot seem to have been important. This is true for example of the decorative use of palm trees and sphinxes (equated by scholars with the biblical 'cherubs') in the Temple, and of lions flanking Solomon's throne. (We shall note the use of such motifs on cult stands and in other Israelite contexts below.) Aegean (Cypriot) traditions evident in the style of the movable lavers in the Temple passed into the Canaanite repertoire earlier. Even more interesting is the occurrence of cult stands of Canaanite derivation in cities which had come under Israelite sway during the period of the early (Solomonic?) monarchy. These stands imitate buildings and are adorned with plastic figures. Two were found at Taanach, one before the First World War by Sellin and another fairly recently by Lapp. The former, restored from fragments, shows a tall rectangular edifice, the two front corners of which are decorated with five superimposed alternate rows of lions and sphinxes. Their bodies are in line with the sides of the stand but the heads project from it in front. Only two caprids leaping up a sacred tree survive from the decoration of the front of the stand.

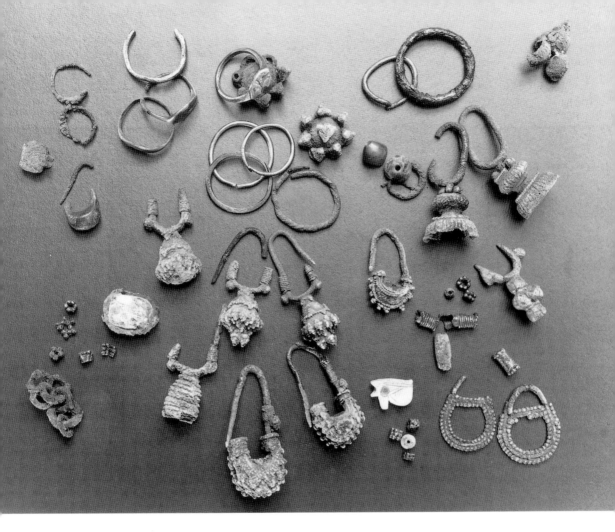

56 Jewelry from the burial caves at Ketef Hinnom, Jerusalem, dating from the final period of the monarchy and later.

57 Mould for casting axe heads and weapons, on the top are recesses for two axe heads. Such moulds were in use during the Bronze and Iron Ages.

Arts and crafts

58, 59 *(Left)* Female figurine holding a tambourine or frame drum, perhaps connected with a fertility cult; and an ivory bottle stopper, carved in the shape of a ram's head – one of the few surviving examples of ivory or bone carving in Judah. From Lachish.

60, 61 *(Below)* Cult stand ornamented with figures of musicians, from Ashdod. While this crudely executed stand is from Philistia, the small orchestra recalls those in Israel (1 Samuel 10, 5; Isaiah 5, 12); pottery cult stand from Taanach, decorated with crude figures of animals.

Opposite

62, 63, 64 Pottery cult stand from Jerusalem (fragment), decorated with the figure of a hero; a pottery fragment from Shiloh, decorated with plastic animal figures (a leopard attacking a deer); and a piece of a terracotta cult stand from Tell en-Naṣbeh, featuring an ibex.

65, 66 Figurine of a woman sitting in a hip-bath, from the cemetery of the Phoenician harbour site at Akhzib – similar methods of ablution were probably used in Israel; terracotta figurine of a horseman from Lachish. Such figurines may have had a religious significance.

67 Ivory openwork plaque from Late Bronze Age Megiddo, with a figure of the Egyptian god Bes.

68 Ivory comb from Late Bronze Age Megiddo, decorated with a carving showing a dog attacking an ibex.

Opposite

69 Ivory receptacle from Late Bronze Age Megiddo, carved with representations of lions and sphinxes.

70, 71 Ivory toilet spoon from Hazor, carved with four Phoenician palmetto ornaments on one side and the simplified figure of a woman in the Syrian style on the other.

Ivory carving

72 Phoenician terracotta figurine, representing a pregnant woman, from Akhzib. It is related to Israelite fertility charms but far more naturalistic.

73, 74 Carved bone handle from Hazor, featuring a four-winged figure, holding on to the branches of a palmetto tree with both hands. The design is wrapped round the handle. The motif is of Egyptian derivation, but the treatment shows Syrian stylistic influence.

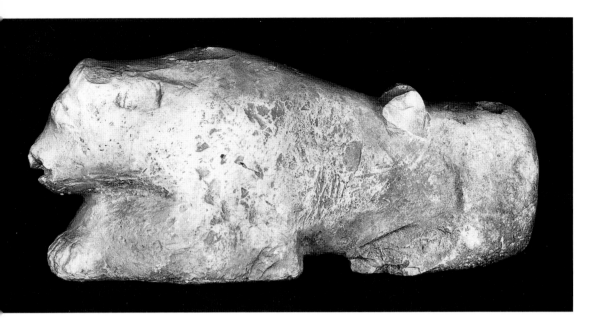

75 Stone figurine of a lion (originally perhaps one of a pair flanking a column or statue base) from Tell Beit Mirsim. It was at first attributed to the Late Bronze Age.

76 Carved bone handle ending in the head of Hathor, from a sistrum (ritual rattle) found at Beitim (Bethel). Late Bronze Age.

77 Fragment of painted pottery from Ramat Rachel, depicting a seated king, perhaps King Jehoiakim of Judah. Artistic influences from Assyria or alternatively Archaic Greece have been suggested.

78, 79 Seal (and a drawing of its impression) of Ya'azanyahu, servant of the king (a high royal official) featuring a fighting cock. From Mizpah (Tell en-Naṣbeh). Late eighth to seventh century BC.

80, 81, 82 *(Above)* Stamped seal impression on a jar handle found in Jerusalem, featuring a prancing horse. *(Above right)* Seal of Shema, servant of Jeroboam, showing a roaring lion. Attributed to the eighth century, though a tenth-century dating has recently again been proposed. *(Right)* Seal of *yrmyhw* (Jeremiah – a fairly frequent name), with a browsing deer. Eighth century BC.

83, 84, 85 *(Below)* Seal of Ma'adanah, the 'king's daughter', featuring a lyre. This so-far unique representation on a seal (if genuine) would offer valuable information about this kind of ancient Judean musical instrument; seal of *ḥmn*, featuring a griffin above a locust (the locust may be a family emblem); seal featuring two birds.

The second stand from Taanach (pl. 53) is much better preserved and has complex decoration arranged in four superimposed tiers – the sides again consisting of alternate rows of lions and sphinxes. A female figure holding the two neighbouring lions at the corners – a 'mistress of animals' (*potnia theron*) – occupies the lowest register of the front. The second register is missing, but the third again has a sacred tree flanked by goats, while the upper zone is decorated with a calf below a winged solar disk. Volutes adorned the two front corners. On top was a basin (perhaps for liquids), the sides of which project outwards in the shape of an Egyptian cavetto cornice and the roundels on it may be derived from roof beams; the other stand may have had a similar top. A fragment of a third, similar stand, found by Yigal Shiloh in (Davidic?) Jerusalem, preserves the upper part of a bare-chested male in frontal view. He has a small pointed beard and wears his hair long in an Aegean or Philistine fashion. Of the two flanking animals which he appears to have held only the paws survive.

These cult stands are remarkable in several respects. The decorative repertoire on which they draw is completely un-Israelite in derivation though it was also drawn on for the decoration of Solomon's Temple. Stylistically, they represent a mixture of traditions blending Canaanite with Egyptian, Syro-Mesopotamian and Aegean elements. Were any of them made by Israelites? This seems perhaps more likely in the case of the first stand, which looks like a crude copy, than the others – especially the second Taanach stand – which appear to be the products of schools of craftsmen trained in long-established traditions.

61 *Fragment of pottery with impressed relief decoration from En Gedi. Such decoration is rare, especially during the Divided Monarchy.*

Fragments of other cult stands were discovered at Megiddo. Two of them could be partly restored and proved also to be decorated with sphinxes, though otherwise they were smaller and less ornamented. They may be contemporary with the Taanach stands, or later, though it appears that such cult implements lost favour in the period of the Divided Monarchy. Relief decoration seems also to have become somewhat unfashionable. Part of a crater bowl from En Gedi (*c.* 600 BC?) once thought to carry its decoration of stamp seal imprints of a seated crowned male adoring a plant, a ram (now taken to be a stag) and a lion(?)

62 *Terracotta model of a shrine from Tell el Far'ah (N), Stratum VIIB (tenth century BC?). This model represents a small cult building open in front with two columns overtopped by volute capitals flanking the opening. Though there is relief decoration above the opening, the profuse representation of living creatures as found on contemporary cult stands is absent.*

head on an applied plastic strip has instead been shown to have the decoration stamped directly on the vessel's body. In any case, such rich decoration was not applied to another kind of cult object – a tenth-century model of a small shrine from Tell el Far'ah (N).

The Solomonic period also saw developments in art. Statues of deities in metal – and images of male deities in particular – went out of fashion, as did plaques representing goddesses. They were replaced by free-standing figurines, mould- or hand-made, which after the division of the United Monarchy displayed differences between north and south. Those in the north attempted to represent realistically a whole female body, while the south was developing 'pillar figurines' consisting of mould-made heads pegged into disproportionally small bell-shaped bodies, hand- or wheel-made, provided with arms usually held to the breasts, more rarely holding a child or a disk-shaped object (probably a frame drum, less probably a cake or loaf). These objects are also represented on some northern figurines ('women with tambourines'). While northern examples show little artistic quality, those in the south do attempt some in the heads, which usually have stiff curls – either natural or a wig – or longer locks; paint may indicate jewelry. Though some faces are enlivened with a slight smile or individual characteristics, few can be rated as art. Derived perhaps from Phoenicia, these figurines were popular in Judah, and especially in Jerusalem, in the eighth and seventh centuries in particular. They may be images of the 'Queen of Heaven' or another female deity worshipped by women; other types may represent mortal females supplicating for divine favour. Also probably cultic are statuettes of horses, or horses and riders – perhaps images of the 'horses of the sun' (2 Kings 23, 11). They are not art, however.

For the disappearance of the rich, but foreign-inspired body of imagery represented on the cult stands, and the discontinuation of the use of male deity statues, we may suspect that religious scruple of the maintainers of official religion were responsible; though they were obviously not totally effective and they did not succeed in suppressing the imagery linked with feminine cult.

Art in the period of the Divided Monarchy

Both in the quantity and quality of artistic production, this period represents the apex in the history of Israelite art. There were reasons for this: in both kingdoms there now existed, in addition to the court and its functionaries, a social élite who could afford a spectacular lifestyle rivalling foreign models, which could be both imitated and improved on. Israelite art would thus comprise both the (selective) copying of foreign models – Egyptian, Phoenician and Syro-Mesopotamian – and also some innovations.

Among the art used to embellish the style of life of the élite we may first of all mention the use of carved ivory to decorate the palaces of the kings and the abodes of nobles – especially in the form of wall panelling or furniture. Those produced by Phoenician craftsmen were especially outstanding – technically very competent, with a wide selection of Egyptian-inspired motifs and a smooth and glossy finish, they were a joy to behold. Those of the Syrian school were only a little inferior. In Israel ivory carvings included flat plaques, often carved in relief or sometimes decorated with incised linear patterns. The former were on occasion embellished by inlays of coloured glass, paste and perhaps jewels and overlays of gold leaf. Alternatively there were ivory carvings in the round, which would have adorned wooden wall panelling or furniture, but might also be independent luxury objects.

Samaria has furnished a particularly important collection of some 500 items, including around 300 carved pieces. They were unfortunately not found in their original context, and their dating is disputed. Some may come from the ninth-century 'Ivory House' of Ahab (mentioned in 1 Kings 22, 39), but others (some scholars think all) date from a century later. The vast majority are Phoenician in style and were executed on the spot by Phoenician craftsmen using stock motifs derived from Egyptian prototypes. However, some Syrian influence is apparent, and one rather crudely executed piece belonging to the Syrian school, a 'cherub' (sphinx) with an over-large head, may be Israelite work. Israelite carving, executed on occasion in cheaper bone rather than costly ivory, has also been identified elsewhere, as at Hazor, where a bone handle featuring a four-winged angel figure holding on to a tree of life combines Syrian and Phoenician features. There are others, too, at Tell en-Naṣbeh and Gezer, and one example has now been found at Tell Abu al-Kharaz (Jabesh of Gilead). A pyxis and a carved ivory spoon from Hazor (pls 70, 71) also show some Syrian as well as Phoenician traits. These may all be examples of a northern Israelite school of carving located perhaps at Samaria and possibly elsewhere. It is worth noting that the Assyrians thought its products worth taking away as booty (some have been found at Nimrud), though technically and aesthetically they did not match the best Phoenician work. Such work was rarer in Judah, though there is a carved ivory bottle top from Lachish, and ivory was part of Hezekiah's tribute to Sennacherib. Ivory inlays in panelling were also substituted in the poorer south by wood using similar patterns, as recent discoveries in Jerusalem demonstrate.

In the field of decorative seals there was an astonishing change from those which had been current in the pre-monarchic period, as early perhaps as the tenth century. The cheap conoid or pyramidal stamp seals were progressively superseded by smaller seals of scarab shape, often made of semiprecious stones or other valuable materials. Designs showed considerable diversification and improvement in quality – some, of Egyptian or Phoenician derivation, were shared with those on ivories, but others were of Syrian types. The Phoenician types dominated in the ninth and early eighth century, while Syrian influence was important later. There were humans and animals, singly or in groups, plant motifs and divine symbols, astral or solar, the latter especially in the seventh century. Not all designs popular in the neighbouring countries found favour in Israel, though some, like the lion (popular in Syria) or the griffin, were; the browsing female deer and the cockerel, on the other hand, were especially favoured in Israel.

Writing was rare on early seals, but from the ninth century onwards it became an increasingly common feature, indicating especially the name of the owner and that of his (or her) father. During the seventh century seals bearing inscriptions but no other design became dominant in Judah. The best of such aniconic seals show not only a skill in execution but also a feeling for balance and flowing line unequalled in the contemporary Semitic-speaking world. Like later Arab calligraphers, ancient Judeans may have satisfied their artistic impulses in this abstract way.

Israelite seal designs were often essentially two-dimensional in intention – the imposition of drawings on fairly flat surfaces. Among the best Israelite seals there are, however, some which combine relief with a fairly naturalistic representation. The famous seal of Shema, the servant of Jeroboam (pl. 81), is a good example of what could be achieved in this way: the roaring lion looks remarkably life-like, even though closer inspection reveals the traditional canon in the stance of the beast, or in the way his mane is represented. In such cases the Israelite seal cutter created genuine works of art. This lion seal has been attributed to the time of Jeroboam I rather than II – the tenth rather than the eighth century BC. Such highly successful artistic creations at such an early period would be quite remarkable. Abstract designs, like those on the *l-mlk* stamps, are unusual during this period.

The next question to be looked at is, to what extent were Israelite seals actually produced by Israelites? For a long time it was thought that practically all such seals were the work of foreign, Phoenician or Syrian, artists; Israelites might perhaps have been responsible for some cheap and undistinguished examples in easily worked raw materials like bone. It is now thought, however, that there were Israelite workshops during the period of the Monarchy producing good seals, for instance at Samaria. This would parallel the assumed production of carved ivories there. There is no reason to exclude the likelihood of the aniconic seals found in Judah having been produced in Jerusalem and perhaps other Judean centres.

Painting is a more problematic subject, both because little has survived and

Painting on a sherd from Kuntillet 'Ajrud showing two ibexes *ling at a sacred tree. It is derived from the Syro–Phoenician *stic tradition, but the motif goes back much further.

64 (Above) *Two 'Bes'-figures and a seated female lyre-player painted on pottery from Kuntillet 'Ajrud. Motifs and execution are largely derived from Syro–Phoenician tradition.*

65 (Left) *Men in procession shown on a pottery jar from Kuntillet 'Ajrud. The rendering of this sketch is impressionistic and abstract and has been compared with North Arabian art, but it is also related to the abstract scribbled drawings in the Judean tomb cave of Khirbet Beit Lei.*

because it is again difficult to be sure what is Israelite work and what is not. The largest collection of painted designs now known was revealed in the desert caravan station and sanctuary at Kuntillet 'Ajrud in the Negeb. Dating from the ninth and eighth centuries BC, they include wall frescoes and pictures on two pithoi which may either be preliminary sketches by fresco artists, or the work of visitors, who appear to have included Phoenicians as well as Israelites. The frescoes (representative perhaps of much similar work elsewhere which has perished) are outlined in black and filled in with black lines or dots, or heightened with yellow and red. Subjects shown include persons on a city wall, a seated figure holding a lotus flower and animal scenes; the sacred tree and lotus chains also figure. Designs on the pithoi include a lion, a cow and calf and other animals, a sacred tree flanked by ibexes, a seated female lyre-player, two peculiar standing Bes(?) figures and a bowman. Whether any were originally part of a group composition is doubtful. Phoenician motifs and designs are strong here, while execution varies from competent to childish abstraction in the case of some human figures in a procession which may owe something to a 'desert art' tradition. Execution furthermore tends towards the abstract; there may occasionally be a touch of humour. Again, we cannot be sure how much of all this is Israelite.

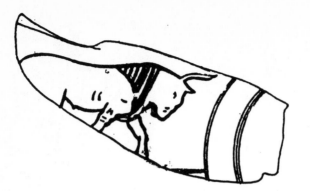

66 Sherd from a Judean round dish, showing a figure of a bull. This is taken from the Phoenician repertoire, where it may be shown on metal vases.

Among later examples of representational drawings and paintings, it is difficult to find work of the same quality and stylistic tradition as the better specimens from Kuntillet 'Ajrud. Graffiti scratched into cave walls, as at (post-Exilic?) Khirbet Beit Lei tend to resemble abstract child art. A painting of a seated, long-bearded male executed in red and black on a potsherd found at Ramat Rachel (Khirbet Ṣaliḥ) near Jerusalem deserves mention, however. It dates from the last century of the Judean monarchy – some have even suggested it may represent King Jehoiakim. Both Assyrian and Greek influences have been assumed, the latter because of the 'archaic smile' on the man's face, but too little is known to permit the linking of this picture with a specific background in Judah or outside (pl. 77).

Other applied arts

A similar juxtaposition of well-executed foreign models and, at least initially, poorer Israelite imitations can be discerned in a number of other fields. Tridacna shells decorated by Phoenician and perhaps Syrian craftsmen were copied rather badly in stone or bone by Israelites. The occasional copy of a Phoenician design on Israelite pottery (like a cow or bull on a sherd from Tell Beit Mirsim) can be rather better. To what extent Israelites were involved in the making of Phoenician-style metal bowls found in Assyria and taken as loot from Israel we cannot tell.

We may finally ask whether sculpture was produced in Israel – either to adorn important buildings, like the sphinxes and other mythological creatures figured on cult stands, which might have been copied from actual buildings found in the neighbourhood; or as portraits of royal personages, such as those produced in Ammon from the ninth to the sixth century; or finally cult statues. From the rather scrappy evidence found, especially at Megiddo, it would appear that some such sculptures did exist, but to a limited extent. Heretical divine images or symbols were occasionally put up: thus both during Asa's and

Manesseh's time there were images of Asherah in the Temple in Jerusalem, where statues(?) of the horses of the sun were also found (1 Kings 15, 13; 2 Kings 21, 7; 23, 11). As they were, not surprisingly, destroyed at times of religious revival we have no idea of what they looked like.

There have, so far, been no discoveries of monumental architectural sculptures forming part of buildings, but there are nevertheless some interesting stray finds. A small and rather crudely executed stone lion – originally possibly one of a pair flanking a pillar or statue base – was found at Tell Beit Mirsim in southern Judah (pl. 75). Once dated to the late Bronze Age it is now attributed to the ninth or eighth century BC; stylistically, it reflects North Syrian or Hittite prototypes. There may have been other architectural sculpture: Psalm 144, 12 appears to liken Israelite daughters to sculpted pillars at the corners of a palace (or temple, if the New English Bible is followed).

Relief carving was also apparently practised occasionally, though there is no sign of anything like its massive employment by Assyrian and other monarchs to eternalize their successes in battle and other achievements. There may have been some heretical reliefs (or paintings) in the Temple in Jerusalem (Ezekiel 8, 10); in any case a representation of a sphinx, carved into the rock wall of the 'Royal Caves' (underground quarries) in Jerusalem recalls Syro–Hittite models. Since the quarries were presumably most intensively used when the city expanded during the period of the Divided Monarchy it may date from that period, though a different date is possible. Outside Jerusalem there are two northern Israelite examples. At Megiddo, a stray sculpted stone slab found in Stratum III (eighth–seventh century BC), but presumably older, is adorned with a flat relief representation of a female figure, reduced to a few simplified

67 Relief figure of a rock-carved sphinx. Originally found in the 'Royal Caves', a former quarry near the northern wall of Jerusalem (it is now in London). The sphinx was probably interpreted by Israelites as a cherub. The time when it was carved is uncertain, but a pre-Exilic origin is possible.

surfaces; its exaggeratedly large head may link it with Aramean traditions in North Syria. Not very far away, at Beth Shean, a far more naturalistic relief showing in two superimposed registers a lion attacked by a dog (or alternatively a lion) and a lioness engaged in amorous play, was originally attributed to the Bronze Age, but an Iron Age date (eighth century?) is now preferred by some. Whether any of the above were officially commissioned we cannot tell; the same is true for a small bronze lion in Egyptian-derived Phoenician style, found as a votive gift at Arad in the temple precincts.

Two other lion sculptures, both from the region east of the Lake of Tiberias, are doubtfully Israelite. One, a complete orthostat which once flanked a gate entry, with projecting head and body along a side wall rather like the figures on the cult stands from Taanach, has long been known at Sheikh Sa'd (ancient Karnain); the surviving head of another has more recently been found at the village of Masharfawi, 4 km (2½ miles) east of Lake Tiberias in the Golan. Of North Syrian derivation, these sculptures, powerful but crude, seem to belong to a local school different from the one whose works inspired the Taanach stands, and it is difficult to be sure that the district in which they were found was Israelite rather than Syrian when they were put up.

We may finally mention a very interesting fragment of a limestone statuette from Megiddo wearing a smock, a tunic and a belt, the ends of which are hanging down in front. This is closely analogous to the corresponding part of a female statue from Khirbet el-Hajjar in Jordan. The example from Megiddo is ascribed to Stratum III but could well be older; the Jordanian statue is dated to the eighth century BC. In any case the two seem nearly contemporary. While the complete statuette from Megiddo would have been only about half the size of the Jordanian one, it is described as wrought with unusual skill; it might well be replica of a fullsize image, perhaps even that of a queen. The implications are tantalizing.

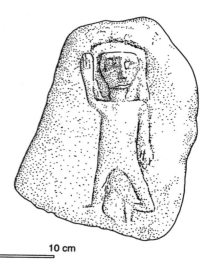

68 (Above) Part of a miniature female stone statue in the round, of good workmanship. The surviving part (head and feet are missing) resembles a larger stone statue found at Khirbet el-Hajjar in Jordan, and, like it, may represent a deity or a queen. Found at Megiddo Stratum III; late eighth/seventh century BC. (Right) A stone slab carrying on its front a crude female figure in relief. The disproportionately large head hints at Syrian influence. Also found at Megiddo III.

0   10 cm

69 *Three unscripted stamp seals, showing:* (left) *a horse with a human figure and a bird, from Lachish;* (centre) *a horse-drawn chariot with three occupants, from Tell Dan; and* (right) *a horse and rider, from Beth Shean. Iron Age II.*

Israelite art: an overall assessment

Our knowledge of Israelite art is thus limited, making a proper assessment of its nature difficult. From the period of the United Monarchy onwards it seems to have been restricted on religious grounds – the absence of statues representing rulers or their achievements, and the transition from seals bearing representations to those carrying writing only, may well be linked with such factors. Yet Israel and even Judah from the seventh century onwards never gave up representational art entirely. In its selection of traditional motifs, and also in execution, it was indebted to Canaanite art and its Phoenician and Syrian offsprings, especially the latter in the fields of non-official and popular art. In attempting to follow such canons, Israelite artists were often imitative newcomers whose level of achievement was, at first at least, not always high. Artistic output was, moreover, limited rather than pervasive, especially where three-dimensional art is concerned: the early promise shown here in the examples of decorated pottery and terracotta from the period of the Judges proved somewhat deceptive.

70 *Seal of Ya'azanyahu, servant of the king, from Tell en-Naṣbeh* (left), *juxtaposed with a cockerel on a proto-Corinthian vase from Perachora, Greece* (right). *They both obviously come from the same tradition of design, though the Greek one offers a more static and heraldic impression.*

In its treatment of motifs, Israelite art often showed a lack of interest in the representation of anatomically correct detail, and a striving after reduction to simple forms. Yet at its best, it could combine close observation of nature with a feeling for elegant flowing lines (expressed also in the best Judean styles of writing, on seals especially) and a surprising sense of movement – caught as it were in a split-second and expressed sometimes with a few strokes. This is true of the rendering of a browsing cervid on a seal (pl. 82), but especially of the magnificent relief drawing of a prancing horse on a seal impression from Jerusalem (pl. 80). A closer look at some individual cases may clarify matters.

The seal of Ya'azanyahu showing a cockerel belongs to a group of representations of this animal stretching from eighth-century Assyria to Archaic

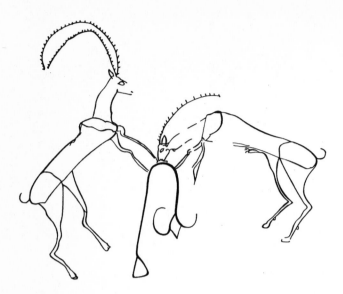

71 *Drawing of two ibexes nibbling at a lotus plant, incised on a jar from Lachish. The motif of two caprids flanking a sacred tree had long been familiar in Levantine art. It is here transformed into a lively and graceful naturalistic sketch in spite of some faults in draughtsmanship (crossing lines). Sixth century BC.*

Greece. Yet the way in which the bird is shown is significantly different from country to country. The Assyrian seal-cutter offered naturalistic detail, including the fluffiness of plumage. Early Greek vase-painters strove for a decorative, almost heraldic, effect. In the Israelite version naturalistic detail in the Assyrian manner is lacking, while the heraldic effect achieved by Greek vase-painters is to some extent paralleled, but its execution is far less involved. Yet the cockerel drawn by the Israelite craftsman in a few schematic lines is the only one giving evidence of life – we can see the bird lowering his head as if to make for his opponent.

A drawing of two ibexes nibbling at a drooping lotus plant, scratched on a jar by some unknown Lachish potter, is comparable. The motif is ultimately derived from the ancient subject of two caprids flanking a sacred tree, but in its execution the Lachish drawing is unique. There are faults in design – the outlines of legs and body cross in a way which no novice should have been guilty of – and the representation is purely two-dimensional, indeed the horns of the gazelles are even reduced to a single line. In spite of all this, however, the drawing possesses a freshness, a truth of observation and a sense of graceful line which lift it into the realm of genuine art.

Such impressionistic vision and rendering may perhaps be regarded as a common tendency in Israelite art. It may also be linked with impressionistic descriptions found sometimes in Israelite literature, as in Nahum (3, 2–3). It was, however, like Israelite art in general, cut short by the fall of the Judean monarchy.

Israelite music

While Israelite visual art does not seem to have enjoyed international esteem, Israelite music, and especially Israelite singing, apparently did. Thus, among

72 (Left) *A detail from an Egyptian fresco from a tomb at Beni Hassan, representing a procession of Asiatic nomads, seeking permission to enter Egypt (early Middle Kingdom). Note the lyre carried by one man, which is basically the type used in Canaan in the second millennium BC.*

73 (Below) *Figures of musicians, from Zinjirli* (right) *and Carchemish* (left), *illustrating musical instruments in use in the Iron Age Levant.*

the tribute received from Hezekiah, Sennacherib lists male and female singers – a very unusual item; later on, Judean exiles in Bablyonia were exhorted by their captors to entertain them with 'songs of Zion' (Psalm 137, 3). Requests of this kind by well-informed masters of large empires are surely significant. Yet there are parallels: the Assyrians also showed interest in Arab music, and Syro–Phoenician music was esteemed in Egypt and elsewhere. Among our sources the Bible is of primary importance, together with comments found in later rabbinical and patristic writings, and in the Jewish historian Flavius Josephus.

All such art is the fruit of lengthy development. By the time Israel first appeared on the stage of history, the Middle Eastern countries from Egypt to Mesopotamia were heirs to well-established musical traditions, employing a considerable range of musical instruments to support the human voice. Music had a place not only in settled societies where palaces and temples employed the services of trained professional singers and musicians organized in guilds, but also (as the famous Beni Hassan pictures remind us) among wandering pastoralists. Israel may well have drawn on both these sources: indeed instruments such as the harp (lyre) and pipe were traced back to Jubal, brother of the first tent-dwelling pastoralist and of the first wandering smith (Genesis 4, 20–22). However, it is difficult to say much about the music of such non-settled people during the second and first millennia BC. It was probably affected by the music found among their settled contemporaries, as it was later. About the latter

we are fairly well informed by archaeological discoveries, ancient pictorial representations and textual references, as far as musical instruments are concerned. Wind instruments included flutes, double pipes (oboes), and ram's horn and metal trumpets. Among stringed instruments there were harps large and small, lyres (a special type with rectangular sound box and outward-curving arms joined by a yoke was in fashion in Canaan) and lutes with a small body and long stem. In addition there were drums and large and small tambourines (perhaps we should call them 'frame drums'), cymbals big and small, sistra and rattles. Various instruments might be used in combination by bands as an accompaniment to singing (stringed instruments in particular) though they do not seem to have been used in purely orchestral music, or in isolation. Such combinations may have involved some polyphony, the main sung melody being accompanied at distances of fourths or fifths, or perhaps by a lower 'drone' note held throughout a sequence. In Egypt musicians seem to have been guided by directors whose detailed 'cheironomical' hand or finger signals may even have indicated to them the individual notes to be played. The melodies and rhythms of the actual music performed remain something of a mystery. Instruments may have been tuned at intervals between notes analogous to those in a modern C Major scale, and various scales were perhaps constructed on this basis.

Music accompanied the most varied occasions – there were working songs (like the song of the well-diggers, Numbers 21, 17–18, or of harvesters in field and vineyard), songs of rejoicing on private or public occasions, or of grief after bereavement, and music accompanying state occasions or public worship. The coming of the Monarchy meant a vital change in the musical sphere. Before, music was largely in the hands of private individuals or popular gatherings (though there may have been some professionals, like the singers of tales and ballads). The establishment of court and Temple led to the foundation of bodies of musicians, professionals organized in guilds on the Canaanite model (those on the religious side were grouped according to Levitical families, such as the sons of Asaph and Korah). The royal court music with its male and female singers was before long imitated among the aristocracy, whose banquets were accompanied by singing and instrumental playing (cf. Amos 6, 5; Isaiah 5, 12).

Musical instruments
In general, Israelites seem to have used the same types of musical instruments as their contemporaries, but equating them with terms used in the Bible has caused problems. Thus, the instrument played by David is now thought not to have been a harp, but a lyre (the tone of which seems to have been somewhat like that of a modern Spanish guitar). Furthermore, Israelites experimented with producing new variants of known types – Amos (6, 5) taunted the nobles of Samaria with devising for themselves new musical instruments like David (which would make such innovations surprisingly early). There is perhaps some archaeological support for this assertion. A Judean seventh-century seal (if genuine, once owned by a king's daughter) depicts a twelve-stringed lyre not conforming to local standard type (pl. 83). The sound box has a rounded rather

than straight bottom and one inward curved side, and, unusually, it is decorated. Its shape may, perhaps, be affected by Greek round-bottomed types, as were the lyres shown on the roughly contemporary reliefs at Karatepe in Anatolia.

74 Musical score, showing the same biblical text chanted according to Oriental Jewish and Gregorian traditions respectively. These show analogies, hinting at a possible common origin, from the religious music of the Second Temple period, and this may in turn perpetuate musical traditions from the time of the First Temple.

Musical practice

Biblical references offer some hints about arrangements involved in different types of music. Thus, where victory celebrations are concerned, Exodus (15) relates that Moses and the Israelites sang their paean, being answered by Miriam and the women with tambourines and dances; 1 Samuel (18, 6–8) tells of a similar chorus of tambourine-playing and dancing women singers welcoming the victorious David. Noble feasting is accompanied by a small orchestra including lyre, harp, tambourine and oboe (Isaiah 5, 12). On the religious side, a band of prophets might also find inspiration from the music of these same instruments (1 Samuel 10, 5). Most of our information in the religious sphere, understandably, concerns religious music in the Temple. Unfortunately many specialist terms in Psalms are badly understood – thus *Sela* has been variously interpreted, and the duties of the 'choirmaster' or 'musical director' (*Menaṣṣeah*) much discussed. They may have included cheironomical direction, perhaps also solo singing. However, some aspects are clearer. Though Psalm 150 refers to a number of musical instruments, the main strength of Temple music seems to have been in singers supported by stringed instruments; 'secular' instruments, like oboes, were little used. We hear, in Psalm 68, 25, of a processional arrangement involving singers followed by instrumentalists and, interestingly, tambourine-playing young women. We are occasionally informed of the proportions of instrumentalists involved in performance: thus 1 Chronicles (15, 19ff.) traces an arrangement comprising three cymbal-players, eight harpists and six lyre-players back to David. It is furthermore worth noting that in a sphere where conservatism would be expected, a new song might be valued – and indeed David is regarded as a creator of songs – though in some cases there are hints that popular melodies were adapted for religious purposes. All this does not tell us, however, what Israelite music, and especially religious music, sounded like (the absence of instruments played with a bow, like violins, must in any case have produced orchestral sounds very different from those produced by modern orchestras). Josephus made some comparisons with Greek music (*Antiquities* XVIII, 6); more useful is the observation by modern musicologists, especially Idelsohn, that the traditional religious music preserved among some isolated Jewish communities, such as the Jews of the Yemen, shows remarkable similarities with early Christian

Gregorian chant, which in its turn probably owes something to Jewish religious music as practised at the time Christianity arose. The underlying system common to both might indeed even go back to the period of the First Temple. This, however, remains supposition. The existence of very old traditions of cheironomy linked with cantillation in such communities has also been noted, but how relevant they are for our period is unclear.

Dance and drama

In ancient Israel as in neighbouring countries, music was often associated with dancing. Yet, though dance was popular, especially on joyful occasions, we are only moderately well informed about it, owing to the absence of pictorial representations such as those found especially in Egypt. We have thus to rely on what the Bible and post-biblical Jewish sources offer, supported by data drawn from art and texts found in neighbouring lands.

Some basic facts are clear. Both men and women danced in ancient Israel, singly or in groups. Group dancing involved processions, dancing in circles and perhaps also dancers side by side or in two lines or groups facing each other. The Song of Songs (6, 13) may allude to this, according to one interpretation, but the passage may well be post-Exilic. Both secular and religious occasions gave rise to dancing. We may here refer to the dances by the maidens in the vineyards (Judges 21, 21) or to the celebrations of victories, when the women would welcome the returning warriors with singing and dancing, as already noted. We are not told whether dancing as well as music enlivened the feasts of the nobles, to which Amos took exception, as in Homeric Greece. Religion was linked with dancing to a surprising extent (cf. Psalm 149, 3; 150, 4). Sometimes it was presumably solemn and stately, as in the circulation of the altar mentioned in Psalm 26, 6, but on occasion it was energetic or even frenzied (as when King David danced before the Ark (2 Samuel 6, 14). Music could also induce a state of ecstasy, as in the case of the band of prophets whom Saul encountered (1 Samuel 10, 5). It is thus perhaps not surprising that the Hebrew vocabulary describing dancing includes a number of terms referring to energetic actions: whirling, leaping, stamping. What we lack is any indication of a set sequence of movements for particular types of dances such as can be found in later centuries.

There is a remarkable gap in our knowledge when it comes to drama. Drama of the cultic variety, acting out well-known myths, existed in both Egypt and Mesopotamia. There is no inherent impossibility in similarly dramatizing events and persons in Hebrew tradition – the existence of plays of this kind in the Hellenistic period, like the one on Exodus by Ezekiel of Alexandria, or of the later Jewish Purim plays dramatizing the story of Queen Esther, or of medieval mystery plays – all prove the point. However, there is up to now no clear trace of Israelite drama, or anything which might have led to it. The suggestions that in works of literature containing a number of personages (such as the Song of Songs or the Book of Job) different 'parts' were spoken by different persons remains unproven.

Epilogue

Israel developed in the course of some six centuries from a society of agriculturalists organized around clans and families into a body politic including an urbanized middle class and élite – craftsmen, traders, scribes, officials, priests, soldiers and landowners. Material standards and technical capacities could in many respects bear comparison with those achieved in neighbouring lands; in both the secular and the religious sphere, intellectual activity was intense and at times innovative. There was, in particular, a high level of literary creativeness, musical proficiency and even representative art with stylistic tendencies of its own which continued in Judah down to the Babylonian Conquest in 586 BC.

We must look at that disaster in some more detail. That there was massive material destruction we learn from the Bible, and archaeology bears this out, in Jerusalem especially but also in many other localities. War, famine, epidemics, flight and deportation must have diminished the population markedly (though we cannot really estimate the loss). Destruction was not complete, however, and Benjaminite territory as well as some parts of Judah were less affected. It seems likely also that in addition to the poorest rural people, whom the Babylonians settled on ownerless land (including the estates of deportees), some members of the middle and upper classes, both lay and priestly, still remained. So probably did the organization of society by clans and families to some extent, and various technical traditions were carried on, as seen in styles of pottery and writing. There are even hints that in this desperately impoverished country some cultural activity was maintained, not indeed in the field of art, but in religious literature, for instance parts of Lamentations. Some maintain also that the 'Deuteronomic History' – which gathered and edited the history of Israel from the time of the Judges down to the fall of Jerusalem in 586 and beyond, with the aim of demonstrating the existence of cycles of apostasy, punishment, repentance and delivery – was composed mainly in Judah during the Babylonian period, to give guidance to a bewildered people. That the Babylonians did not dilute this Judean remnant by settling colonists from elsewhere among them as the Assyrians had done left the field open for a possible future revival. Meanwhile, Palestinian Jewry took second place to the exiles in Babylonia, who included what had been the cream of Judean society. Literary output here included not only the writings of Ezekiel, but by nearly universal consent, also the splendid writings of 'Deutero-Isaiah' (Isaiah chapters 40ff., up to 56 perhaps). It is somewhat difficult to account for such a literary flowering there. Many of the exiles will have been fully occupied and the supply of Hebrew books among them is likely to have been limited. The position in that latter respect should have been better in Palestine, for the Babylonians would have found it advantageous to preserve records likely to be of use for the administration they were about to install. In due course, individuals favoured by the authorities might have been allowed access to such texts, which would be helpful in composing historical writings.

The decisive influences for future development came, however, from the interpretation of the recent past. It had been a widely held popular belief that, in the end, the Lord would not abandon His people, His city and His sanctuary. Events proved that this confidence had been grievously misplaced. There could be several possible explanations for such a deeply shocking state of affairs. Either the Lord was not interested in His people, or He was even powerless to help. In that case it would be best to seek help elsewhere, either among the traditional gods of Canaan (if one lived in Palestine) or among the Babylonian deities (if one lived in Babylonia); association of such gods with the worship of the God of Israel might also be prudent. Alternatively, however, a radically different explanation was possible. Israel's prophets had foretold that disobedience to the commands of the Lord would be terribly punished. Events had proved them right, and the only hope for the future lay in strict obedience to divine writ. Such thinking was to command decisive influence among the community of exiles in Babylonia where, incidentally, the strict adherence to the observance of the Sabbath and of the rite of circumcision had their effect in maintaining the separate identity of the exiles. With the 'Return to Zion', associated with the names of Ezra and Nehemiah, this ideology became dominant in Jerusalem. It led to the establishment there of a community bound to the strict and punctilious observance of the Law, and of an existence separate from other nations. This was a society very different from the Judah of the past, but it was to its members that the future was to belong. The three great monotheistic religions – Judaism, Christianity and Islam – are, in various ways, its progeny, and the world-wide influence of the Bible stems from this modified offshoot of the old order which had come to an end in 586 BC.

Select Bibliography

ABBREVIATIONS

AASOR — *Annual of the American Schools of Oriental Research*

ABD — *Anchor Bible Dictionary*

ADAJ — *Annual of the Department of Antiquities of Jordan*

AJA — *American Journal of Archaeology*

ANET — *Ancient Near Eastern Texts Relating to the Old Testament*, Pritchard, J.B. (ed.), 1969 (3rd ed.) (Princeton, N.J.)

BA — *The Biblical Archaeologist*

BARev — *Biblical Archaeology Review*

BAR Int. Ser. — *British Archaeological Reports, International Series*

BASOR — *Bulletin of the American Schools of Oriental Research*

BRL — *Biblisches Reallexicon. Handbuch zum Alten Testament I/1*, Galling, K. (ed.), 1977 (2nd ed.) (Tübingen)

BZAW — *Beiheft zur Zeitschrift für die alttestamentliche Wissenschaft*

CAH — *Cambridge Ancient History*

Enc. Jud. — *Encyclopedia Judaica*

EI — *Eretz-Israel*

HThR — *Harvard Theological Review*

IDB — *The Interpreter's Dictionary of the Bible*

IDBS — *The Interpreter's Dictionary of the Bible, Supplementary Volume*

IEJ — *Israel Exploration Journal*

JA — *Journal Asiatique*

JAOS — *Journal of the American Oriental Society*

JBL — *Journal of Biblical Literature*

JCS — *Journal of Cuneiform Studies*

JESHO — *Journal of the Economic and Social History of the Orient*

JNES — *Journal of Near Eastern Studies*

JNWSL — *Journal of Northwest Semitic Languages*

JQR — *Jewish Quarterly Review*

JSOT — *Journal of the Society of Old Testament Studies*

JSOTSS — *Journal of the Society of Old Testament Studies Supplementary Series*

Mazar 1990 — Mazar, A., 1990, *Archaeology of the Land of The Bible, 10,000–586 B.C.E.* (New York & London)

MMA — *Monographs in Mediterranean Archaeology*

NEAEHL — *The New Encyclopaedia of Archaeological Excavations in the Holy Land*

OBO — *Orbis Biblicus et Orientalis*

PEQ — *Palestine Exploration Quarterly*

Qedem — *Monographs of the Institute of Archaeology, the Hebrew University of Jerusalem*

SAOC — *Studies in Ancient Oriental Civilization*

SHAJ — *Studies in the History and Archaeology of Jordan*, Hadidi, A. (ed.), 1982, 1985 & 1987 (Amman, London & New York)

SMA — *Studies in Mediterranean Archaeology*

SVT — *Supplements to Vetus Testamentum*

SWBA — *Social World of Biblical Antiquity*

Symposia — *Symposia Celebrating the Seventy-Fifth Anniversary of the American Schools of Oriental Research (1900–1975)*, Cross, F.M. (ed.), 1979 (Cambridge, Mass.)

TA — *Journal of Tel Aviv University Institute of Archaeology*

TAVOB A — *Beihefte zum Tübinger Atlas des vorderen Orients, Reihe A: Naturwissenschaften*

VT — *Vetus Testamentum*

Weippert 1988 — Weippert, H., 1988, *Palästina in vorhellenistischer Zeit (Handbuch der Archäologie, Vorderasien II, Band I)* (Munich)

ZDPV — *Zeitschrift des Deutschen Palästina-Vereins*

Introduction (pp. 7–20)

This section of the bibliography is fuller than for succeeding chapters, since it provides guidance for a number of basic issues relevant to the whole book. (H) = in Hebrew; (E) = English translation.

I On the Bible and Biblical Criticism: For general orientation, see *Enc. Jud.* 4, 'Bible', cols. 514ff. From the vast literature we select: Soggin, J.A., 1976, *Introduction to the Old Testament* (London); Eissfeldt, O., 1965, *The Old Testament: An Introduction* (Oxford) represents older views, while Knight, D.A. & Tucker, C.H. (eds), 1985, *The Hebrew Bible and its Modern Interpreters* (Philadelphia, Pa. & Chico, Cal.) offer recent ideas. Gottwald, N.K., 1985, *The Hebrew Bible: a Socio-Literary Introduction* (Philadelphia, Pa.) follows a special approach, but is full and detailed (helpful bibliography). For summaries of recent developments in source criticism cf. *ABD*, entries 'Elohist', II, 478–82; 'Deuteronomy', II, 168–83; 'Yahwist ('Y') source', VI, 1012–70; 'Priestly ('P') source', V, 454–61. See further: 'Canon of the O.T.', *IDB* I, 499–520; *IDBS*, 150–60; 'Biblical Criticism', *IDB* I, 407–16; *IDBS*, 98–100; Tov, E., 'The Text of the Old Testament' in Van der Woude, A.S. (general editor) & Mulder, M.J. et al. (eds), 1986, *The World of the Bible*, Bible Handbooks, vol. I (Grand Rapids), 156–90. For a detailed recent discussion of the books contained in the Bible see Van der Woude, A.S. (ed.), *The World of the Bible*, Bible Handbooks, vol. II (Grand Rapids), 97–296, by various authors. Statistical details concerning the Bible are given by Ullendorff, E., 1977, *Is Biblical Hebrew a Language? Studies in Semitic Languages and Literatures* (Wiesbaden), 3–17. For a critical review of the new tendency to regard biblical historians as late, and of little value, see Dever, W.G., 1995, 'Will the Real Israel Please Stand Up? Archaeology and Israelite Historiography Part I', BASOR 297, 61–80.

For the recent tendency to date Pentateuchal and other biblical books and sources late and to question their value as historical evidence, cf. Davies, P.R., 1997, *In Search of Ancient Israel* (*JSOTSS* 148, Sheffield); Whybray, N., 1987, *The Making of the Pentateuch. A Methodological Study* (*JSOTSS* 53, Sheffield); and van Seters, J., 1975, *Abraham in History and Tradition* (New Haven & London); id., 1983, *In Search of History: Historiography in the Ancient World and the Origins of Biblical History* (New Haven & London); Thompson, T.L., 1974, *The Historicity of the Patriarchal Narratives: The Quest for the Historical Abraham* (Berlin & New York); id., 1987, *The Origin Traditions of Ancient Israel (Vol. I: The Literary Foundation of Genesis and Exodus 1–23)* (*JSOTSS* 55, Sheffield); Welten, P., 1974, *Geschichte und Geschichtsdarstellungen in den Chronikbüchern* (Neukirchen-Vluyn). For an overview of recent applications of various types of literary criticism to the Bible, cf. House, P.-R. (ed.), 1972, *Beyond Form Criticism. Essays in Old Testament Literary Criticism* (Winona Lake, Ind.), especially the introduction, 3–22. A useful general overview is found with reference to the framework in the other ancient texts, 22ff., and *passim*, in Tigay, J.H. (ed.), 1985, *Empirical Models for Biblical Criticism* (Philadelphia, Pa.), especially in his own contribution.

II Hebrew and Other Relevant Inscriptions: Most main inscriptions of interest to us are contained in Smelik, K.A.D., 1991, *Writings from Ancient Israel. A Handbook of Historical and Religious Documents* (Edinburgh) (E) where references to the specialist literature will be found. A wider selection of texts translated into English from various ancient languages is available in Pritchard, J.B. (ed.), 1969 (3rd ed.) *Ancient Near Eastern Texts Relating to the Old Testament* (Princeton, N.J.).

III General Cultural Background: For an overview see Roberts, J.J., 'The Ancient Near Eastern Environment' in Knight, D.A. & Tucker, G.N. (eds), see above under I, 75–121; and for detail cf. *CAH* (2nd ed.), 1970ff. See also Hallo, W.W., 1996, *Origins: The Ancient Near Eastern Background of Some Modern Western Institutions* (Leiden, New York & Cologne). For the special topics of Mari and Ugarit consult, respectively, Malamat, A., 1989, *Mari and the Israelite Experience* (Oxford), and Young, G.D. (ed.), 1985, *Ugarit in Retrospect. Fifty Years of Ugarit and Ugaritic* (Winona Lake, Ind.), especially 'Ugarit and the Bible', 99–111; Loretz, O., 1990, *Ugarit und die Bibel* (Darmstadt). For the ancient Near East in general, see: Pritchard, J.B., see above under II; id., 1969, *The Ancient Near East in Pictures* (Princeton, N.J.), and Wiseman, D. (ed.), 1973, *Peoples of the Old Testament* (Oxford).

IV Classical Texts: See, in general, Stern, N., 1978–80–84, *Greek and Latin Authors on Jews and Judaism*, I–III (Jerusalem). For Josephus, see Attridge, H.W., 1976, *The Interpretation of Biblical History in the Antiquitates Judaicae of Flavius Josephus* (Missoula, Mont.). On Eusebius, see Wallace-Hadrill, D.S., 1960, *Eusebius of Caesarea* (London); for the Onomastica, cf. Wolf, D.S., 1964, 'Eusebius of Caesarea and the Onomastica', *BA* 27, 66–96.

V The Coming of Modern Interests and Research: Ben-Arieh, Y., 1979, *The Rediscovery of the Holy Land in the Nineteenth Century* (Jerusalem); Moorey, P.R.S., 1991, *A Century of Biblical Archaeology* (Cambridge); Silberman, N.A., 1982, *For God and Country: Exploration, Archaeology, and the Secret Struggle for the Holy Land, 1799–1914* (New York). See also De Geus, H., in Van der Woude et al. (eds), 1986 (see above, under I), 65–74. See further contributions in Drinkard, J.F. et al. (eds), 1988, listed below under VIa.

VI Archaeology
(a) General Surveys and Handbooks: The following four books cover practically the whole field treated by this book to varying extents, and should be consulted throughout: Ben-Tor, A. (ed.), 1992, *The Archaeology of Ancient Israel* (E) (New Haven & London); Levy, T.E. (ed.), *The Archaeology of Society in the Holy Land* (Leicester); Mazar, A., 1990, *Archaeology of the Land of The Bible, 10,000–586 B.C.E.* (New York & London); Weippert, H., 1988, *Palästina in vorhellenistischer Zeit* (*Handbuch der Archäologie, Vorderasien II, Band I*) (Munich). The following are very helpful for references to sites: *The New Encyclopaedia of Archaeological Excavations in the Holy Land*, I–IV, ed. E. Stern (Jerusalem, 1995) (*NEAEHL*); Myers, E.M. (ed.), 1997, *The Oxford Encyclopaedia of Archaeology in the Middle East* (Oxford). Among Bible dictionaries, the following have been widely referred to: Freedman, D.N. (ed.), 1992, *The Anchor Bible Dictionary* (New York & London) (*ABD*); Buttrick, G.A. (ed.), 1962, *The Interpreter's Dictionary of the Bible* (New York & Nashville (Tenn.)) (*IDB*) (Supplementary Volume ed. K. Crim, 1976 (Nashville, Tenn.) (*IDBS*).

The following offer recent views of archaeology in the land of Israel and nearby countries: Amitai, J. (ed.), 1985, *Biblical Archaeology Today, Proceedings of the International Congress on Biblical Archaeology, Jerusalem 1984* (Jerusalem); Biran, A. & Aviram, J. (eds), 1990, *Biblical Archaeology Today, Proceedings of the Second International Congress on Biblical Archaeology, Jerusalem, June 1990* (Jerusalem). See further Drinkard, J.F., Mattingly, C.L., Maxwell Miller, J. (eds), 1988, *Benchmarks in Time and Culture. An Introduction to Palestinian Archaeology dedicated to Joseph A. Calloway* (Atlanta, Geo.); Fritz, V., 1994, *An Introduction to Biblical Archaeology* (*JSOTSS* 372, Sheffield);

Gitin, S. & Dever, W.G. (eds), 1989, *Recent Excavations in Israel: Studies in Iron Age Archaeology* (*AASOR* 49); Harris, R.L., 1995, *Exploring the World of the Bible Lands* (London and New York).

(b) On Archaeological Methods: Moorey, P.R.S., 1981, *Excavations in Palestine* (Guildford, Surrey); id., 1991, *A Century of Biblical Archaeology* (Cambridge); Franken, H.J., 1985, 'Archaeology of Palestine: Problems and Tasks' in Van der Woude & Mulder, M.J. (eds) referred to above under I, 50–62; Chapman, R.L., 1986, 'Excavation Techniques and Recording Systems: A Theoretical Study', *PEQ* 118, 5–26. W.G. Dever has repeatedly dealt with problems of method; among his recent publications, we may mention Gitin, S. & Dever, W.G., see above, VI (a), 143–52; *EI* 20, 1985, 44–51; *BASOR* 277/8, 1990, 120–30; and earlier in Knight, D.A. & Tucker, G.M. (eds) (quoted above under I), 31–74. The contributions by various authors to *BASOR* 277/8, 1990, illustrate the present state of the debate. Archaeological techniques and the applications of various types of scientific investigation are reviewed in Drinkard, J.F. et al. (eds), 1988, quoted above under VI (a). The total retrieval of finds is discussed by Van Beek, G. in *EI* 20, 1989, 12*–29*.

(c) Absolute Chronology, and the Regnal Years of the United Monarchy, Israel and Judah: Middle Eastern chronology has been under discussion recently (cf. Åhlström, P. (ed.), 1987, 1989, *High Middle, or Low*, Parts 1, 2 and 3 (Gothenburg)), and suggested lower datings for Egyptian Pharaohs like Ramses II, Merneptah and their successors are of direct interest to Israelite history. Problems in Egyptian chronology in the first millennium BC also concern Israel, but Assyrian chronology from the 9th century onwards, and Babylonian, are essentially established within 1 year. For the dates of Israelite and Judean kings, see Cogan, M., 'Chronology', *ABD* II, 1011–17, who discusses problems and the various systems of dating. The system of H. Tadmor (underlying Cogan's) is widely respected, but in this book the chronology offered by Maxwell Miller, J. & Hayes, J.H., 1986, *A History of Ancient Israel and Judah* (London) is followed.

(d) Archaeological Periodization of the Iron Age: The subdivision adopted in *NEAEHL* is popular, and followed here: Iron Age IA 1200–1150 BC; Iron Age IB 1150–1000 BC; Iron Age IIA 1000–900 BC; Iron Age IIB 900–700 BC; Iron Age IIC 700–586 BC.

Alternative proposals have been made by Ben-Tor, A. (ed.), 1992, *The Archaeology of Ancient Israel* (E) (New Haven & London); Mazar 1990; and Weippert 1988. A fundamentally different system has been proposed by P. James et al., 1991, *Centuries of Darkness* (London). In order to obviate 'dark ages', drastic lowerings in the dates of archaeological periods are suggested: thus, the Palestinian Late Bronze II is equated with the Age of Solomon. These suggestions have not found general acceptance (cf. K. Kitchen et al. 1991, 'Centuries of Darkness', *Cambridge Archaeological Journal* 1, 227–53). More recently, I. Finkelstein ('The Archaeology of the United Monarchy: an Alternative View', *Levant* 18, 177–87) has suggested that the datings of certain key Iron Age II strata in Israel, (e.g. Megiddo VA–IVB), could be lowered by *c*. one century, from the 10th to the 9th, with a corresponding lowering of the previous levels. See now Finkelstein, I., 1998, 'Bible Archaeology or Archaeology of Palestine in the Iron Age? A Rejoinder', *Levant* 30, 167–74, contra Mazar, A., 1997, 'Iron Age Chronology: A Reply to I. Finkelstein', Levant 29, 155–65.

(e) The relationship between the Bible and Archaeology: Darrell Lance, H., 1981, *The Old Testament and the Archaeologist* (Philadelphia, Pa.); Kenyon, K.M. (revised by Moorey, P.R.S.),

1987, *The Bible and Recent Archaeology* (London); Dever, W.G., 1990, *Recent Archaeological Discoveries and Biblical Research* (Seattle & London).

Chapter One: Geography: The Land and its Resources (pp. 21–47)

I Atlases: Aharoni, Y. & Avi-Yonah, M. (eds), 1970, *The Macmillan Bible Atlas* (London); Grollenberg, L.H., 1965, *Atlas of the Bible* (London); May, H.G. (ed.), 1987, *Oxford Bible Atlas* (Oxford); Pritchard, J.B. (ed.), 1989, *The Times Atlas of the Bible* (London); Rogerson, J. (ed.), 1989, *Atlas of the Bible* (Oxford).

II General Geography: Aharoni, Y., 1979, *The Land of the Bible: A Historical Geography*, 2nd ed. (London); Alexander, P.S., 'Early Jewish Geography', *ABD* II, 977–88; Baly, D., 1963, *Geographical Companion to the Bible* (London); Bintliff, J.L. & van Zeist W. (eds), 1988, *Palaeoclimates, Palaeoecology and Human Communities in the Eastern Mediterranean Region in Later Prehistory* (*BAR* Int. Ser. 133); Braudel, F., 1972, *The Mediterranean and the Mediterranean World in the Age of Philip II*, vol. I (London); Cansdale, G., 1970, *Animals of Bible Lands* (Exeter); Kallai, Z., 1986, *Historical Geography of the Bible; The Tribal Territories of Israel* (Jerusalem); Karmon, Y., 1971, *Israel: A Regional Geography* (Jerusalem); Orni, E. & Efrat, E., 1980, *Geography of Israel*, 4th ed. (Jerusalem); Raphael, C.N., 'Geography of Palestine', *ABD* II, 964–77; Smith, G.A., 1894 (and later reprints), *Historical Geography of the Holy Land* (London); Zohary, M., 1982a *Vegetation of Israel and Adjacent Areas* (*TAVOB* A/7) (Wiesbaden); id., 1982b, *Plants of the Bible* (Cambridge).

III Travel: Betzel, B.J., 'Roads and Highways (Pre-Roman Roads and Highways)', *ABD* V, 776–82; id., 'Travel and Communications (Old Testament World)', *ABD* VI, 644–8; Boyden, P.B., 1978–9, 'A System of Communications throughout each County', *National Army Museum Report*, 8–13, esp. p.11; Casson, L., 1986, *Ships and Seamanship in the Ancient World*, 2nd ed. (Princeton, N.J.); id., 1989, *The Periplous Mari Erythrei* (Princeton, N.J.); Crown, A.D., 1974, 'Tidings and Instructions: how news travelled in the ancient Near East', *JESHO* 17, 3, 244–71; Dorsey, D., 1991, *The Roads and Highways of Ancient Israel* (Baltimore & London); Grant, C.F., 1937, *The Syrian Desert. Caravans, Travel and Exploration* (London); Hallo, W.W., 1964, 'The Road to Emar', *JCS* 18, 57–88.

Chapter Two: Origins and Affinities of the Israelites (pp. 48–64)

Ahlström, G.W., 1986, *Who Were the Israelites?* (Winona Lake, Ind.); id., 1993, *The History of Ancient Palestine from the Palaeolithic Period to Alexander's Conquest* (*JSOTSS* 146, Sheffield); Albright, W.F., 1949, *The Archaeology of Palestine* (Harmondsworth); Alt, A., 1966/1967, *Essays on Old Testament History and Religion* (Oxford & Garden City, N.Y), 135–69 (E); Bienkowski, P. (ed.), 1992, *Early Edom and Moab: the Beginning of the Iron Age in Southern Jordan* (Sheffield Archaeol. Mon. 7, Sheffield); Bimson, J.J., 1978, *Redating the Exodus and the Conquest* (Sheffield); Boling, R.G., 1988, *The Early Biblical Community in Transjordan* (*SWBA* 6, Sheffield); Coote, R.B. & Whitelam, K.W., 1987, *The Emergence of Early Israel in Historical Perspective* (*SWBA* 5, Sheffield); Dornemann, R.H., 1982, 'The Beginnings of the Iron Age in Transjordan', *SHAJ* 1, 135–40; id., 1985, *The Archaeology of Transjordan in the Bronze and Iron Ages* (Milwaukee, Wisc.); Finkelstein, I., 1988, *The Archaeology of the Israelite Settlement* (Jerusalem);

Freedman, D.N. & Graf, D. (eds), 1983, *Palestine in Transition. The Emergence of Ancient Israel* (*SWBA* 2, Sheffield); de Geus, C.H.J., 1976, *The Tribes of Israel* (Amsterdam); Gottwald, N.K., 1979, *The Tribes of Yahweh* (New York); Halpern, B., 1983, *The Emergence of Israel in Canaan* (Chico, Cal.); Hopkins, D.C., 1985, *The Highlands of Canaan* (*SWBA* 3, Sheffield); Isserlin, B.S.J., 1983, 'The Israelite Conquest of Canaan: A Comparative Review of the Arguments Applicable', *PEQ* 115, 85–94; Ji, C.C., 1995, 'Iron Age I in Central and Northern Transjordan: Interim Summary of Archaeological Data', *PEQ* 127, 122–40; Kempinski, A., 1992, 'How Profoundly Canaanized were the Israelites?', *ZDPV* 108, 1–7; Kitchen, K.A., 1966, *Ancient Orient and Old Testament* (Chicago); id., 1993, 'The Tabernacle – A Bronze Age Artefact', *EI* 24, 119*–129*; Lemaire, A., 1982, 'Recherches actuelles sur les origines de l'ancien Israël', *JA* 270, 5–24; Lemche, N.P., 1985, 'Early Israel' (*SVT* 37); Malamat, A., 1989, *Mari and the Israelite Experience* (Oxford); Mendenhall, G.E., 1962, 'The Hebrew Conquest of Palestine', *BA* 25, 66–8; Millard, A.R. & Wiseman, D.J. (eds), 1983, *Essays on the Patriarchal Narratives* (Leicester); Mittmann, S., 1970, *Beiträge zur Siedlungs- und Territorialgeschichte des Ostjordanlandes* (Wiesbaden); Oren, E., 1984, "Governors' Residencies' in Canaan under the New Kingdom. A Case Study in Egyptian Administration', *Journal for the Study of Egyptian Antiquities* 14, 37–56; Redford, D.B., 1992, *Egypt, Canaan and Israel in Ancient Times*, (Princeton, N.J.); Rendsburg, G.A., 1992, 'The Date of the Exodus and the Conquest/Settlement: the Case for the 1100s', *VT* 42, 510–27; Rowley, H.H., 1950, *From Joseph to Joshua* (Oxford); Stager, L.E., 1985a, 'The Archaeology of the Family in Israel', *BASOR* 260, 1–38; id., 1985b, 'Merenptah, Israel and the Sea Peoples. New Light on an Old Relief', *EI* 18, 56*–64*; Thompson, T.L., 1992, *Early History of the Israelite People from Written and Archaeological Sources* (Leiden, New York & Cologne); Ussishkin, D., 1987, 'Lachish – Key to the Israelite Conquest of Canaan', *BARev* 13, 1, 18–39; de Vaux, R., 1978, *The Early History of Israel* I, II (London); Weinstein, J.M., 1981, *The Egyptian Empire in Palestine: A Reassessment*, *BASOR* 241, 1–28; Weippert, M., 1971, *The Settlement of the Israelite Tribes in Palestine* (London); Whitelam, K.W., 1989, 'Israel's Tradition of Origin: Reclaiming the Land', *JSOT* 44, 19–42; Yadin, Y., 1982, 'Is the Biblical Account of the Conquest of Canaan Reliable?', *BARev* 7, 16–23; Yurco, F.J., 1990, '3200-Year-Old Picture of Israelites, Found in Egypt', *BARev* 16, 5, 20–38; see also id., 1991, *BARev* 17, 6, 54–5 & 61, in reply to Rainey, A.F., *BARev* 17, 6, 56–60, 93. Frerichs, E.S. & Lesko, L.H. (eds), 1997, *Exodus: The Egyptian Evidence* (Winona Lake, Ind.) is a recent work on the subject.

Chapter Three: History (pp. 65–92)

The following will be found helpful (a fuller list is in Maxwell Miller, J. & Hayes, J.H., 1986, *A History of Ancient Israel and Judah* (London), 477–8): Ahlström, G.W., 1993, *The History of Ancient Palestine from the Paleolithic Period to Alexander's Conquest* (*JSOTSS* 146, Sheffield); Arnold, P.M., 1990, *Gibeah: The Search for a Biblical City* (*JSOTSS* 79, Sheffield); Bright, J.A, 1985, *A History of Israel*, 3rd ed. (Philadelphia, Pa. & London); Ben-Sasson, H.H. (ed.), 1976, *History of the Jewish People* (London & Cambridge); Garbini, G., *Law and Ideology in Ancient Israel* (London); Halpern, B. & Hobson, D.W., *Law and Ideology in Monarchical Israel* (*JSOTSS* 124, Sheffield); Hayes, J.H. & Maxwell Miller, J. (eds), 1977, *Israelite and Judean History* (Philadelphia, Pa. & London); Heaton, E.W., 1974, *Solomon's New Men* (London); Malamat, A., 1987, 'The Last Days of the Kings of Judah', in Malamat, A., Perdue, T.G., Tombs, L.E. & Johnson, G.L., *Archaeology and Biblical Interpretation. Essays in Memory of D. Glen Rose* (Atlanta, Geo.), 287–314; Maxwell Miller, J. & Hayes, J.H., 1986, *A History of Ancient Israel and Judah* (London); Mazar, B. & Malamat, A. (eds), 1961ff. *The World History of the Jewish People* (esp. vols. II; III; IV.1 & IV.2) (vols I & II,ed. Mazar; vols. IIIff., Malamat; Jerusalem); Mettinger, T.N.D., 1971, *Solomonic State Officials: A Study of the Civil Government Officials of the Israelite Monarchy* (Lund); Na'aman, N., 1986, 'Hezekiah's Fortified Cities', *BASOR* 261, 5–21; Noth, M., *The History of Israel*, 2nd ed., 1969 (London) (E); Pitard, W.T., 1987, *Ancient Damascus: Historical Study of the Syrian City State from the Earliest Times until the Fall of the Assyrians* (Winona Lake, Ind.); Schley, D.G., 1989, *Shiloh: a Biblical City in Tradition and History* (*JSOTSS* 63, Sheffield); Shanks, H. (ed.), 1989, *Ancient Israel. A Short History from Abraham to the Roman Destruction of the Temple* (London); Soggin, J.A., 1984, *A History of Israel from the Beginnings to the Bar Kochba Revolt AD 135* (London); Strange, J., 1975, 'Joram, King of Israel and Judah', *VT* 25, 191–201; Thompson, T.L. 'Historiography (Israelite)', *ABD* III, 206–12; Ussishkin, D., 1982, *The Conquest of Lachish by Sennacherib* (Tel Aviv).

See also: 'Israel (History)', *ABD* III, 526–76 – pre-monarchic period: N.P. Lemke, 526–45; archaeology and the Israelite 'conquest': W.G. Dever, 545–52; monarchic period: W.J. Hoppe, 553–67; post-monarchic period: G.A. Herion, 567–76; and relevant chapters in *CAH* vols. II.1, II.2, III.1, III. 2 (2nd ed. Cambridge, 1973–91) by Kenyon, K.M., Eissfeldt, O., Franken, H.J. & Mitchell, T.C., respectively; see also Plates to Vol. III (1984).

For the period of the Judges, see also de Vaux, R., 1978, *The Early History of Israel* (E). Among histories not in English, Donner, H., 1987, *Geschichte des Volkes Israel und seiner Nachbarn in Grundzügen* (Göttingen) deserves special mention. For historical atlases see above, Chapter One, I.

Chapter Four: Social Structure, Constitutional Ideas and Government (pp. 93–110)

The most comprehensive survey of matters dealt with in this chapter will be found in de Vaux, R., 1962, *Ancient Israel, its Life and Institutions* (London). The following more recent works will offer guidance on various aspects: Ahlström, G.W., 1986, *Who were the Israelites?* (Winona Lake, Ind.); Becker, H.J., 1980, *Law and the Administration of Justice in the Old Testament and Ancient East* (London); Bird, P.A., 1992, 'Women', *ABD* VI, 947–57, esp. 95off.; Brenner, A., 1985, *The Israelite Woman: Social Role and Literary Type in Biblical Narrative* (*The Biblical Seminar* 2, Sheffield); Broshi, M. and Finkelstein, I., 1992, 'The Population of Palestine in Iron Age II', *BASOR* 287, 47–60; Chaney, M.L., 1986, 'Systemic Study of the Israelite Monarchy', *Semeia* 37, 55–76; Chirichigno, G.C., 1993, *Debt-Slavery in Israel and the Ancient Near East* (*JSOTSS* 141, Sheffield); Clements, R.E. (ed.), 1989, *The World of Ancient Israel. Sociological, Anthropological and Political Perspectives* (Cambridge); Coote, R.B. & Whitelam, K.W., 1987, *The Emergence of Early Israel* (*SWBA* 5, Sheffield); Finkelstein, I., 1988, *The Archaeology of the Israelite Settlement* (Jerusalem); Flanagan, J., 1981, *David's Social Drama: A Hologram of Israel's Early Iron Age* (*SWBA* 9/*JSOTSS* 73, Sheffield); Frick, F.S., 1985, *The Formation of the State in Ancient Israel: A survey of Models and Theories* (Decatur, Ga.); Fritz, V. & Davies, P.R. (eds), 1985, *The Origins of the Ancient Israelite States* (*JSOTSS* 228, Sheffield); de Geus, C.H.J., 1976, *The Tribes of Israel: An*

Investigation into some of the Presuppositions of Martin Noth's Amphictyony Hypothesis (Assen); Gottwald, N.K., 1979, *The Tribes of Yahweh. A Sociology of the Religion of Liberated Israel, 1250–1050 BCE* (London); Halpern, B., 1983, *The Emergence of Israel in Canaan* (Chico, Cal.); Heaton, E.W., 1956, *Everyday Life in Old Testament Times* (London); Ishida, T., 1977, *The Royal Dynasties in Ancient Israel: A Study of the Formation and Development of Royal-Dynastic Ideology* (*BZAW* 142); Kessler, R., 1992, *Staat und Gesellschaft im vorexilischen Juda* (*SVT* XLVII); Leachley, N.P., 1985, *Early Israel. Anthropological and Historical Studies on Israelite Society before the Monarchy* (London); Mettinger, T.N.D., 1976, *King and Messiah. The Civil and Sacral Legitimation of the Israelite Kings* (Lund); Smith, P., 1995, 'People of the Holy Land from Prehistory to the Recent Past', in Levy, T.E. (ed.), *The Archaeology of Society in the Holy Land* (London), 58–75; Stager, L.E., 1985, 'The Archaeology of the Family in Ancient Israel', *BASOR* 260, 1–35; Weinfeld, M., 1993, *The Promise of the Land. The Inheritance of the Land of Canaan by the Israelites* (Berkeley, Cal.); Whitelam, K.W., 1979, *The Just King. Monarchical Judicial Authority in Ancient Israel* (*JSOTSS* 12, Sheffield).

Chapter Five: Towns and Villages: Planning and Architecture (pp. 111–47)

I General surveys: The following are comprehensive; individual subjects are dealt with under headings: Herzog, Z., 'Fortifications (Levant)', *ABD* II, 844–52 (esp. 848ff.); Kempinski, A., Reich, R., Katzenstein, H. & Aviram, J. (eds), 1992, *The Architecture of Ancient Israel from the Prehistoric to the Persian Periods* (Jerusalem); Kenyon, K.M., revised by Moorey, P.R.S., 1987, *The Bible and Recent Archaeology* (London): a shorter but interesting summary.

II Individual Topics:
(a) Rural Settlement: Finkelstein, I., 1988, *The Archaeology of Israelite Settlement* (Jerusalem); Hopkins, D.C., 1965, *The Highlands of Canaan* (*JSOTSS* 68, Sheffield); Dar, S., 1986, *Landscape and Pattern. An Archaeological Survey of Samaria 800 B.C.E.– 636 C.E.* (*BAR Int. Ser.* 308, i, ii) (Oxford); Stager, L.E., 1985, 'The Archaeology of the Family in Ancient Israel', *BASOR* 260, 1–35; Thompson, T.L., 1992, *Early History of the Israelite People from Written and Archaeological Sources* (Leiden, New York & Cologne), esp. 215ff.

(b) Towns and Town Planning: Frick, F.S., 1977, *The City in Ancient Israel* (Missoula, Mont.); Geva, S., 1989, *Hazor, Israel: An Urban Community of the 8th Century B.C.E.* (*BAR Int. Ser.* 543, Oxford); Herzog, Z., 'Cities', *ABD* I, 1031–43 (esp. 1037ff.); Kenyon, K.M., 1971, *Royal Cities of the Old Testament* (London); Lampl, P., 1968, *Cities and Town Planning in the Ancient Near East* (London); Shiloh, Y., 1978, 'Elements in the Development of Town Planning in the Israelite City', *IEJ* 28, 36–51; id., 1980, 'The population of Iron Age Palestine in the Light of a Sample Analysis of Urban Plans, Areas and Population Density', *BASOR* 239, 25–35.

(c) Buildings, general surveys: Braemer, F., 1982, *L'architecture domestique du Levant à l'Âge du Fer* (Paris); Wright, G.R.H., 1985, *Ancient Buildings in South Syria and Palestine* (Leiden & Cologne).

(d) Houses: In addition to the above, see Holladay, J.S., 'Houses, Israelite', *ABD* III, 308–18; Shiloh, Y., 1970, 'The Four Room House – Its Situation and Function in the Israelite City', *IEJ* 20, 180–90. For some more recent views, see Finkelstein, I., 1988, esp. 255–60, and Stager, L., 1985, both referred to in II (a).

(e) Palaces: Fritz, V., 1983, 'Paläste während der Bronze-und Eisenzeit in Palästina', *ZDPV* 99, 1–42; Herzog, Z., 1992, 'Administrative structures in the Iron Age' in Kempinski et al. 1992, 223–30; Reich, R., 1992, 'Palaces and Residencies in the Iron Age', in Kempinski et al. 1992, 202–22, referred to above in I.

(f) Citadels: Mazar 1990, 406ff., 412, 438ff., 450.

(g) Other Fortifications: Mazar 1990, 453ff.

(h) Town Walls and Gates: Herzog, Z., 1986, *Das Stadttor in Israel und in den Nachbarlandändern* (Mainz).

(i) Store Houses and Stables: Davies, G.I., 1988, 'Solomonic Stables at Megiddo After All?' *PEQ* 120, 130–41; Holladay, J.S., 'Stable, Stables', *ABD* VI, 178–83; Holladay, J.S., 1986, 'The stables of Ancient Israel' in Geraty, T. & Herr, L.G. (eds), *The Archaeology of Jordan and Other Studies (Siegfried Horn Festschrift)* (Berrien Springs, Mi.), 103–65.

(j) Public Water Supply: Oleson, J.P., 'Waterworks', *ABD* VI, 883–93; Shiloh, Y., 1992 'Underground Water Systems in the Land of Israel in the Iron Age', in Kempinski, A. et al., referred to above in I, 275–93; Wilkinson, J.C., 1974, 'Ancient Jerusalem: its Water-supply and Population', *PEQ* 106, 33–51.

(k) Tombs: Barkay, G. & Kloner, A., 1986, 'Jerusalem Tombs from the Days of the First Temple', *BARev* 12, 22–39; Bloch-Smith, E., 1992, *Judahite Burial Practices and Beliefs about the Dead* (*JSOTSS* 123, Sheffield); Rahmani, L.Y., 1981, 'Ancient Jerusalem's Funerary Customs and Tombs: Part II', *BA* 44, 229–35; Ussishkin, D., 1970, 'The Necropolis from the Time of the Kingdom of Judah at Silwan', *BA* 33, 34–6; id., 1986, *The Village of Silwan: The Necropolis from the Period of the Judean Kingdom* (Jerusalem) (H).

Chapter Six: Agriculture (pp. 149–59)

Borowski, O., 1987, *Agriculture in Iron Age Israel* (Winona Lake, Ind.); id., 1992, 'Agriculture' *ABD* I, 95–8; Bruins, H.J., 1986, *Desert Environment and Agriculture in the Central Negev and Kadesh-Barnea during Historical Times* (Nijkerk); Dar, S., 1986, *Landscape and Pattern. An Archaeological Survey of Samaria 800 B.C.E.–636 C.E.* (*BAR Int. Ser.* 308, Oxford); Evenari, M., Shanan, L., Tadmor, N., et al., 1971, *The Negev: The Challenge of a Desert* (Cambridge, Mass.); Finkelstein, I., 1995, *Living on the Fringe. The Archaeology and History of the Negev, Sinai and Neighbouring Regions in the Bronze and Iron Ages* (*MMA* 6, Sheffield); Finkelstein, I. & Na'aman, N. (eds), 1994, *From Nomadism to Monarchy. Archaeological and Historical Aspects of Early Israel* (Jerusalem); Frick, F.S., 1989, 'Ecology, agriculture, and patterns of settlement' in Clements, R.E. (ed.), *The World of Ancient Israel: Sociological, Anthropological and Political Perspectives* (Cambridge), 67–93; Frankel, R., Avitsur, S. & Ayalon, E., 1994, *History and Technology of Olive Oil in the Holy Land* (Arlington, Va., & Tel Aviv); Heltzer, M. & Eitam, D., 1987, *Olive Oil in Antiquity. Israel and Neighbouring Countries. Conference 1987* (Haifa); Herzog, Z., 1994, 'The Beersheba Valley: From Nomadism to Monarchy', in Finkelstein, I. & Na'aman, N. (eds), 1994, op. cit., 122–49; Hopkins, D.C., 1985, *The Highlands of Canaan: Agricultural Life in the Early Iron Age* (*SWBA* 3, Sheffield); Rosen, B., 1984, 'Subsistence Economy in Iron Age I', in Finkelstein, I. & Na'aman, N. (eds), 1994, op. cit., 339–51; Turkowski, L., 1969, 'Peasant Agriculture in the Judean Hills', *PEQ* 101, 21–33.

Chapter Seven: Industries and Crafts (pp. 160–80)

I General: In addition to Weippert 1988 and Mazar 1990, the following are especially useful: Lucas, A. & Harris, J.R., 1962,

Ancient Egyptian Materials and Industries (London); Moorey, P.R.S., 1994, *Ancient Mesopotamian Materials and Industries* (Oxford); Singer, C., Holmyard, E.J., Hall, A.R. et al. (eds), 1954, *A History of Technology from the Earliest Times to the Fall of Ancient Empires* (Oxford).

II Metal: Artzy, M., 1983, 'Tin Bars in the Sea near Haifa', *BASOR* 250, 51–5; Conrad, H.G. & Rothenberg, B., 1980, 'Antikes Kupfer im Timna-Tal. 4000 Jahre Bergbau und Verhüttung in der Arabah (Israel)', *Der Anschnitt Zeitschrift für Kunst und Kultur im Bergbau, Beiheft* 1 (Bochum); Curtis, J. (ed.), 1988, *Bronzeworking Centres of Western Asia c. 1000–539 BC* (London), especially chs. 14 'Phoenicia as a bronzeworking centre in the Iron Age' by G. Falsone (pp. 222–50), and 15 'The role of the Sea Peoples in the bronze industry of Palestine/Transjordan in the Late Bronze-Early Iron transition' by J.N. Tubb (pp. 251–70); Horne, L., 1982, 'Fuel for the Metal Worker. The Role of Charcoal and Charcoal Production in Ancient Metallurgy', *Expedition* 25, 6–13; Lupu, A. & Rothenberg, B., 1970, 'The Extractive Metallurgy of the Early Iron Age Copper Industry in the 'Arabah, Israel', *Archaeologia Austriaca* 47, 91–130; Madden, R., Wheeler, T. & Muhly, J.D., 1977, 'Tin in the Ancient Near East: Old Questions and New Finds', *Expedition* 19, 35–47; McNutt, P.M., 1990, *The Forging of Israel. Iron Technology, Symbolism and Tradition in Ancient Society*, (*JSOTSS* 108, Sheffield); Negbi, O., 1974, 'The Continuity of the Canaanite Bronzework of the Latest Bronze Age into the Early Iron Age', *TA* 1, 159–72; Pigott, V.C. & Notis, M.R., 1982, 'The Earliest Steel from Transjordan', *MASCA Journal* 2, 35–39; Rothenberg, B., 1962, 'Ancient Copper Industries in the Western Arabah', *PEQ* 94, 5–71; Stech, T. et al., 1981, 'Iron at Taanach and Early Iron Metallurgy in the Eastern Mediterranean', *AJA* 85, 245–68; Waldbaum, J.C., 1978, *From Bronze to Iron: Transition from the Bronze Age to the Iron Age in the Eastern Mediterranean* (*SMA* 54, Göteborg); Wertime, I.A. & Muhly, J.D., 1980, *The Coming of the Age of Iron* (New Haven). See also Weippert, M., 'Metall und Metallbearbeitung', *BRL* (2nd ed.), 219–24.

III Stone: Amiran, R., 1956, 'The Millstone and the Potter's Wheel', *EI* 4, 46–9 (H); Lucas, A. & Harris, J.R., referred to above in I, 406–28; Moorey, P.R.S., 1994, *Ancient Mesopotamian Materials and Industries* (Oxford), 21–73; Thompson, H.O., 1971, 'Iron Age Cosmetic Palettes', *ADAJ* 16, 61–70; Thompson, H.O., 1972, 'Cosmetic Palettes', *Levant* 4, 148–50.

IV Mineral substances: Lucas, A. & Harris, J.R., 1962, referred to above in I, esp. pp. 8, 34ff., 82–4, 501–2, 512; Moorey, P.R.S., 1994, referred to above in I, 139, 240–2; Gibson, S., 1984, 'Lime Kilns in North-East Jerusalem', *PEQ* 116, 94–102; Weippert, H., 1977, 'Stein und Steinbeartbeitung' *BRL* (2nd ed.) , 317–21.

V Pottery:
(a) General, including typology: Amiran, R., 1970, *Ancient Pottery from the Holy Land from its Beginnings in the Neolithic Period to the End of the Iron Age* (Jerusalem & Ramat Gan); Lapp, N.L., 'Chronology of Palestinian Pottery', *ABD* V, 433–44, esp. 441–2; Tappy, R.E., 1992, *The Archaeology of Israelite Samaria*, I (Atlanta, Geo.), 231ff. and *passim*, offers a valuable analysis of Palestinian Iron I and II ceramics.
(b) Technical aspects: Anderson, W.P., 1989, 'The Pottery Industry at Phoenician Sarepta (Sarafand, Lebanon) with Parallels from Kilns from other East Mediterranean Sites', in McGovern, P.E., Notis, M.D. & Kingery, W.D (eds), *Cross-Craft and Cross-Cultural Influences in Ceramics* (*Ceramics and Civilisation*, Vol. IV) (Westerville, Oh.), 197–245; Dever, W.G.,

1990, *Gezer III, A Ceramic Typology of the Late Iron II, Persian and Hellenistic Periods at Gezer* (Jerusalem); Franken, H.J., 1974, *In Search of the Jericho Potters: Ceramics from the Iron Age and from the Neolithic* (Amsterdam); Franken, H.J., 1992, 'Pottery', *ABD* V, 428–33, esp. 431–2; Franken, H.J., 1990, in Franken, H.J. & Steiner, M.L., 1990, *Excavations in Jerusalem 1961–1969, II. The Iron Age Extramural Quarter on the South-East Hill* (London), 61–131; Hankey, V., 1968, 'Pottery Manufacture at Beit Shabab, Lebanon' *PEQ* 100, 27–32 for pottery kilns; Holladay, J.L., 1990, 'Red Slip, Burnish, and the Solomonic Gateway at Gezer', *BASOR* 277/8, 23–70; Johnston, R.H., 1974, 'The Biblical Potter', *BA* 37, 86–106; Kelso, J.L. & Thorpe, J.P., 1943, 'The Potter's Technique at Tell Beit Mirsim, particularly in Stratum A', in Albright, W.F., *The Excavation of Tell Beit Mirsim, AASOR*, XXI–XXII, 86–142; Rast, W.E., 1978, *Taanach I. Studies in the Iron Age Pottery* (Cambridge, Mass.); Tappy, R.E., 1992, *The Archaeology of Israelite Samaria*, I (Atlanta, Geo.); Wood, R.G., 1992, 'Potter's Wheel', *ABD* V, 427–8.

VI Frit and faience: Lucas, A. & Harris, J.R., 1962, see above I, 155–78, and see index, p. 505; Moorey, P.R.S., 1994, see above I, 168–89; Weippert, H., 1988, 'Fayence', *BRL* (2nd ed.), 74–7.

VII Glass: Barag, D., 1972, 'Cosmetic Glass Palettes from the Eighth–Seventh Century BC', *Journal of Glass Studies* 24, 11–19; id., 1988, *A Catalogue of Glass in the Department of Western Asiatic Antiquities in the British Museum, 1 Ur III–AD 200* (London); Moorey, P.R.S., 1994, see above I, 189–215; Weippert, H., 1977, 'Glas', *BRL* (2nd ed.), 98–9.

VIII Woodworking: Weippert, H., 1977, 'Holzbearbeitung', *BRL* (2nd ed.), 147–9.

IX Leather: Reed, R., 1972, *Ancient Skins, Parchments and Leathers* (London); Weippert, H., 1977, 'Leder, Lederbearbeitung', *BRL* (2nd ed.), 203–4.

X Spinning and weaving: Crowfoot, G.M., 1941, 'The Vertical Loom in Palestine and Syria', *PEQ* 73, 141–51; Galling, K., 1977, 'Weben und Weberei', *BRL* (2nd ed.), 360–1; Irving, D., 1977, 'Spinnen', *BRL* (2nd ed.), 311–13; 'Stoff', 325–7; Weir, S., 1970, *Spinning and Weaving in Palestine* (London).

XI Jewelry and ornament: Maxwell-Hyslop, K.R., 1971, *Western Asiatic Jewellery c. 3000–612 BC* (London); Weippert, H., 1977, 'Schmuck', *BRL* (2nd ed.), 282–9.

XII Seals: Welten, P., 1977, 'Siegel und Stempel', *BRL* (2nd ed.), 299-307.

XIII Bone and ivory: Moorey, P.R.S., 1994, see above I, 112–27; Lucas, A. & Harris, J.R., 1962, see above I, index; Weippert, H., 1977, 'Elfenbein', *BRL* (2nd ed.), 56–72.

XIV Productivity:
(a) Iron and steel. Forbes, R.J., 1967, in Matz, F. & Buchholz, H-G. (eds), *Archaeologia Homerica*, 11, *Bergbau, Steinbruchtätigkeit und Hüttenwesen* (Göttingen), esp. p. K31 for civilian requirements. For state requirements (armour), Moorey, P.R.S., 1994, see above I, 290, gives a Mesopotamian helmet weight (3 kg.); while Ventzke, W., 1986, 'Der Schuppenpanzer von Kamid-el-Loz', in Hachmann, R., *Bericht über die Ergebnisse der Ausgrabungen in Kamid el-Loz in den Jahren 1977 bis 1984* (Bonn), 161–82 and esp. 178–9, gives weights (9.6–26.6 kg) for bronze armour suit of varying lengths; Prof. A. Eitan (*in litt.*, 7.2. 1995) gives a weight for the iron sword from Vered Jericho (0.85 kg; originally more). Moorey, P.R.S., see above I, 1994, 281, quotes Jankowska, N.B., 1969, 'Socio-Economic History',

in Diakonof, J.M. (ed.), *Ancient Mesopotamia* (Moscow), 253–67 for the amounts of iron delivered as tribute by Levantine states to Assyria.

(b) Pottery: see Franken, 1992, *ABD* V, 430, for annual breakage rates for a family of four; and cf. Anderson, W.P., 1989, 203, and Hankey, 1968, 29, (quoted above in Vb) for the number of pots fired in ancient and modern kilns.

(c) Olive oil: figures by Heltzer, in Heltzer, M. & Eitam, D., 1987, *Olive Oil in Antiquity. Israel and Neighbouring Countries. Conference 1987* (Haifa), 115, are comparable with figures offered by Mattingly, D.J., 1988, 'Oil for Export? A Comparison of Libyan, Spanish and Tunisian olive oil production in the Roman Empire' *Journal of Roman Archaeology* 1, 33–56, esp. 33–4 & nn. 4–5.

(d) Wool fibre: Rosen, B., 1986, in Finkelstein, I., '*Izbet Sartah: An Early Iron Age Site near Rosh ha'Ayin, Israel* (*BAR Int. Ser.* 229, Oxford), 156–85 and esp. 180 for clothing requirements; *Annual Reports of the Dept. of Agriculture, Forestry and Fisheries, Palestine* for 1925 and 1926 for the numbers of sheep and goats in Palestine during the early Mandate.

Chapter Eight: Trade and the Economic System (pp. 181–91)

Elat, M., 1977, *Kishrei Kalkalah ben artsot ha-Mikra bi-yeme Bayit rishon* (*Economic Relations in the Lands of the Bible ca. 1100–539 B.C.E.*) (Jerusalem) (H); Finkelstein, I., 1988, 'Arabian Trade and Socio-Political Conditions in the Negeb in the Twelfth–Eleventh Centuries B.C.E.', *JNES* 47, 241–52; id., 1995, *Living on the Fringe: The Archaeology and History of the Negev, Sinai, and Neighbouring Regions in the Bronze and Iron Ages* (*MMA* 6, Sheffield), esp. 144–53; Hawkins, J., 1977, *Trade in the Ancient Near East* (London); Na'aman, N., 1979, 'The Brook of Egypt and Assyrian Policy on the Border of Egypt', *TA* 6, 68–90; Knauf, E.A., 'Ishmaelites', *ABD* III, 513–20 (useful information about the ancient Arabs and the incense trade); Oppenheim, A.L., 1967, 'Essay in Overland Trade in the First Millennium', *JAOS* 21, 236–54; Silver, M., 1995, *Economic Structures of Antiquity* (Westport, Ct. & London); Snell, D.C., 'Trade in the First Millennium B.C.E.', *ABD* VI, 622–9; Waldbaum, J.C., 1979, 'The Chronology of Early Greek Pottery: New Evidence from Seventh-Century Destruction Levels in Israel', *AJA* 101, 23–40 (offers useful data concerning the distribution of Greek pottery in Israel, esp. the map, fig. 1, p. 24); id., 1981, 'Greeks in the East or Greeks *and* the East', *BASOR* 305, 1–17.

Chapter Nine: Warfare (pp. 192–203)

Aharoni, Y., 1975, *Arad Inscriptions* (Jerusalem); Bartlett, J.B., 1982, 'Edom and the Fall of Jerusalem, 587 BC', *PEQ* 114, 15–24; Biran, A. & Naveh, J., 1993, 'An Aramaic Stele Fragment from Tel Dan', *IEJ* 43, 81–98; id., 1995, 'The Tel Dan Inscription: A New Fragment', *IEJ* 45, 1–18; Buchholz, H.-G. & Wiesner, J. (eds), 1977, *Archaeologia Homerica, Kriegswesen, Teil 1, Schutzwaffen und Wehrbauten* (Göttingen); id., 1980, *Teil 2, Angriffswaffen* (Göttingen); Chambon, A., 1984, *Tell el-Far'ah 1. L'Age du Fer* (Paris); Dalley, S., 1985, 'Foreign Chariotry and Cavalry in the Armies of Tiglath-Pileser III and Sargon II', *Iraq* 47, 59–84; Davies, R.W., 1971, 'The Roman Military Diet', *Britannia* II, 122–42; Eitan, A., 1994, 'Rare Sword of the Israelite Period found at Vered Jericho', *Israel Museum Journal* 12, 61–2; Eph'al, I., 1974, 'Arabs in Babylonia in the 8th century BC', *JAOS* 94, 108–15; Eretz, M.I., 1992,'Weapons and Implements of Warfare', *ABD* VI, 893–4; Galling, K., 1966, 'Goliath und seine Bewaffnung', *VT* 15, 150–69; Hallock, M., 1989, *Persepolis Fortress Tablets, O.I.P.* 92

(Chicago) (ration information); Herzog, C. & Gichon, M., 1997, *Battles of the Bible*, 2nd ed. (London & Mechanicsburg, Pa.); Hobbs, T.R., 1989, *A Time for War: A Study of Warfare in the Old Testament* (Wilmington, M.); Jones, C.H., 1989, 'The Concept of Holy War', in Clements, R.E., *The World of Ancient Israel* (Cambridge), 299–320; Lemaire, A., 1977, *Inscriptions Hébraïques. Tome 1. Les Ostraca* (Paris); Marion, H., 1961,'Early Eastern Steel Swords', *AJA* 65, 175–84; Mazar, A., 1982, 'Iron Age Fortresses in the Judean Hills', *PEQ* 114, 87–109; Mendenhall, G.E., 1958,'The Census Lists of Numbers 1 and 26', *JBL* 77, 52–66; Milik, J.T. & Cross, F.M., 1956, 'A Typological Study of the el-Khadr Javelin and Arrow Heads', *ADAJ* 5, 15–25; Miller, P.D., 1975, *The Divine Warrior in Early Israel* (*Harvard Semitic Monographs* 5) (Cambridge, Mass.); Mittman, S., 1993, 'Gib den Kittäern 3 b(at) Wein. Mengen und Güter in den Arad-Briefen', *ZDPV* 109, 39–48; Na'aman, N., 1986, 'Hezekiah's Fortified Cities and the LMLK Stamps', *BASOR* 261, 5–21; Neiman, D., 1969–70, 'URBI – 'Irregulars' or 'Arabs', *JQR* 60, 237–58; Von Rad, G., 1991, *Holy War in Ancient Israel* (Grand Rapids, Mich.); Tadmor, C., 1958, 'The Campaigns of Sargon II of Assur: A Chronological Historical Study', *JCS* 2, 22–40, 77–100; Ussishkin, D., 1982, *The Conquest of Lachish by Sennacherib* (Tel Aviv); de Vaux, R., 1965, *Ancient Israel, its Life and Institutions* (London); Yadin, Y., 1965, *The Art of Warfare in Biblical Lands* (London).

Chapter Ten: Language, Writing and Literature (pp. 204–33)

1 Language: A helpful overall study is offered by Sáenz-Badillos, A., 1993, *A History of the Hebrew Language* (Cambridge). For a recent survey see also *ABD* IV, 203–17, ('Languages: Hebrew'): sections A–D in this entry – A, 'Hebrew as a Language Name', 203–4 (G. Schramm); B, 'Linguistic Affiliations', 204–5 (P.C. Schmitz); C, 'Early History of Hebrew', 205–6 (P.C. Schmitz); D, 'Structural Overview', 206–8 – are particularly relevant here. See further: Baumgartner, W., 1955, *Ausgewählte Aufsätze* (Leiden), esp. 208–39, 'Was wir heute von der hebräische Sprache und ihrer Geschichte wissen'; Blau, J., 1971, 'Hebrew Language', *Enc. Jud.* 16, 1568–83; Davies, G.I., 1991, *Ancient Hebrew Inscriptions: Corpus and Concordance* (Cambridge); Driver, G.R., 1936, *Problems of the Hebrew Verbal System* (Edinburgh); Garbini, G., 1960, *Il semitico di nord-ouest* (Naples); Garr, W.R., 1985, *Dialect Geography of Syria-Palestine 1000–586 B.C.E.* (Philadelphia, Pa.); Harris, Z.S., 1959, *Development of the Canaanite Dialects. An Investigation in Linguistic History* (New Haven); Kutscher, E.Y., 1982, *A History of the Hebrew Language* (ed. R. Kutscher) (Jerusalem); Moran, W. L., 1961, 'The Hebrew language in its Northwest Semitic Background', in G.E. Wright (ed.), *The Bible and the Ancient Near East. Essays in Honor of William Foxwell Albright* (Garden City, N.Y.), 54–72; Polzin, R., 1976, *Late Biblical Hebrew. Towards an Historical Typology of Biblical Prose* (Missoula, Mont.); Rabin, C., 1970, 'Hebrew', in Sebeok, T.A. (ed.), *Current Trends in Linguistics, vol. 6: Linguistics in Southwest Asia and North Africa*, 197–203, 304–46; id., 1973, *A Short History of the Hebrew Language* (Jerusalem); id., 1979, 'The Emergence of Classical Hebrew', in Malamat, A. (ed.), *The World History of the Jewish People, First Series, V: The Age of the Monarchies, II: Culture and Society* (Jerusalem), 71–8, 293–5; Rendsburg, G.A., 1990, *Diglossia in Ancient Hebrew* (New Haven); id., 1991, 'The Structure of Biblical Hebrew', *JNWSL*, 81–99; id., 1992, 'Morphological Evidence for Regional Dialects in Ancient Hebrew' in Bodine, W.R. (ed.), *Linguistics and Biblical Hebrew* (Winona Lake, Ind.); Ullendorff, E., 1977, *Is Biblical Hebrew a Language?*

(Wiesbaden). Waldman, N.M., 1989, *The Recent Study of Hebrew. A Survey of the Literature with Selected Bibliography* (Cincinnati-Winona Lake, Ind.) offers fairly extensive bibliographies for each topic dealt with here.

II Writing: Baines, J., 1992, 'Literacy, Ancient Near East', *ABD* IV, 333–7; Cross, F.M., 1967, 'The Origin and Early Evolution of the Alphabet', *EI* 8, 8–24; id., 1979, 'Early Alphabetic Scripts', in Cross, F.M. (ed.), *Symposia*, 97–121; id., 1980, 'Newly found inscriptions in Old Canaanite and Early Phoenician Scripts', *BASOR* 238, 1–20; Cross, F.M. & Freedman, D.N., 1952, *Early Hebrew Orthography. A Study of the Epigraphic Evidence* (American Oriental Series 36); Davies, G.I., 1991, *Ancient Hebrew Inscriptions. Corpus and Concordance* (Cambridge); Demski, A., 1985, 'On the Extent of Literacy in Ancient Israel', in Amitai, J. (ed.), *Biblical Archaeology Today...*, 349–53; Driver, G.R., 1976, *Semitic Writing. From Pictogram to Alphabet*, 3rd ed. (London); Gibson, J.C.L., 1973, *Textbook of Syrian Semitic Inscriptions. I. Hebrew and Moabite Inscriptions*, 2nd ed. (Oxford); Isserlin, B.S.J., 1982, 'The Earliest Alphabetic Writing', *CAH* III, 1, 794–816; Jamieson-Drake, D.W., 1991, *Scribes and Schools in Monarchic Judah. A Socio-Archaeological Approach* (*JSOTSS* 109, Sheffield); Lemaire, A., 1977, *Inscriptions Hébraïques. Tome I, Les Ostraca* (Paris); id., 1981, *Les Écoles et la formation de la Bible dans l'ancien Israël* (*OBO* 39) (Fribourg-Göttingen); id., 1992, 'Education', *ABD* II, 305–12; id., 1992, 'Writing and Writing Materials', *ABD* VI, 999–1008; Millard, A.R., 1972, 'The Practice of Writing in Ancient Israel', *BA* 35, 98–111; id., 1982, 'In Praise of Ancient Scribes', *BA* 45, 143–53; id., 1985, 'An Assessment of the Evidence for Writing in Ancient Israel', in Amitai, J. (ed.), *Biblical Archaeology Today...*, 301–12; id., 1986, 'The Infancy of the Alphabet', *World Archaeology* 17, 390–8; id., 1992, 'Literacy', *ABD* IV, 337–40; Naveh, J., 1968, 'A Palaeographic Note on the Distribution of the Hebrew Script', *HThR* 61, 68–74; id., 1970, 'The Scripts in Palestine and Transjordan in the Iron Age', in Sanders, J.A. (ed.), *Near Eastern Archaeology in the Twentieth Century. Essays in Honor of Nelson Glueck* (New York), 277–83; id., 1982, *Early History of the Alphabet. An Introduction to West Semitic Epigraphy and Palaeography* (Jerusalem & Leiden); Sass, B., 1988, *The Genesis of the Alphabet and Its Development in the Second Millennium* BC (Wiesbaden); Shiloh, Y., 1987, 'South Arabian Inscriptions from the City of David, Jerusalem', *PEQ* 119, 9–18; Smelik, K.A.D., 1991, *Writings from Ancient Israel. A Handbook of Historical and Religious Documents* (Edinburgh) (E).

III Texts and Literature: in general, see: Alter, R. & Kermode, F. (eds), 1987, *The Literary Guide to the Bible* (London).

(a) poetry, see: Alonso Schoekel, L., 1988, *A Manual of Hebrew Poetics* (*Subsidia Biblica* 11, Rome); Alter, R., 1990, *The Art of Biblical Poetry* (Edinburgh); Berlin, A., 1983, *Dynamics of Biblical Parallelism* (Bloomington, Ind.); id., 'Parallelism', *ABD* V, 152–5; Culley, R., 1970, 'Metrical Analysis of Classical Hebrew Poetry' in Weers, J.W. & Redford, D.B. (eds), *Essays on the Ancient Semitic World* (Toronto); Follis, E.R. (ed.), 1987, *Directions in Classical Hebrew Poetry* (*JSOTSS* 40, Sheffield); Freedman, D.N., 1980, *Pottery, Poetry and Prophecy: Studies in Early Hebrew Poetry* (Winona Lake, Ind.); Gevirtz, S., 1963, *Patterns in the Early Poetry of Israel* (*SAOC* 32, Chicago); Hrushovski, B., 1971, 'Prosody, Hebrew', *Enc. Jud.* 13, 1200–3; Kugel, J.L., 1981, *The Idea of Biblical Poetry: Parallelism and its History* (New Haven & London); Loretz, O. & Kottsieper, I., 1987, *Colometry in Ugaritic and Biblical Poetry. Introduction, Illustrations, and Topical Bibliography* (Winona Lake, Ind.); Meer, van der, W., & Moor, de, J.C. (eds), 1988, *The Structural*

Analysis of Biblical and Canaanite Poetry (*JSOTSS* 74, Sheffield); Watson, W.G.E., 1994, *Traditional Techniques in Classical Hebrew Verse* (*JSOTSS* 170, Sheffield).

(b) Prose, see: Alter, R., 1981, *The Art of Biblical Narrative* (London); Bar Efrat, S., 1989, *Narrative Art in the Bible* (*JSOTSS* 26, Sheffield); Berlin, A., 1991, *Poetics and Interpretations of Biblical Narrative* (Winona Lake, Ind.); Bodine, W.N. (ed.), 1992, *Linguistics and Biblical Hebrew* (Winona Lake, Ind.); Exum, J.C. & Clines, D.J.A. (eds), 1993, *The New Literary Criticism and the Hebrew Bible* (*JSOTSS* 143, Sheffield); Davison, D.A., 1994, *Text-Linguistics and Biblical Hebrew* (*JSOTSS* 177, Sheffield); Fewell, D.N. & Gunn, D.M., 'Narrative, Hebrew', *ABD* IV, 1023–7; Gunn, D.M. & Fewell, D.N. (eds), 1989, *Old Testament Narrative* (Oxford); Sternberg, M., 1985, *The Poetics of Biblical Narrative* (Bloomington, Ind.).

Chapter Eleven: Religion (pp. 234–60)

Ackerman, S., 1992, *Under Every Green Tree. Popular Religion in Sixth-Century Judah* (Harvard Semitic Monographs 46, Atlanta, Ga.); Ahlström, G., 1963, *Aspects of Syncretism in Israelite Religion* (Lund); Albertz, R., 1994, *A History of Israelite Religion in the Old Testament Period. I From the Beginning to the End of the Monarchy* (London) (E); Barkai, G., 1986, *Ketef Hinnom: A Treasure Facing Jerusalem's Walls'* (Israel Museum Catalogue 274, Jerusalem), 34–5; Biran, A. (ed.), 1981, *Temples and High Places in Biblical Times* (Jerusalem); id., 1994, *Biblical Dan* (Jerusalem); Busink, T.A., 1970, *Der Tempel von Jerusalem von Salomon bis Herodes. Eine archäologisch-historische Studie unter Berücksichtigung des westsemitischen Tempelbaus* (Leiden); Coogan, M.D., Exum, J.C. & Stager, L.E. (eds), 1994, *Scripture and Other Artifacts. Essays on the Bible and Archaeology in Honour of Philip J. King* (Louisville, Kentucky); Cryer, F.H., 1994, *Divination in Ancient Israel and its Near Eastern Environment* (*JSOTSS* 142, Sheffield); Dietrich, W. & Klopfenstein, N.A., 1993 (eds), *Ein Gott allein? JHWH-Verehrung und Monotheismus im Kontext der israelitischen und altorientalischen Religionsgeschichte* (Fribourg & Göttingen); Fowler, J.D., 1988, *Theophoric Personal Names in Ancient Hebrew* (*JSOTSS* 49, Sheffield); Haran, N., 1978, *Temples and Temple Service in Ancient Israel* (Oxford); id., 1981, 'Temples and Cultic Open Areas as Reflected in the Bible' in Biran, A. (ed.), 1981, op. cit., 31–7; Holland, T.A., 1977, 'A Study of Palestinian Iron Age Baked Clay Figurines with Reference to Jerusalem: Cave 1', *Levant* 9, 121–55; Kaufmann, Y., 1961, *The Religion of Israel from the Beginnings to the Babylonian Exile* (London); Lang, B., 1983, *Monotheism and the Prophetic Minority. Essays in Biblical Society* (*SWBA* 1, Sheffield); Lemche, N.P., 1991, 'The Development of the Israelite Religion in the Light of Recent Studies on the Early Religion of Israel', *SVT* XLIII, 97–115; Loretz, O., 1990, *Ugarit und die Bibel. Kanaanäische Götter und Religion im Alten Testament* (Darmstadt); Meshel, Z., 1978, *Kuntillet 'Ajrud: A Religious Centre from the Time of the Judaean Monarchy on the Border of Sinai* (Israel Museum Catalogue 175, Jerusalem); Miller, P.D., Hanson, P.D., McBride, S.D. (eds), 1987, *Ancient Israelite Religion. Essays in Honor of Frank Moore Cross* (Philadelphia, Pa.); De Moor, J.C., 1990, *The Rise of Yahwism. The Roots of Israelite Monotheism* (Leuven); Niehr, H., 1990, *Der höchste Gott. Alttestamentlicher JHWH-Glaube im Kontext syrisch-kanaanäischer Religion des 1. Jahrtausends v. Chr.* (*BZAW* 190); Ottosson, M., 1980, *Temples and Cult Places in Palestine* (Uppsala); Pritchard, J.B., 1943, *Palestinian Figurines in Relation to Certain Goddesses known through Literature* (New Haven); Shiloh, Y., 1969, 'Iron Age Sanctuaries and Cult Elements in Palestine' in Cross, F.M. (ed.), *Symposia*, 147–57;

Smelik, K.A.D., 1991, *Writings from Ancient Israel. A Handbook of Historical and Religious Documents* (Edinburgh) (E); Smith, M.S., 1990, *The Early History of God. Yahweh and the other Deities in Ancient Israel* (San Francisco); Tadmor, M., 1982, 'Female Cult Figurines in Late Canaan and Early Israel: Archaeological Evidence', in Ishida, T. (ed.), *Studies in the Period of Solomon and Other Essays*, (Winona Lake, Ind.), 139–73; Tigay, J.H., 1987, 'Israelite Religion: The Onomastic and Epigraphic Evidence' in Miller, P.D., Hanson, P.D. & McBride, S.D. (eds), 157–94; Tigay, J.H., 1986, *You Shall Have No Other Gods. Israelite Religion in the Light of Hebrew Inscriptions* (Atlanta, Ga.); van der Toom, K., Becking, B. & van der Horst, P.W. (eds), 1995, *Dictionary of Deities and Demons in the Bible (DDD)* (Leiden, New York & Köln); de Vaux, R., 1963, *Israel, its Life and Institutions* (London); Zwickel, W., 1990, *Räucherkult und Räuchergeräte: Studien zum Räucheropfer im Alten Testament* (Fribourg & Göttingen).

Chapter Twelve: Israelite Art (pp. 261–86)

Amiet, P., 1980, *Art of the Ancient Near East* (New York); Barnett, R.D., 1982, *Ancient Ivories in the Middle East and Adjacent Countries* (*Qedem* 14, Jerusalem); Bayer, B., 1967, *Material Relics of Music in Ancient Palestine and its Environs*, (Tel Aviv); id., 'Music', *Enc.Jud.*, 12, 554–65; Beck, P., 1982, 'The Drawings from Horvat Teiman', *TA* 9, 3–68; Dever, W.G., 1995, 'Art' in Levy, T.E. (ed.), *The Archaeology of Society in the Holy Land* (London), 423–5; Eaton, J.H., 1975, 'Dancing in the Old Testament', *Expository Times*, 86, 136–40; Frankfort, H., 1954, *The Art and Architecture of the Ancient Orient* (London); Haïk-Vantoura, S., 1975, *The Music of the Bible Revealed* (Sheffield); Henton Davies, G., 'Dancing', *IDB* 1, 760–1;

Hestrin, R. & Dayagi-Mendels, M., 1979, *Inscribed Seals. First Temple Period: Hebrew Ammonite, Moabite, Phoenician and Aramaic. From the Collections of the Israel Museum and the Israel Department of Antiquities and Museums* (Jerusalem); Isserlin, B.S.J., 1961, 'Israelite Art during the Period of the Monarchy', in Roth, C. (ed.), *Jewish Art. An Illustrated History* (Tel Aviv); Jones, I.H., 'Musical Instruments', *ABD* 4, 934–9; Keel, O. & Uehlinger, C., 1992, *Göttinnen, Götter und Göttesymbole. Neue Erkentnisse zur Religionsgeschichte Kanaans und Israels aufgrund bislang unerschlossener ikonograpischer Quellen* (Fribourg-Basel-Vienna); Keel, O., Shuval, M., Uhlinger, C., 1990, *Studien zu den Stempelsiegeln aus Palästina / Israel, III. Die frühe Eisenziet. Ein Workshop, OBO* 100 (Fribourg & Göttingen); Keel, O., 1994, *Studien zu den Stempelsiegeln aus Palästina / Israel, IV, OBO* 135 (Fribourg & Göttingen); Kilmer, A.D., 'Music', *IDBS* 610–12; Matthews, V.H., 'Music in the Bible', *ADB* 4 930–34; Sass, B. & Uehlinger, C. (eds), 1993, *Studies in the Iconography of Northwest Semitic Inscribed Seals. Proceedings of a Symposium Held in Fribourg on April 17–20, 1991, OBO* 125 (Fribourg & Göttingen); Schroer, S., 1987, *In Israel gab es Bilder. Nachrichten von der darstellenden Kunst im Alten Testament* (Fribourg & Göttingen); Sendrey, A., 1969, *Music in Ancient Israel* (London); Stern, L., 1978, 'New Types of Phoenician Style Decorated Pottery From Palestine', *PEQ* 110, 11–21; Werner, E., 'Music', *IDB* 3, 457–69; id., 'Musical Instruments', *IDB* 3, 469–76; Werner, E. et al., 'Jewish Music', in S. Sadie (ed.), *The New Grove Dictionary of Music and Musicians*, esp. vol. 9, 614–21; Winter, J., 1976, 'Phoenician and North Syrian Ivory Carving in Historical Context', *Iraq* 38, 1–22; id., 1981, 'Is there a South Syrian Style of Ivory Carving in the Early First Millennium BC?', *Iraq* 43, 101–30.

Acknowledgments

Producing a book of this kind has not been easy, and the author has benefited from help in a variety of ways and subjects. Not all individuals can be listed here, but it is hoped that this comprehensive note will be accepted by those not specially mentioned. I have to thank the Brotherton Library of Leeds University; the British Library; the Library of the Institute of Archaeology in London; and the Palestine Exploration Fund and its library (and in particular Dr R. Chapman III, Dr Shimon Gibson and Miss H. Bell). I am also grateful to the British School of Archaeology in Jerusalem; and in Israel to the Hebrew University of Jerusalem (especially Prof. Y. Tsafrir and Prof. A. Eitan); the Israel Antiquities Authority and its predecessor there, the Dept. of Antiquities; and to the Israel Museum (and there especially Dr I. Lewitt and Dr M. Dayagi-Mendels). I must also thank the late Dr (later Dame) Kathleen Kenyon for training in archaeological method during a number of happy weeks at her excavations in Sabratha in Libya and Sutton Walls in England – I have tried to apply her methods in my own diggings in Israel and especially to my excavations at the Phoenician-Punic city of Motya in Sicily. I owe a great deal to my brief but happy experience as a temporary Inspector of Ancient Monuments in Israel (for which I must thank the late Dr S. Yeivin, then Head of the Department of Antiquities) and as a participant in the late Prof. Yigal Yadin's excavations at Hazor.

Individual thanks are due for a considerable variety of help. The late Prof. N. Avigad, Prof. I. Finkelstein, Prof. S. Gitin and Prof. T. Dothan and Prof. D. Ussishkin have all made illustrations available. Dr G.I. Davies read the first half of the manuscript in an earlier version, and offered valuable criticisms and suggestions. Prof. C. Rabin similarly saw an early form of the chapter on Hebrew language. Prof. P.R.S. Moorey arranged for a number of swords, daggers and arrowheads from Deve Hüyük in the Ashmolean Museum in Oxford to be weighed for comparative background information. Dr H. Catling gave advice on ancient Aegean armour. Dr V. Hankey and Dr D. Evely kindly answered questions on ancient potters' kilns, and the former helped with the relevant bibliography. Prof. A.R. Millard, Prof. K. Kitchen, Dr H.J. Bruins and Dr H. Curtis all helped with information. Prof. J. Rogerson gave kind permission to reproduce an illustration, and Prof. N. Postgate supplied a vital reference. My sincere thanks go to them all. My son Raphael, himself an archaeologist, drew many of the line drawings for this book, and thanks several colleagues for advice. Thanks are also due to a succession of ladies (and in particular Mrs Audrey Harrison) who transformed unwieldy manuscripts into orderly typescripts.

Sources of Illustrations

Plates

1 F.N. Hepper, Royal Botanic Gardens, Kew; 2–3 Palestine Exploration Fund; 4 Prof. Y. Tsafrir, Hebrew University Jerusalem; 5 Palestine Exploration Fund; 6-7 Prof. D. Ussishkin, Institute of Archaeology, University of Tel Aviv, photo: David Harris; 8 The City of David Archaeological Project, Prof. Y. Tsafrir, Hebrew University Jerusalem; 9 The City of David Archaeological Project (T. Harari); 10 The City of David Archaeological Project, Prof. Y. Tsafrir, Hebrew University Jerusalem; 11–12 photo courtesy The Oriental Institute, University of Chicago; 13 The City of David Archaeological Project, Prof. Y. Tsafrir, Hebrew University Jerusalem; 14 Copyright British Museum, London; 15 Israel Museum, Jerusalem; 17 The Ancient Art and Architecture Collection Ltd; 18 Prof. A. Biran, Nelson Glueck School of Biblical Archaeology, Jerusalem; 19–20 Prof. D. Ussishkin, Institute of Archaeology, University of Tel Aviv; 21 photo courtesy The Oriental Institute, University of Chicago; 22 Palestine Archaeological Museum; 23–5 Copyright British Museum, London; 26–7 Prof. D. Ussishkin, Institute of Archaeology, University of Tel Aviv; 28 Philip Winton; 29 Copyright British Museum, London; 30 Palestine Archaeological Museum; 31–2 Prof. D. Ussishkin, Institute of Archaeology, photo: Avraham Hay; 33 Copyright British Museum, London; 34–5 Archives Photographiques; 36 Prof. A. Biran, Nelson Glueck School of Biblical Archaeology, Jerusalem; 37–8 Israel Museum, Jerusalem; 39 Courtesy of the Trustees of the late Sir Henry S. Wellcome; 40 Prof. Y. Tsafrir, Hebrew University Jerusalem; 41 Israel Antiquities Authority; 42 Palestine Archaeological Museum; 43 Courtesy of the Trustees of the late Sir Henry S. Wellcome; 44 Dept. of Antiquities, Israel; 45 Prof. D. Ussishkin, Institute of Archaeology, University of Tel Aviv; 46 Copyright British Museum, London; 47–9 Prof. D. Ussishkin, Institute of Archaeology, University of Tel Aviv; 50 photo courtesy The Oriental Institute, University of Chicago; 51 Israel Antiquities Authority, photo: Israel Museum, Jerusalem; Nachum Slapak; 52 The Ancient Art and Architecture Collection Ltd; 53 collection of the Archaeological Staff Officer, Judaea and Samaria, photo: David Harris; 54 Palestine Archaeological Museum; 55 Dept. of Antiquities, Israel; 56 Israel Antiquities Authority, Israel Museum; 57 Palestine Archaeological Museum; 58 Israel Museum, Jerusalem; 59 Prof. D. Ussishkin, Institute of Archaeology, University of Tel Aviv; 60 Israel Museum, Jerusalem; 61 Archaeological Museum, Istanbul; 62 The City of David Archaeological Project, Prof. Y. Tsafrir, Hebrew University of Jerusalem; 63 Prof. I. Finkelstein, Institute of Archaeology, University of Tel Aviv; 64–6 Israel Antiquities Authority; 67 photo courtesy The Oriental Institute, University of Chicago; 68–9 Palestine Archaeological Museum; 70–1 Israel Antiquities Authority; 72 Dept. of Antiquities, Israel; 73–4 Israel Museum, Jerusalem; 75–6 Israel Antiquities Authority; 77 photo: Helene Bieberkraut; 78 Palestine Archaeological Museum; 79 Israel Antiquities Authority; 80 Prof. N. Avigad; 81 Israel Museum, Jerusalem; 82 Private Collection, courtesy of Teddy Kollek, Jerusalem; 83 Prof. N. Avigad; 84–5 Israel Antiquities Authority.

Line illustrations

1, 2 compiled by the author from various sources; 3 redrawn mainly after Rogerson, J., 1989, *Atlas of the Bible* (Oxford), 59; 4 redrawn mainly after Orni, E. & Efrat, E., 1980, *Geography of Israel* (Jerusalem), 145; 5 a) redrawn after Rogerson, J. & Davies,

P., 1989, *The Old Testament World* (Cambridge), 27; 6 redrawn mainly after Dorsey, D., 1991, *The Roads and Highways of Ancient Israel* (Baltimore & London), endpapers, and Aharoni, Y. & Avi-Yonah, M. (eds), 1970, *The Macmillan Bible Atlas* (London); 7 compiled by the author; 8 redrawn mainly after Finkelstein, I., 'The great transformation: the conquest of the highland frontiers and the rise of the territorial states', in Levy, T.E. (ed.), 1995, *The Archaeology of Society in the Holy Land* (London), 356, fig. 3, and Ji, C.C., 1995, 'Iron Age I in Central and Northern Transjordan: Interim Summary of Archaeological Data', *PEQ* 127, 122–40, and Mittmann, S., 1970, *Beiträge zur Siedlungs- und Territorialgeschichte des Ostjordanlandes* (Wiesbaden); 9 redrawn mainly after Finkelstein, I., 1988, *The Archaeology of the Israelite Settlement* (Jerusalem), and Oren, E., 1984, "Governors' Residencies' in Canaan under the New Kingdom. A Case Study in Egyptian Administration', *Journal for the Study of Egyptian Antiquities* 14, 37–56, and Weinstein, J.M., 1981, 'The Egyptian Empire in Palestine: A Reassessment', *BASOR* 241, 1–28; 10 redrawn after Rogerson, J., 1989, *Atlas of the Bible* (Oxford), 29; 11 redrawn after Maxwell Miller, J. & Hayes, J.H., 1986, *A History of Ancient Israel and Judah* (London), 140, map 13, and Aharoni, Y. & Avi-Yonah, M. (eds), 1970, *The Macmillan Bible Atlas* (London), 61, map 90; 12 redrawn after Maxwell Miller, J. & Hayes, J.H., 1986, *A History of Ancient Israel and Judah* (London), 181, map 15, and Aharoni, Y. & Avi-Yonah, M. (eds), 1970, *The Macmillan Bible Atlas* (London), 68, maps 104 and 105 (inset); 13 redrawn after Maxwell Miller, J. & Hayes, J.H., 1986, *A History of Ancient Israel and Judah* (London), 181, map 15 and 215, map 17; 14 redrawn after Maxwell Miller, J. & Hayes, J.H., 1986, *A History of Ancient Israel and Judah* (London), 248, map 19, and Aharoni, Y. & Avi-Yonah, M. (eds), 1970, *The Macmillan Bible Atlas* (London), 91, map 142; 15 redrawn after Bordreueil, P., 1985, 'Sigillaires ouest-Sémitiques, III...', *Syria* LXII, 21–29, figs 1A, 2, 7 and 8, and Mazar, A., 1990, *Archaeology of the Land of the Bible, 10,000–586 B.C.E.* (London & New York), 519, fig. 11.36; 16 George Taylor, © Thames and Hudson; 17 redrawn after Aharoni, Y. & Avi-Yonah, M. (eds), 1970, *The Macmillan Bible Atlas* (London), map 130; 18 Herzog, Z., *Beersheba II. The Early Iron Age Settlement* (Tel Aviv), 80, fig. 35; 19 George Taylor, © Thames and Hudson; 20 redrawn after Finkelstein, I., 1988, *The Archaeology of the Israelite Settlement* (Jerusalem), 259, fig. 88; 21 George Taylor, © Thames and Hudson; 22 redrawn after McClellan, T.L., 1983, 'Town Planning at Tell en Naṣbeh', *ZDPV* 99, fig. 1; 23 Herzog, Z., in *NEAEHL* (Jerusalem), fig. 17; 24 redrawn after Bahat, D., *The Illustrated Atlas of Jerusalem* (London & New York), 25, with additional information from Avigad, N., 1984, *Discovering Jerusalem* (Oxford), 50, fig. 30, and Prag, K., 1989, *The Blue Guide to Jerusalem* (London), 22; 25 George Taylor, © Thames and Hudson; 26 redrawn after Tufnell, O., 1953, *Lachish III. The Iron Age. The Plates* (Oxford), pl. 29, nos. 19 & 22; 27 Tracy Wellman, © Thames and Hudson; 28 George Taylor, © Thames and Hudson; 29 Mazar, A., 1990, *Archaeology of the Land of the Bible, 10,000–586 B.C.E.* (London & New York), 425, fig. 10.12; 30 Mazar, A., 1990, *Archaeology of the Land of the Bible, 10,000–586 B.C.E.* (London & New York), 475, fig. 11.28; 31 Ben-Tor, A. (ed.), 1992, *The Archaeology of Ancient Israel* (E) (New Haven & London), 342, fig. 9.33; 32 after Ben-Tor, A. (ed.), 1992, *The Archaeology of Ancient Israel* (E) (New Haven & London), 342, fig. 9.34; 33 Herzog, Z., *Das Stadttor in Israel und in den Nachbarlandändern* (Mainz), 114, abb. 91, 97, abb. 82, 109, abb. 89; 34 Loud, G., 1948, *Megiddo II. The Expeditions of 1935–39.* University of Chicago Oriental Institute Publications LXII (Chicago), 50, fig. 107; 35 Ben-Tor, A. (ed.), 1992, *The Archaeology of Ancient Israel* (E) (New Haven &

London), 314, fig. 9.10; 36 Lamon, R.S. & Shipton, G.M., 1939, *Megiddo I. The Expedition of 1925–31.* University of Chicago Oriental Institute Publications XLII (Chicago), 36, fig. 43; 37 George Taylor, © Thames and Hudson; 38 Tracy Wellman, © Thames and Hudson; 39 redrawn after Mazar, A., 1990, *Archaeology of the Land of the Bible, 10,000–586 B.C.E.* (London & New York), 391, fig. 9.3, and author; 40 author; 41 Turkowski, L., 1969, 'Peasant Agriculture in the Judean Hills', *PEQ* 101, 39, fig. 2; 42 E. Cohen, Tel Miqne-Ekron excavations, courtesy S. Gitin & T. Dothan; 43 redrawn after Gunneweg, J., Perlman, I. & Meshel, Z., 1985, 'The Origin of the Pottery at Kuntillet 'Ajrud', *IEJ* 36, 271, fig. 1; 44 Wood, B.G., 1990, *The Sociology of Pottery in Ancient Palestine, JSOTSS* 103 (Sheffield), 105, fig. 7; 45 Singer, C., Holmyard, E.J., Hall, A.R. et al. (eds), 1954, *A History of Technology from the Earliest Times to the Fall of Ancient Empires* (Oxford), 413, fig. 269 (a) & (c); 46 redrawn after after Wood, B.G., 1990, *The Sociology of Pottery in Ancient Palestine, JSOTSS* 103 (Sheffield), 114, fig. 17 and 120, fig. 23; 47 Mazar, A., 1990, *Archaeology of the Land of the Bible, 10,000–586 B.C.E.* (London & New York), 362, fig. 8.33; 48 Philip Winton, © Thames and Hudson; 49 redrawn after Mazar, A., 1982, 'Iron Age Fortresses in the Judean Hills, *PEQ* 114, 87, fig. 1, with additional data from Lemaire, A., 1977, *Inscriptions Hébraïques. Tome 1. Les Ostraca* (Paris); 50 Philip Winton, © Thames and Hudson; 51 Ben-Tor, A. (ed.), 1992, *The Archaeology of Ancient Israel* (E) (New Haven & London), 300, fig. 8.29; 52 Dever, W.G., 1990, *Recent Archaeological Discoveries and Biblical Research* (Seattle & London), 150, fig. 50; 53 redrawn after Yadin, Y., 1961, *Hazor III–IV. An account of the third and fourth seasons of excavations 1957–58* (Jerusalem), pl. CCCXLVI; 54 A. Biran, Nelson Glueck School of Biblical Archaeology, Jerusalem; 55 Biran, A., 1994, *Biblical Dan* (Jerusalem), 190, fig. 150; 56 Ben-Tor, A. (ed.), 1992, *The Archaeology of Ancient Israel* (E) (New Haven & London), 340, fig. 9.30; 57 George Taylor, © Thames and Hudson; 58 Weippert, H., 1992, 'Die Kesselwagen Salamos' *ZPDV* 108, 18, abb. 5 and 25, abb. 12; 59 Tracy Wellman, © Thames and Hudson; 60 Tracy Wellman, © Thames and Hudson; 61 Stern, L., 1978, 'New Types of Phoenician Style Decorated Pottery from Palestine', *PEQ* 110, 13, fig. 1; 62 Dever, W.G., 1990, *Recent Archaeological Discoveries and Biblical Research* (Seattle & London), 154, fig. 54; 63 Harris, R.L., 1995, *Exploring the World of the Bible Lands* (London & New York), 52; 64 Dever, W.G., 1990, *Recent Archaeological Discoveries and Biblical Research* (Seattle & London), 145, fig. 47; 65 Dever, W.G., 1990, *Recent Archaeological Discoveries and Biblical Research* (Seattle & London), 144, fig. 46; 66 Stern, L., 1978, 'New Types of Phoenician Style Decorated Pottery from Palestine', *PEQ* 110, 17, fig. 7; 67 Vincent, H., 1954, *Jerusalem de l'Ancien Testament Recherches d'Archéologie et d'Histoire*, I Texte (Paris); 68 redrawn after May, H.G., 1935, *Material Remains of the Megiddo Cult.* Oriental Institute of Chicago Publications XXVI (Chicago), pl. XXXII; 69 Schroer, S., 1987, *In Israel gab es Bilder. Nachrichten von der darstellenden Kunst im Alten Testament* (Fribourg & Göttingen), abb. 113, 114, 117; 70 (l) redrawn from Hestrin, R. & Dayagi-Mendels, M., 1979, *Inscribed Seals...* (Jerusalem), fig. 5; (r) Payne, H., 1931, *Necrocorinthia. A Study of Corinthian Art in the Archaic Period* (Oxford), fig. 21f; 71 Tufnell, O., 1953, *Lachish III. The Iron Age. The Plates* (Oxford), pl. 50, 1; 72 Philip Winton, © Thames and Hudson; 73 Galling, K. (ed.), 1977, *Biblisches Reallexicon*, (Tübingen), 235, 236, fig. 57; 74 Buttrick, G.A. (ed.), 1962, The Interpreter's Dictionary of the Bible (New York and Nashville (Tenn.)), 467. The following maps were redrawn, in addition to the sources specified individually, after the endpapers from *The Times Atlas of the Bible*, Pritchard, J.B. (ed.), 1989: 3; 4; 5; 6; 8; 9; 10; 11; 12; 13; 14; 17; 39; 46; 49.

Index